1990

C0-AWE-591
Traditions and innovations :
3 0301 00088938 2

Traditions and Innovations

Traditions and Innovations

Essays on British Literature of the Middle Ages and the Renaissance

Edited by
David G. Allen and Robert A. White

Newark: University of Delaware Press
London and Toronto: Associated University Presses

LIBRARY
College of St. Francis
JOLIET, ILLINOIS

© 1990 by Associated University Presses, Inc.

All rights reserved. Authorization to photocopy items for internal or personal use, or the internal or personal use of specific clients, is granted by the copyright owner, provided that a base fee of $10.00, plus eight cents per page, per copy is paid directly to the Copyright Clearance Center, 27 Congress Street, Salem, Massachusetts 01970. [0-87413-335-6/90 $10.00 + 86 pp, pc.]

Associated University Presses
440 Forsgate Drive
Cranbury, NJ 08512

Associated University Presses
25 Sicilian Avenue
London WC1A 2QH, England

Associated University Presses
P.O. Box 488, Port Credit
Mississauga, Ontario
Canada L5G 4M2

The paper used in this publication meets the requirements
of the American National Standard for Permanence of Paper
for Printed Library Materials Z39.48-1984.

Library of Congress Cataloging-in-Publication Data

Traditions and innovations : essays on British literature of the Middle Ages and the Renaissance / edited by David G. Allen and Robert A. White.
p. cm.
Includes index.
ISBN 0-87413-355-6 (alk. paper)
1. English literature—Early modern, 1500–1700—History and criticism. 2. English literature—Middle English, 1100–1500–History and criticism. I. Allen, David G., 1953– . II. White, Robert A., 1943
PR423.T7 1990
820.9—dc20 88-40599
CIP

PRINTED IN THE UNITED STATES OF AMERICA

820.9
A376

Contents

136,929

Preface

The literary-historical period covered by the essays in this volume begins with Chaucer, ranges through Spenser, Shakespeare, Jonson, and Milton, and ends with the collapse of the Renaissance tradition of letters in the eighteenth century. The first forum for these studies was the Fifth Citadel Conference on literature, held in Charleston, South Carolina, in March 1985, and the call to which their authors responded was almost as broad as the time period that is their subject: papers on any aspect of medieval and Renaissance literature, but particularly on the continuity and discontinuity between the two periods.

Since the whole range of this broad call is reflected in the volume, it is likely that readers will first come to *Traditions and Innovations* as they work on individual subjects; for the primary strength of the collection is the sustained high quality and significance of its scholarship on various topics rather than in the presentation of a single thesis. Three essays that together illustrate both the variety and the importance of the scholarship in the volume are those by David Hiscoe, Richard Griffith, and Kathleen Kelly. Hiscoe shows that the motif of separation in *Troilus and Criseyde* should be understood in the context of St. Paul's thorn in the flesh; Griffith uses some exciting detective work to show *which* Thomas Malory was probably the author of *Le Morte Darthur* (and in the process uncovers the earliest autograph of a major British author); and Kelly presents an incisive explanation for the demise of the Renaissance love lyric in the seventeenth century. The essays that begin and end the collection are by influential scholars whose work has been respected by students of these fields for decades: Robert Kaske offers a new reading of *The Knight's Tale* and *The Man of Law's Tale,* and Alvin Kernan describes the end of the tradition of courtly letters.

However, *Traditions and Innovations* not only gathers significant scholarship on disparate topics, but also seeks to be true to the original call by inviting readers to consider how the literature of one period can illuminate that of the other. Dorothea Kehler and Michael Wentworth, for example, discuss Renaissance dramatists' use of the medieval mystery and morality plays: Kehler shows that 5.3 of *Richard II* echoes but inverts the comforting central message of the early plays; and Wentworth places Heywood's *A Woman Killed With Kindness* squarely in the tradition of the morality.

Charlotte Spivack shows how Jacobean playwrights often gained dramatic effect by reversing the familiar, traditional roles of women. Lorrayne Baird-Lange and Pamela Macfie define the progress of the ancient myths of Ganymede and Arachne through the Middle Ages into the work of Peacham and Spenser. Together, these essays underscore the importance to Renaissance literature of medieval heritage and tradition, and stress the continuity between the two periods.

Even though the sequence of the essays is chronological, readers will find other useful patterns in the collection. For example, the essays by Kelly, Parks, Strout, and Wentworth deal with genre; those by Spivack and Strout address some of the concerns of feminism. Halli, Halio, and Linkin focus upon the language of poetry; Brown and Matalene work with social context; and Matalene, Evans, and Kernan focus more specifically upon the presence and effects of patronage.

The title of the volume, *Traditions and Innovations,* seeks to characterize not only its content but also its approach. Its content helps both to define the literary traditions in which the works under discussion were composed and to show how poets and playwrights drew upon the traditions they inherited. And in its approach, this collection is likewise traditional: as a group, the essayists clearly prefer, for example, the methods and assumptions of new criticism to those of deconstruction. However, the volume is also concerned with innovations. The papers emphasize the ways in which great artists used tradition without being smothered by it; and while some of the essayists do reflect the interests of contemporary critical theory in feminism and social problems, all approach their subjects with an innovative eye and draw new insights from familiar words. The result is a volume that successfully combines traditional literary-historical approaches and sensitive, innovative reading to broaden our understanding of the British literature of the Renaissance and Middle Ages.

In assembling the collection, we relied on the good services of more colleagues and friends than we have space to name. However, chief among these were the scholars who helped us evaluate the submissions: Professors Malcolm Brennan, Anne Eesley, Jeffrey Loomis, C. B. Moore, Nan Morrison, Deborah D. Rubin, B. Jane Stanfield, and E. F. J. Tucker. We would also like to acknowledge the alumni and friends of The Citadel whose support of The Citadel Development Foundation made possible the whole enterprise.

Traditions and Innovations

Causality and Miracle: Philosophical Perspectives in the *Knight's Tale* and the *Man of Law's Tale*

R. E. KASKE

Whenever I approach Chaucer's *Knight's Tale* these days, I am reminded of the time while I was a graduate student at the University of North Carolina during the late 1940s, when one of my fellow students celebrated his mother's sixtieth birthday by giving her a copy of what was then the latest translation of the *Canterbury Tales*—a translation, be it said, that accomplished the difficult feat of making most of Chaucer's bawdy passages sound worse than they really are. I remember saying to him, "My God, Jack, are you trying to become an orphan overnight? What's going to happen when your dear old mother hits the *Miller's Tale?*" He looked at me coldly and replied, "You don't remember the *Canterbury Tales* as well as you think you do. Never forget that before the *Miller's Tale* comes the *Knight's Tale*. Mother will get halfway through the *Knight's Tale,* yawn, fall asleep, and when she wakes up thank me for a lovely gift. I guarantee you she'll go to her grave innocent of the very existence of the *Miller's Tale*." He later reported with unseemly glee that it had worked out just as he predicted, with one minor exception: his mother had gotten only a third of the way through the *Knight's Tale*.

I tell this story because I think it sums up rather neatly what was once a popular attitude toward the *Knight's Tale*. The reason, I suspect, was that for a long time readers approached the tale as if it were in some way a story of romantic love; and read in that way, it probably justifies all the uncharitable judgments ever heaped upon it. Today, though there are about as many interpretations of the *Knight's Tale* as there are interpreters, the approaches are a great deal more sophisticated; and it is perhaps a tribute to the critical adventurousness of our students that year after year I receive more term papers on it than on any other part of the *Canterbury Tales.*

Everybody know that the story of the *Knight's Tale* is ultimately part of the legendary history of Thebes following the downfall of Oedipus: that it was told near the end of the first century by Statius in his *Thebaid* and subsequently became part of the enormous repertory of medieval romance; and that Chaucer's direct source for it is Boccaccio's *Teseida.*[1] The usual characterization of *Il Teseida* and the *Knight's Tale* is that Chaucer has taken what in Boccaccio's telling was "courtly epic" and turned it into something much like medieval romance. I should remind you at this point that the popular notion of medieval romance as a light, essentially frivolous genre, always at one remove from reality and having little to say about life as we know it, does not really hold for romances written by sophisticated authors. On the contrary, the best medieval romances seem to be trying to sketch out real patterns, problems, situations, and the like, but in the fictional garb of the unreal or unfamiliar—the long ago, the far away, the wondrous, and so on. I would begin with the not altogether novel suggestion that in the *Knight's Tale* Chaucer has turned Boccaccio's narrative of event into a work of somewhat this kind—with Boethian wisdom as its thematic center, and love as the good in respect to which this wisdom is being dramatized. As P. M. Kean aptly puts it, "While in the *Troilus* . . . Chaucer gives us a philosophical treatment of a love story, in the *Knight's Tale* a love story forms the pretext for a philosophical poem."[2] This purpose will, of course, account for many of Chaucer's drastic alterations from the *Teseida*—for example, his famous transformation of Boccaccio's Emilia from a credible young woman into something of a puppet. If the *Knight's Tale* is at center a narrative poem about wisdom, the essential importance of Emily will be not as a developed character with whom we are invited to sympathize, but as a "good" to be striven for wisely; her realness as a woman must be muted to keep the love interest from running away with the story.

That Chaucer himself translated Boethius's *Consolation of Philosophy* into Middle English, and that his poetry is also saturated with its thought, will be news to no one; and I suppose it is equally obvious that the *Knight's Tale* is especially full of Boethian echoes.[3] In particular, as R. M. Lumiansky pointed out more than thirty years ago,[4] nearly everything that happens in the tale seems motivated or set in action by some member of the famous "Boethian hierarchy": Providence, Destiny, Fortune, Nature, and their earthly results, which Chaucer calls *cas* or *aventure*. At the beginning of the tale the suppliant Theban ladies ascribe to Fortune both Theseus's power and their own wretched plight—the two factors from which the subsequent action springs:

> . . . "Lord, to whom Fortune hath yiven
> Victorie, and as a conqueror to lyven. . . .
> Now be we caytyves, as it is wel seene,
> Thanked be Fortune and hire false wheel. . . ."
> (I.915–16, 924–25)[5]

After the imprisonment of Palamon and Arcite, Emily's crucial walk in the garden is inspired by Nature: "The sesoun priketh every gentil herte. . . ." (1043). And in a more general way, I wonder whether the continual references to nature and its observances in the early part of the poem (e.g., 1500–1512)—emphasized, for example by John Halverson[6]—are not also to be seen as glancing allusions to Nature in the Boethian hierarchy. At any rate, when Palamon looks out the prison window and sees Emily, it is "by aventure or cas" (1074). After Arcite has been released from prison, he says of Palamon, who is still confined,

> "Wel hath Fortune yturned thee the dys,
> That has the sighte of hire, and I th'absence.
> For possible is, syn thou hast hire presence,
> And art a knyght, a worthy and an able,
> That by som cas, syn Fortune is chaungeable,
> Thow maist to thy desir somtyme atteyne."
>
> (1238–43)

Arcite is at length directed to return to Athens by a dream of Mercury (1384–92), whom I would interpret as a messenger of Providence in classical garb. Palamon's breaking out of prison—an act normally calling for a fair amount of initiative—is attributed rather oddly to chance or destiny:

> It fel that in the seventhe yer, of May
> The thridde nyght, (as olde bookes seyn,
> That all this storie tellen moore pleyn)
> Were it by aventure or destynee—
> As, whan a thyng is shapen, it shal be—
> That soone after the mydnyght Palamoun,
> By helpyng of a freend, brak his prisoun. . . .
>
> (1462–68)

Arcite's discovery of Palamon in the grove, and apparently also its results, are blamed on Fortune:

> Now wol I turne to Arcite ageyn,
> That litel wiste how ny that was his care,
> Til that Fortune had broght him in the snare.
>
> (1488–90)

By chance, Palamon is hiding near his path:

> And in a path he rometh up and doun
> Ther as by aventure this Palamoun
> Was in a bussh, that no man myghte hym se. . . .
>
> (1515–17)

In a striking passage possibly echoing Boethius's' *Consolation,*[7] Theseus's decision to go hunting that morning is attributed to Destiny and Providence:

> The destinee, ministre general,
> That executeth in the world over al
> The purveiaunce that God hath seyn biforn,
> So strong it is that, though the world had sworn
> The contrarie of a thyng by ye or nay,
> Yet somtyme it shal fallen on a day
> That falleth nat eft withinne a thousand yeer.
> For certeinly, oure appetites heer,
> Be it of werre, or pees, or hate, or love,
> Al is this reuled by the sighte above.
>
> (1663–72)

The tournament to win Emily is described by Theseus as an appeal to Fortune:

> "Thanne shal I yeve Emelya to wyve
> To whom that Fortune yeveth so fair a grace. . . ."
>
> (1860–61)

At the council of the gods on the eve of the tournament, Saturn makes the promise that will result in the defeat of Palamon, the death of Arcite, and Palamon's eventual winning of Emily (2453–78); I take Saturn here to be a classical figure of Providence, exercising its power of foreordaining human affairs. After the tournament, Arcite dies of injuries clearly received through the operation of Saturn; his death is described in a grisly passage analyzing the workings of Nature under the domination of Saturn (2743–60) and ending,

> Nature hath now no dominacioun.
> And certeinly, ther Nature wol nat wirche,
> Fare wel phisik! Go ber the man to chirche!
>
> (2758–60)

And finally, there is Theseus's famous pronouncement in his great summarizing speech (2987–3089):

> "Thanne is it wysdom, as it thynketh me,
> To maken vertu of necessitee. . . ."
>
> (3041–42)

Necessitee I understand as the sum total of what is sent to man, or inflicted on him, by the whole of the Boethian hierarchy—the "givens" of human life which it is impossible to avoid and against which it is pointless to rebel. Though the *Teseida* includes many references to Fortune, and though some of the passages I have cited seem based on hints provided by the *Teseida,* I think it is fair to say that the total pattern is an addition by Chaucer to the story he is adapting from Boccaccio. As a further grace note, we may observe that the selection of the Knight to tell his Boethian tale is by way of those earthly aspects of Fortune, accident, luck, and chance:

> Were it by aventure, or sort, or cas,
> The sothe is this: the cut fil to the Knyght. . . .
>
> (844–45)

Now in the Boethian universe, as in medieval thought generally, the great ruling power is of course love, conceived of as a cosmic unifying force; and the supreme virtue is wisdom, particularly the wisdom to bear with resignation and fortitude the varying fortunes imposed by the workings of Providence, Destiny, Nature, and Fortune. Both love and wisdom receive their climactic emphasis in the *Knight's Tale* in the final speech of Theseus (2987–3089), beginning

> "The Firste Moevere of the cause above,
> Whan he first made the faire cheyne of love. . . ."
>
> (2987–88)

and including the prominent reference to wisdom quoted above (3041–42). Within this Boethian scheme of things, the story we are told is of the two young men, Palamon and Arcite, and their love for Emily. Though it has sometimes been assumed that Palamon and Arcite are completely undifferentiated, like a kind of medieval Rosencrantz and Guildenstern, I follow the opinion of a growing number of scholars that the difference between them is not only clearly developed but also of major thematic importance in the tale.[8] As I see the pattern, Palamon is presented as an instinctive idealist, who when we first meet him, however, shows no sign of philosophical perspective; this lack of philosophical orientation is reflected most strongly in a long speech clearly based on an unphilosophical lament by the character Boethius in Book I of the *Consolation:*

> . . . "O crueel goddes that governe
> This world with byndyng of youre word eterne,
> And writen in the table of atthamaunt
> Youre parlement and youre eterne graunt,
> What is mankynde moore unto you holde
> Than is the sheep that rouketh in the folde?
> For slayn is a man right as another beest,

And dwelleth eek in prison and arreest,
And hath siknesse and greet adversitee,
And ofte tymes giltless, pardee.
"What governance is in this prescience,
That giltelees tormenteth innocence?
And yet encresseth this al my penaunce,
That man is bounden to his observaunce,
For Goddes sake, to letten of his wille,
Ther as a beest may al his lust fulfille.
And whan a beest is deed he hath no peyne;
But man after his deeth moot wepe and pleyne,
Though in this world he have care and wo.
Withouten doute it may stonden so.
The answere of this lete I to dyvynys,
But wel I woot that in this world greet pyne ys. . . ."
(1303–24)

In the course of the poem Palamon, through idealistic love and the sufferings he endures for love, gradually achieves the wise acceptance that lies at the heart of Boethian wisdom. Arcite, on the other hand, is presented as a man of more practical and appetitive bent, who when we first meet him talks a plausible though as yet untested game of Boethian philosophy—somewhat like a freshman who has just passed the introductory survey. His initial lip service to the Boethian system is dramatized most elaborately in a long speech which, as P. M. Kean remarks, is "built up from scraps from several different parts of the *de Consolatione,* used in an altered sense":[9]

"Allas, why pleynen folk so in commune
On purveiaunce of God, or of Fortune,
That yeveth hem ful ofte in many a gyse
Wel bettre than they kan hemself devyse?
Som man desireth for to han richesse,
That cause is of his mordre or greet sikness;
And som man wolde out of his prisoun fayn,
That in his hous is of his meynee slayn.
Infinite harmes been in this mateere.
We witen nat what thing we preyen heere;
We faren as he that dronke is as a mous.
A dronke man woot wel he hath an hous,
But he noot which the righte wey is thider,
And to a dronke man the wey is slider.
And certes, in this world so faren we;
We seken faste after felicitee,
But we goon wrong ful often, trewely. . . ."
(1251–67)

In the course of the poem, through the sufferings inflicted by his more appetitive love, Arcite declines in Boethian wisdom. To put it another way, each of the two young men has certain psychological traits which, when acted on by sexual love, push their development in different directions, with different implications for their wisdom. I might add that Douglas Brooks and Alastair Fowler, in one of the best studies on the *Knight's Tale* to date, arrive at a somewhat similar conclusion in terms of astrological influence—with Palamon as the sanguine man produced by the planetary influence of Venus, and Arcite as the choleric man produced by the influence of Mars and the Sun.[10] More recently A. J. Minnis, interpreting Chaucer's characters by way of the mythography of their patron gods, has proposed a distinction that again is broadly comparable.[11]

Time forbids the detailed analysis this important theme deserves, but to hit a few high spots: When Palamon first catches sight of Emily through the prison window he cries out, prompting from Arcite an acceptable Boethian admonition:

> "For Goddes love, taak al in pacience
> Oure prisoun, for it may noon oother be.
> Fortune hath yeven us this adversitee.
> Som wikke aspect or disposicioun
> Of Saturne, by som constellacioun,
> Hath yeven us this, although we hadde it sworn;
> So stood the hevene whan that we were born.
> We moste endure it; this is the short and playn."
>
> (1084–91)

Palamon, describing Emily, takes her for a goddess, probably Venus:

> "I noot wher she be womman or goddesse,
> But Venus is it soothly, as I gesse,"
> And therwithal on knees doun he fil,
> And seyde: "Venus, if it be thy wil
> Yow in this gardyn thus to transfigure
> Bifore me, sorweful, wrecched creature
> Out of this prisoun help that we may scapen. . . ."
>
> (1101–7)

Arcite's response, once he sees her, contrasts strongly both with Palamon's speech and with his own earlier one:

> "The fresshe beautee sleeth me sodeynly
> Of hire that rometh in the yonder place;
> And but I have hir mercy and hir grace,

That I may seen hire atte leeste weye,
I nam but deed; ther nis namoore to seye."

(1118–22)

A little later, Arcite draws the comparison explicitly:

". . . Thos woost nat yet now
Wheither she be a womman or goddesse!
Thyn is affeccioun of hoolynesse,
And myn is love, as to a creature. . . ."

(1156–59)

In what is certainly a touch of dramatic irony, he quotes the rhetorical question that in Boethius serves as a melancholy comment on the disastrous tale of Orpheus and Eurydice:

"Wostow nat wel the olde clerkes sawe,
That 'who shal yeve a lovere any lawe?' "

(1163–64)

Throughout the exchange of speeches, the problem for Arcite remains the practical one of how to "get" the lady; he sums the matter up in a tellingly unromantic simile:

"We stryve as dide the houndes for the boon;
They foughte al day, and yet hir part was noon.
Ther cam a kyte, whil that they were so wrothe,
And baar awey the boon bitwixe hem bothe."

(1177–80)

Even Arcite's long Boethian speech (1251–67, quoted above) is undercut by the non-Boethian outburst with which it ends:

"Syn that I may nat seen you, Emelye,
I nam but deed; ther nys no remedye."

(1273–74)

After Arcite has been freed and gone to Thebes, the teller concludes Part I with a *question d'amour,* asking which of the two now has the worse fate:

Yow loveres, axe I now this questioun:
Who hath the worse, Arcite or Palamoun?
That oon may seen his lady day by day,
But in prison he moot dwelle alway;
That oother wher hym list may ride or go,
But seen his lady shal he nevere mo.

(1347–52)

The ironic point, I take it, is that the reverse would suit each one's temperament better. The more idealistic lover has the sight of his lady, which presumably he could do without; the more appetitive lover is deprived even of that.

During Arcite's exile in Thebes, he is physically shattered by the ravages of love (1358–79),[12] and after "a yeer or two" (1381) returns to Athens. Palamon endures the woes of love in prison for "Thise *seven* yeer" (italics mine; 1452, 1462), and the contrast seems underscored by the remark that he is a prisoner "Perpetually, noght oonly for a yer" (1458). We have already noticed the teller's apparent attempt to mute the initiative of his escape from prison (1462–69). A curious difference between Palamon and Arcite in this part of the poem is that while both are characterized to some extent as jealous, the jealousy of Palamon seems emphasized much more strongly and frequently than that of Arcite.[13] The first hint of Palamon's jealousy has appeared in the initial dispute over Emily, where he says,

> "And now thow woldest falsly been aboute
> To love my lady, whom I love and serve. . . ."
>
> (1142–43)

When he is left alone in prison after Arcite's release,

> . . . the fyr of jalousie up sterte
> Withinne his brest, and hente him by the herte
> So woodly that he lyk was to biholde
> The boxtree or the asshen dede and colde.
>
> (1299–1302)

The jealousy of Palamon is contrasted with the attitude of Arcite in their parallel speeches (as emphasized, for example, by lines 1591 and 1601) just before their battle in the grove. Palamon's speech (1580–95) includes the declaration,

> "I wol be deed, or elles thou shalt dye.
> Thou shalt nat love my lady Emelye.
> But I wol love hire oonly and namo. . . ."
>
> (1587–89)

Arcite's (1599–1619) includes the sharply contrasting remark,

> "And if so be that thou my lady wynne,
> And sle me in this wode ther I am inne,
> Thow mayst wel have thy lady as for me."
>
> (1617–19)

Still another striking example is Palamon's long, desperate speech (1715–41) to Theseus after he has found them fighting in the grove—unmatched by any corresponding speech from Arcite—which concludes,

> "I am thy mortal foo, and it am I
> That loveth so hoote Emelye the brighte
> That I wol dye present in hir sighte.
> Wherfore I axe deeth and my juwise;
> But sle my felawe in the same wise,
> For bothe han we deserved to be slayn."
>
> (1736–41)

It has always seemed to me that jealousy, though certainly not confined to the more idealistic forms of love, does have a special closeness to idealistic love; the more idealistic the love, the more intolerable will be anything that threatens to mar its perfection. The tremendously influential treatise *De amore,* written in the twelfth century by Andreas Capellanus, leaves no doubt that jealousy is a necessary concomitant of the apparently idealized love he is describing.[14] I suspect, then, that the greater emphasis on Palamon's jealousy is a further touch differentiating the attitudes of the two lovers. It may be worth suggesting also that Palamon's despairing speech to Theseus mentioned above (1715–41) may in fact represent an initial rudimentary turn in the direction of wisdom—a relinquishing of earthly hopes and an as yet imperfect acceptance of what must be, born out of adversity, thwarted love, and their resulting exasperation. He is, I would suggest, in the position of one who knows he cannot fall off the floor—which, though not precisely wisdom, can by its very loosening of wordly attachments provide some of the conditions for the development of wisdom.

However that may be, the two young men are surely differentiated by their prayers in the temples of their respective gods. Palamon's prayer (2221–60) is for what he really wants—the love of Emily—and in its lack of concern for victory seems to show a greater acceptance of the ruling powers:

> "Ne I ne axe nat tomorwe to have victorie,
> Ne renoun in this cas, ne veyne glorie
> Of pris of armes blowen up and doun;
> But I wolde have fully possessioun
> Of Emelye, and dye in thy servyse.
> Fynd thow the manere hou, and in what wyse:
> I recche nat but it may bettre be
> To have victorie of hem, or they of me,
> So that I have my lady in myne armes. . . ."
>
> (2239–47)

Arcite (2373–2420) seems at least as interested in victory itself, whether because he has confounded ends and means or because he has been carried away by the pomp of the occasion; his prayer actually concludes, "Yif me the victorie, I aske thee namoore" (2420).[15] The difference is heightened by an obviously parallel pair of references to past loves of the two gods themselves—Palamon's a discreet one-line allusion to the unfilled love of Venus for Adonis (2224), Arcite's a tactlessly expanded account of an embarrassing moment from Mars's past:

> "For thilke peyne, and thilke hoote fir
> In which thow whilom brendest for desir,
> Whan that thow usedest the beautee
> Of faire, yonge, fresshe Venus free,
> And haddest hire in armes at thy wille—
> Although thee ones on a tyme mysfille,
> Whan Vulcanus hadde caught thee in his las,
> And foond thee liggynge by his wyf, allas!—. . ."
>
> (2383–90)

I have already suggested that Palamon in the course of the tale progresses from unphilosophic rebellion to a Boethian acceptance of the state of things, and that Arcite declines from a nominally philosophic outlook to something like Palamon's original condition. Such a pattern seems borne out in Arcite's long dying speech (2765–97)—primarily an outcry at leaving life and earthly love, epitomized in the lines,

> What is this world! what asketh men to have?
> Now with his love, now in his colde grave
> Allone, withouten any compaignye."
>
> (2777–79)

The development I have proposed for Palamon, on the other hand, would approximate that of Wolfram von Eschenbach's Parzival: *er küene, traeclîche wîs,* "he the brave one, slowly wise." There is in fact some reason for suspecting that the ubiquitous heroic ideal *sapientia et fortitudo,*[16] clearly reflected in Wolfram's epitome, may contribute also to the portrayal of the characters in the *Knight's Tale*. Theseus, like the Knight himself in the *General Prologue* (67–68), has been characterized in the opening lines of the tale as embodying the ideal: "What with his wysdom and his chivalrie . . ." (865). Early in the tale, after Arcite's release from prison, he is credited by Palamon with having "wisdom and manhede" (1285); late in the tale, just before Arcite's death, he declares that Palamon has, among other virtues, "knyghthede, / Wysdom . . ." (2789–90). Are we to understand that Arcite has possessed both heroic virtues (with emphasis on wisdom) only in the early part of the tale, and Palamon only in the later part? This difference in their final development might be supported also by the fact that in the first test to win Emily—the tournament—the victory goes to Arcite, while in the second and more enduring one—which I would identify as wise acceptance—it goes to Palamon. The "processe and . . . lengthe of certeyn yers" (2967) by which Theseus's final speech and the outcome of the tale are separated from the rest of its major events might, I suppose, imply that this eventual wise acceptance is at least partly the result of Palamon's having matured over an extended period of time. But if this whole outline has been an accurate reflection of what happens to the two young men in the course of the *Knight's Tale,* it may fairly be asked why the story ends with the more appetitive lover winning Emily and not getting her, and the more idealistic lover having her, so to speak, in the flesh. Surely the point would be still another comment on the working of the Boethian hierarchy, dramatizing one more way in which Providence governs us and not we it. Such as emphasis would, I take it, eliminate the cheaply platitudinous by giving Palamon's finally winning Emily the kind of philosophical perspective it otherwise seems to lack. The whole theme is parodied rather cruelly in the *Miller's Tale* which follows, with Absolon as the burlesque counterpart of Palamon, and Nicholas, of Arcite; and it goes without saying that in the Miller's world the outcome is reversed, with the more appetitive and practical lover possessing the lady.

I have been concentrating on Palamon and Arcite because the differences between them are central to the interpretation I am proposing; let us now glance more briefly at some of the other components of this complex tale. First of all, I would interpret Theseus as the embodiment of mature Boethian wisdom, against whom the limitations of the two young lovers are projected. The traditional associations of his city (Athens) with wisdom, and the city of Palamon and Arcite (Thebes) with passion can hardly be overlooked. The temples of Venus, Diana, and Mars into which Palamon, Emily, and Arcite go to pray can, I suspect, be seen as aspects of the world of human experience; the three petitioners, as seekers after different kinds of temporal felicity; and the elaborate portraiture within the temples (1918–2088), as surveys of the woes inflicted by these pursuits.[17] Palamon's prayer to Venus wins out in the end because of the three, love is the one that lends itself to a higher development; by perfecting one side of man's nature it can lead him to the fuller perfection of wisdom, as Palamon's prayer to Venus ultimately reaches the ear of Saturn (2470–78). The pattern of parallels between gods and men in the poem seems generally accepted: Venus with Palamon, Diana with Emily, Mars with Arcite, and some combination of Saturn and Jupiter with some combination of Egeus and Theseus.[18] A parallel between Saturn and Theseus seems particularly inviting. For example, both clearly represent aspects of wisdom combined with power; both, as rulers, realize certain obligations to the force of love; Theseus sees more deeply than Palamon and Arcite, just as Saturn sees more deeply than Venus and Mars; and Theseus at the end of the tale finds a solution to the problem of love and the results of strife, just as Saturn has found a solution to the dispute of Venus (love) and Mars (strife). I would, however, hesitantly suggest that there may be another dimension to the pattern, in which the gods are figuratively associated with elements in the Boethian hierarchy. The two father-and-son combinations—Saturn and Jupiter on the level of the gods, Egeus and Theseus on the level of the men—have always presented difficulties, mainly because two of the figures are so muted: among the gods, the son, Jupiter, and among the men, the father, Egeus. If we were to suppose an association of the two fathers (Saturn and Egeus) with Providence, and of the two sons (Jupiter and Thesus) with Destiny—which can, after all, be thought of figuratively as the "offspring" of Providence—we would have a pattern in which Destiny is appropriately muted on the divine level, and Providence on the earthly. If this sort of thing is at all worth speculating about, Venus would seem an appropriate enough counterpart of Nature, with emphasis on the inevitable connection between nature and love; and Mars a counterpart of Fortune, with emphasis on the traditional idea of the fortunes of war.

This analysis of the *Knight's Tale* has, of course, provided only the barest sketch of my interpretation; and other major themes (like, for example, the principle of order that has been persuasively proposed as the thematic center of the tale)[19] can be related to it or combined with it in various ways. In any case such a reading, with its emphasis on the workings of the Boethian hierarchy and the frame of "Boethian optimism" that that implies, may on the face of it appear suspiciously facile beside the darker and more questioning interpretation that seems to be coming into fashion for both the *Consolation* and the *Knight's Tale*.[20] I would suggest that the Boethian universe itself, for all its superstructure of philosophical optimism, presents in human terms a bleak enough picture, with its ultimate "consolation" attainable only through a wholesale acceptance of the greatest horrors life has to offer; and that it is this same stoic outlook that pervades the *Knight's Tale*—including grim details like the picture of Saturn inexorably drowning Arcite in the fluid from his own damaged lungs. Boethian optimism, both in the *Consolation* and in the *Knight's Tale,* presupposes a strong philosophical digestion.

Before proceeding to the *Man of Law's Tale,* let us pause briefly to consider the Knight himself as teller of his tale. As I see him, he is presented as a rather uncertain and inept storyteller—the person who is such a gentleman, and so anxious to tell his story properly, that his telling becomes a little tedious.[21] (I suppose I need not comment on Chaucer's neat trick of characterizing the teller as tedious without letting the story itself slip into tedium.) An example of the Knight's storytelling that will occur to everyone is his continual use of *occupatio*—the rhetorical device of passing over a thing without describing it, usually in the name of brevity. Though Chaucer does in fact use *occupatio* in the *Knight's Tale* partly to help him condense leisurely parts of *Il Teseida,* he manages to do it in a way that often leaves the Knight in the position of telling us at length what he is not going to tell us. The most elaborate instance is the forty-five–line account of what he is not going to tell us about the funeral ceremonies for Arcite, beginning,

> But how the fyr was maked upon highte,
> Ne eek the names that the trees highte,
> As ook, firre, birch, aspe, alder, holm, popler,
> Wylugh, elm, plane, assh, box, chasteyn, lynde, laurer,
> Mapul, thorn, bech, hasel, ew, whippeltree,—
>
> (2919–23)

At this point—having begun a sentence clearly intended to say that he is not going to tell us the names of the trees, and then uncontrollably reeled off the names of twenty-one trees—he breaks it off and concludes bravely if somewhat lamely, "How they weren feld, shal nat be toold for me" (2924). The same long *occupatio* ends with the Polonius-like declaration,

> But shortly to the point thanne wol I wende,
> And maken of my longe tale an ende.
>
> (2965–66)

Again, there is the Knight's studiously reflective and carefully qualified recitation of clichés about the behavior of women, betraying, one suspects, no great familiarity with the subject:

> (For wommen, as to speken in comune,
> Thei folwen alle the favour of Fortune). . . .
>
> (2681–82)

And a little later,

> For in swich cas wommen have swich sorwe,
> Whan that hir housbondes ben from hem ago,
> That for the moore part they sorwen so,
> Or ellis fallen in swich maladye,
> That at the laste certeinly they dye.
>
> (2822–26)

In somewhat the same vein is his attempt to describe Emily's performance of her lustral rites before her prayer to Diana. He begins cautiously,

> This Emelye, with herte debonaire,
> Hir body wessh with water of a welle.
> But hou she dide hir ryte I dar nat telle,
> But it be any thing in general. . . .
>
> (2282–85)

Then he is seized by a daring thought—

> And yet it were a game to heeren al.
> To hym that meneth wel it were no charge;
> But it is good a man been at his large.
>
> (2286–88)

Fortified by this reflection, he starts off boldly,

> Hir brighte heer was kembd, untressed al;
> A coroune of a grene ook cerial
> Upon hir heed was set ful fair and meete.
> Two fyres on the auter gan she beete. . . .
>
> (2289–92)

At which point he gets cold feet again and concludes with an embarrassed summary:

> And dide hir thynges, as men may biholde
> In Stace of Thebes and thise bookes olde.
>
> (2293–94)

Finally, there is the famous refusal to speculate about the destination of Arcite's spirit, sometimes interpreted as evidence of religious skepticism on Chaucer's part:

> His spirit chaunged hous and wente ther,
> As I cam nevere, I kan nat tellen wher.
> Therfor I stynte; I nam no divinistre;
> Of soules fynde I nat in this registre,
> Ne me ne list thilke opinions to telle
> Of hem, though that they writen wher they dwelle.
>
> (2809–14)

Here again I think we can hear the voice of the teller I have been suggesting—ill at east with the business of storytelling, and obsessively careful not to tell us anything he cannot footnote.[22]

Let us turn now to the *Man of Law's Tale*—which, though it belongs to a

136,929
College of St. Francis Library
Joliet, Illinois

different block of the *Canterbury Tales,* follows the block containing the *Knight's Tale, Miller's Tale, Reeve's Tale,* and usually *Cook's Tale* in all significant manuscripts.[23] Chaucer's immediate source for it is one part of the early fourteenth-century Anglo-Norman *Chronicle* by Nicholas Trivet, with possibly some influence from Gower's telling of the same story in the *Confessio Amantis.*[24] Chaucer's treatment of the story as told by Trivet is broadly similar to what we have observed in his derivation of the *Knight's Tale* from the *Teseida.* Here, by drastically reducing certain features of Trivet's story and overlaying it, so to speak, with new material, he turns a rather shambling chronicle-account into thematic romance. Its unifying theme, in the words of a classic article by Edward A. Block, is "the philosophical concept that although the stars are potent in human affairs, in the final analysis they are controlled by the far greater power of God."[25] The tale begins as though it were going to be dominated, like the *Knight's Tale,* by the Boethian hierarchy, specifically the power of the heavens. Immediately after the Sultan has fallen in love with Custance by hearing about her (II. 155–80), the teller speculates,

Paraventure in thilke large book
Which that men clepe the hevene ywriten was
With sterres, whan that he his birthe took,
That he for love sholde han his deeth, allas!
For in the sterres, clerer than is glas,
Is writen, God woot, whose koude it rede,
The deeth of every man, withouten drede.

(190–96)

Just before Custance boards the ship that will take her to Syria for her marriage, the teller laments the unfavorable configuration of the heavens and the fact that no attention has been paid to it by her father:

O firste moevyng! Crueel firmament,
With thy diurnal sweigh that crowdest ay
And hurlest al from est til occident
That naturelly wolde holde another way,
Thy crowdyng set the hevene in swich array
At the bigynnyng of this fiers viage,
That crueel Mars hath slayn this mariage.

(295–301)

And again,

Imprudent Emperour of Rome, allas!
Was ther no philosophre in al thy toun?
Is no tyme bet than oother in swich cas?
Of viage is ther noon eleccioun,

> Namely to folk of heigh condicioun?
> Noght whan a roote is of a burthe yknowe?
> Allas, we been to lewd or to slowe!
>
> (309–15)

Shortly after Custance arrives in Syria, the mother of the Sultan, enraged that her son has renounced Mohammed and embraced Christianity, has him and all his followers slain at a feast (323–437); and Custance is set adrift in a rudderless ship (438–45). From this point on, we hear nothing about the heavens or the Boethian hierarchy; rather, just as events in the *Knight's Tale* are motivated by elements of the Boethian hierarchy, so here they are motivated by God's setting aside the workings of the hierarchy and acting directly in Custance's defense. The theme is announced in a prayer by the teller, emphasizing God's rulership over the Fortune that has played so powerful a part in the *Knight's Tale:*

> O my Custance, ful of benigyntee,
> O Emperoures yonge doghter deere,
> He that is lord of Fortune be thy steere!
>
> (446–48)

Custance prays that she may be protected by the Cross of Christ (451–62). The teller asks rhetorically,

> Men myghten asken why she was nat slayn
> Eek at the feeste? who myghte hir body save?
>
> (470–71)

The answer is a long historical survey of God's Providence as manifested to Daniel, Jonas, the Israelites at the Red Sea, and Mary of Egypt, as well as in Christ's feeding of the five thousand (472–504). Particularly relevant is a stanza stressing the mysterious working of Providence:

> God liste to shewe his wonderful myracle
> In hire, for we sholde seen his myghty werkis;
> Crist, which that is to every harm triacle,
> By certeine meenes ofte, as knowen clerkis,
> Dooth thyng for certein ende that ful derk is
> To mannes wit, that for oure ignorance
> Ne konne noght knowe his prudent purveiance.
>
> (477–83)

The rest of the tale is permeated by references to God and His Providence, Christ, and Mary at crucial points in the action. Custance is cast ashore in Northumberland because "The wyl of Crist was that she sholde abyde" (511). She remains there

Til Jhesu hath conveted thurgh his grace
Dame Hermengyld, constablesse of that place.

(538–39)

When Custance is accused of the murder of Hermengild, the teller stresses her dependence on Christ:

Allas! Custance, thou hast no champioun,
Ne fighte kanstow noght, so weylaway!
But he that starf for our redempcioun,
And boond Sathan (and yet lith ther he lay),
So be thy strong champion this day!
For, but if Crist upon myracle kithe,
Withouten gilt thou shalt be slayn as swithe.

(631–37)

When the false knight swears to Custance's guilt, a mysterious hand smites him on the neck, and a voice is heard declaring her innocence (666–79). The king, Alla, is converted "thanked be Cristes grace!" (686); and Christ makes him wed Custance:

And after this Jhesus, of his mercy,
Made Alla wedden ful solempnely
This hooly mayden, that is so bright and sheene;
And thus hath Crist ymaad Custance a queene.

(690–93)

When Custance is about to be put adrift again through the machinations of Donegild, she places herself under the protection first of God and then of Mary:

"He that me kepte fro the false blame
While I was on the lond amonges yow,
He kan me kepe from harm and eek fro shame
In salte see, althogh I se noght how.
As strong as evere he was, he is yet now.
In hym triste I, and in his mooder deere,
That is to me my seyl and eek my steere."

. . . .

"Mooder," quod she, "and mayde bright, Marie . . .
Rewe on my child, that of thy gentillesse,
Rewest on every reweful in distresse."

(827–33, 841, 853–54)

The teller thanks God for her provisions and prays to God for her safety:

And othere necessaries that sholde nede
She hadde ynogh, heryed be Goddes grace!

For wynd and weder almyghty God purchace,
And brynge hire hoom! . . .

(871–74)

She is adrift "Fyve yeer and moore, as liked Cristes sonde . . ." (902). When she finally arrives at a heathen land, the teller prays,

Almyghty God, that saveth al mankynde,
Have on Custance and on hir child som mynde. . . .

(907–8)

While still on shipboard, she is assaulted by a steward but is saved from harm by Mary and Christ:

But blisful Marie heelp hire right anon;
For with hir struglyng wel and myghtily
The theef fil over bord al sodeynly,
And in the see he dreynte for vengeance;
And thus hath Crist unwemmed kept Custance.

(920–24)

The teller asks how such a thing was possible and once more finds the answer in God's Providence:

How may this wayke womman han this strengthe
Hire to defende agayn this renegat?
O Golias, unmesurable of lengthe,
Hou myghte David make thee so maat,
So yong and of armure so desolaat?
Hou dorste he looke upon thy dredful face?
Wel may men seen, it nas but Goddes grace.

Who yaf Judith corage or hardynesse
To sleen hym Olofernus in his tente,
And to deliveren out of wrecchednesse
The peple of God? I seye, for this entente,
That right as God spirit of vigour sente
To hem and saved hem out of meschance,
So sente he myght and vigour to Custance.

(932–45)

Her ship sales on,

Til Cristes mooder—blessed be she ay!—
Hath shapen, thurgh hir endelees goodnesse,
To make an ende of al hir hevynesse.

(950–52)

She eventually makes her way to Rome, and the teller attributes it to Mary:

> Thus kan Oure Lady bringen out of wo
> Woful Custance, and many another mo.
>
> (977–78)

Alla comes to Rome, and when he sees Custance's son asks whether Christ has sent his wife back to him:

> "What woot I if that Crist have hyder ysent
> My wyf by see, as wel as he hire sente
> To my contree fro thennes that she wente?"
>
> (1041–43)

And the concluding prayer of the tale adds a summarizing reference to Christ's governance of human affairs:

> Now Jhesu Crist, that of his myght may sende
> Joye after wo, governe us in his grace,
> And kepe us alle that been in this place! Amen
>
> (1160–62)

Though some of these passages are approximated in Trivet's *Chronicle,* most of them, including all the most prominent, are Chaucer's additions;[26] and in general, while God's Providence and his protection of Custance are mentioned frequently enough in the *Chronicle,* they attain nothing like the thematic insistence they are given in the *Man of Law's Tale*. It may be worth adding that Mary, who is appealed to so repeatedly in the *Man of Law's Tale,* is never mentioned by Trivet.

If these analyses of the *Knight's Tale* and the *Man of Law's Tale* have been at all revealing, the two tales emerge as a closely complementary pair of philosophical narratives, with the action of the *Knight's Tale* ordered by the Boethian hierarchy and that of the *Man of Law's Tale* ordered by God's power to transcend such causality and operate directly in man's behalf. The wisdom of the *Knight's Tale* is an essentially natural, philosophical wisdom, allied to reason and the Boethian tradition; that of the *Man of Law's Tale* is an essentially Christian, theological wisdom, allied to faith and what might be called the Augustinian tradition. In the *Knight's Tale,* the mediators between God's Providence and human affairs are God's regents over the material world, Nature and Fortune; in the *Man of Law's Tale,* the same role is filled by Mary in her familiar Christian function as mediatrix. And both tales are narrated by tellers whose limitations bear an ironic relation to these profound themes. The Knight, as we have seen, falls intellectually shy of being the perfect teller for his tale; the shortcomings in the Man of Law's moral outlook are hinted at unmistakably in his Prologue, where he dutifully echoes Innocent III's *De contemptu mundi* in his lament over poverty (99–121), but then contradicts it blatantly in his praise of wealth:

> O riche marchauntz, ful of wele been yee,
> O noble, o prudent folk, as in this cas!
> Youre bagges been nat fild with ambes as,
> But with sys cynk, that renneth for youre chaunce;
> At Cristemasse myrie may ye daunce!
>
> (122–26)

This basic pattern may, in turn, throw into relief other possible parallels and contrasts. Most obviously, both tales emphasize man's relative powerlessness in the presence of great rulling schemes, the one essentially pagan, the other Christian. Again, it is not difficult to see a thematic relation—at least partly ironic—between the conflicting prayers of Palamon, Emily, and Arcite to their respective deities, and the single-minded prayers to God, Christ, and Mary throughout the *Man of Law's Tale*. As a more specific correspondence, there is the menacing role of Mars in both poems, particularly in view of Mars's generally baleful reputation in medieval astrology. Palamon's seven years in prison and Custance's five years adrift may hold a meaningful parallel, as portrayals of suffering endured for human and divine love respectively. The relative brevity of Custance's wedded happiness, as against the apparent length of Palamon's, allows the *Man of Law's Tale* to end on a note beyond mere temporal felicity; Custance ends her trials not so much in happiness as in holiness. The emphasis on universal mortality in Theseus's long final speech may be seen as foreshadowing also the eventual death of all the characters at the end of the *Man of Law's Tale*. Emily's ill-fated wish to remain a virgin may give unexpected relevance to the curious stanza concerning Custance's marriage to Alla:

> They goon to bedde, as it was skile and right;
> For thogh that wyves be ful hooly thynges,
> They moste take in pacience at nyght
> Swiche manere necessaries as been plesynges
> To folk that han ywedded hem with rynges,
> And leye a lite hir hoolynesse aside,
> As for the tyme,—it may no bet bitide.
>
> (708–14)

The point, that is, may be that in both world views certain great realities remain inescapable. And finally—so obvious that it is apt to be overlooked—let us observe that the *Knight's Tale* is divided into four parts and the *Man of Law's Tale* into three.[27] In medieval number symbolism the most common significance of the number four is the four elements, and through them the material world; the most common significance of three is the Trinity, and through it the spiritual realm. Can it be that Chaucer has used even the formal division of the two tales to point up subtly his contrasting pictures of natural and supernatural causality?

Though a thematic relationship between the *Knight's Tale* and the *Man of Law's Tale* has occasionally been hinted at (most pointedly, perhaps, by Paul G. Ruggiers),[28] I do not think they have so far been seen as the developed philosophical diptych I am proposing. Such a pattern, if it can be accepted, will of course take its place with other partial designs—like those formed by the *Knight's Tale, Miller's Tale,* and *Reeve's Tale,* the *Friar's Tale* and *Summoner's Tale,* and the tales of the Marriage Group—and so contribute at least one more piece to the imperfect jigjaw puzzle of the *Canterbury Tales.*

Notes

This paper epitomizes an interpretation that I have been presenting in my classes, with the usual cumulative embellishments, for the past thirty years—a fact that produces an awkward relationship between it and some of the scholarship from this period. I have tried to note places where the interpretations of other scholars have virtually coincided with my own, but inevitably a great many approximations and similarities of this kind will be unrecorded. Since the Fifth Citadel Conference, the paper has been presented as the Address to the Fellows at the meeting of the Medieval Academy of America at Albuquerque, New Mexico, 18 April 1986.

1. For convenient summaries, see Robert Armstrong Pratt, "The Knight's Tale," in *Sources and Analogues of Chaucer's Canterbury Tales,* ed. W. F. Bryan and Germaine Dempster (1941; reprint, New York: Humanities Press, 1958), 82–105; and "Chaucer's Use of the Teseida," *PMLA* 62 (1947): 613–21.
2. *Chaucer and the Making of English Poetry* (London: Routledge & Kegan Paul, 1972), 2:2.
3. For a checklist and comparative table, see Bernard L. Jefferson, *Chaucer and the Consolation of Philosophy of Boethius* (Princeton: Princeton University Press, 1917), 142–43 and 150; and for critical analyses of particular passages, Kean, *Chaucer and the Making of English Poetry,* 2:1–52, passim.
4. "Chaucer's Philosophical Knight," *Tulane Studies in English* 3 (1952): 52–68; substantially repeated in his *Of Sondry Folk: The Dramatic Principle in the Canterbury Tales* (Austin: University of Texas Press, 1955), 34–49.
5. Quotations are from *The Riverside Chaucer,* ed. Larry D. Benson (Boston: Houghton Mifflin, 1987). Hereafter cited as Benson.
6. "Aspects of Order in the Knight's Tale," *Studies in Philology* 57 (1960): 606–12.
7. Chaucer, trans., *Boece* 4, prosa 6, 53ff. (Benson, 451); but note also Dante, *Inferno* 7.78ff. In any case, this passage provides a good example of Chaucer expanding the barest hint from Boccacio in a strongly Boethian direction; its basis in *Teseida* 5.77.1–2, ed. Aurelio Roncaglia, *Teseida delle nozze d'Emilia,* Scrittori d'Italia, 185 (Bari: Laterza, 1941), 148, is the simple proverbial comment, "Ma come noi veggiam venire in ora / cosa che in mill'anni non avvene. . . ."
8. For example William Frost, "An Interpretation of Chaucer's Knight's Tale," *Review of English Studies* 25 (1949): 292–97; Lumiansky, "Chaucer's Philosophical Knight," 57–67, and *Of Sondry Folk,* 38–47; Douglas Brooks and Alastair Fowler, "The Meaning of Chaucer's

Knight's Tale," *Medium Aevum* 39 (1970): 134–39; and A. J. Minnis, *Chaucer and Pagan Antiquity,* Chaucer Studies, 8 (Cambridge: D. S. Brewer, 1982), 109–16.

9. *Chaucer and the Making of English Poetry,* 2:12. For a detailed analysis, see J. A. W. Bennett, ed., *The Knight's Tale,* 2d ed. (London: Harrap, 1958), 116–17, notes to his lines 393–409.

10. "Meaning of Chaucer's *Knight's Tale,*" 124–36, especially 135.

11. As in note 8 above.

12. Arcite's malady, as analyzed by Edward C. Schweitzer, "Fate and Freedom in *The Knight's Tale,*" *Studies in the Age of Chaucer* 3 (1981): 20–30, would presumably support my interpretation of him as the more appetitive of the two lovers.

13. There are, of course, exceptions; note, e.g., lines 2257–58 and 2629.

14. See 1.6. Dialogue F (or 7); 2.2; and 2.8, Rules 2, 21, 22. E. Trojel, ed., *Andreae Capellani . . . De amore libri tres,* 2d ed. (Munich: Wilhelm Fink, 1972), 145–47, 243, 310–11; John Jay Parry, trans., *The Art of Courtly Love by Andreas Capellanus* (New York: Columbia University Press, 1941), 102–3, 153, 184–85. Dante in the *Convivio,* 1.10.5–10, ed. G. Busnelli and G. Vandelli, *Opere di Dante,* vol. 4, 2d ed. (Florence: Le Monnier, 1964), 1:61–63, says that he was moved to use the vulgar tongue "per lo naturale amore de la propria loquela," explains that "lo naturale amore principalmente muove l'amatore a tre cose," the second of which "è ad esser geloso di quello," and adds, "La gelosia de l'amico fa l'uomo sollicito a lunga provedenza"; though his immediate subject is love for his native tongue, his remarks seem intended also to define the relationship between love and jealousy themselves. A fourteenth-century treatise by Jehan le Bel, *Li ars d'amour, de vertu et de boneurté,* 1.4.11, ed. Jules Petit (Brussels: Victor Devaux, 1867–69), 1:170–72, distinguishing between *jalousie malvaise* and *jalousie bonne,* makes a somewhat similar pronouncement about commendable jealousy accompanying sexual love: "En l'amour honeste est une autre manière de jalousie ki est bonne; en tel amor li amis quiert le bien del ami; et quant ce quiert durement et aigrement, si se muet li amans contre tot çou ki est contraire au bien del amet, et ensi dist-on: 'Je suis tous jalous de vous aidier contre celui, et de vous servir et valoir.' " I am grateful to Mary F. Wack of Stanford University for reminding me of the passage from Dante, and to Alfred Karnein of the Johann Wolfgang Goethe–Universität, Frankfurt am Main, for referring me to the treatise of Jehan.

15. Perhaps the prayers of Palamon and Arcite are to be viewed against Boethius's remarks on goods as means to other goods (Chaucer, trans., *Boece* 3, prosa 10, 227–33; Benson, 352).

16. For bibliography and some applications to other literature, see my articles *"Sapientia et Fortitudo* as the Controlling Theme of *Beowulf,*" *Studies in Philology* 55 (1958): 423–56; *"Beowulf,"* in *Critical Approches to Six Major English Works: Beowulf through Paradise Lost,* ed. R. M. Lumiansky and Herschel Baker (Philadelphia: University of Pennsylvania Press, 1968), 3–40; *"Sapientia et Fortitudo* in the Old English *Judith,*" in *The Wisdom of Poetry: Essays in Early English Literature in Honor of Morton W. Bloomfield,* ed. Larry D. Benson and Siegfried Wenzel (Kalamazoo, Mich.: Medieval Institute Publications, 1982), 13–29 and 264–68; and *"Sir Gawain and the Green Knight,"* in *Medieval and Renaissance Studies: Proceedings of the Southeastern Institute of Medieval and Renaissance Studies* [*no. 10*], *Summer, 1979,* ed. George Mallary Masters (Chapel Hill: University of North Carolina Press, 1984), 24–44.

17. A somewhat similar interpretation is proposed by Richard Neuse, "The Knight: The First Mover in Chaucer's Human Comedy," *University of Toronto Quarterly* 31 (1962): 302–3.

18. See for example Neuse, "The Knight," 304; Brooks and Fowler, "Meaning of Chaucer's *Knight's Tale,*" 125–28; and Minnis, *Chaucer and Pagan Antiquity,* 109–21.

19. In various forms by, for example, Dale Underwood, "The First of *The Canterbury Tales,*" *ELH* 26 (1959): 455–69; Charles Muscatine, *Chaucer and the French Tradition: A Study in Style and Meaning* (Berkeley: University of California Press, 1960), 175–90; Halverson, "Aspects of Order"; and Robert W. Hanning, " 'The Struggle between Noble Designs and Chaos': The Literary Tradition of Chaucer's Knight's Tale." *Literary Review* 23 (1979/80): 519–41.

20. For example Winthrop Wetherbee, *Platonism and Poetry in the Twelfth Century: The*

Literary Influence of the School of Chartres (Princeton: Princeton University Press, 1972), 82; Minnis, *Chaucer and Pagan Antiquity*; and V. A. Kolve, *Chaucer and the Imagery of Narrative: The First Five Canterbury Tales* (Stanford: Stanford University Press, 1984), 85–157.

21. Noted by Hanning, "Struggle," 520 and 530, who adds a brilliant analysis (534–38) of the Knight's telling as that of a professional soldier.

22. Noted by Paul T. Thurston, *Artistic Ambivalence in Chaucer's Knight's Tale* (Gainesville: University of Florida Press, 1968), 40–41.

23. See the convenient tables of Manly and Rickert, reproduced most recently by Larry D. Benson, "The Order of *The Canterbury Tales*," *Studies in the Age of Chaucer* 3 (1981): 118–20.

24. For a convenient summary, along with the pertinent parts of Trivet's *Chronique* and Gower's *Confessio*, see Bryan and Dempster, *Sources and Analogues*, 155–206; and for a detailed analysis of the relationship between the *Chronique* and the *Man of Law's Tale*, Edward A. Block, "Originality, Controlling Purpose, and Craftsmanship in Chaucer's *Man of Law's Tale*," *PMLA* 68 (1953): 572–616.

25. "Originality," 598.

26. For Chaucer's additions emphasizing God's protection of Custance, see Block, "Originality," 596–98.

27. These divisions appear in all major editions and are supported in the critical edition by John M. Manly and Edith Rickert, *The Text of the Canterbury Tales* (Chicago: University of Chicago Press, 1940), which cites no variants of them. I am indebted to Helen Cooper for reminding me that in the Hengwrt manuscript the *Knight's Tale* is divided into three parts, while the *Man of Law's Tale* has no divisions. See *The Canterbury Tales . . . A Facsimile and Transcriptions of the Hengwrt Manuscript, with Variants from the Ellesmere Manuscript*, ed. Paul G. Ruggiers (Norman: University of Oklahoma Press, 1979), 70, 97, 141, 462, 490; or *The Canterbury Tales . . . Edited from the Hengwrt Manuscript*, ed. N. F. Blake, York Medieval Texts, 2d series (London: Edward Arnold, 1980).

28. "The Form of *The Canterbury Tales: Respice Fines*," *College English* 17 (1956): 442–44; and *The Art of the Canterbury Tales* (Madison: University of Wisconsin Press, 1965), 173.

Separations and St. Paul's Thorn in Chaucer's *Troilus*

DAVID W. HISCOE

Troilus and Criseyde—almost surrealistically so—is a poem about separations. On the most obvious level, the lovers' separation moves the narrator to tell his tale. This parting is the narrative germ of the poem; and from the seed grows an amazing crop of recurring manifestations of the motif. A partial catalogue can give some sense of the extent to which severances pervade all levels of Chaucer's story.

The poem's plot, to begin with, is set against the mythic background of both Helen's abduction from Greece and the war that divides the Greeks and the Trojans. When the Palladium is separated from the town. Troy will fall. The narrator's first contact with his audience speaks of the time "er that I parte fro ye" (1.5), and the first action he recounts is Calkas's successful attempt to "departen softely" (1.78)[1] from Troy, a severance that dangerously estranges Criseyde from the town's defenders. The intrigue that engenders the love affair itself moves through a seemingly endless series of separations. Falling in love initially leaves Troilus "in swich disjoynte" (3.496), a situation Pandarus diagnoses when he insists that "he that departed is in everi place / Is nowhere hol" (1.960–61). Offering to cure such psychic separations, Criseyde's uncle strategically accuses Troilus of distancing himself from true friendship (1.617ff.) and warns him that the role of friends is "To entreparten wo as glad desport" (1.592); Troilus's suffering will soon disappear, since Pandarus "wol parten with the al thi peyne" (1.589). Softening his niece up for the final seduction, Pandarus convinces Criseyde that Troilus is nearly parted from his reason by love-longing and by a deadly jealousy induced when she sundered her vows to the fictitious Horaste. Later, the uncle's clever separation of Criseyde from her watchful companions allows the lover their first night of secret love.

The manifold separations in the plot of *Troilus* are intellectual as well as merely physical. The first secret meeting between the lovers is prepared for by the contrived moral distinctions that Troilus offers himself to ease his own suspicions of impropriety. Trysts, as planned by Pandarus, may seem a little like "bauderye," but Troilus carefully divorces "felawship" from such nastiness:

> Departe it so, for wyde-wher is wist
> How that ther is diversite requered
> Bytwixen thynges like, as I have lered.
>
> (3.404–6)

Both Criseyde and the narrator pander to similar philosophic divisions. Proper lovers, the heroine argues, either know that man's joys are fleeting or are naively ignorant of this natural law: "it mot ben oon of tweye" (3.823). The narrator assures his audience that the human community, at least in the ways of amorous practice, is a diversity of separate behaviors, "for to wynnen love in sondry ages, / In sondry londes, sondry ben usages" (2.27–28).

Such sunderings may allow the lovers to find their joys during their "wele," but when "twynned be [they] tweyne" (4.476). Troilus is quick to find fault in learned separations of ideas into categories: "Love hym made al prest to don hire byde," but "resoun" requires that he let Criseyde be traded for Antenor; he is "with desir and reson twight" (4.572). After leaving Troy, Criseyde finds herself in an equivocal world where calculating men "lede . . . with ambages, / That is to seyn, with double wordes slye, / Swiche as men clepen a word with two visages" (5.897). Apparently adapting well to such a world, she leaves the poem very adept herself at separating the word from the deed as she ends her final and all-too-short letter to Troilus by claiming that "Th'entent is al, and nat the lettres space" (5.1630). Indeed, the only plot detail that escapes this multiplication of separations might seem to be Criseyde's unfashionably joined eyebrows.

The ubiquitous separations in *Troilus* also converge on places other than the poem's plot. The sunderings in the story itself, for example, beget an analagous narrative technique. Chaucer's narrator incessantly complains that he is fundamentally separated from his subject material. He knows nothing of love "for [his] unliklynesse" (1.16), and the God of Love is "fer . . . from his help in derknesse" (1.18). This separation produces, aside from the ambiguities that his sliding attitude toward his story generates,[2] a strange retelling of the Troy story. Coming to *Troilus* with a set of responses cultivated by the myth and its expected manner of presentation, the audience is cut off from the usual ways in which the tale might take on its meanings. Though the traditional meanings of the rape of Helen cannot help but provide the background of the poem's consideration of love, Helen herself is oddly severed from her usual and expected role. Instead of the face that brought ruin to a civilization, the narrator presents us with what Mark Lambert has called "the maternal Helen," a stately, gracious woman well in control of both her emotional and political ties.[3] Even the mode the speaker uses to address his audience is severed from the usual generic expectations. As Charles Dahlberg has pointed out, the poem starts with epic promise only quietly to ambush its listeners by substituting themselves, the "ye" of the first stanza, for the Muses that are conventionally addressed at this point.[4]

Having carefully placed a multitude of separations both in the plot and in the narrative techniques of the poem, Chaucer brings the pattern to fulfillment in the narrator's palinode where Chaucer's persona abruptly distances himself from the fictive world he has sympathetically presented for five long books and disappears into final prayer beseeching the love of God and the Virgin Mary. The rift that the narrator tries to put between his story and its stated moral may be the most openly dramatic of the severances around which Chaucer's tale is constructed. Yet it in turn creates an even more troublesome split. The apparent separation between the story's deeds and its stated moral gapes so wide that the narrator finally can solve his dilemma only by condemning all of pagan literature—"the forme of olde clerkis speche / In poetrie" (5.1854–55)—as unworthy of presentation to a Christian audience. In writing the poem that ends with the narrator's condemnation, Chaucer the poet, however, has rather obviously thought it necessary to use pagan subject matter. In not taking his own narrator's advice, Chaucer insists upon the possibility that his persona, and perhaps that persona's moral, stand separate from himself.

The narrator's strenuous attempt to divide pagan literature cleanly from Christian revelation parallels and prepares for the fundamental separation in *Troilus and Criseyde,* the severance to which all others call attention. As he placed Troilus in the heavens and bestows his tacit approval upon the hero's contempt for "This wrecched world" (5.1817), the narrator leaves his audience with an almost Manichaean rift between "the pleyn felicite" (5.1818) of the heavenly and the world of "floures faire" (5.1841), the world that has interested us in the lovers' story to begin with. Chaucer's speaker ends his poem demanding a militantly held and easily distinguished separation of the earthly and the heavenly, the natural and the supernatural. One, it would seem, must lay "his herte al holly" (5.1846) on Christ, or one must wholeheartedly weep for the earthly pains and sorrows of the likes of the Trojans and Greeks. The Christian world is separated clearly and definitely from the "rascaille" of the earthly world; and the surface of Chaucer's poem is left as far away from its revelatory moral as the world of Christ is from the universe of nature.

The act of severance, for which Troilus's loss of Criseyde is only the most obvious metaphor, is, then, a central organizing principle of the poem's universe; and the ultimate focus of the organization is to force the audience to define, as must the narrator, the proper relationship between things of this world and those of the City of God—between the earthly and the heavenly. The narrator's rather desperate solution is to swing wildly between a firm attachment to the earthly during the tale's plot and an equally exclusive and determined attachment to the heavenly in its palinode. In the middle of the narrator's equivocal wrestlings with such distinctions Chaucer wittily submerges a telling biblical comment on the poem's creation of a world abundant with such separations. As the narrator waxes enthusiastic in praise of the lovers' consummation, he drops an almost casual remark that gives us a solid place from which to watch the comic inadequacies of his own attempt to understand and control the traditional Christian distinctions between the two spheres. As he waits in exuberant expectation of Criseyde's submission to the powers of sexual love, Chaucer's persona proclaims that though "she hath hard ben herebyforn" there will be cause for rejoicing in the near future:

> To God hope I, she hath now kaught a thorn,
> She shal not pulle it out this nexte wyke.
> God sende mo swich thornes on to pike!
>
> (2.1271–74)

As John Fisher has pointed out, the thorn for which the narrator so gleefully thanks God is suspiciously reminiscent of St. Paul's thorn in the flesh (2 Cor. 12:7).[5] Supplying an authoritative explanation of the relationship between the heavenly and the earthly, Paul's understanding of the role of the thorn in the flesh in his own spiritual life provides an ironic and illuminating foil to the narrator's inability to keep the two realms from splitting his story apart.

Perhaps the central issue in 2 Corinthians is Paul's defense of his authority as a prophetic speaker, an authority apparently under pervasive attack from elements of his flock in Corinth as he begins to write his letter. The thorn in his flesh becomes, in the course of a strategically convoluted rhetorical argument, the crucial metaphor used to explain the source of the preacher's ability to do God's work. The heavenly is, to be sure, the end of the earthly pilgrimage for Paul. But the relationship that he delineates between the holy and the mundane as he prepares for his climactic thorn metaphor is far from either a dualistic or a simplistic one. In fact, his defense of his pastoral effectiveness demands an essential place for both realms in the divine scheme. The parable of the thorn in the flesh that Chaucer's narrator invokes in the course of his manifold severances is, above all, a parable of the inadequacy of glibly separating the divine and the earthly.

Paul begins his balancing of the two realms by first clearly giving the City of God its due. The Corinthians surely must "not be mismated with unbelievers," for "what partnership have righteousness and iniquity?"

Again, "what has a believer in common with an unbeliever," or "What agreement has the temple of God with idols?" Fundamentally separate from iniquity, the Christian is to "touch nothing unclean" (6:14–17); and while defending the City of God, the Church's "weapons of . . . warfare are not worldly but have divine power" (10:4). And as Paul knows from his own experience, the Christian has access to the heavenly in the most unequivocal manner possible: in what appears a mystical vision he himself was "caught up into Paradise" where he "heard things that cannot be told, which man may not utter" (12:3–5).

With this pole of his argument carefully stated, however, Paul moves to complicate the relationship between the two realms by introducing one of the most productive biblical sources for the doctrine of the fortunate fall. Paul is capable of experiencing a rise into the paradisiacal "third heaven" (12:2), into an immediate unity with God. But such a manner of engagement with the celestial is, in itself, profoundly double-edged: one might distance oneself from earthly life into the heavenly vision, but that vision's very lack of communicableness leaves the probability that, indeed, it might be a hindrance rather than a blessing for an earthly flock in need of spiritual guidance here in this life.[6] The vision, after all, is of things that may not be told, of things that may not be uttered.

Paul makes the same point earlier when he warns that while those in the congregation who speak in tongues might "utter mysteries in the Spirit," they just as likely fail to speak a useful language to those around them. "If the bugle gives an indistinct sound," he argues by metaphor, "how will any know what is played?" (1 Cor. 14:8). Or, "if you in a tongue utter speech that is not intelligible, how will any one know what is said? For you will be speaking into the air" (14:9). Utterances, for the preacher most particularly, must be told so that they might be understood.

By refusing to speak in tongues and by renouncing his disembodied trips to third heavens, Paul makes clear that his effectiveness as a speaker for the City of God comes directly from his own painful entanglement in the affairs of this world. Paul draws emphasis to the crucial interconnections between the earthly and the heavenly by creating a paradoxical play of ideas that deftly reinterprets his own concept of what constitutes "the flesh." Fools, quite certainly, "glory after the flesh" (2 Cor. 11:18–19); and Paul will have none of this foolish glorification of the worldly. Disembodied trips into the third heaven are dramatically useful for sundering such fleshly attachments. But having set up an easy distinction, Paul quietly destroys it by presenting another sort of exaltation one can find in the worldly life. The massive catalogue of the suffering he endures in the course of carrying out his pastoral duties unexpectedly redefines the glories of the flesh for which he is willing to give up his mystical visions. While distancing the saint from the immediate joys of divine union, Paul's entirely human life as a persecuted preacher draws him closer to his neighbors and forces upon him a voice that his flock can hear and presumably heed. The robberies, near-drownings, imprisonments, the weariness and the pain of his temporal rounds of teaching, the infirmities, reproaches, necessities, and humiliating escapes from persecution (12:10) are his undeniable connections with life as both he and his flock must live it after the Fall. Instead of speaking in tongues or in the unutterable words of the third heaven, Paul commands a language grounded in the pain that all humans share. He can speak to his flock, as the salutation to the letter shows, because both he and they "share abundantly in Christ's sufferings" (1:6). And because he has shared their sufferings, he can also effectively share his knowledge of Christ's comfort (1:7).

The image of the thorn in the flesh provides the encapsulating metaphor both for Paul's suffering and for that suffering's ability to serve as the origin of his power as a speaker to his pastoral charges. If the heavenly is opened up to Christians, there is a danger that a consuming interest in the celestial will cut them off from the lives of those who surrounded them. To keep the saint, and all of humankind, solidly on the earthly road where they must earnestly confront and attempt to reform their fallen natures amid all the daily rigors of the average life, God bestows the thorn: "to keep me from being too elated by the abundance of revelations, a thorn was given me in the flesh, a messenger of Satan, to harass me, to keep me from being too elated" (12:7). Paul, in short, does not reach Christ or his flock by climbing into heavenly revelations. Instead, accepting the gift of the thorn as God bestows it, he is "content with weaknesses, insults, hardships, persecutions, and calamities" (12:10). Momentarily giving up the celestial, temporarily forced to entangle himself with the earthly, Paul discovers the paradoxes central to the fortunate fall: to go up, he must go down; to live the heavenly life, he must live the earthly one. In this fortunate thorn, Paul ultimately finds not only humility, but also his strength as a man and as a preacher: "for when I am weak, then I am strong" (12:10).

An emblematic numerological contrast provides the final paradigmatic statements of the relationship between the celestial and the earthly that Paul expresses in the metaphor of the thorn in the flesh. Having once dwelt at least temporarily in paradise, Paul finds himself sorely stuck with the agonizing prickings of mundane life. Naturally he initially rankles at the descent and questions the wisdom of God's gift: "Three times I besought the Lord about this, that [the thorn] should leave me" (12:8). Rather than giving Paul an easy deliverance into the third heaven, his three pleas produce an entirely different sort of saving grace. Instead of disappearing into the unutterable, Paul ends his letter to his flock by assuring them that he is ready for the third time to come before the Corinthians to berate, haggle, argue, exhort, beg, and harass in his attempt to keep them dedicated to their spiritual well-being. The replacement of the journey to the third heaven with Paul's willingness to return to Corinth for the third time clearly underlines the value of the earthly in Paul's delicate balance.

The audience that originally heard Chaucer's narrator rejoice in Criseyde's thorn would have understood Paul's story through the lens of a traditional exegesis, which, with Augustine and Gregory the Great, focused unequivocally on the mysterious point of convergence the story offers between the celestial and the mundane.[7]

For Augustine the parable provides a biblical answer to the central question every preacher must face: "what can we do . . . when we are conveying lessons of spiritual things to carnal men."[8] Since Paul obtains his authority as a speaker from an immersion in the trials of daily life, Augustine's discussion of the thorn continually stresses that any attempt to win humankind for the City of God must not ignore the subtle knot that makes us human. The essence of that humanity, even for those as saintly as Paul, is the interpenetration of the heavenly and the earthly disclosed by the thorn in the flesh: "We are men, let us acknowledge the holy Apostles to be men; chosen vessels, but as yet frail, as yet in the pilgrimage in this flesh, not yet triumphant in the heavenly country."[9] Being able to travel to the third heaven and still be brought low by the thorn, Paul is representative of all who share his faith. Christians simultaneously hold within themselves both a heritage from original creation and an inheritance from the Fall: "Is . . . the very same person at once spiritual and carnal? The very same undoubtedly, as long as he liveth here, so he is."[10] The thorn in the flesh presents an image of humankind that will not easily brook a separation of the divine and the earthly. Augustine steadfastly plants the beginning of self-understanding and of his own ability to use that understanding to influence others in the knowledge that "there are not two contrary natures but, of both, one man."[11] *Here,* firmly in what he calls "the solitude of this present pilgrimage," the thorn leaves the spiritual inextricably intertwined with the carnal. The "I myself" that is at the center of Augustine's reading of Paul is the paraxodical "I in the mind, I in the flesh."[12]

Since Job suffers a series of Old Testament types for the thorn in the flesh, Gregory the Great repeatedly employs Paul's metaphor in the *Moralia in Job*. And again, what Gregory finds useful in the emblem is its ability to reveal the inseparability of the celestial and the mundane. With the thorn implanted, Paul becomes, in fact, the very principle of paradoxical opposites held together in one figure:

> Paul, do you already see Jesus in heaven, and do you still fly man on earth? Are you carried into Paradise, are you made acquainted with secret words of God, and are you still tempted by a messenger of Satan?

> Whence so strong, that you art caught up to heavenly places, whence so weak that you fly from man on the earth, and still endure hard handling from an angel of Satan?[13]

All humanity, Gregory argues, follow the same pattern of fortunate paradoxes: God "applies the allurements of vices to promote virtues, and wounds our healthy state in order to preserve it that we who fly from humility when we run, may cling to it at least when falling. . . . By the wonderful course of the dispensation, when they are tempted, they are humbled; when they are humbled they cease at once to be [Satan's]. The jaws of this Behemoth . . . lose the Elect of God by crushing them, by attempting to destroy, he keeps them from perishing."[14] The balancing of the heavenly and the earthly revealed by the thorn is, as Gregory explains further, the essence of God's plan for salvaging the fallen humankind: "if the Spirit lifted us above, while the flesh did not tempt, it would by that very uplifting prostrate us the worse in the fall of pride."[15] This providential suspension between utter degradation and destructive pride becomes inscribed as a central universal principle in one of the most eloquent passages in the *Moralia:* "by a certain regulation it takes place, . . . by a strange method it is brought to pass, . . . by the exactest regulating of the Interior Judgment, the soul is balanced in a kind of mean above the things below, and below the things above."[16] God's painful but ultimately benevolent regulating thorn grants the human soul the ability to "at one and the same time enjoy the gifts of a firm state, and humbly acknowledge her own state of infirmity."[17] Having been granted the thorn, Paul finds himself then in a spiritually fruitful balance between the calls of the earthly and the demands of the heavenly.

Most importantly, Gregory also unequivocally teaches that Paul's ability to live in the flesh instead of merging into some sort of unutterable mystical vision is the bedrock on which the saint's ability to speak to his flock rests: "Who lifts you on high, again limits you with the minutest measuring, that both in your miracle you should preach to us the power of God, and again in your fear cause us to remember our own infirmity."[18] The certain regulating power of Paul's thorn grants him not only the knowledge of heavenly things, but also the knowledge of earthly ways to transmit celestial guidance to an earthly flock.

At first glance, the narrator's invocation of Paul's thorn seems to show that he has absorbed the essence of the saint's metaphorical marriage between the celestial and the mundane. Though the narrator borrows his words from the language of courtly love, the essence of his often-repeated conviction that "sondry peynes bryngen folk in heavene" (3.1204) is Pauline to the core. So is the vehicle on which these folk are to ride to their paradises. Paul's thorn bestows the humility by which, as Gregory insists, "they who could perish from pride, are, by being humbled, preserved from destruction."[19] The poem's first two references to the thorn in the flesh—one oblique and one explicit—show the main characters brought low from a prideful disdain of love and, now humble, able to enter the blissful world of human *amor.* In his joy that Criseyde "hath now kaught a thorn," the narrator is merely fulfilling a pattern which starts earlier in the poem as Troilus, mocking those under love's control, receives his version of the Saint's pricking. "Moost in pride above" in the temple of Pallas Athena (1.230), the proud knight soon finds that he must "Wax sodeynly moost subgit unto love" (231) when he is pierced with an arrow from Cupid's bow. Metaphorically pulling the feathers from the peacock (210), the dart from the God of Love rescues Troilus from "surquidrie and foul presumpcioun" (213) and brings him within the humbling and nourishing realm of love.

When Criseyde's pride is finally pricked by the humbling thorn in Book II, the narrator happily looks forward to the once-proud lovers reaping the fruits—sexual and otherwise—of humility. But if the parable of the thorn in the flesh teaches, as Gregory and Paul argue, that humility will save us from destruction, the fact that the narrator has begun his story well knowing that Troilus's life will end in what amounts to a suicide and that Criseyde will lose all claims to honor and innocence suggests the comic inadequacy of his understanding of the biblical story that he himself invokes. The tale that should lead to a fortunate convergence of the City of God and the cities of men produces a multitude of separations; the story that should grant us protection from destructive pride breeds a series of disasters. The blunderingly scrambled version of Paul's parable that the narrator presents in his prayer for Criseyde's thorn thus produces a resonant commentary on his own inabilty throughout *Troilus and Criseyde* to achieve a poise between the heavenly and the earthly.

The poem is, in fact, a comic catalogue of every possible way a jangler might tip Paul's careful balance either too far toward the mundane or too far toward the celestial. When Paul insists that the thorns of his earthly life are more valuable to his flock than mystical visions, he metaphorically shifts the celestial in the direction of the earthly. The narrator's favorite distortion of the saint's maneuver is to accelerate this movement wildly until the City of God is nowhere in sight. The convergence of the two realms in Paul becomes their separation in *Troilus;* and the narrator leaves no doubt which end of the scale he prefers. In the preeminent separation in *Troilus,* Pandarus, arguing early in the poem that love is a force that all humans must heed, strategically divides all amorous impulses into "loves hete, / Celestial, or elles love of kynde" (1.978–79). Love of God is neatly and glibly divided from man's natural instincts; following one, it would seem, inevitably precludes following the other, and both are presented as equally worthy. It is clearly "love of kynde" that Pandarus promotes and that the narrator gleefully celebrates throughout much of his tale.

The poem's last explicit reference to Paul's thorn highlights the narrator's inability to control the implications of Pandarus's crucial separation of the earthly from the heavenly. With Troilus sprawled across Criseyde's bed in little but his undershirt, Pandarus twists Paul's divine malady into a very thinly disguised sexual proposition: "Yee, nece, wol ye pullen out the thorn / That striketh in his herte?" (3.1104–5). The uncle clearly reads his Bible in the Vulgate where *thorn in the flesh* appears as *stimulus carni;* his reductive revision of Paul's metaphor discloses only the carnal stimulation, as Fisher notes, of "the thorn of sexual need."[21] Yet in his enthusiastic devotion to and stimulation by his own characters and their quite earthly pursuits, the narrator does not notice even the most glaring inconsistencies in the story he himself is telling. Pandarus wants Criseyde to pull out Troilus's thorn; the narrator, referring to Criseyde's own pricking, has earlier rejoiced that "She shal nat pulle it out this next wyke" (2.1273). The reader can hardly be expected to trust the authority of a speaker who cannot seem to keep his own metaphors from splitting apart. Unsure where the thorn should be or what to do with it once it is there, Chaucer's persona has reduced Paul's metaphorical deferral of heavenly consummations to only a comically salacious delight in the immediately forthcoming pleasures of the entirely fleshly life. And, if Paul's ability to accept the thorn grants him the power to speak effectively to his flock, the narrator's inability to understand God's gift of the thorn surely accounts for some of the contradictions and confusions that keep creeping into his story.

At the same time that Chaucer's narrator shifts Paul's balance unduly toward the earthly, however, he also places an equally suspect weight on the celestial end of the scale. While in the process of evoking the terrible and painful beauty of the fortunate fall, the narrator ironically creates a fictive world in which paradise is always easily within reach just around every corner. When he enthusiastically prays that his deity will bestow the thorn on Criseyde, the obvious implication is that the imminent sexual consummation will quickly produce an instant abundance of third heavens right here on earth. In place of the saint's painful and circuitous route to the heavenly, the narrator allows his characters and his audience to enter the "thridde heven faire" (3.2) that Venus freely offers to all "who nede hath" of the certain "gladnesse" that the excursion will surely create (3.49). So while Paul is deferring the immediate pleasure of heavenly visitations for the arduous struggle to communicate successfully with his congregations, the narrator of *Troilus* has his characters briskly going about preparing themselves for a more pleasant version of the saint's heavenly trips. As soon as Criseyde's thorn is securely in place, Pandarus confidently advises Troilus that he should "Make . . . redy right anon," since in no time at all he will be in his lady's bed where the lovers shall "into heven blisse wende" (3.703–4). And sure enough, it takes only the relatively painless fall of his faint onto Criseyde's pillow before Troilus quickly finds himself stroking her long "flesshly" sides in what the narrator assures us is "this hevene" (3.1251). Similar celestial joys abound everywhere in the poem. When Criseyde listens to her lover speak, "It was an hevene his wordes for to here" (3.1742); and "Paradis," the narrator tells us in his formal portrait of the heroine, "stood formed in hire yën," (5.817).

With such a plethora of visits to heaven resulting from Criseyde's pricking, the narrator's delight in his characters' thorns is quite understandable. But even this joy comically shows his fundamental misunderstanding of Paul's balance. Although Paul insists that an "abundance of revelations" is available to Christians, God bestows the thorn on the Saint "to keep [him] from being too elated." The narrator's version of the Fall seems a good deal too merry; and it is clearly all too easy to enter his kingdoms of heaven.

The final irony is that the narrator's naive overvaluation of both the heavenly and the earthly produces a story that ultimately undervalues each realm. Paul's visit to the third heaven finally works to confirm the value of his earthly life. The trips the narrator and his characters make into the celestial leave them only unfit for or even contemptuous of the world around them. The narrator, for instance, follows Troilus's famous aubade against the return of day and the mundane world that will take him away from Criseyde's bed with Pandarus's insistence that "he / That ones may in hevene blisse be, / He feleth other weyes . . . / Than thilke tyme he first herde of it seye" (3.1656–59). Having been on divine journeys, Troilus hardly wants to return to Troy at war. When the dead hero actually experiences the "hevenyssh melodye" of the eighth sphere after his death, the narrator's parodic thorn has left Troilus even less able to value properly the earthly life than he was at the poem's beginning. In Athena's temple he would "smyle and holden it folye" (1.194) when others endured the travails of love. His contempt for earthly suffering has only escalated by the poem's ending when he "lough right at the wo" (5.1821) of those who mourn his death and "fully gan despise / This wrecched world" (5.1816–17).[22]

But if the narrator's comic aversion to the earthly causes him to tilt Paul's balance mightily toward the heavenly, it paradoxically spoils his characters' ability to be comfortable in their fictive City of God. Appeals to the heavenly, in fact, become oddly ironic celebrations of only the earthly. Paul's parable of the thorn in the flesh shows the proper appreciation of the heavenly design behind the fortunate fall: the worldly is only a necessary means to an end, since it provides the saint with the earthly experiences that can allow his heavenly revelations to penetrate into the lives of his flock. By contrast the narrator asks for falls by the dozen, failures world without end. Paul rebels against, but then accepts, the one thorn God bestows: the narrator stumbles close to blasphemy when he prays that "God sende mo swich thornes on to pike" (2.1274).

The light into which Paul's careful interlacing of the heavenly and the earthly casts *Troilus* also provides an implicit commentary on the poem's controversial ending. The narrator's recoil from the effects his characters suffer from their attachment to the earthly merely allows him once again to vacillate between the two realms, this time retreating into the heavenly. If he has valued the earthly too much in the body of the poem, he now sends his *moralitas* too far in the opposite direction. Paul is willing, for the good of his neighbors, to return to the earthly even after glimpsing the abundance of the heavenly. The narrator's final prayer for union with the celestial should surely be seen as a last ironic reversal of Paul's example, Asking for too many thorns in his love story, he ends in the palinode by supposing a world in which Paul's redemptive thorn is totally superfluous. After earlier diminishing Paul's thorn into merely a metaphor for sexual delight, the narrator advises his listeners to forgo "blynde lust" (5.1824) and fix their eyes on "the pleyn felicite / That is yn hevene above" (5.1818–19). With the complexity of human pain and blundering reduced to only earthly lust, the narrator sees little problem with pulling out the thorn altogether. Having asked for an abundance of thorns, the narrator finds himself with more than he can handle; and, stunned by the complexities inherent both in his story and in human life as a whole, he ends his poem in a most un-Pauline retreat into his world of separations and his glib version of a thornless heaven.

Since Paul's ability to understand his own thorn ultimately provides him with the base from which to communicate with his flock, it is no accident that Chaucer ends *Troilus and Criseyde* by exposing his persona's inability to speak with real authority. Having retreated into an easy separation of the earthly and the heavenly, the narrator can only end his poem enmeshing both himself and his audience in strategy after strategy of rhetorical equivocation and evasion. In the course of five of the last stanzas, for instance, he brings his narrative to the point of Troilus's death, careens off to tell how nasty men are to women, breaks unpredictably into the envoi for his "litel bok" of over eight thousand lines, takes a leap into historical linguistics and the mechanics of manuscript reproduction, and without benefit of transition finally returns to the "purpos of my rather speche / . . . as I began yow for to seye" (5.1799–1800). His hero, after disappearing for almost fifty lines, finally dies. In addition to this almost surrealistic failure to order his speech, the narrator also cannot end it. As Monica

McAlpine points out, there are at least four desperate attempts to bring the work to a conclusion in its last several hundred frantic lines.[23] Filling his work with separations, Chaucer's speaker has an appropriately agonizing time finding a proper closure.

In the last separation in *Troilus,* this lack of an authoritative voice provides perhaps the most comic indictment of the narrator's disastrous attempt to sunder the heavenly and the earthly. Having removed the thorn from the flesh and vanished into the disembodied heavens, he quite naturally has little use for pagan love stories. But the narrator's final passionate dismissal of exactly the sort of earthly "feigned" tale that he has just told produces a separation that Chaucer himself pointedly refuses to make. *Troilus,* after all, is a story of the pagan world; and Chaucer has obviously not considered it necessary to give up the tale. His refusal to accept his own narrator's advice to abandon the pagan, to separate the earthly and the Christian, leaves us with a symbolic remedy for the multitude of divisions that have threatened to engulf the narrator's story. By weaving together the pagan and the Christian, by interlacing the earthly and the heavenly, Chaucer bestows upon up a complex and difficult poem, a prick in our critical sides. But in making it difficult for us to accept the sort of separations on which his narrator thrives, Chaucer both demonstrates his own understanding of Paul's thorn in the flesh and affirms the use of feigned storytelling as one of the most powerful tools of communication left in human hands after the Fall.

Notes

1. *The Riverside Chaucer,* ed. Larry Benson, (Boston: Houghton Mifflin, 1987). All further references to *Troilus* are from this edition.

2. An extensive body of commentary has shown how, in Robert M. Jordan's words, the narrator is in "decisive ways . . . central to the life of the poem"; "The Narrator in Chaucer's *Troilus,*" *ELH* 25 (1958): 233. For a review of the criticism see Thomas J. Garbaty, "The Degradation of Chaucer's 'Geffrey,' " *PMLA* 87 (1972): 97–104.

3. "*Troilus,* Books I–III: A Criseydan Reading," in *Essays on Troilus and Criseyde,* ed. Mary Salu (Cambridge: D. S. Brewer, 1979), 117.

4. "The Narrator's Frame for *Troilus,*" *Chaucer Review* 15 (1980): 87.

5. *The Complete Poetry and Prose of Geoffrey Chaucer* (New York: Holt, Rinehart and Winston, 1977), 443. Middle English *stimulus carni* as "the pricke of fleisch." The thorn metaphor is not, in fact, made explicitly clear until the King James version. But evidence abounds that the idea of a thorn contained within the Latin *stimulus* was an inherent part of the notion captured by the Middle English "pricke." See, for instance, the entries under "prick" and "prikel" in the *Middle English Dictionary.* When the context is a sexual one, the connection becomes a very common one. Wycliff's sermons, for example, warn that lustful thoughts "prychen and wounden þe soule, as þornes done to þe fleishe"; *Select English Works of John Wycliff,* ed. T. Arnold (Oxford: Clarendon, 1869), 1:103. The *Ayenbite of Inwyt,* speaking of Christ's approbation of St. John's virginity, easily slips into the metaphor while explaining the saint's ability to resist exactly the sort of desires that Criseyede is falling prey to at this point in Chaucer's poem. John is the lily among the thorns that the Song of Song praises; and the thorns are "þe þornes of uondingges of þe ulesse":

Vor þet uless is ase a donghel / þet ne carkeþ asemoche ase if of him-zelue / bote þornes / and netlen. þet byeþ kueade meniynges / þet ofte prekieþ þane gost. Ac þe flour of maydenhod ne heþ hede of þo þornes. uor hi is wel y-roted ine godes loue / þet hire wereþ uram þe þornes of uondinge.

Ayenbite of Inwit, ed. Richard Morris, EETS, o.s., no. 23 (London: Trübner, 1866), 230.

The coupling of the prick of the flesh with the image of thorns is such an assumed one that Robert of Brunne can use it as the organizing metaphor for the section on fleshly temptations in *Handlyng Synne;* in the "Tale of St. Benedict's Temptation," Benedict, seeing a "feyre womman" (7499) outside his cell, is struck with what Robert calls "a ful hard prykel" (8485). The saint protects himself from this prick in his flesh by, appropriately enough, rolling energetically in the thorns and nettles that grow outside his monastery:

. . . naken hymself he wrappe
Among þe þornes þat were sharpe,
And among þe netles echone,
Tyl hys temptacyun was al gone.
Đe þornes prykked, þe netles dyd byte,
Of flesshly temptacyun þey made hum quyte,
So clene, þat neuer aftyrward
was he tempted more so hard
Of hys flesshe, þat was hys fo.

(7517–25)

Robert of Brunne's "Handlyng Synne", ed. Frederick J. Furnivall, EETS, o.s., no. 119 (London: Paul, Trench, Trübner, 1901).

6. For a discussion of Paul's heavenly visitation, see A. T. Lincoln, " 'Paul the Visionary': The Setting and Significance of the Rapture to Paradise in II Cor. xii: 1–10," *New Testament Studies* 25 (1979): 204–20; and Russell P. Spittler, "The Limits of Ecstasy: An Exegesis of 2 Corinthians 12:1–10," in *Current Issues in Biblical and Patristic Interpretation,* ed. Gerald F. Hawthorne (Grand Rapids: Eerdmans, 1975), 259–66.

7. Various exegetes do, of course, stray from this central focus. A large group of commentators concentrate exclusively on deciding what particular disease Paul suffered from or what rival Corinthian faction plagued his preaching. Tertullian, for instance, identifies the thorn with chronic headaches or ear troubles (*De pudicitia* 13; J. P. Migne, ed., *Patrologia Latina* [hereafter *PL*] 2. 1004). The search for a particular malady has been continued by modern commentators. See A. Hisey, "A Paragnostic View of Paul the Apostle," *Unitarian Universalist Christian* 33 (1978): 12–19; and J. Bernard, "Lorsque je suis faible, c'est alors que je suis fort (2 Cor. 12, 7–10)," *Assemblées du Seigneur* 45 (1974): 34–39. Chrysostom concludes that the thorn refers to Alexander, Hymenaeus, and Philetus mentioned in 1 Timothy 1:20 (*Homilia in II Cor.* 26.7; *Patrologia Graeca* 61.519), a concern for identifying particular trangressors that is also taken up by modern commentators; see M. L. Barre, "Qumran and the 'Weakness' of Paul," *Catholic Biblical Quarterly* 42 (80): 216–27. And a good number of exegetical and mystical treatments reduce the metaphor until it designates only fleshly pursuits. See, for example, Ambrose, *De Isaac et anima* 4.11 (*PL* 14.508); *The Early English Versions of the Gesta Romanorum,* ed. Sidney J. H. Herrtage, EETS, e.s., no. 33 (London: Trübner, 1879), 48; and Walter Hilton, *The Goad of Love,* ed. Clare Kirchberger (London: Faber and Faber, 1952), 48.

8. "Et quid facimus . . . quando carnalibus spiritualia insinuamus." *Sermo CXVII* 5.7 (*PL* 38.665); John Henry Parker, trans. and ed., *Sermons or Selected Lessons on the New Testament* (Oxford: Oxford University Press 1845), 2:492.

9. "Homines sumus, Apostolos sanctos homines agnoscamus; vasa electa, sed adhuc fragilia; adhuc in hac carne peregrinantes, nondum in coelesti partria triumphantes." *Sermo CLIV* 5.6 (*PL* 38.836); Parker, *Sermons,* 2:740.

10. "Idem . . . ergo ipse et spiritualis et carnalis? Idem plane, quamdiu hic vivit, sic est." *Sermo CLIV* 5.7 (*PL* 38.836); Parker, *Sermons,* 2:740.

11. "Non enim duae naturae contrariae, sed ex utraque unus homo." *Sermo CLIV* 8.9 (*PL* 38.837); Parker, *Sermons,* 2:742.

12. "Ego in mente, ego in carne." Ibid.

13. "Paule, in coelo jam Jesum conspicis, et in terra adhuc hominem fugis? In paradisum

duceris, secreta Dei verba cognoscis, et adhuc a Satanae angelo tentaris? Unde sic fortis, ut ad coelestia rapiaris? Unde sic infirmus, ut in terra hominem fugias, et adhuc a Satanae angelo adverse toleres." *Moralia in Job* 19.6.11 (*PL* 76.102).

14. "Ille vitiorum illecebras assumit in artem virtutum, et salutis statum percutit ut servet, ut qui humilitatem currentes fugimus, ei saltem cadentes haereamus. . . . Miro dispensationis ordine dum tentantur humiliantur, dum humiliantur ejus esse jam desinunt. . . . Maxilla Behemoth istius . . . electos Dei unde counterit, inde amittit; unde tentat ut perdat, agit inde ne pereant." *Moralia in Job* 33.11.25–26 (*PL* 76.688–89); John Henry Parker, trans., *Morals on the Book of Job* (Oxford: Rivington, 1844), 2:580–81.

15. "Si non tentante carne ad summa nos spiritus sublevaret, in superbiae casu ipsa nos pejus sublevatione prosterneret." *Moralia in Job* 19.6.12 (*PL* 76.103), Parker, *Morals*, 2:403.

16. "Fit certo moderamine, . . . miro modo agitur, . . . subtilissimo judicii interni moderamine, infra summa, et supra infima in quodam medio anima libratur." Ibid.

17. "Ut ergo et firmitatis dona habeat, et infirmitatem suam humiliter agnoscat." *Moralia in Job* 8.29.48 (*PL* 75.831); Parker, *Morals*, 2:455.

18. "Qui te sublevat rursum subtilissima te mensura moderatur, ut et in miraculis tuis nobis praedices virtutem Dei, et rursum in timore tuo reminisci nos faciat infirmitatis nostrae." *Moralia in Job* 19.6.11 (*PL* 76.102).

19. "Qui elati perire poterant, humiliati a perditione serventur." *Moralia in Job* 33.14.28 (*PL* 76.690), Parker, *Morals*, 2:583.

20. See Samuel Schuman, "The Circle of Nature: Patterns of Imagery in Chaucer's *Troilus and Criseyde*," *Chaucer Review* 10 (1975): 99–112; and Peggy A. Knapp, "The Nature of Nature: Criseyde's 'Slydying Corage,' " *Chaucer Review* 15 (1978): 133–40.

21. *The Complete Poetry and Prose of Geoffrey Chaucer*, p. 470.

22. See Edmund Reiss, "Troilus and the Failure of Understanding," *Modern Language Quarterly* 29 (1968): 131–55, for a further discussion of the ironies Chaucer sets in motion when he has his narrator invoke the *contemptus mundi* motif at this point in the poem. Monica McAlpine, in *The Genre of Troilus and Criseyde* (Ithaca: Cornell University Press, 1978), 178, has asserted that "at least our reading must be subtle enough to distinguish this laughter of the transformed prince from the laughter of the callous young man," but Paul's parable of the thorn suggests that the transformation is not as beneficial as McAlpine would have it.

23. *The Genre of Troilus*, 179.

Fragment VII of Chaucer's *Canterbury Tales* and the "Mental Climate of the Fourteenth Century"

EMERSON BROWN, JR.

Whatever validity the terms *Middle Ages* and *Renaissance* may have, any accurate assessment of the continuities and discontinuities between those periods must acknowledge the crucial role of the fourteenth century. In a valuable essay, David Knowles identified and examined an important "characteristic of the mental climate of the fourteenth century."[1] So fundamental is this characteristic that it would be difficult to make much sense out of either the late Middle Ages or the Renaissance without taking it into consideration.

By the "fourteenth century" Knowles means essentially the period between Aquinas and Wyclif. By "mental climate," he means "certain ways and methods of approach to problems which the thinkers of that age applied to every branch of intellectual discipline." The "chief characteristic or tendency" of these methods of approach is "the drastic extension of an idea, by what is an apparently irrefutable logical process, to the furthest extremes of which it is capable, even when this implies taking it over the horizon, so to say, beyond the bounds of what is reasonably practical or even possible."[2] The "first adumbration of this tendency" is the thought of Siger of Brabant and his followers at Paris in the 1260s, those thinkers long known as the "Latin Averroists." These philosophers desired to discover not necessarily the truth but what Aristotle taught: "In their view the aim of a Parisian philosopher was not to criticize Aristotle, nor to attempt to harmonize his teaching with revealed truth, but to expound him in absolute integrity. This was their task as philosophers; as Christians they would give the assent of faith to revealed truth."[3] Off they went following Aristotle, then, and they followed him to dangerous extremes.

Concerning church and state, Knowles continues, the fourteenth century saw the most extreme claims both for supremacy of the papacy and for supremacy of the secular state. Similar polarities appear in controversies over the questions of poverty and dominion and grace, over legal jurisdiction, over administrative control and finance, and over such issues as the nature and comprehension of universals and the absolute freedom of God. The supreme examples of this tendency Knowles seeks in Ockham and his followers, on one side, and Thomas Bradwardine on the other: "While to Ockham the whole universe of spirit is freedom in indeterminacy, to Bradwardine everything is the reflection and consequence of the inexorable working of the unalterable laws of God. . . . Between them, Ockham and Bradwardine shattered to bits the mighty scholastic synthesis. . . . Each has taken a dynamic idea, driven it to the limit, and used it to annihilate a whole climate of opinion."[4]

Knowles might have extended his survey to cover developments in the arts as well. In music, the fourteenth century was a period of extraordinary innovation and audacity. That was the period of the *Ars Nova,* the *Ars Subtilior* and, as at least one musicologist would have it, the *Ars Subtilissima.*[5] Early in the century such trends so alarmed Pope John XXII that he tried to put an end to them in the bull *Docta sanctarum,* but the trouble was just beginning. As the century moved on, tonal and rhythmic complexity increased. According to David Monrow, late fourteenth century "extremists" like Solage or Matheus de Perusio "produced works which in harmonic daring and rhythmic complexity have not been equalled until the twentieth century." Some parts of songs "are at loggerheads" with others: the "dissonance and syncopation" of Matheus's' "Le greygnour bien" are "so extravagant that the three parts often appear totally unrelated and the composer seems to be attempting to cram into one piece all the notational subtleties and intricate cross rhythms of which music is capable."[6] In his discussion of late fourteenth-century mannerist style, Richard Hoppin describes a "polyphony in which the individual lines achieved a maximum of rhythmic independence [and] a wide variety of rhythmic complications, sometimes to the point of destroying all feeling of a consistent metrical organization."[7] Like the opposing points of view in the fourteenth-century intellectual disputes Knowles examines, each part of the song goes its own way, even to extremes, however threatening that may be to the harmony of the piece as a whole.

With this tendency briefly explored in fourteenth-century thought and music, we turn to Chaucer and that strange sequence of tales conjecturally known as Fragment VII. This part of the *Canterbury Tales* is strange because of the relatively low intrinsic quality of most of the tales—the Shipman's, the Prioress's, Chaucer's tales of Thopas and Melibee, and the Monk's—and the unsurpassed quality of the links that join them together and of the last tale in the group, the Nun's Priest's.[8]

Why would the poet who wrote the *Miller's Tale* or the *Wife of Bath's* produce something like the *Prioress's Tale* or the *Monk's?* Whatever virtues such tales may have in context, in isolation they seem almost deliberately, perversely, weak. Common explanations are that these tales are early work, as their verse forms suggest, and hence should be forgiven, or that by medieval tastes, they weren't as bad as we think. But even if they are early work, as they may be, why did Chaucer weave them into the *Canterbury Tales* with such care? And even if they would appear better to a medieval audience, as they no doubt would, how well, finally, does such an explanation support our conviction that Chaucer is a great poet of universal appeal? What is Chaucer doing with this sequence of tales? And what does this sequence of tales have to do with fourteenth-century ideas?

Although Chaucer was up to the minute in his reading of French and Italian literature, and although he enlivens his poetry with allusions to contemporary men and events, seeking the excitement of fourteenth-century ideas in his works can be disappointing. Chaucer will allude to burning philosophical and theological issues, but rather than wrestle with such questions himself, as a philosopher would, or as Dante did, Chaucer often seems content to use such material to reveal the intellectual or moral condition of his characters. Troilus's hilarious ramblings on the theme of free will and predestination do not advance our grasp of that impossibly difficult philosophical problem. Rather, we learn how Troilus's mind works, or tries to work. Similar, I think, is the Knight's apparent unwillingness to accept the disparagement of human endeavor implied by the divine perspective Boccaccio gives to the soul of Arcite. So also with Dorigen's adolescent musings concerning the presence of evil in a world created by a just and good God. While Dante fills the *Comedia* with examples of contemporary thought concerning the most complex philosophical issues, we search Chaucer's works in vain for a serious glimpse of the sophisticated argumentation carried on at Oxford during Chaucer's years, the kind of "logyk" unto which Chaucer's Clerk "hade longe ygo." Although some valuable scholarly work has been done in recent years in relating Chaucer's poetry to some of the great philosophical controversies of his time, especially his connections with nominalism, we realize that Chaucer operates not as a philosopher but as a narrative and dramatic poet.[9] He creates characters whom he gives—and who gleefully accept—lives of their own, lives Chaucer seems unwilling, and pretends to seem unable, to control. It is the behavior of Chaucer's characters as storytellers that reveals what Knowles declares to be the chief characteristic of fourteenth-century thought.

Knowles said that the Latin Averriosts belived "the aim of a Parisian philosopher was not to criticize Aristotle, nor to attempt to harmonize his teaching with revealed truth, but to expound him in absolute integrity."[10] Had Knowles directed his attention to the tales in Fragment VII, he might have put it this way: "In Chaucer's view the aim of a storyteller is not to criticize his fictional narrators nor to attempt to bring harmony to their tales through a proper balance of art and morality but to let them express themselves in absolute integrity."

The stories in Fragment VII comprise an anthology of different genres—pious tale, risqué fabliau, saint's legend, popular romance, aristocratic moral allegory, *de casibus* tragedy, and beast fable. But with the exception of the *Nun's Priest's Tale,* as they push the potentialities of their different genres to their logical extremes, the tales turn dark in their implications about art and morality. The tendency to extremism characteristic of the age seems embodied in these stories, and we are aware that the freedom Chaucer allows his flawed narrators produces tales that are themselves morally flawed. Through explicit talk about literature in the links and through literature itself in the tales, this fragment unfolds as a dramatized *ars poetica* through which Chaucer demonstrates many ways in which literature goes wrong and one way in which literature goes right. To support such a thesis adequately would require lengthier treatment than is possible here, but a brief look at these tales may give it some substance.

Although only one manuscript put the Shipman in the Epilogue to the *Man of Law's Tale,* and hence makes that Epilogue also the link between the tale and the *Shipman's Tale,* rejecting that assignment may demand too high a price: either canceling the Epilogue entirely or emending it (with no manuscript authority) to link it with the *Wife of Bath's Tale*.[11] Therefore, while acknowledging the fragility of the supporting evidence, I assume in this discussion that the Shipman belongs to this Epilogue and that this Epilogue leads to his tale.

In the neglected bit of splendid drama the Epilogue presents, the Parson rebukes Harry Bailey for his swearing; to shift attention from himself Harry calls the Parson a Lollard; the Shipman takes Harry's bait, and, on the grounds that the good Parson might corrupt his fellow pilgrims, the Shipman refuses to let him speak. The Shipman then says that his "jolly body" will tell a tale and that his tale will contain nothing of philosophy. He implies that it is not ony possible but desirable for literature to be entirely without "philosophy"—to be what we might call "pure entertainment"—the kind of art produced by (and perhaps for) a jolly body with nothing by (or for) the spirit.[12]

That is what the *Shipman's Tale* proves to be. In explicit language and action it doesn't approach Chaucer's other fabliaux in obscenity, and yet its overall effect is more shocking. In the Shipman's world, love, sex, marriage, adultery, and financial wheeling and dealing are almost interchangeable transactions. And, as Robert Adams has recently shown, unlike the usual fabliau, the *Shipman's Tale* ends with no "cataclysmic denouement," no "exposure scene," no punishment, no retribution, no assertion of even the most primitive morality.[13] The Shipman takes a theory about literature—that ideas might be dangerous and that the safest tale is one told by the body alone—and pushes that theory to its logical extreme. As if to make certain that we not miss his point, Chaucer has the heroine of the tale repeat that phrase—"my jolly body"—in an ugly context at the end of the tale, the only other time that phrase occurs in Chaucer's works:

> Ye shal my joly body have to wedde;
> By God, I wol nat paye yow but abedde!
>
> (VII.423–24)[14]

Crudely alluding to that body with which, in a Christian universe, one should be primarily concerned, and with unconscious thematic insight superior to his Latin grammar, Harry Bailey recapitulates that theme: " 'Wel seyd, by *corpus dominus,*' quod oure Hoost" (435).

If the *Shipman's Tale* shuns the spirit, the Prioress attempts to redress the balance with a spiritually uplifting tale. The *General Prologue* prepares us for this contrast, for the Shipman "took no keep" of "nyce conscience" while with the Prioress "al was conscience and tendre herte." But, as many have observed, the Prioress's tender heart bleeds more profusely for the suffering of mice—creatures emblematic of her own besetting vice of gluttony.[15] As has long been recognized, her conscience proves to be mere sentimentality. With a view of life in which satanic evil perversely seeks out and destroys helpless Christian innocence, undisciplined sentimentality pushes literature to another extreme. This kind of Christian literature is pious in intention and pious in its reception by the more mindless and sentimental members of the audience, but it is Christian literature likely to stir up hatred and violence against non-Christians, in this case against the Jews. Lest her audience conclude that the "cursed" Jewish child-murderers of her tale exist only in faraway lands, in the last stanza the Prioress reminds them that "yonge Hugh of Lyncoln" was also slain by "cursed Jewes," and that "but a litel while ago," though Hugh's death actually occurred a hundred and thirty years before the Prioress speaks.[16]

With the two tales of Chaucer the pilgrim, the tendency to push literature to extremes becomes more pronounced. Harry Bailey asks for a "tale of myrthe," and, in the *Tale of Thopas,* he gets the best rhyme that pilgrim Chaucer has to offer. Although *Thopas* is important beyond its function as literary parody, on that level Chaucer demonstrates another way literature can go wrong.[17] Of a different genre, *Thopas* resembles the *Shipman's Tale* as a work almost totally lacking in doctrine. Harry Bailey attributes the failure of the tale to Chaucer's shaky grasp of poetic techniques—"thy drasty rymyng is nat worth a toord!" (930)—and commands him to "telle in prose" something "in which ther be som murthe *or* som doctryne" (my italics). With his "litel thyng in prose," the *Tale of Melibee,*

Chaucer then entertains his fellow pilgrims for just under two hours. Although the *Tale of Melibee* may come close to revealing Chaucer's own deepest convictions, on the storytelling level it fails through its lack of literary merit. It is as extreme as *Thopas* but in the opposite direction. As many readers have observed, *Thopas* is entertainment without doctrine, *Melibee,* at least to our tastes, doctrine without entertainment.

When the *Tale of Melibee* has skipped lightly to its conclusion, Harry Bailey, showing little progress in either spiritual growth or accuracy of Christian allusion, swears by the incomprehensible "precious corpus Madrian," amuses us briefly with a view of his domestic situation, and then turns to the Monk for the next tale. Continuing the explicit reference to literary practice common in the links in this fragment, the Monk pompously displays his familiarity with the genre of tragedy and then narrates a series of thumbnail tragedies that few hearers, least of all the Knight, have ever wished longer. Here, too, literature pushes to the extreme—a morbid reiteration of the tragic view of life as a fall from "greet prosperitee . . . into myserie." Unlike either the more heroically pessimistic tragedy of ancient Greece or the more religiously optimistic tragedy that one might expect from medieval Christendom, the Monk's view of tragedy is unrelieved by the conviction either that in confronting such a fall man reveals his greatest dignity or that the apparent tragedy of such a fall fades in the light of Boethian philosophy.[18]

Only the last tale of Fragment VII rescues storytelling from the extremes to which earlier narrators carried it. In the *Nun's Priest's Tale,* mirth and doctrine blend to form an indissoluble whole. In his gentle view of near-tragedy made laughable by nearly divine perspective, the Nun's Priest presents the most thorough refutation of the Monk's view of life and the most thoroughly Boethian work Chaucer ever wrote, far more Boethian, I believe, than works embodying more explicitly Boethian language, such as the *Knight's Tale* or *Troilus and Criseyde*. Teasingly rejecting the assumption that in such a masterpiece one should, or could, separate "the moralite" from the storytelling, at the end of the tale Chaucer has the Nun's Priest invite us to take "the fruyt, and lat the chaf be stille." The fruit and the chaff are inseparable, and efforts to reduce the tale of Chauntecleer and the fox to a kernel of truth and thus read it as a simple allegory inevitably cast out with the chaff much of what gives the tale both its "murthe" and its "doctryne." As E. T. Donaldson puts it, the fruit of the tale *is* its chaff.[19]

Should all this suggest that, contrary to what many Chaucer scholars believe, some or most of the tales in Fragment VII are not products of Chaucer's earlier years? Not at all. But far from weakening their effect in the *Canterbury Tales,* Chaucer's earlier telling of these tales in his own person would only increase their power in their new context. As he attributes these tales to morally flawed narrators and as he joins them with links describing different aspects of the literary process, Chaucer separates himself from warped views of the human condition he might once have entertained. Perhaps he did tell, in his own person, the ugly, amoral tale the Shipman tells or the dangerously anti-Semitic tale the Prioress tells. Perhaps influenced by what we would call an affliction (depression) and the Parson would call sin ("wanhope"—*accidia*), he did assemble a series of gloomy tragedies like the Monk's. But in his last great work he confesses that such tales are told by such people, and he judges the Chaucer who told such tales.

We walk through life "always meeting ourselves," said Joyce's Stephen Dedalus in his talk about Shakespeare. On the way to the holy place, through the pilgrims of his imagination Chaucer meets features of his own character, his own history, and his own artistry. He meets them and judges them. And at the end of the process, as Chaucer recognized in his Retraction, there is no longer any place for stories. As the fourteenth century drew to a close, Chaucer glimpsed the dangerous tendencies of fourteenth-century thought David Knowles describes, recognized them and offered, in effect, two solutions for them. One, the Nun's Priest's, is the solution of Chaucer still on his journey, a moral man, but one glorying in the full brillance of his artistic virtuosity: a Chaucer, we might almost say, more of the Renaissance than of the Middle Ages. The other solution, more medieval, is the solution of Chaucer at the end of his journey, anticipating judgment, the Chaucer of the *Parson's Prologue and Tale* and the Retraction. Having put mirth and doctrine together in the tale of Chauntecleer and the Fox, Chaucer must separate them forever in the end. "Thou getest fable noon ytoold for me," says the Parson as he rejects all literature in favor of pure "moralitee and vertuous mateere." That was not the solution of the Renaissance, nor is it ours. But from Chaucer's perspective, at least, that solution was his only salvation.

Notes

1. David Knowles, "A Characteristic of the Mental Climate of the Fourteenth Century," in *Mélanges offerts à Étienne Gilson, de l' Académie française* (Toronto, Paris, Limoges, 1959), 315–25.

2. Ibid., 315–16.

3. Ibid., 316.

4. Ibid., 323. Knowles's essential point is sound even if the "mighty scholastic synthesis" itself is more postmedieval invention than medieval reality. Richard E. Sullivan argues that the thirteenth century was not a time of "creative processes leading toward an organic, holistic, harmonious synthesis. Rather, what happenes in this era was the fixing of a set of widely generalized institutional and ideological patterns that accommodated on a massive scale basically contradictory elements. . . . The energies of the era were not directed toward the construction of a balanced, harmonious, monolithic civilization in an Innocentian or Aquinian mode. Rather, they were consumed in the incorporation—often forced and tortured incorporation—of everything that was a part of the times into civilizational structures that

took their essential shape from the juxtaposition of contradictions and discordances" ("The Middle Ages in the Western Tradition: Some Reconsiderations," in *Essays on Medieval Civilization* [Austin: University of Texas Press, 1978], 22–23).

5. An excellent general introduction is Richard H. Hoppin, *Medieval Music* (New York: Norton, 1978); for our concerns here see especially chapters 17–19. His discussion of the *Ars Subtilissima* occurs in the section on "The Mannerist Style of the Late Fourteenth Century," 472–76. Also useful is the entry in the *New Catholic Encyclopedia,* s.v. "Music, Sacred, History of"; see especially the section "Polyphonic Music: Origins to 1450" (10:109–112). Some contemporary analyses of trends in medieval music are found in Oliver Strunke, *Source Readings in Music History: From Classical Antiquity through the Romantic Era* (New York: Norton, 1950); see especially the excerpts from the last book of Jacob of Liège's encyclopedic *Speculum musicae,* pp. 180–90, which "is at once an eloquent defence of the music of the Ars Antiqua and an impassioned tirade against the Ara Nova and all its works" (Strunk, 180). Jacob is at special pains to attack the "imperfections" in the "notes, modes, and measures" of the new art, imperfections discussed in a treatise by Jean de Muris (excerpts of which may be found in Strunk, 172–79). That metrical innovations and "imperfections" in late fourteenth-century music should be taken into account in our study of fourteenth-century poetic meter, particularly Chaucer's, is a topic I have explored in papers presented at SAMLA and the Medieval Academy, papers that may eventually get worked into shape for publication.

6. David Monrow, from notes accompanying his record album *The Art of Courtly Love: Machaut and His Age—14th Century Avant-Garde—The Court of Burgundy* (Seraphim 51C-6092), p. 23. Hoppin agrees: "Not until the twentieth century did music again reach the most subtle refinements and rhythmic complexities of the mannerist style" *Medieval Music,* (473).

7. Hoppin, *Medieval Music,* 475.

8. Talk about literature is a recurring theme in the links joining the tales of this fragment, as Alan T. Gaylord observed in an important essay, "*Sentence* and *Solaas* in Fragment VII of the *Canterbury Tales:* Harry Bailey as Horseback Editor," *PMLA* 82 (1967): 226–35. Such talk begins, prominently, in Fragment II, in the Introduction to the *Man of Law's Tale,* and this essay might be expanded to reinforce the thematic grounds that support retaining the Epilogue to the *Man of Law's Tale* (with the Shipman as the Parsons's antagonist and next narrator) and considering Fragments II and VII as a single group. It might, that is, defend the "Bradshaw Shift." The most impressive argument against the Bradshaw Shift is now Larry D. Benson, "The Order of *The Canterbury Tales,*" *Studies in the Age of Chaucer* 3 (1981): 77–120; Benson argues that the "order of the tales in the Ellesmere MS (and others) represents Chaucer's own final arrangement" (79). His careful display of the manuscript evidence is very nearly convincing, and all further discussion of tale order will have to take it into consideration. Crucial points, however, are still arguable. Does the Retraction prove that "unfinished as *The Canterbury Tales* is [Chaucer] was finished with it" (80)? Couldn't Chaucer have written the Retraction and then gone back to work on the tales and links, especially if by doing so he might make the Retraction all the more effective? Accepting the Ellesmere order also requires believing that Chaucer canceled the Man of Law's Endlink (which Professor Benson believes he did for reasons of tract, see 100–101 n. 14, but also see below, n. 11). Defending the Bradshaw Shift is beyond the scope of of this paper and probably beyond my powers. For hints of one approach such a defense might take, see Robert Adams, "The Concept of Debt in *The Shipman's Tale,*" *Studies in the Age of Chaucer* 6 (1984): 100 n. 14.

9. See, for example, Sheila Delaney, *Chaucer's House of Fame: The Poetics of Skeptical Fideism* (Chicago: University of Chicago Press, 1972); Winthrop Wetherbee, "Some Intellectual Themes in Chaucer's Poetry," in *Geoffrey Chaucer: A Collection of Original Articles,* ed. George D. Economou (New York: McGraw-Hill, 1975), 75–91; and Russell Peck, "Chaucer and the Nominalist Questions," *Speculum* 53 (1978): 745–60.

10. Knowles, "Mental Climate," 316.

11. The Epilogue to the *Man of Law's Tale* appears in no manuscripts of the A group. In only one, a manuscript generally given little authority, is it the Shipman who refuses to let the Parson preach (the Summoner and the Squire play that role in the other manuscripts that

contain this link). To Fred N. Robinson, the use of "thrifty" at II.46 and 1165 makes it "very probable that the *Epilogue* was written to follow the tale of the Man of Law"; see the second edition of his *The Works of Geoffrey Chaucer* (Boston: Houghton Mifflin, 1957), 696. Repetition of "My joly body" (II.1185, VII.423) and other thematic concerns discussed below seem to connect the Epilogue with the *Shipman's Tale*. I don't know why it does not appear in the Ellesmere manuscript and the others of that group. No one doubts that Chaucer wrote it. With thoughts of touching it up to make it join *MLT* and *ShT* more perfectly, he may have removed it temporarily from the collection of the Tales that became the basis for the "final" order that the MSS support. It is one of the greatest passages in the *Canterbury Tales*, and I cannot believe that he wished it to disappear.

12. That this tale is, on the narrative level, a tale of body without spirit does not mean that Chaucer did not imbue it with moral significance, significance beyond the intentions of the narrator, as several astute studies have shown, most recently—and most importantly—Robert Adams, "The Concept of Debt," 85–102.

13. Adams, "Concept of Debt," 90, 93. Professor Adams convincingly argues that "the uniquely inpenitent, thoroughly amoral-sounding conclusion" (86) of the tale is part of a design that prominently displays the crucial missing element in the lives of the characters—penance.

14. Larry D. Benson, ed., *The Riverside Chaucer* (Boston: Houghton Mifflin, 1987). All Chaucer citations are from this edition.

15. See Stephen P. Witte, "*Muscipula Diaboli*, Chaucer's Portrait of the Prioress," *Papers on Language and Literature* (1977): 227–37; David H. Brumble III, "Chaucer's General Prologue: Canterbury Tales," *Explicator* 37, no. 1 (1978): 45; and Emerson Brown, Jr., "Of Mice and Women: Thoughts on Chaucerian Allusion," in *Chaucer and the Art of Fiction*, ed. Leigh Arathoon (Rochester, Mich.: Solaris Press, 1986), 63–84.

16. We may now know far more of the circumstances surrounding little Hugh's death than Chaucer could have known, thanks to the fine scholarly detective work of Gavin I. Langmuir, "The Knight's Tale of Young Hugh of Lincoln," *Speculum* 47 (1972): 459–82, and now "Thomas of Monmouth: Detector of Ritual Murder," *Speculum* 59 (1984): 820–46.

17. Recent students have explored the intelligence and subtlety that makes of *Sir Thopas* something far greater than delightful literary parody, though it is that, too, of course. See, for example, Mary Hamel, "And Now for Something Completely Different: The Relationship between the *Prioress's Tale* and the *Rime of Sir Thopas*," *Chaucer Review* 14 (1980): 251–59, and Alan Gaylord's essays on the tale, most recently "The 'Miracle' of Sir Thopas," *Studies in the Age of Chaucer* 6 (1984): 65–84.

18. Although there are exceptions, most readers now agree that the Monk's tragedies reveal an attitude toward life pointedly lacking in the philosophical optimism that sympathetic study of Boethius's *Consolatio* might provide. Still of central importance in understanding Chaucer's artistry in dealing with Boethian ideas in general and the Monk in particular is R. E. Kaske, "The Knight's Interruption of the *Monk's Tale*," *ELH* 24 (1957): 249–68.

19. E. Talbot Donaldson, "Patristic Exegesis in the Criticism of Medieval Literature: The Opposition," in *Critical Approaches to Medieval Literature: Selected Papers from the English Institute, 1958–1959*, ed. Dorothy Bethurum (New York: Columbia University Press, 1960), 20.

The Flyting Contract and Adversarial Patterning in the Alliterative *Morte Arthure*

WARD PARKS

One of the most visible characteristics of heroic narrative in its appearances throughout world literature consists in the place of honor it accords to the heroic contest. Indeed, wide panoramas of narrative in the *Iliad,* the *Mahabharata, Beowulf, La Chanson de Roland,* the Alliterative *Morte Arthure* (hereafter cited as *AMA*), and other works in this mode are devoted to nothing else.[1] Perhaps because bellicose displays of this variety do not appeal to modern aesthetic sensibilities, the meaning and structure of the contest per se has often been ignored, although many scholars have attended to the *use* of particular contest episodes within individual poems.[2] My aim here will be to dilate upon a particular facet of the heroic contest, *flyting,* or the exchange of insults and boasts commonly associated with scenes of martial combat. I will argue that, in the *AMA* as in other works of traditional heroic narrative, the eristic or querulous motive that predominates on the surface of flyting operates on a contractual foundation. That is, even as the heroes vie with one another for personal glory, they are tacitily or explicitly negotiating the terms of a trial of arms that will determine which of them has won.[3]

Before we turn to a more detailed analysis of the flyting theme, some justification should be offered for my assumption that instances of this phenomenon can legitimately be studied from a comparative perspective.[4] The basis for such comparison resides in the poem's probable affiliation with oral tradition. In fact, scholars have consistently seized upon the *AMA* as the best exemplar of a poem exhibiting oral-formulaic tendencies in Middle English literature.[5] In 1957 Ronald A. Waldron cited many examples and performed a "formulaic analysis" of the first twenty-five lines from the *AMA* in what represented the first application of oral-formulaic methods to Middle English literature.[6] John Finlayson devoted one of his many articles on this poem to its "formulaic technique," concluding (among other things) that the *AMA,* while composed in writing, retains an "oral character."[7] In the mid-1960s Karl Heinz Göller and Laila Gross wrote articles on oral formulas;[8] into his 1969 dissertation James D. Johnson incorporated a complete formulaic analysis of the

AMA, and in two subsequent articles he examined occurrences of the famous "hero on the beach" theme and proposed a new version of Parry's "formulaic thrift."[9] Jean Ritzke-Rutherford examined formulaic patterning at both the microstructural level of the "cluster" and the macrostructural level of the battle theme in a pair of articles in 1981;[10] and in what represents the strictest application to date of the Parry-Lord model to any Middle English poem, Valerie Krishna examined in statistical detail the *AMA*-poet's proclivities regarding parataxis, formulaic density, and thrift.[11] While these scholars obviously do not stand together in harmonious accord on all issues, their collective efforts do suggest that the *AMA*, if not necessariy "oral" in the Parry-Lord sense, is at least "oral-derived," that is, composed in geographical or historical proximity to an oral tradition and drawing many of its materials and assumptions from an oral poetics.[12]

Most of this research has focused on the level of the verbal formula; as Göller points out, "little work has been done on formulaic themes in the poem."[13] Of course, many scholars have treated the "theme of battle" in the sense that an assessment of the character of Arthur inevitably entails an interpretation of the *AMA*-poet's attitudes toward war, particularly imperialistic conquest.[14] Yet most attuned to the poem's formulaic underpinnings is Ritzke-Rutherford's "Formulaic Macrostructure: The Theme of Battle," which identifies a general battle sequence (composed of such elements as "challenge," "strong emotion," "preparations or arming for battle," "dawn," "arraying of troops," etc.) and then analyzes the innovative and antitraditional treatment to which the *AMA*-poet subject this theme. Ritzke-Rutherford's thesis, argued through a close examination of antitypal elements and ironic contexting patterns, is that the *AMA*-poet is engaged in a covert attack on the martial glory motive, perceiving "war as an instrument of corruption and a thing of growing horror, a law unto itself."[15]

Since martial idealism seems to exert a perennial appeal on the human psyche, particularly in ages of nationalistic endeavor, and since one could hardly engage in the kind of knightly enterprise that the fourteenth century regularly demanded without a compatible belief system, I wonder at times to what extent such interpretations arise from a truly disinvolved and balanced perception of medieval realities.[16] Yet my central aim here is not so much to interpret the *AMA*'s particular realization of adversarial patterning as to identify generically what those patterns are, in the manner of an anatomist whose illuminations concerning, say, bone structure are hardly intended to deny the existence of individual human beings; and in this connection Ritzke-Rutherford's "theme of battle" scheme brings to light obvious affinities between the *AMA* and other works of heroic narrative.[17] And the particular elements in her pattern that provide my principal subject, the flyting and the martial encounter, recur—in the Old English and Homeric traditions at least—in a consistent and rule-governed relationship.[18] Whatever might be the personal ideological orientation of its poet, then, it would seem that the *AMA* is drawing (for its material at least) on a primary-oral narrative pattern with a rather archaic significance.

Since flyting cannot meaningfully be studied in isolation from its larger narrative and dramatic context, let us begin by defining some of the parameters of heroic contests in general. Rooted in an agonistic impulse that man seems to share with many animal species, contesting has as its underlying objective the public establishment of personal identity.[19] Heroes are seldon pragmatists. Of course, one cannot banish pragmatic considerations altogether: Arthur clearly stands to benefit from the increase in feudal tributes resulting from his conquests, and Beowulf might eventually find it to his benefit to redeem his father's debt to Hrothgar. Yet neither hero follows the straight and easy path to success: to the contrary, both men seem at times bent an multiplying their dangers and worsening the odds at every opportunity.[20] Their reason for doing so lies in the greater attainment of glory, fame, reputation, called *kléos* in the Greek, cognate with *klúein,* "to hear."[21] In a world where merit is inseparable from meritorious action and where judgment is anchored in communally held values, the glory accruing from success in combat facilitates what we might characterize as the ritualized valorization of selfhood.

The contest paradigm has a fairly simple structure, though in the narrative realization it often lends itself to considerable elaboration and complication. The primary participants are the two adversaries, who are ideally comparable in their standing within their respective communities and in their martial attainments. Thus much of the action in the *AMA* is predicated upon and culminates in the struggles between Arthur and Lucius, in the first half of the poem, and between Arthur and Mordred in its final segment. All three heroes can claim preeminence in their respective armies; and as Arthur at several points makes clear, he stakes his very manhood on the outcome of these trials.[22] Though the contestants themselves play the most active roles, equally indisensable are the *witnesses;* indeed, the very word *contest* contains the meaning "witness" in its Latin etymology.[23] Witnessing requires that the contest take place in a public setting. Old English and Homeric narrative features three of these: the intracommunal council setting, as in the Achilles-Agamemnon quarrel; the guest-host setting, as in the Beowulf-Unferth flyting or in the Odysseus-Euryalos exchange in Book 8 of the *Odyssey;* and the battlefield setting, as in the showdowns between Achilles and Hector or between Byrhtnoth and the Viking messenger in *The Battle of Maldon.*[24] The *AMA* adds to this list a mediated composite setting, as proxies like the Roman senator in 78–115 or Gawain in 1299–1350 flyt on behalf of their masters in the course of an embassy to the enemy king.[25]

The orientation toward the winning of personal glory through formalized, public contesting is common to most heroic narrative. Yet two noteworthy ideological shifts do nonetheless distinguish contests in the *AMA* (and, significantly, other high or late medieval works such as *La Chanson de Roland*) from their Anglo-Saxon and Homeric counterparts. First, a fuller assimilation of Christian values seems to have created a tension between the glory motive and the demands of humility, between the need to prove oneself and the Christian imperative to forgive one's enemies. Thus while Arthur freely indulges in the favorite heroic pastimes of boasting and flyting, unlike Achilles he refrains from taunting fallen enemies (although Arthur's subordinates do not always exhibit a similar restraint).[26] The other difference can be related to the establishment of feudal monarchies and the growth of nationalism. Verbal contests in the *AMA,* as in *Beowulf* and the *Iliad,* continue to focus primarily on matters of personal heroic worthiness, as displayed in one's deeds and genealogy. Yet bonds of feudal loyalty have to a certain degree assimilated knights and vassals into the cause and, more significantly, the very person of their master. Thus while Cador, Gawain, Clegis, Priamus, the Roman senators, and other feudal subordinates implicate their own manhoods in the course of verbal sparring, the personal qualities of Lucius and Arthur figure in as well; indeed, the battle-cry "Arthure!" on several occasions launches a flyting match or a martial exchange.[27] In the *Iliad* and *Beowulf,* by contrast, the identities of the contestants themselves supply the matter of debate.

Most of the discussion so far has pertained to the ideology and structure of the contest as a whole; at this juncture we will need to concentrate on its verbal or flyting aspect more narrowly. I must begin with several qualifications. First, the verbal context accompanies combat irregularly at best and thus must be judged an optional element of the contest theme; it seems to crop up most frequently in contest episodes that are for some reason specially featured. Second, flyting, though paradigmatically dialogic in character, cannot altogether be differentiated from the boasts, insults, oaths, and other speech acts that regularly make it up;[28] indeed, in my analysis below I have occasionally treated as "flyting," interactions in which only one adversary actually speaks. Third, my comments are meant to apply only to what we might characterize as "heroic flyting." Poems such as "The Flyting of Dunbar and Kennedie" or "Polwart and Montgomerie Flyting," or verbal dueling such as we find in "sounding" or "playing the dozens," all belong to another kind of interaction (not found in the *AMA*) that we might call "ludic flyting," distinguished by a nonserious mode of reference and by a lack of martial entailments.[29]

Yet when flyting and fighting do occur simultaneously, they stand in a definable relationship to each other. In brief, flyting proposes, fighting disposes; flyting enunciates publicly the meaning of the contest and defines its terms, while combat provides the resolution. For example, Beowulf and Unferth in *Beowulf* 449–610, even as they insult each other, are tacitly agreeing that the winner of their quarrel will be determined by the outcome of a projected fight between Beowulf and Grendel; similarly, Achilles and Aeneas in *Iliad* 20.158–352 are, in effect, contracting on a direct mortal encounter.[30] Thus the flyting exchange is based on both eristic (or querulous) and contractual motives. Its eristic aspect manifests in the insults and boasts of the contestants who are laying claims to personal superiority over their adversaries. The contractual aspect comprises the negotiations (tacit or explicit) over future course of action. Heroic flyting can be defined, then, as "an adversative verbal exchange in which the heroes, even as they contend with each other for *kléos* or glory, are contracting on some future course of action from a range of possibilities at least one of which entails a trial of arms."[31]

Let us turn now to several examples, beginning with a few smaller scale flyting-fighting sequences, and graduating to a far more developed adversarial pattern that structures much of the first half of the poem. A relatively simple flyting exchange in 2525–40 precedes the fight between Gawain and Priamus, strangers to one another at the outset who identify themselves later in the encounter.[32] The flyting begins with Gawain's cry of "Arthure!" (2529): thus the Briton knight identifies himself with the cause and person of his master. The flyting proceeds as follows:

> "Whedyr prykkes thow, pilouur, þat profers so large?
> Here pykes thowe no praye, profire when þe lykes!
> Bot thow in þis perell put of the bettire,
> Thow all be my presonere, for all thy prowde lates!"
> "Sir," sais Sir Gawayne, "so me Gode helpe,
> Siche glauerande gomes greues me bot lyttill!
> Bot if thowe graythe thy gere, the will grefe happen,
> Or thowe goo of þis greue, for all thy grete wordes!"[33]

Now this exchange illustrates in rather stark terms the quarrel-contract dichotomy in the motivational structure of flyting. From the eristic standpoint, the two flyters adopt similar strategies: each introduces a term of insult, each proclaims the vacuity of his adversary's bold display, and each predicts for himself victory in a fight that is to follow. In short, the contestants are pitting rival claims for personal superiority. The contract they are establishing comprises the ground of concord on the basis of which their quarreling proceeds. For both boasts contain common elements, in the proposition that battle should ensue, and further, in the assumption that its outcome should provide the proof and judgment of their quarrel. Thus the contractual process defines the framework in which the fight will occur and by which it will acquire its meaning.[34]

This simple pattern, variously transmuted and adapted, recurs repeatedly in the poem's many battle sequences.[35] For another example on a small scale, consider the brief flyting between Feraunt's cousin and Floridas (2772–79) in the course of a general melee between the forces of Arthur and those of the Duke of Lorraine. In the preceding passage, Feraunt first flytes with and then is killed by Florent, the leader of Arthur's expeditionary force. After praising his kinsman and condemning his killing, Feraunt's cousin boasts,

> "Thou schall dye for his dede with my derfe wapen,
> And all þe doughtty for dule þat in ȝone dale houes!"[36]

A Briton comrade takes up the quarrel on Florent's behalf:

> "Fy," sais Sir Floridas, "thow fleryande wryche!
> Thow wenes for to flay vs, floke-mowthede schrewe!"[37]

Now the interactions of these two speeches is instructive. For while the boast of Feraunt's cousin contains no explicit term of abuse, Floridas's abuse contains no explicit boast. The fact is that insults and boasts serve the same function of asserting one's superiority over one's adversary. Verbally abusing one's foe in effect commits one to fight with him. Thus in its contractual substructure the exchange negotiates between two courses of action—fighting and fleeing: Feraunt's cousin proposes the former, and Floridas rejects the latter. Having completed, then, this fairly ritualized interaction, these two knights engage in a trial of arms in which Feraunt's cousin is slaughtered.

These two encounters illustrate the flyting activity in a rather minimal form, in that the flyters confine themselves to name calling and boasting within the compass of a few lines. A slightly more developed flyting speech appears in 1059–73, in which Arthur verbally assaults the giant of St. Michael's Mount.[38] In the course of this speech the British king several times invokes divine powers and adds curses to an assortment of abusive names. Yet particularly interesting is his condemnation of the monster for killing women and children—clearly in his perception an unheroic and unmanly pastime. In fact, flyters frequently "retroject"—cast back and recall past incidents in the personal histories of the contestants—as a means of establishing heroic claims.[39] In the final lines of the speech, Arthur, by challenging the giant to battle and by predicting his own victory (1068–73), is initiating the contractual process: a death-struggle will provide judgment on the issues that he has raised. The monster does not ratify this contract proposal verbally—like Grendel he is never humanized to the extent of enjoying powers of the *reordberende* ("speechbearers"); and yet his "body language," described by the *AMA*-poet in graphic detail (1074–1103), conveys unmistakably that the prospect of a fight is quite acceptable to him.[40]

All of these cases show that flyting provides the *AMA*-poet with a highly serviceable theme in the generation of his narrative; yet the flyting-fighting association has a role beyond this, in the orchestration of large-scale narrative movements. The most dramatic example of this, dominating the first 2,400 lines of the poem, is the prolonged and much mediated struggle between Lucius and Arthur, to which I would now like to devote some attention.[41] This exchange opens with Lucius's challenge presented through messengers at Arthur's court (86–115). Asserting his rights as a feudal overlord, Lucius (through his proxies) insists that his British vassal present himself at the emperor's court at Rome to give accounting for his longstanding failure to pay appropriate tributes and dues. Should Arthur refuse, Lucius will attack militarily, burn Britain, and take its king captive. Thus Lucius has extended two contractual options: acknowledgment of his claims, or combat. Arthur takes counsel with his men, who urge him to fight (243–406). Thanking them for upholding his "menske" and "manhede" ("honor" and "manhood," 399), Arthur returns to the senator and his men, boasts that he will conquer Roman lands, and challenges Lucius to redeem, once again, his honor and manhood by meeting him on the battlefields of France (419–66). When he receives this messages, Lucius announces his own war plans (554–69). Through this extended flyting mediated by messengers, the complementary co-functioning of the eristic and contractual motives plainly emerges. For on the one hand, the interaction from its incipience is a rivalry from which neither king can withdraw without a forfeiture of honor; on the other hand, a principal aim of the embassy is to negotiate some joint course of action. Since Arthur has scornfully rejected accession to Lucius's demands, only the rival boasts now stand, the common presumption of which is that a military struggle will ensue. Thus the two monarchs, through their flyting, have contracted on war.

The initial phase of this encounter between Arthur and the Roman senator contains another feature of interest. After he has heard the emperor's message, Arthur's face, we are told, takes on such a fearsome expression that the Romans fall on the floor and beg, in effect, for diplomatic immunity (116–31). Arthur grants this request and entertains them as honored guests[42]—but not without first calling them cowards who dare not even look upon his face (133–35). In reply the senator acknowledges that he is a "lyon" (139) and "þe lordlyeste lede þat euer I one lukyde" ("the lordliest man that even I looked on," 138), a general sentiment that he reiterates to Lucius later on (515–53). Here we see a contest that is aborted by one party's capitulation and, to some degree, by a recognition of a distinction between a master and his messenger. Yet another principle is at work also. The senator, as a feudal subordinate, is no worthy adversary for the king of the Britons. In an earlier example we saw how the problem of dealing with Feraunt's cousin is referred from Florent, the leader of the British force, to Floridas, the next in the line of prominence. Thus the matching of context adversaries seems to proceed with some regard for feudal hierarchies and orders of precedence.

This exchange between Arthur and Lucius's emissaries has a counterpart approximately a thousand lines later as Gawain and others are deputized with the office of delivering Arthur's message of defiance directly to the Roman emperor.[43] Discharging his function with vigor, Gawain embroiders his master's core message, "fight or flee!" with several of his own additions, including a pair of curses (1303–6 and 1311–12) and such less-than-flattering denominations as "fals heretyke" (1307) and "cukewalde" (1312). Gawain's speech is clearly designed both to reinitiate the contractual process and to compare the personal merits of his lord with those of his lord's adversary.[44] In a reply (1326–41) that structurally corresponds rather closely to Arthur's declaration to the Roman senator earlier, Lucius refuses to flee and chooses to fight, boasting, in fact, of his own projected conquests. So once more the contract is sealed. Yet at the same time, while like Arthur he addreses several insults to the messenger, he disdains to punish him directly. Once more, a complex of motives is involved: on the one hand, he explicitly acknowledges the principle of diplomatic imunity (1327–29: cf. 125–27); on the other, Gawain, as Arthur's mere vassal, does not rank as a fit adversary.

At this juncture the whole affair gets referred down the feudal hierarchy. Gawain introduces the notion of immediate combat by calling the emperor an "oaf" ("alfyn," 1343) and expressing the wish that he could fight with him on the battlefield directly (1344–45)—a cutting insult, coming as it does from a social inferior. Now Lucius's uncle, Gayous, enters the fray, labeling the Briton a "boy" (1351) and "braggart" (1348). Having found an adversary on his own level, Gawain takes up the challenge instantly, lopping off the Roman's head and galloping away (1352–55). In sum, then, this episode, when viewed as a continuation of the flyting between Arthur and Lucius, mirrors the earlier interaction between the senator and Arthur and completes the pattern of mediated flyting between the two monarchs. At the same time Gawain, by engaging in the flyting process personally and consummating his boasts with a martial demonstration, exhibits an initiative that the senator plainly lacked.

The culmination of this vast adversarial pattern arrives approximately at the midpoint of the poem (2242–2370) as the two principals match off and go at each other head to head. "Flyting" is at this juncture reduced to a minimum: Lucius has already addressed a boastful speech (2223–25) to Gawain, serving perhaps as Arthur's surrogate, while the British king contributes merely the cry of "Arthure!" (2245). Naturally Arthur prevails, although the special significance of this encounter may be registered in Lucius's success at least in wounding him in the nose. Arthur draws the pattern to a ritual closure through speech and symbolic action: he returns the bodies of the fallen with treasure to Rome and insists that the Romans now renounce their claims (2290–2352). It is sometimes assumed that this message to the Romans, both as speech and gesture, amounts to an insult.[45] And yet the poet takes pains to depict Arthur treating Lucius's body with considerable honor; indeed, by heroic standards he is exhibiting extraordinary restraint and deference.[46] At the same time, in view of the fact that a major war has just been concluded, one could hardly expect him not to stamp the verbal seal on a victory that is, after all, an accomplished political and military reality.

All of the patterns that we have examined so far occur prior to Arthur's dream of the Wheel of Fortune in 3218–3393, universally regarded as the turning point in the poem.[47] And in fact the final thousand-line sequence, though dominated by another adversarial pattern in the matching off of Arthur and Mordred, features flyting in only its most reduced and minimal forms. For example, the two principals never engage in an elaborate exchange of embassies such as we saw earlier in the Arthur-Lucius struggle. When Arthur first learns of Mordred's betrayal, though he vows revenge (3559–60), he does not "flyt" in that he sends no message to this effect to his rebel vassal; and his subsequent exhortations to his men (3565–90 and 3636–43), though at times echoing some of the invective and abusive style of earlier exchanges, substitute injunctions to battle in the place of open boasts.

Two flyting episodes do nonetheless succeed in rekindling something of the old heroic fire. In the first of these Gawain, once again leading an advance party, vilifies Mordred in harsh terms (3776–79):

> "Fals fosterde foode, the Fende haue thy bonys!
> Fy one the, felone, and thy false werkys!
> Thow shall be dede and vndon for thy derfe dedys,
> Or I shall dy this daye, ȝif destayne worthe!"[48]

Here we find most of the elements of classic flyting: Gawain curses and name-calls, condemns Mordred's descent and actions, and proposes battle. And yet the Briton does not project any certitude of victory, but only that one of the two of them will die in the coming encounter. Arthur himself, when at last he meets Mordred in the poem's climactic duel, has fewer reservations (4227–29):

"Turne, traytoure vntrewe—þe tydes no bettyre;
By gret Gode, thow sall dy with dynt of my handys!
The schall rescowe no renke, ne reches in erthe."[49]

Here the British king urges his foe to meet him in battle and definitely predicts his death. And yet, both of these flytings are one-sided: in neither case does Mordred reply. Indeed, at no juncture does the unfaithful "leuetenaunte" (646) embroil himself in flyting or invective in any form, but confines his remarks to what is in effect a eulogy of Gawain (3875–85). In sum, then, Arthur and his party in this final sequence indulge in flyting and invective comparatively rarely (by the standards of the poem), employ terms of abuse that highlight Mordred's very real and damnable sin of treason, curb hyperbolic tendencies in their boasting, phrase their predictions carefully and in terms that they are able literally to fulfill, and provoke no rebuttal from an enemy who, we gather, privately admits the justice of their claims. In all these ways the flyting spirit has been muted; and this effect is further reinforced by the dominant elegiac mood generated in the speeches of lamentation, which, through their sheer number and bulk, tend to overshadow such few flyting passages as there are.

How, then, are we to account for the *AMA*-poet's sudden disinclination to depend on the verbal contest theme for the development of his narrative matter, despite the fact that a contest structure—Arthur versus Mordred—still underlies and motivates the narrative movement? This question, concerned as it is with authorial intention, propels me across the boundary into what is undoubtedly literary interpretation; and since so many critics have written so ably on such matters, I will confine myself here to a few suggestions arising out of the perspective that it has been the aim of this essay to explore. The poet's deemphasizing of flyting at the end of his narrative in favor particularly of scenes of lamentation has its roots in his larger thematic designs. As we have seen, the aesthetic and thematic effect of flyting scenes is to foreground the winning of glory and the establishment of personal identity. Yet for Arthur and his men these aims have already been achieved through his overthrow of the Roman empire. Moreover, the dream of Fortune's Wheel was intended precisely to relativize achievements of this kind, to point out that glory and high attainment inevitably lead to a downfall. By continuing to build his narrative around flyting and the flyting contract, by continuing to tap into the archaic associations of this theme, the poet would simply have been reinforcing the very standard of measure whose limitations it is now his purpose to expose. This does not necessarily mean that either the *AMA*-poet or Arthur has rejected the heroic ethos: to the contrary, Arthur and Gawain continue to flyte in a limited way; and their very restraint in doing so seems to be a mechanism by which the poet keeps them from discrediting themselves. At the same time, the action of the poem clearly shows that eventual failure and death are endemic to the human condition; and to this problem the path of heroic endeavor can ultimately provide no solution.

Yet however one ultimately chooses to assess the *AMA*-poet's intentions, there can be no doubt that the flyting and contest patterns provided one of his chief literary resources. It aided him considerably in the generation of narrative incident; and through the binding force of the flyting contract he was able to create coherencies over long narrative sequences. At the same time, the flyting motif brought with it a concept of the human warrior individual and the valorization of selfhood that he could work with. Whatever else might be said about his sources and influences, the *AMA*-poet clearly understood the power inhering in traditional forms and did not hesitate to make the exploitation of this potentiality one of the central principles in his narrative artistry.

Notes

1. All citations from the Alliterative *Morte Arthure,* hereafter cited as *AMA,* refer to Valerie Krishna, ed., *The Alliterative Morte Arthure: A Critical Edition* (New York: Burt Franklin, 1976).

2. The principal exceptions to this rule appear mostly in the scholarship of the oral-formulaic school: see, for example, Jean Rychner's discussion of traditional themes and motifs in *La chanson de geste: Essai sur l'art épique des jongleurs,* Société de Publications Romanes et Françaises, 53 (Geneva and Lille: E. Droz and Giard, 1955), esp. 127–53; or Albert B. Lord's analysis of the "arming for battle" theme in *The Singer of Tales* (New York: Atheneum, 1965), 86–91; or Albert C. Baugh's discussion of the same motif in "Improvisation in the Middle English Romances," *Proceedings of the American Philosophical Association* 103 (1959): 418–54, and esp. 425–27 and 440–54. Obviously I am not disparaging attempts to interpret particular passages and works of art. Yet such endeavors proceed on a surer foundation when informed by a thorough understanding of the traditional dimensions of the material under review.

3. I propound this view more fully, as it pertains to Old English and Homeric narrative, in "Flyting and Fighting: Pathways in the Realization of the Epic Context," *Neophilologus* 70 (1986): 292–306; see also my "The Flyting Speech in Traditional Heroic Narrative," forthcoming in *Neophilologus,* which concentrates on the level of the individual speech unit. In fact, some excellent scholarship on flyting and contesting has appeared in recent years, especially with regard to the Germanic language traditions. Joaquin Martinez Pizarro provides the best comprehensive survey of relevant material in "Studies on the Function and Context of the Senna in Early Germanic Narrative," (Ph.D. diss., Harvard University, 1976); less descriptive and more theoretical are Joseph Harris, "The *senna:* From Description to Literary Theory," *Michigan Germanic Studies* 5 (1979): 65–74, and Carol J. Clover, "The Germanic Context of the Unferþ Episode," *Speculum* 55 (1980): 444–68. More socio-historical and restricted in focus to Icelandic narrative is Jesse Byock, *Feud in Icelandic Saga* (Berkeley: University of California Press, 1982). For a remarkable general study of the contest motive in its wide-ranging cultural manifestations, see Walter J. Ong, *Fighting for Life: Contest, Sexuality, and Consciousness* (Ithaca: Cornell University Press, 1981). I propose criteria for the differentiation of heroic flyting from other verbal context genres, such as academic debate or "playing the dozens," in "Flyting, Sounding, Debate: Three Verbal Contest Genres." *Poetics Today* 7 (1986): 439–58.

4. For a more detailed exposition on the intercultural character of heroic flyting than I will be able to offer here, see "Flyting and Fighting." Alain Renoir has written many articles defending what he calls "oral-formulaic context" as the basis for a critical method; for a

statement on this theme, see "Oral-Formulaic Context: Implications for the Comparative Criticism of Mediaeval Texts," in *Oral Traditional Literature: A Festschrift for Albert Bates Lord,* ed. John Miles Foley (Columbus, Ohio: Slavica, 1980), 416–39.

5. For a detailed bibliographic survey of relevant Middle English scholarship through 1984, see my article, "The Oral-Formulaic Theory in Middle English Studies," in *Oral Tradition* 1 (1986). Outstanding adaptations of oral-formulaic concepts to the conditions of Middle English Literary production include Baugh's "Improvisation in the Middle English Romance" and "The Middle English Romance: Some Questions of Creation, Presentation, and Preservation," *Speculum* 42 (1967): 1–31. It should be noted that Baugh does not argue that any extant Middle English poem represents the direct transcription of an oral performance: in fact, to my knowledge no scholar has made such a claim. The oral theory has, naturally, had its critics; perhaps the most articulate of these in Middle English studies is Thorlac Turville-Petre, in *The Alliterative Revival* (Totowa: N.J.: Rowman and Littlefield, 1977). For a comprehensive review of scholarship concerned with the oral theory, see John Miles Foley, *Oral-Formulaic Theory and Research: An Introduction and Annotated Bibliography* (New York: Garland, 1985).

6. "Oral-Formulaic Technique and Middle English Alliterative Poetry," *Speculum* 32 (1957): 792–804.

7. "Formulaic Technique in *Morte Arthure," Anglia* 81 (1963): 372–93. In fact, Finlayson takes Waldron to task for what he sees as the excessive looseness in that scholar's treatment of formulaic language; he is particularly critical of Waldron's "rhythmical syntactical moulds." For another perspective on this dispute, see R. F. Lawrence, "The Formulaic Theory and its Application to English Alliterative Poetry," in *Essays on Style and Language: Linguistic and Critical Approaches to Literary Style,* ed. Roger Fowler (London: Routledge and Kegan Paul, 1966), 166–83.

8. See Göller's "Stab und Formel im *Alliterierenden Morte Arthure," Neophilologus* 49 (1965): 57–67, and Gross, "The Meaning and Oral-Formulaic Use of *Riot* in the Alliterative *Morte Arthure," Annuale Mediaevale* 9 (1968): 98–102.

9. "Formulaic Diction and Thematic Composition in the Alliterative *Morte Arthure," DAI* 30 (1970): 3462A; "'The Hero on the Beach' in the Alliterative *Morte Arthure," Neuphilologische Mitteilungen* 76 (1975): 271–81; and "Formulaic Thrift in the Alliterative *Morte Arthure," Medium Aevum* 47 (1978): 255–61. Also pertinent is Hugh Ward Tonsfeldt's dissertation, "Medieval Narrative and the Alliterative *Morte Arthure," DAI* 36 (1975): 1489A.

10. "Formulaic Microstructure: The Cluster," and "Formulaic Macrostructure: The Theme of Battle," in *The Alliterative Morte Arthure: A Reassessment of the Poem,* ed. Karl Heinz Göller (Cambridge: D. S. Brewer, 1981), 70–82 and 167–69, and 83–95 and 169–71. Also useful is Göller's introductory "A Summary of Research," 7–14 and 152–57. Several other articles in this volume are marginally relevant to oral studies.

11. "Parataxis, Formulaic Density, and Thrift in the *Alliterative Morte Arthure," Speculum* 57 (1982): 63–83; Krishna's statistics on formulaic density are based on Johnson's 1969 dissertation (see note 9 above). Krishna attends to several oral-formulaic aspects of the poem in a section entitled "Formulas and Rhetorical Style" (27–34) in the introduction to her edition.

12. On oral-derived poetry see John Miles Foley, "Oral Texts, Traditional Texts: Poetics and Critical Methods," *Canadian-American Slavic Studies* 15 (1981): 122–45. The problem of "oral aesthetics" is broached in several of the essays in *Current Research in Oral Traditional Literature,* ed. John Miles Foley (Columbus, Ohio: Slavica, forthcoming).

13. "A Summary of Research," 11; exploratory efforts in this area include Finlayson, "Formulaic Technique," Tonsfeldt, "Medieval Narrative," and Johnson, "Hero on the Beach." "Theme" in oral-formulaic usage carries quite a different sense than in general literary studies; for seminal discussions, see Lord's "Homer and Huso II: Narrative Inconsistencies in Homer and Oral Poetry," *Transactions of the American Philological Association* 69 (1938): 439–45 (his definition of "theme" appears on 440), and *The Singer of Tales,* 68–98; and Donald K. Fry, "Old English Formulaic Theme and Type-Scenes," *Neophilologus* 52 (1968): 48–54. John Foley provides a detailed summary of the work of Parry and Lord (28–51) as well as a survey of Anglo-Saxon scholarship concerned with oral themes

(79–91) in his introduction, "The Oral Theory in Context," to *Oral Traditional Literature*, 27–122.

14. The view that the *AMA*-poet intends to undercut Arthur's character and martial ambitions has become in various forms established in recent criticism largely due to William Matthews's' influential study, *The Tragedy of Arthur: A Study of the Alliterative Morte Arthure* (Berkeley: University of California Press, 1960). For several important later articles touching on this subject from various viewpoints, see Larry D. Benson, "The Alliterative *Morte Arthure* and Medieval Tragedy," *Tennessee Studies in Literature* 11 (1966): 75–88; Finlayson, "The Concept of the Hero in *Morte Arthure*," in *Chaucer und seine Zeit: Symposion für Walter F. Schirmer*, ed. Arno Esch, Buchreiche der *Anglia, Zeitschrift für englische Philologie* 14 (Tübingen: Max Niemeyer, 1968), 249–74; Robert M. Lumiansky, "The Alliterative *Morte Arthure*, the Concept of Medieval Tragedy, and the Cardinal Virtue Fortitude," in *Medieval and Renaissance Studies: Proceedings of the Southeastern Institute of Medieval and Renaissance Studies, Summer, 1967*, ed. J. M. Headley (Chapel Hill: University of North Carolina Press, 1968), 95–118; George Robert Keiser, "The Theme of Justice in the Alliterative *Morte Arthure*," *Annuale Mediaevale* 16 (1975): 94–109; several of the contributions to Göller, ed., *AMA: A Reassessment*, especially Manfred Markus, "The Language and Style: The Paradox of Heroic Poetry," 57–69 and 164–67; and J. Eadie, "The Alliterative *Morte Arthure:* Structure and Meaning," *English Studies* 63 (1982): 1–12. For further citations, see below, as well as Michael Foley, "The Alliterative *Morte Arthur:* An Annotated Bibliography, 1950–75," *Chaucer Review;* 14 (1979): 166–87, and Göller, "A Summary of Research," in his collection of essays.

15. "Formulaic Macrostraucture," 95.

16. Elizabeth Porter in "Chaucer's Knight, the Alliterative *Morte Arthure*, and Medieval Laws of War: A Reconsideration," *Nottingham Medieval Studies* 27 (1983): 56–78, has recently argued that Arthur's conduct of war would have been perceived as admirable during the fourteenth century. She further cautions against the tendency too readily to assume that "Chaucer and the unknown poet or *Morte Arthure* had the same preconceptions and the same ideals as late twentieth century liberal intellectuals. In our age the military hero has suffered an eclipse; neither can we espouse the ideal of a war to further the cause of religion. It was not so at the end of the fourteenth century. The Knight and Arthur are heroes created out of the needs and aspirations of their own age" (78). For another recent interpretation that construes the poem as a celebration of the British king, see Eadie, "*AMA:* Structure and Meaning."

17. Patterns of this type have been recognized in heroic narrative for some time; compare, for example, Ritzke-Rutherford's sequence with that identified by Dorothy L. Sayers in the introduction to her translation of *The Song of Roland* (Middlesex, England: Penguin, 1957), 34–37, or by J. B. Hainsworth in "Joining Battle in Homer," *Greece and Rome*, 2d ser., 13 (1966): 158–66.

18. Again, see "Flyting and Fighting" (note 3 above) for a detailed exposition.

19. Ong argues for the connection between contesting and identity—particularly sexual identity—in *Fighting for Life*. For seminal studies on the ritual character of aggression, human and animal, see Konrad Lorenz, *On Aggression*, trans. Marjorie Kerr Wilson (New York: Harcourt, Brace & World, 1963), and Niko Tinbergen, *The Herring Gull's World: A Study of the Social Behavior of Birds* (New York: Basic Books, 1961), esp. 44–96.

20. One is reminded of Beowulf's disdainful rejection of armor prior to his fight with Grendel, or Arthur's conniving so that he might fight the giant of St. Michael's Mount alone.

21. See Gregory Nagy's discussion of *kléos* in *The Best of the Achaeans: Concepts of the Hero in Archaic Greek Poetry* (Baltimore: Johns Hopkins University Press, 1979), 16–18, 35–41, 94–106, 111–15, and passim.

22. See, for example, line 399, where he compliments his knights for their warlike spirit by saying "My menske and my manhede ȝe mayntene in erthe" ("my honor and my manhood you uphold on the earth"); or again, a few lines later, where he urges Lucius to defend his "menske" and "manhede" (433–34) militarily by meeting him in battle in the fields of France.

23. See Ong's discussion of the etymology of "contest" and its derivation from "testis," a "witness" or "third stander," in *Fighting for Life*, 45–47.

24. These examples and the types that they represent are discussed in detail in "Flyting and Fighting." These categories assume that contest settings can be more meaningfully distinguished by the character of the interactions between the communities involved than by features in the actual physical environment. For other discussions of setting, see Pizarro, "Function and Context of the Senna," esp. 75–102, and Clover, "Germanic Context," 447–49. Clover finds "two standard settings, one outdoors over what Phillpotts called the 'sundering flood' (a body of water separating the contenders), the other indoors in the hall—at drinking, often in court (or, in Iceland, at the Alþing)" (447). Her reference is to Bertha S. Phillpotts, *The Elder Edda and Ancient Scandanavian Drama* (Cambridge: Cambridge University Press, 1920), 158.

25. This "flyting by proxy" is a composite pattern in the sense that the social groups represented are—or soon will be—at war with each other, as in the battlefield setting; on the other hand, the initiators in the exchange, as messengers in the enemy's stronghold, can claim entitlement to protection and hospitality (see the negotiations between Arthur and the Roman senator on this point, lines 116–230).

26. After killing Lucius, for example, Arthur keeps boasting to a minimum, refrains altogether from insulting his fallen enemy, and treats his body honorably. By contrast, both Britons and Romans vaunt over fallen enemies during their battle in lines 1637–1881.

27. Gawain initiates a prebattle flyting with Sir Priamus with this cry (2529); and even Arthur himself resorts to it as he charges down on the Emperior Lucius (2245).

28. For an important study in one of these related areas, see Alain Renoir, "The Heroic Oath in Beowulf, the *Chanson de Roland,* and the Nibelungenlied," in *Studies in Old English Literature in Honor of Arthur G. Brodeur,* ed. Stanley B. Greenfield (Eugene: University of Oregon Press, 1963), 237–66. See also Dwight Conquergood, "Boasting in Anglo-Saxon England: Performance and the Heroic Ethos," *Literature in Performance* 1 (1981): 24–35.

29. This distinction between "serious" and "ludic" modes of reference is one of the four principles of generic differentiation pertaining to the larger class of verbal contests that I identify in "Flyting, Sounding, Debate: Three Verbal Contest Genres" (see note 3 above). On the Scottish flyting tradition, see Priscilla Bawcutt, "The Art of Flyting," *Scottish Literary Journal* 10, no. 2 (1983): 5–24. For a superb treatment of "playing the dozens" among inner city black adolescents, see William Labov, *Languge in the Inner City: Studies in Black English Vernacular* (Philadelphia: University of Pennsylvania Press, 1972), 297–396. On a related phenomenon in another culture, see Alan Dundes, Jerry W. Leach, and Bora Ozkok, "The Strategy of Turkish Boys' Verbal Dueling Rhymes," in *Directions in Sociolinguistics: The Ethnography of Communication,* ed. John J. Gumperz and Dell Hymes (New York: Holt, Rinehart & Winston, 1972), 130–60.

30. These examples (and others) receive more detailed attention in "Flyting and Fighting" and "The Flyting Speech in Traditional Heroic Narrative" (see note 3 above). Homeric scholarship provides no systematic analysis of the verbal contest per se, though there are some excellent treatments of particular episodes or battle incident generally. For several important examples, see Bernard C. Fenik, *Typical Battle Scenes in the Iliad: Studies in the Narrative Techniques of Homeric Battle Description* (Wiesbaden: Franz Steiner, 1968), and G. S. Kirk, "The Formal Duels in Books 3 and 7 of the *Iliad,*" in *Homer: Tradition and Invention,* ed. Bernard C. Fenik (Leiden: E. J. Brill, 1978), 18–40.

31. See my "Flyting and Fighting," 915. In her essay on the Unferþ episode (see note 3 above), Carol Clover maintains that the flyting and the fighting are fully separable and distinct narrative units; my point is that they are connected through the flyting *contract*. Of course, contracts are not always fulfilled. Also, the trial of arms can take various forms; and in certain circumstances it can be circumvented. All these matters are discussed further in my article cited above.

32. For a recent discussion of this episode with a view to Priamus's religious affiliations, see Mary Hamel, "The 'Christening' or Sir Priamus in the Alliterative *Morte Arthure,*" *Viator* 13 (1982): 295–307. While in the sources for this episode Priamus is a Saracen, according to Hamel he is a Christian—probably Greek Orthodox—in the *AMA*.

33. "Where are you riding, plunderer, you who offer battle so boldly? Here you will seize no prey, display yourself as you please! Unless you parry the better in this peril, you will be my prisoner, for all your proud bearing!" "Sir," says Sir Gawain, "so help me God, such

blathering men grieve me but little! But if you make ready your gear, injury will befall you, before you depart from this grove, despite all your great words!" (2533–40).

34. The exchange takes a curious turn later as the two heroes, after fighting vigorously, in effect embark in a new contractual process that entails a genealogy and life history by Priamus and self-identifications by both heroes and that culminates in Priamus's defection to the British cause. As I point out in "Flyting and Fighting," flyting in certain circumstances can modulate into other modes of interaction. The Priamus-Gawain exchange might bear comparison in this regard with the Diomedes-Glaucus encounter in *Iliad* 6.119–236, or better, with the Hector-Ajax contest in 7.219–307.

35. Considerable densities of flyting occur in the course of the ambush which Lucius's men set for the Britons under Sir Cador in 1637–1881, and in the battle between the followers of the young Sir Florent and the army of the Duke of Lorraine (2752–3015), an episode from which is discussed below.

36. "[To atone] for his death you will die by my cruel weapon, along with all the valiant men that remain in the valley yonder!" (2776–77).

37. "Fie, says Sir Floridas, "you grimacing wretch! You hope to put us to flight, you flat-mouthed shrew!" (2778–29).

38. Finlayson characterizes this episode as a vindication of Arthur (at this stage of the story) as "the champion of Christianity and the redeemer of his people," in "Arthur and the Giant of St. Michael's Mount," *Medium Aevum* 33 (1964): 112–20; the quoted passage appears on 119.

39. Compare, for example, the rival accounts of Beowulf's swimming match with Breca in the Beowulf-Unferth exchange, or Achilles' unpleasant reminder to Aeneas of their previous meeting in *Iliad* 20.178–98. I described retrojection as one of a number of principal topics of invention or avenues of discursive elaboration within flyting speeches in "The Flyting Speech in Traditional Heroic Narrative" (see note 3 above).

40. In the martial encounter that follows, Arthur stabs the giant in the genitals (1122–23). One is reminded here of Ong's thesis in *Fighting for Life* that sexual identity is very much the concern of contestants. In fact, as Dundes, Leach, and Ozkok point out in "Strategy of Turkish Boys' Verbal Dueling," the objective of the adolescent Turkish verbal duelers is to represent the adversary as playing the female victim role in an aggressive homosexual assault. One is further reminded of Skarp-Hedin's famous insult to Flosi at the Althing when he accuses him of being the "mistress of the Svinafell Troll, who uses you as a woman every ninth night," in *Njal's Saga,* trans. Magnus Magnusson and Hermann Palsson (Middlesex, England: Penguin, 1960), 256. All of this may or may not bear on that curious knight "Sir Ienitall" (emended by Krishna to "Ionathal") who makes his brief appearnce in *AMA,* line 2112.

41. The organization of the first segment of this struggle is discussed by Keiser in "Narrative Structure in the Alliterative *Morte Arthure,* 26–720," *Chaucer Review* 9 (1974): 130–44.

42. Flyting exchanges are, in fact, extremely susceptible to guest-host associations as I argue in "Flyting and Fighting," discussing cases where flyting is terminated on account of former guest-host relations among ancestors of the present contestants. I examine guest-host patterning from a comparative perspective in "Generic Identity and the Guest-Host Exchange: A Study of Return Songs in the Homeric and Serbo-Croatian Traditions," *Canadian-American Slavic Studies* 15 (1981): 24–41. On an associated problem, see John M. Hill, "Beowulf and the Danish Succession: Gift Giving as an Occasion for Complex Gesture," *Medievalia et Humanistica,* n.s., 11 (1982): 177–97.

43. Arthur gives these orders and propounds his message in 1263–78; the flyting between the Romans and Britons occupies 1301–51, with an extended battle sequence following.

44. Gawain compares the two explicitly in their genealogical claims to overlordship (1307–13) and in their moral qualifications to rule over subjects (1314–18).

45. See, for example, Benson, "*AMA* and Medieval Tragedy," 77.

46. Compare Arthur's behavior with, for example, that of Achilles towards the body of Hector. For an excellent treatment of this subject, see Charles P. Segal, *The Theme of the Mutilation of the Corpse in the Iliad* (Leiden: E. J. Brill, 1971).

47. For a recent study of this pivotal episode see Anne Janssen, "The Dream of the Wheel

of Fortune," in Göller, *AMA: A Reassement,* 140–52 and 179–81. See also Karl Josef Höltgen's treatment of the motif of the Nine Worthies in his article by that name, "Die 'Nine Worthies,'" *Anglia* 77 (1959): 279–309.

48. "False-bred offspring, the Fiend take your bones! Fie on you, felon, and your false works! You will be dead and undone for your wicked deeds, or I will die this day, if destiny brings this about!"

49. "Turn, false traitor, no better will befall you; by great God, you will die by the strength of my hands! No man, no riches of the earth will rescue you."

Caxton's Copy-Text for *Le Morte Darthur*: Tracing the Provenance

RICHARD R. GRIFFITH

In 1985 we celebrated the quincentenary of the publication of Malory's *Morte Darthur,* which was issued by Caxton's press in early August, 1485. Calculations as to the number of full-run-of-an-edition pages Caxton was capable of printing per day by this, his eleventh year in business, yield different answers—probably six, possibly as many as eight. But since the *Morte* runs to almost a thousand pages, whatever figure one uses leads to the conclusion that, about five hundred years ago in the printing area behind Westminster Abbey, pages of Sir Thomas's great book were being peeled off the forms and hung to dry. Caxton's was a busy establishment. It used to be thought that his shop, "at the sign of the Red Pale," served only as a sort of "outlet store" for the products of his own press. We now know that he ran a "full-service" bookstore; he sold manuscripts; he was affiliated with a binder and sold books "hard bound" as well as in the usual basted-gatherings format; he imported both printed books and manuscripts from the continent; and there is no reason to doubt that—as I shall suggest later—he could arrange to have a scribe make manuscript copies of books for which the shop's supply of printed volumes was exhausted.

When the Winchester Manuscript was discovered back in 1934, it was immediately recognized as independent of Caxton's printed version, and scholars produced various analyses of the differences between the published volume and the handwritten text. However, when the British Library purchased the manuscript almost ten years ago, Lotte Hellinga noted smudges on a few pages and—in a piece of scholarly detective work that actually involved Scotland Yard, whose laboratories provided the specialized ultraviolet photography—she demonstrated that the marks were actually letters, the result of the manuscript's having come in contact with page-sheets on which the ink had not completely dried. Moreover, the letter-forms could be identified with specific typefaces used by Caxton at different periods, indicating that this manuscript was actually in Caxton's establishment for some years before and after the printing of the *Morte*.[1] Yet the textual arguments against its being the very copy-text used by Caxton's typesetters remained as strong as before. An obvious suggestion is that the printer employed the manuscript that survives for consultation in cases of hiatuses or questionable readings in his base text, which had reached him later by a different route.

Printing practices provide a satisfactory explanation for the rejection of the Winchester copy for use by the typesetters. In a volume like the *Morte*, gathered in eights, pages one and sixteen would be printed at the same time, and one would work toward the center of the gathering, finishing up with pages seven and eight; immediately after these would come pages seventeen and thirty-two, printed together. Thus it would appear that a minimum of twenty-six pages (thirty-two minus the first six, type for which could be thrown back and reused) would have to be set in type at any given time in order to keep the work flowing—and it's unlikely that Caxton had anything like this much type. Fortunately, there was a way around the problem; a skilled foreman could estimate quite accurately the amount of handwritten wordage which would make up a printed page and mark it off on the manuscript, while a clever typesetter (judiciously using spaces, contractions, and variant spellings) could bring that estimate in exact to the single letter. This had the additional advantage of permitting more than one typesetter to work on a single project, essential if two or more presses were being employed. The disadvantage was that the blocking off of pages required making marks on the manuscript, and spreading the work out required disassembling the copy so that sections could be distributed among several compositors. The Winchester Manuscript, characterized by such refinements as having all proper names rendered in red, is a rather luxurious piece of work. Presumably it didn't belong to Caxton, and its owner would hardly have been happy to have it marked up and taken apart. This could well be an important factor in the printer's decision not to publish the *Morte* immediately upon obtaining a manuscript of the work.

The actual copy-text used by the typesetters doubtless received the treatment described; it was marked up, disassembled, and—being considered of little value, more than adequately replaced by the ultimate printed version—was then discarded. Now *any* professionally copied thousand-page manuscript executed for an individual client would have been quite valuable. A mass-produced book obtained from a scriptorium would have been cheaper, but no analysis of the printed text has turned up the sort of errors characteristic of mass copying, and there's no indication that the work had any extensive circulation in manuscript prior to Caxton's printing. A *possible* explanation is that the printer somehow came into possession of the author's own master manuscript, the "fair copy" he would have made from drafts (probably written in wax with a stylus), textually sound but nothing much as a specimen of calligraphic artistry. Caxton's sprawling sentence describing the circumstances of his publication of the *Morte* has been quoted many times, but no scholar has noted that, reduced to essentials, it actually asserts that he used the author's own manuscript: "I have . . . emprysed to enprynt a book of . . . Kyng Arthur . . . *after a copye unto me delyverd, whyche copye syr Thomas Malorye dyd take out of certeyn bookes of Frensshe* . . ." (my italics).[2] This may be too literal a reading of the printer's words, but the possibility seems worth testing through a search for some line of transmission between the author and Caxton—a line that might at the same time cast some light on the dispute over *which* Thomas Malory was actually responsible for writing *Le Morte Darthur.*

Caxton was out of the country serving as Governor of the English Merchant Adventurers in Flanders during the period when the *Morte* was being written, not returning until six years after its completion—by which time every reasonable candidate for the work's authorship was dead. Furthermore, Caxton was resident in London for the period immediately before he went overseas, whereas the possible authors were living in Warwickshire, Yorkshire, or Cambridgeshire. A connection between him and Malory must therefore be sought through the two men's families and associates.

In his generally admirable biography of Caxton, George Painter attempts to resolve the long-standing question of the printer's family home, which he locates in Causton, Norfolk. Painter's argument is based simply on his having located a fourteenth-century Londoner named Causton who, like the printer, belonged to the Mercers' Company, and demonstrating that this individual indeed had family back in the Norfolk town.[3] But since Norfolk was an important center for the wool and cloth trade, and since that trade's headquarters and chief marts were the London Staple and Mercers' Company, it is no more than would be expected that some denizen of Causton should set up in business at England's chief city. Painter (in company with several other scholars) has assumed that, because the printer's name was often rendered as *Caston* or *Causton* instead of *Caxton* (the form he himself invariably used), the name variants are completely interchangeable. This is not the case. Linguistics has a tenet, usually called "the principle of least effort," which asserts simply that a form difficult to pronounce may well be modified to an easier variant, but not the reverse. In short, *Caxton* might easily be converted into *Caston* or *Causton,* but these forms would never turn into the more difficult *Caxton*. (There is an exception to this principle, but the circumstances governing it are inapplicable here.)

As Crotch established in his edition of Caxton's *Prologues and Epilogues* some sixty years ago, there is only one place in England named Caxton—a village in western Cambridgeshire, on the borders of Huntingdonshire.[4] It's a common experience even in modern England to find denizens of one community bearing surnames derived from the names of other nearby towns,[5] and there was indeed a Caxton family that held land in Cambridgeshire, although its main manor was just across the Suffolk border, in a village called Little Wratting (see fig. 1). A series of deeds connected with this family instances a second son named William, who sold his interest in the estate in 1438, the same year that William the printer is first listed as an apprentice in London's foremost livery guild, the Mercers' Company. Apprenticeships for the sons of nonmembers of a guild entailed a substantial gift to the master accepting their service, so it's an obvious inference that young William swapped his share in the family property for the chance to prepare for a career in trade. A large number of the individuals involved in the Little Wratting land transactions have later associations with William the printer, which caused these deeds to be hailed initially as solving the mystery of Caxton's youth. However, there was one serious difficulty: involved in the property deal was a man described as "William Caxton, alias Causton, saddler," who was assumed to be the same individual as William, the family's younger son; since William the printer had unquestionably belonged to the Mercers' Company, this was accepted as demonstrating that the deeds were not connected with the "right" Caxton family.[6]

A close reading of the deeds, however, reveals that the part played by this saddler is not consistent with his being a family member owning an interest in the property. Other researchers have asserted that no records of a William Caxton, saddler, exist. They have, however, failed to pursue standard variants of the surname and thus missed a William Coddeston, or Cottiston, whose name once appears as Coston.[7] Students of onomastics will recognize here an instance of the phenomenon which has been dubbed a "familiarity metonym"—in an area where *Caxton* is a well-known name, *Coston* or *Cotston* is likely to be converted into the more familiar form. (My own name, *Griffith,* is regularly turned into *Griffin* by students and strangers acquainted with the more common variant.) This move from *Coston* to *Caxton* would seem to violate that linguistic "principle of least effort" cited earlier, but such a change can be accounted for linguistically as well as onomastically; it comes under the heading of "folk etymology," in the special category dubbed "false reconstruction" or "false correction"—the process by which Welsh *Rabbit* on menus becomes Welsh *Rarebit,* or, in an area where Wellington or Skeffington are familiar names, the dialect pronounciation of the word for a body's bony structure becomes *skellington*. *Coston* was assumed simply to be a sloppy pronounciation of *Caxton,* and duly corrected. The legal secretary responsible for recording the names of those involved in the land transaction was not, as any medieval Englishman would have understood, implying that the saddler belonged to the same *family* as the principals, merely that he

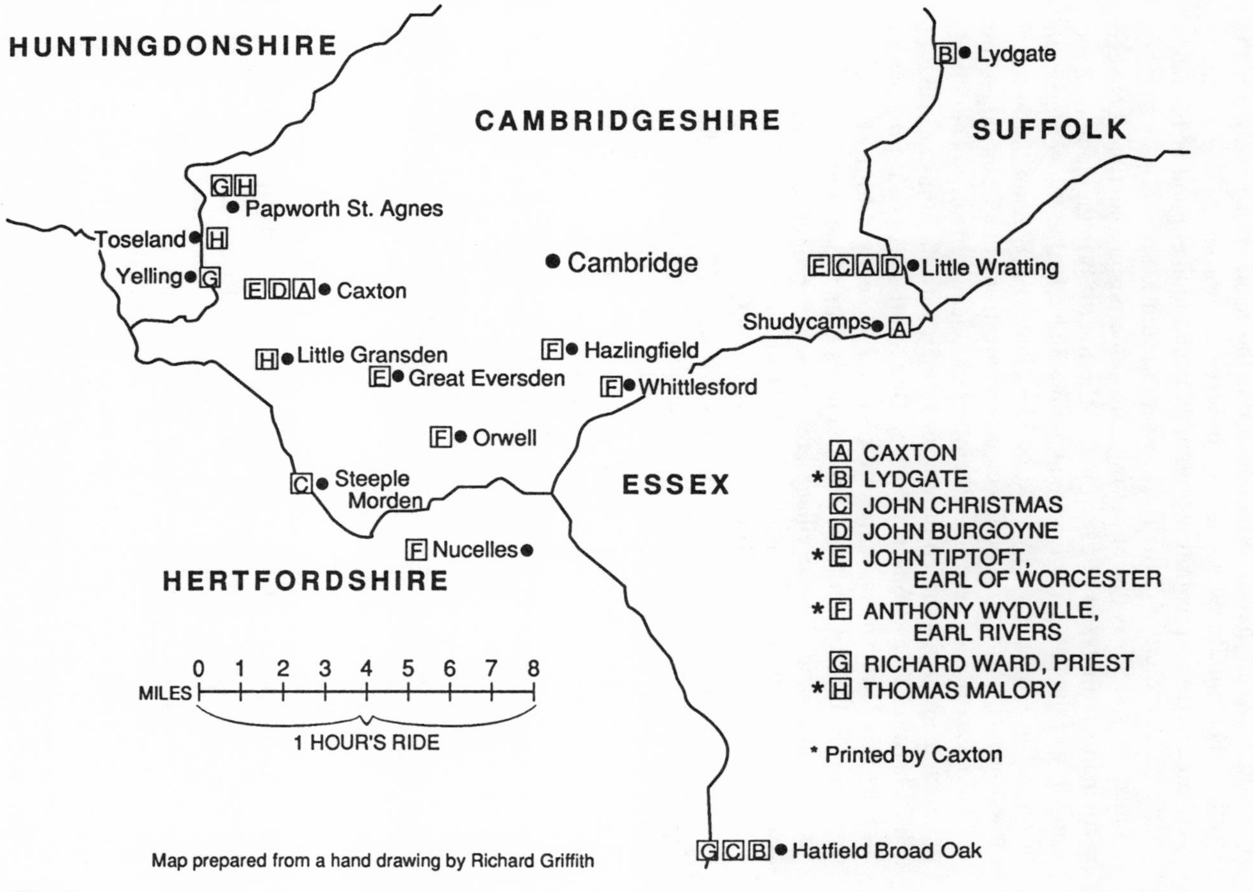
HUNTINGDONSHIRE
CAMBRIDGESHIRE
SUFFOLK
ESSEX
HERTFORDSHIRE
B Lydgate
G H Papworth St. Agnes
Toseland H
Yelling G
E D A Caxton
Cambridge
E C A D Little Wratting
Shudycamps A
H Little Gransden
E Great Eversden
F Hazlingfield
F Whittlesford
F Orwell
C Steeple Morden
F Nucelles
G C B Hatfield Broad Oak
A CAXTON
* B LYDGATE
C JOHN CHRISTMAS
D JOHN BURGOYNE
* E JOHN TIPTOFT, EARL OF WORCESTER
* F ANTHONY WYDVILLE, EARL RIVERS
G RICHARD WARD, PRIEST
* H THOMAS MALORY
* Printed by Caxton
MILES
0 1 2 3 4 5 6 7 8
1 HOUR'S RIDE
Map prepared from a hand drawing by Richard Griffith

Fig. 1.

or some ancestor hailed originally from the same village. Coston the saddler, incidentally, was shortly to serve as warden of the Saddlers Company, a senior position, which adds to the unlikelihood of his being young William Caxton of the Little Wratting family.

Once the saddler is out of the way, the numerous connections between participants in this land transaction and Caxton the printer, along with the suitability of the dates involved, make it highly likely that the younger son of the Little Wratting family is to be identified with William the Mercer-turned-printer. And this family clearly came from the Cambridgeshire village of Caxton, for several of the other individuals involved came from the immediate area—the co-purchaser (a man with the unusual name of John Christmas) was from nearby Dry Drayton (he also held property in Steeple Morden), and a witness, John Burgoyne, was lord of Caxton manor itself. In between the Caxton family's Cambridgeshire property at Shady Camps and Caxton village are the Scales properties which were acquired through marriage by the printer's future patron, Anthony Wydville, Lord Scales and Earl Rivers (three of whose translations Caxton printed). Just west of these manors lies the seat of John Tiptoft, Earl of Worcester, two of whose works Caxton published, and whom he eulogizes in a preface. A few miles to the north is the home of John Lydgate and Bury St. Edmonds Abbey, where the poet spent most of his life—and Caxton not only printed several of Lydgate's works, he writes of him as though he knew him.[8]

Right beside the village of Caxton, but across the county border of Huntingdonshire, is a hamlet named Yelling, and the rector of Yelling church was a priest named Richard Ward.[9] Several centuries of scholarly burrowing have failed to turn up William Caxton's will, but we do have one piece of information about it arising from a lawsuit instituted by Caxton's son-in-law after the printer's death: the person designated to distribute bequests of the printer's published volumes was a priest named Richard Ward.[10] In modern terms, Ward was Caxton's "literary executor." This use of a priest whose early turf was a bare mile from the town that gave Caxton's family its name recalls Shakespeare's use of a Warwickshire printer who had moved to London and unquestionably ties the printer to Caxton town, and thus to the Caxtons of Little Wratting, who had demonstrably maintained their contacts with the home village.

Over ninety years ago G. L. Kittredge proposed as author of *Le Morte Darthur* a Thomas Malory who lived in Newbold Revel, Warwickshire.[11] Researchers over the years since have investigated this man more thoroughly than any nonroyal Englishman of his century, turning up evidence of a remarkable criminal career, but they have found nothing to suggest he might have written a work like the *Morte*—or even that he was literate enough to write his own name. One piece of evidence that would have strengthened the case for this candidate immeasurably would be some connection between Thomas of Newbold and the printer who published his book fifteen years after he stopped working on it; but no such connection has been found. There are two other Thomas Malorys in armigerous families of appropriate age to have written the *Morte;* one is from Yorkshire,[12] and the other is from western Cambridgeshire—from Papworth St. Agnes, the next village north of Caxton town. This man's will *is* extant. He provides carefully for the education of his minor children, specifying that the boys shall be schooled in letters and suggesting careers for them in law or the priesthood—certainly reflecting concerns appropriate for a literary artist.[13] One son, Anthony, joined the Mercers' Company, to which Caxton had belonged (and Anthony's son, Sir Richard, became head of the Mercers and lord mayor of London).[14] The most significant evidence comes at the end of Thomas of Papworth's will; he names as one of his executors *a priest named Richard Ward*[15]—surely the same man as Caxton's literary executor (and his use by Caxton in this capacity suggests that he might well have served Malory in the same way). Here, then, we have an individual[16] who would have known of the existence of Malory's work, and who would have been in a position of authority as to the disposition of the author's master manuscript, who has come to London and is associated with Caxton.

It is apparent from Malory's advice on sources for those who want to finish up the *Morte*[17] that he was still working on it when he died, and thus his master manuscript would not have existed as a bound volume, but rather as a group of loose gatherings. These would have been protected during storage or transport by a paper wrapper, perhaps tied with a ribbon or thong. It is my suggestion that these gatherings were delivered to Caxton by Richard Ward (presumably the two men became acquainted, or reacquainted, after Caxton's return from abroad and Ward's move to London), and that the printer used it as his copy-text in preference to the Winchester Manuscript because it was a rough piece of work (not a valuable "fair copy" done by professional scribes), and could be taken apart for distribution among his compositors and afterward discarded.

A major problem for early printers was estimating how many copies of a given work they should print. All these publishing enterprises were, by modern standards, impossibly undercapitalized, and tying up too much expensive paper and labor in unsold stock resulted in bankruptcy for most of them. It was sounder business practice to print small editions, and reprint if a work was so popular it sold out. Caxton reprinted at least four of his publications, and there are hints of others. The problem with this approach is that a printer who is also a bookseller needs to keep his customers happy in order to keep them as customers for his shop, and a customer who wanted a specific work that was out of print would be unhappy. Caxton would naturally want to keep a "shelf copy" of every volume he had published, for his record and as a copy text for possible reprinting, a "sample" that would not be for sale. But it would be possible to employ a scribe (perhaps a copyist actually under contract with the shop to produce those manuscripts it also sold) to make a transcription of the shelf copy for the disappointed customer—not as inexpensive as the printed version would have been, but comparable in price to other manuscripts. This is the most reasonable explanation for the existence of a manuscript containing two devotional works, *The Game and Play of Chesse* (despite its title, a moral allegory) and *The Curial,* both based directly upon Caxton's printed texts of a few years earlier, which were copied by "Master Grace" for "Dame Margaret Woodward" in 1484.[18] Certainly Caxton's shop was the likeliest place for someone to find *both* these works together, and certainly it would be foolish to undertake the expense (and delay in obtaining the works) entailed by commissioning a scribe to copy a pair of printed volumes one had borrowed without visiting the "source" establishment to find out whether they were available in print. A London goldsmith named William Woodward is mentioned in a 1474 document from Westminster, where Caxton's shop was located; a Richard Woodward, saddler, was living in St. Clement Dane's Parish Without Temple Bar (right between London proper and Westminster) in 1484 (there is also a contemporary chancery clerk of this name); and a draper named Ralph Woodward was supervising a Westminster building project[19] about the time Dame Margaret's manuscript was copied, but I have not been able to ascertain whether any of these men had a wife or female relative named Margaret.

My suggestion is that Dame Margaret came to Caxton's shop (possibly in conjunction with a visit to one of the Woodward males mentioned above), chose for purchase a couple of those devotional works considered suitable for female readers, and then—finding them "out of print"—arranged through the shop to have them copied. When the scribe had finished his work and the manuscript was ready for delivery to the customer, Caxton (or one of his helpers) looked around for something to use as a protective wrapper. Large blank sheets of paper were too valuable to waste, as printers well knew. (Paper suppliers who had not received their money for previous shipments accepted printed sheets—sufficient to make up complete works, of course—as payment in kind, planning to sell the volumes themselves; in extreme cases, the deal they offered was only two blank sheets for one printed sheet!) Consequently, wrappers would have been reused rather than thrown away—rather as we use brown bags to carry out the garbage. What was used to wrap Dame Margaret's purchase, I propose, was the wrapper left over from a manuscript that had been delivered to Caxton shortly before, no longer needed because that manuscript had been disassembled for printing—the protective sheet that had been around the author's manuscript of *Le Morte Darthur.* This may seem an extraordinary coincidence, but what makes it extraordinary is entirely a consequence of our modern concern with the *Morte* and its author; the actions involved would have been quite routine to fifteenth-century booksellers and purchasers.

Dame Margaret received her wrapped unbound gatherings and doubtless read the text, but (like many medieval bibliophiles) she never got around to taking the volume to the bookbinder. Still in its protective paper cover, it passed from owner to owner for almost two centuries. That wrapper, smudged with dirt from doing its job of keeping the contents clean, was used as a handy place to test a pen point, figure a problem in addition, or try out a line of poetry. Finally some antiquary decided such a manuscript was worth something and had it bound. The antiquarian impulse valued a thing simply because it was *old,* and accommodating bookbinders regularly did their best to preserve absolutely everything old they were given, managing to make standard-sized volumes out of odd-sized materials by trimming or folding pieces that were too large and binding in smaller scraps. In this case, I suggest, they bound in the wrapper as the volume's endleaves.

Figure 2 shows what appears on the final endleaf (fol. 155v.) of Dame Margaret's volume. Halfway down the right side can be seen the name, *Thomas Malory.* It is written clearly and carefully, whereas elsewhere on the leaf are several scrawled practice *Thomas*es and another complete name. This argues strongly that the carefully executed version is a signature—one does not "doodle" a name other than one's own (moonstruck adolescents excepted). It is also apparent that this putative signature, with its associated practice versions, is among the earliest pieces of writing on the page, for the scrawled *Thomas*es have been written over in some instances, and have been intentionally avoided in others. It may further be deduced that the sheet was considerably larger at the time the *Thomas Malory* was written, for: (1) the lines of poetry at the top, which are spaced to avoid practice *Thomas*es (surely written just before the careful signature) and must therefore have been written after them, disappear into the gutter and even curl back from within the binding—an impossibility if the sheet was basted in with the rest of the gatherings when these lines were written, or even if it was the same size as the other leaves; and (2) the neatly executed signature is itself so near the gutter that it would be cramped and awkward to inscribe it in that position, and absurd to have scribbled practice versions on the open, flat sheet and then attempt the final, best rendition, in such a difficult spot. This tends to confirm the hypothesis that the sheet was a wrapper, and permits the possibility that it had served in that capacity on a previous occasion. Since the likeliest

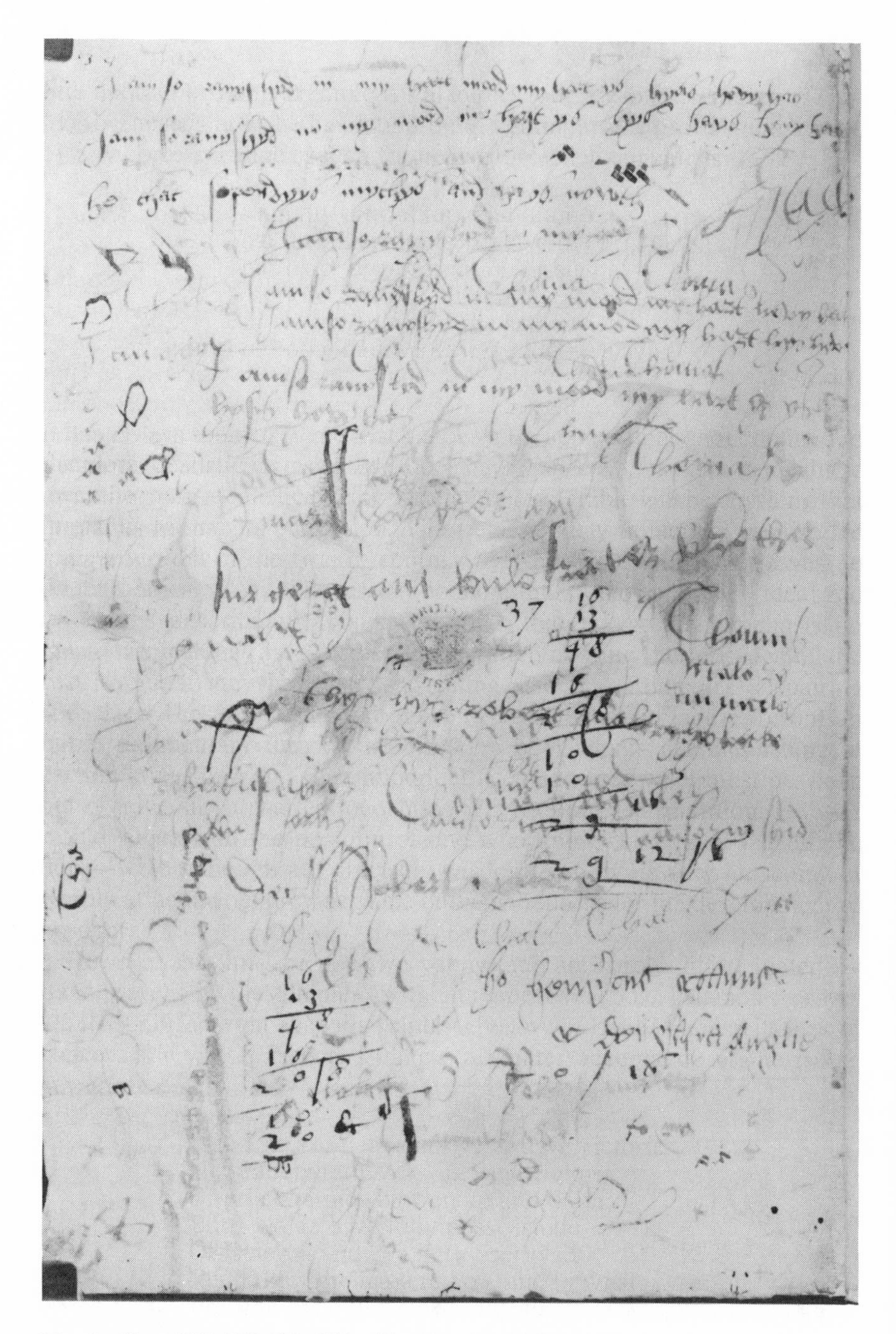

Fig. 2. Sloan MS. 779, fol. 155v. (Courtesy of The British Library.)

source for Dame Margaret's manuscript is Caxton's shop, and since we know beyond question that the manuscript (probably delivered in a protective wrapper) of a work written by Thomas Malory had arrived in that shop shortly before and was at this time (1484–85) being readied for publication (so its wrapper was no longer needed), it seems fair to propose that the appearance of the signature of a man named Thomas Malory on the wrapper of her manuscript implies a connection with that work, *Le Morte Darthur.*

Although it is possible to date the hands of professional scribes, especially those working in centers of manuscript production like London and the university towns, with considerable accuracy, signatures are so individual and idiosyncratic they are notoriously hard to date. The signature of a hinterlands knight and amateur author cannot be placed with assurance even as to century. A nineteenth-century edition of the Paston letters, "authenticated by engravings of autographs," provides some help; almost every letter-form represented in the *Thomas Malory* on Sloane 779 can be matched in signatures dated during the reigns of Henry VI and Edward IV.[20] So the autograph *could* have been written during the 1460s—but it could equally well have been executed a century later.

The geographical propinquity of the town of Caxton (original home of the printer's family) and the village of Papworth St. Agnes, where one Thomas Malory resided, has already been noted, as has the use of a priest named Richard Ward as "literary executor" by both William Caxton, printer, and the lord of Papworth manor. The obvious question is whether other Malory-related writing on the Sloane 779 end-leaf is consistent with its being this particular Thomas Malory as writer of the signature. The name *Robert Malory,* quite faded and carelessly written to begin with, can be seen in the center of the sheet, and ending just below Thomas's signature is the sentence, "Thys hys robert malory hys booke." Thomas of Papworth's second son, eventually his heir, was named Robert, and throughout the 1470s up until Caxton acquired it around 1484 this Robert Malory would have owned his father's manuscript (if the thesis presented here is valid). Immediately below Thomas's "signature," in the same hand, is a barely legible squiggle which appears to read "an malor"; this might be an abbreviated reference to Thomas of Papworth's sister, Anne, with whom he seemingly had an affectionate relationship (he leaves her a specific bequest in his will, rare treatment of a sister during the period), or to his third son, Anthony. Whatever the reference, its position is puzzling.

Ultimately, the surviving evidence is too sparse, and the alternative possibilities too numerous, to conclude with absolute assurance that the *Thomas Malory* on the Sloane 779 endleaf is the signature of *Le Morte Darthur*'s author. A number of Thomases, Roberts, Annes, and even Anthonys appear in later generations of the various branches of the

Malory clan.[21] All that can be said is that the hypothesis presented here successfully accounts for all the evidence, which cannot be said of any other immediately obvious explanation. If it is the correct answer, then (1) the case for Thomas Malory of Papworth as author of *Le Morte Darthur* is immeasurably strengthened, and (2) Figure 2 reproduces the earliest (by many decades) autograph of a major English author.

Notes

1. Lotte Hellinga, "The Malory Manuscript and Caxton," in *Aspects of Malory,* ed. Toshiyuki Takamiya and Derek Brewer (Totowa, N.J.: Rowman and Littlefield, 1981), 127, 131–33.
2. William Caxton, "Preface," *The Works of Sir Thomas Malory,* 2d ed., ed. Eugene Vinaver (Oxford: Clarendon Press, 1967), cxlv; hereafter cited as *Works.*
3. George D. Painter, *William Caxton: A Biography* (New York: G. P. Putnam's and Sons, 1977), 2–3.
4. W. J. B. Crotch, ed., *The Prologues and Epilogues of William Caxton,* EETS, o.s., no. 176 (1928; reprint, London: Oxford University Press, 1956), xxix–xxx.
5. Basil Cottle, *The Penguin Dictionary of Surnames,* 2d ed. (Harmondsworth, Middlesex: Penguin, 1978), 19–21; Gabriel W. Lasker and Bernice A. Kaplan, "English Place-name Surnames Tend to Cluster near the Place Named," *Names* 31 (September 1983): 167–77.
6. Norman F. Blake, "William Caxton and Suffolk," *Suffolk Institute of Archaeology Proceedings* 29 (1962): 139–53, and 30 (1964): 112–15.
7. *Calendar of Patent Rolls* (1446), 408; *Calendar of Close Rolls* (1448), 36, 93; *Calendar of Fine Rolls* (1452), 359.
8. See the Preface to *The History of Troy,* Book 2, in Crotch's edition.
9. A. B. Emden, s.v. "Ward, Richard," *A Biographical Register of the University of Cambridge to A.D. 1500* (Cambridge: Cambridge University Press, 1963), 616; Ward graduated from Cambridge with a Bachelor's degree in canon law in 1454. Emden believes he was dead by 1482 because he vacated Yelling in 1481, but Ward also held a living in Essex, where he is recorded as still alive in 1484 (*Calendar of Close Rolls,* 309), so there is no objection to his having come to London after he left Yelling.
10. Crotch, *Prologues and Epilogues,* cxxvii–viii.
11. G. L. Kittredge, s.v. "Malory, Sir Thomas," *Johnson's Universal Encyclopedia* (1894), 5:498.
12. William Matthews, *The Ill-framed Knight* (Berkeley and Los Angeles: University of California Press, 1966).
13. A. T. Martin, "The Identity of the Author of *Le Morte Darthur,*" *Archaeologia* 55 (1898): 161–77.
14. S. V. Mallory Smith, *A History of the Mallory Family* (Chichester, Sussex: Phillimore, 1985), 65–66, 135–57.
15. Prob. 11/5. 28. Printed by Martin, "Identity of the Author," 176–77.
16. Malory scholarship is plagued by similarities in name. As P. J. C. Field has pointed out to me, there was another priest by the name of Richard Ward, a native of Bristol (on England's west coast, far from the East Anglian habitat of Caxton and Thomas of Papworth), who attended Oxford. He was admitted to All Souls College in 1437, so he must have been thirteen or more years older than the Cambridge Richard Ward, which makes it less likely that he survived until Caxton's death in 1492. This Oxford man seems to have stayed in academe—he became a Fellow of All Souls, and was still there in 1479. See A. B. Emden, *A Biographical Register of the University of Oxford to A.D. 1500* (Oxford: Clarendon Press, 1959), 3:1980–82. I am indebted to F. Barry Karger for help in straightening out the two Richard Wards.
17. *Works,* 180; Richard R. Griffith, "The Authorship Question Reconsidered: A Case for

Thomas Malory of Papworth St. Agnes, Cambridgeshire," in *Apsects of Malroy,* ed. Takamiya and Brewer, 169.

18. British Library MS Sloane 779.

19. *Calendar of Patent Rolls* (1474), 384; *Calendar of Close Rolls* (1484), 387.

20. John Fenn, ed., *Paston Letters* (London: Charles Knight and Co., 1840), 2 vols.

21. Smith, *Mallory Family,* 135–57. H. Kelliher argues for a sixteenth-century Thomas Malory of Litchborough, Northamptonshire; see his "The Early History of the Malory Manuscript," in *Apsects of Malory,* 150–51.

Text and *Textura:* Spenser's Arachnean Art

PAMELA ROYSTON MACFIE

References to tapestry and embroidery are common in Spenser's poetry. From the formal compression of the sonnets to the expansive sweep of the epic, the poet manifests an interest in interwoven design. The *Amoretti* include two weaving sonnets; *The Faerie Queene* unfolds Malecasta's and Busirane's tapestries of love; *Muiopotmos* rewrites the Ovidian weaving contest between Arachne and Minerva. Given the well-developed association between tapestry and poetry in classical, medieval, and Renaissance texts, it should not be surprising that Spenser returns to the motif of the loomed or embroidered object with persistent variety.

The figure of the poet as weaver is a Renaissance commonplace. Sidney states in the *Apology* that "Nature never set forth the earth in so rich tapestry as divers poets have done"; Ariosto confesses that he uses many threads to extend the great web that he is weaving (*Orlando Furioso,* 37); Cervantes speaks of his "hackled, twisting, winding thread of plot" (*Don Quixote,* 1.38). From Virgil's oceanids who weave and sing of universal history (*Georgics,* 4.345–47) to Sannazaro's nereids who display marvelous cloths of woeful meaning (*Arcadia,* Prosa 12), the activity of weaving is variously defined by its motivations for and strategies of narration.

At the center of Spenser's consideration of text as *textura* reside his adaptations of the myth of Arachne. Ovid's story of the low-born weaver who measures her workmanship against that of Minerva is glossed throughout the Middle Ages as a tale of pride.[1] The *Ovide moralisé* reads the story as a warning against self-concerned and self-consuming presumption. Therein Minerva emerges not merely as an exemplary model of divine intelligence and contemplation, but also as an analogue to Christ, who dispenses the counsel of God to those who seek salvation. Arachne, on the other hand, is castigated as a demonically willful hypocrite, one who scorns belief and pursues a life of vanity.[2]

A number of readers have pointed out that Spenser employs these meanings in his references to the myth in *The Faerie Queene* 2.7.28, 2.12.77, and in *Muiopotmos,* 256–352.[3] But Spenser's Arachne, a recurrent, arresting presence in both poems, would seem to evoke a greater complex of issues than those delineated within the moralistic tradition.

Consistently incorporating Arachne within his disclosure of an artistry that threatens to deceive, suspend, and entrap, Spenser would seem to read the myth's full significance in relation to those concerns with furious composition and metamorphic art central in its Ovidian rendition. Although Spenser reshapes what we might call Arachne's poetic, his Arachnean allusions accrue full meaning only in relation to the explorations of the prior poet.

The story of Arachne's contest with Minerva opens Book 6 of the *Metamorphoses,* although the final episode of *Metamorphoses* 5, wherein Minerva hears the Muses sing of their contest with and victory over the Pierides, is relevant to its emphases. Convinced that divinity must scourge mortal presumptions to supramundane artistry, Minerva journeys from Helicon to Hypaepa, seeking the maiden who reportedly refuses to defer to her superior artistic skill. The emphasis upon mortal/divine contest is often noted as a link between the Pierides and Arachne episodes.[4] But I would suggest that the link is equally aesthetic, inasmuch as both episodes present contests in narrative artistry. Minerva and Arachne, no less than Calliope and the Pierides, weave ancient tales with their threads: *"Illic et lentum filis immittitur aurum / Et vetus in tela deducitur argumentum"* (6.68–69).[5]

Minerva' tapestry, which Ovid describes first, depicts the goddess's contest with Neptune over Athens. Minerva is victorious over Neptune, and this victory looks forward to her victory over Arachne. In the center of the cloth, Jupiter, surrounded by the other Olympian deities, sits in judgment of Neptune's and Minerva's displays of power. Neptune smites a cliff with his trident, creating a torrent of water, while Minerva, piercing the earth with her spear, produces an olive tree immediately ripe with fruit: *"Percussamque sua simulat de cuspide terram / Edere cum bacis fetum canentis olivae"* (6.80–81). Thus, Minerva's creative demonstration appears to surpass that of Neptune, and the gods look on in awe, according to the controlling hand of the weaver. Having recorded the power of her authority at the center of her artifact, Minerva proceeds to move outward, filling the corners of her panel with the deformative metamorphoses of other mortals who have dared vie with divinity. Minerva glosses her text with these punitive inscriptions, suiting it to the situation at hand, to the creative presumption of Arachne, not Neptune. With the final movements of her shuttle, the goddess borders her tapestry with the foliage of her own tree: *"Circuit extremas oleis pacalibus oras / (Is modus est) operisque sua facit arbore finem"* (6.101–2).

The motives that animate Arachne's cloth, the heavenly crimes of Jupiter, Apollo, Bacchus, and others, are familiar. For the reader, they summarize selected episodes of *Metamorphoses* 1–5, suggesting that the images of divine love and transformation have been completed. Like Ovid,

Arachne contests with an inherited narrative tradition (as well as with the goddess who sets her to her loom). And like Ovid, she rewrites a furious past. She reinterprets heavenly—and violent—acts of love and reveals Minerva's august and awful gods in the capering pursuits of disorderly desire. Her art, like Ovid's, is metamorphic. Opposed to the poise and balance of Minerva's creation, it swirls with one example after another of a masculine god seducing a mortal woman.[6] Jove transforms from bull to eagle to swan to satyr to golden shower to flame to shepherd to mottled snake. Neptune, Apollo, and Bacchus are similarly transformed. Theocentricity is displaced by discontinuous revolution. Where Minerva binds her narrative with the olive-wreath, Arachne borders hers with ivy and clinging flowers twined together: *"Ultima pars telae tenui circumdata limbo / Nexilibus flores hederis habet intertextos"* (6.127–28). The double spondee with which the passage ends and the interconnections of the word order reinforce the sense of interlacement.[7] Arachne defines her narrative with a luxuriant expansiveness of growth. Her signature of ivy suggests the garlands that crown Dionysus and the poets.

Arachne's art is equal to that of Minerva. Neither the goddess of weaving nor the goddess of envy can discover its lack or flaw. In his description of her creation, Ovid stresses Arachne's capacity for immediacy and verisimilitude: *"Maeonis elusam designat imagine tauri / Europam: verum taurum, freta vera putares"* (6.103–4). [Arachne pictures Europa cheated by the disguise of the bull: a real bull and real waves you would think them.] Although Ovid seems to hint that Arachne inspires Minerva's anger because she reveals the crimes of the gods, his reference to *caelestia crimina* (6.131) is brief, almost casual. Ultimately, it would seem that it is Arachne's success in mimesis rather than her irreverent interpretation of divinity that provokes Minerva's indignation. Confronted with the irony that the artistic verisimilitude of this humble maid exposes the false art of the gods, Minerva tears apart the tapestry and beats its maker, viciously and obsessively, with the shuttle, their shared symbol of productivity. Ovid underscores this action with the verb *percussit* (6.132–33), the same verb he employed to describe Minerva's miraculous creation of the full-fruited olive tree (6.80). The irony is clear. In Minerva's self-confirming art, the percussion of her spear blesses; against realities that threaten the efficacy of her aesthetic, the percussion of the shuttle destroys.

Unable to endure such indignity, Arachne prepares to hang herself from her broken web, but the goddess moves to prevent her suicide. Minerva's intercession, however, ends not in sympathy but in judgment. The goddess dooms the maiden to hang forever from the ruined text. Transformed into a spider, reduced to a body that is almost all belly, Arachne eternally pours forth her creative energy, emptying herself in a process that creates an all-entrapping web. Ovid's metamorphosis places her at the center of a perpetual and destructive artifact.[8]

Arachne's miscreated web, alternately secreted by the body and distilled by dew, is variously designed in Spenser's *Faerie Queene*. Its first appearance, described within the cave of Mammon episode, completes Minerva's translation of Arachne's perfect art into a perversion of nature:

> That houses forme within was rude and strong,
> Like an huge caue, hewne out of rocky clift,
> From whose rough vaut the ragged breaches hong,
> Embost with massy gold of glorious gift,
> And with rich metall loaded euery rift,
> That heauy ruine they did seeme to threat;
> And ouer them *Arachne* high did lift
> Her cunning web, and spred her subtile net,
> Enwrapped in fowle smoke and clouds more blacke then Iet.[9]
> (2.7.28)

Here, Arachne's work remains subtle and artful, but its artfulness is clearly deceptive. There is something abortive about this spinning. Arachne lifts her net over the gold-encrusted stalactites with overreaching contortion. Exemplifying pride, this Arachne looms her artistry on high and yet looms it in an underworld. Her weaving, formerly inspired, is rendered infernal. Smoking and vaporous, foul and black, it partakes of the general atmosphere of decay where all is "darkned with filthy dust" (2.7.4). Like "self-consuming Care" who watches the door, Arachne is both guardian and denizen of hell. She shrouds the rough spires, disguising their oppressive aspect and hiding their riches, but the ambiguous verse suggests also that she wraps herself in infernal vapors. In canto 7, Arachne's web is presented as a small image of Mammon's elaborately structured cave, a prisonhouse of darkness and dross where the hero feeds his eye on the temptations of riches, glory, and knowledge.[10] In canto 12, her web extends the subterfuge of Acrasia.

Arachne's artistry appears to regain its superlative qualities in the Bower of Bliss, "a place pickt out by choice of best aliue / That natures work by art can imitate" (2.12.42). There, a quintessence of dew and exhalation replaces the cave's sulphurous vapors, and Arachne's subtle net shimmers over the enchantress in a mysterious and powerful imitation of nature:

> Vpon a bed of Roses she was layd,
> As faint through heat, or dight to pleasant sin,
> And was arayd, or rather disarayd,
> All in a vele of silke and siluer thin,

That hid no whit her alablaster skin,
But rather shewd more white, if more might bee:
More subtile web *Arachne* cannot spin,
Nor the fine nets, which oft we wouen see
Of scorched deaw, do not in th'aire more lightly flee.

(2.12.77)

But the veil, simultaneously suggesting array and disarray, concealment and exposure, order and disorder, is ambiguous. The very qualities that determine its success in mimesis define it as fragile, mutable, and ephemeral.[11] Acrasia's Arachnean art is seductive, creating an experience that threatens to leave the reader, like the disarmed Verdant, suspended in faerie fantasy. But Spenser exposes and destroys the enchantress's subterfuge. At the end of Book 2, Guyon and the palmer enter the scene of luxury to throw over Acrasia and her thrall "a subtile net, which onely for the same / The skilfull palmer formally did frame" (2.12.81). This net, impervious to destruction, captures Verdant and Acrasia in a Mars/Venus relation. Like Arachne's net, it is subtle, but its formally determined, symmetrical design traps the deviser of false love and frees the victim. The palmer's net makes good Arachne's Ovidian web.

The presence of Arachne's artistry in the Bower of Bliss is not restricted to the canto's conclusion. Spenser opens his description of Acrasia's garden with reference to details that frame and define Arachne's Ovidian cloth. The ivory gate, an example of ecphrasis, the very mode of Ovid's tapestry description, re-creates Arachne's waves and their realistic effect:

Ye might haue seene the frothy billowes fry
Vnder the ship, as thorough them she went,
That seemd the waues were into yuory,
Or yuory into the waues were sent;

(2.12.45)

Arachne's signature, the richly interwoven ivy, is present, too:

And ouer all, of purest gold was spred,
A trayle of yuie in his natiue hew:
For the rich mettall was so coloured,
That wight, who did not well auis'd it vew,
Would surely deeme it to be yuie trew:

(2.12.61)

In creating and destroying the Bower of Bliss, Spenser explores two different sides of Arachne's meaning in Ovid. He demonstrates the powerful ecstatic and mimetic capabilities of her art. But he also considers such art's capacity to degenerate and questions its appropriateness for the ethical lessons of humanist poetry. In order for the hero and the poem to progress, Acrasia's bower and its Arachnean art must be destroyed.[12] Spenser employs the Arachne myth in *Faerie Queene* 2 to urge us to the difficult, but necessary, interpretation of "life-resembling" art. There, he refers to the myth in a narrative that evaluates, in the terms of the proem, how one may properly determine what is "painted forgery" and what is a "matter of just memory." In *Muiopotmos,* he retells Ovid's story as part of a similar disclosure of interpretive necessity.

Muiopotmos, which submits Arachne's miscreated web to its most monstrous extension, represents Spenser's most sustained consideration of the myth. Here, Spenser radically revises Arachne's contest with Minerva, privileging the artistry of Minerva and reducing the potential of Arachne throughout. Unlike Ovid, Spenser describes Arachne's tapestry before Minerva's. He removes the possibility that the reader might perceive Arachne's furious cloth as a protest against Minerva's static design and suggests that the goddess's tapestry comments upon the insufficiency of Arachne's art. Spenser's Arachne represents only one story within her cloth:

> *Arachne* figur'd how *Ioue* did abuse
> *Europa* like a Bull, and on his backe
> Her through the sea did beare; so liuely seene,
> That it true Sea, and true Bull ye would weene.
>
> (277–80)

Although she retains her capacity to render verisimilitude, she loses her power to metamorphose her configurations. The dizzying cataract of changing forms so evident in the Ovidian description has disappeared. Arachne's violent protest against the monstrous crimes of divine desire is replaced by precious, romanticized decoration:

> Before the Bull she pictur'd winged Loue,
> With his yong brother Sport, light fluttering
> Vpon the waues, as each had been a Doue;
> The one his bowe and shafts, the other Spring
> A burning Teade about his head did moue,
> As in their Syres new loue both triumphing:
> And manie Nymphes about them flocking round,
> And manie *Tritons,* which their hornes did sound.
>
> (289–96)

Minerva's tapestry, by contrast, fully reproduces the story of her contest with Neptune as described in Ovid. It retains its allegory of authority. Spenser does not reduce, but enriches, the goddess's design. Her border includes a butterfly made

> With excellent deuice and wondrous slight,
> Fluttring among the Oliues wantonly,
> That seem'd to liue, so like it was in sight.
>
> (330–32)

With the device of the butterfly, the verisimilitude of Minerva's art surpasses that of Arachne's. Lively emblem of flight and change, the butterfly opened in the final leaves of Minerva's text stops Arachne cold. "[M]astered with workmanship so rare" (338), schooled by the fiat of a superior maker, the humbled contestant stands silent and dismayed until a "poysonous rancor" (344) deforms her to a "hideous shape of dryrihed" (347). In *Muiopotmos,* Minerva neither rends Arachne's cloth nor beats the weaver. Arachne does not attempt to hang herself, and Minerva does not change her into a spider. The metamorphosis is completely self-generated.

Muiopotmos does present a divinely wrought, downward metamorphosis in a section that precedes the Arachne/Minerva episode. There, Venus turns Astery into a butterfly because she suspects that Cupid has been helping the maiden gather flowers. Misled by rumor and overcome with jealousy, Venus makes Astery suffer because she fears that the nymph approaches godliness; she fears that Astery has attracted the admiration of divinity. In broad terms, Venus's crisis is reminiscent of that of Minerva in Book 6 of the *Metamorphoses.* In each story, rumor inspires a jealous goddess to act; in each, the threatened goddess creates a new form of life from an offending mortal; in each, the changed form retains some attribute of the mortal's old identity. The spider's spinning repeats Arachne's weaving, and the butterfly's petal-like wings display the flowers gathered by Astery.

The Venus/Astery episode is important to Spenser's revision of the Arachne/Minerva contest in a number of ways. The name of the punished nymph evokes that Astery represented by Ovid's Arachne, but removed from the tapestry of her Spenserian counterpart. By contrast, the image of the butterfly anticipates that butterfly represented by Spenser's Minerva, but unattempted by Ovid's. The episode foregrounds the terms of Minerva's artistic victory. It suggests that the goddess's new signature may be a warning, as well as a marker of successful mimesis. Finally, the episode initiates the history of Clarion, a descendant of Astery who will be destroyed in a net created by Arachne's son.

Clarion and Aragnoll are oppositely drawn in *Muiopotmos.* Clarion's beauty surpasses "all Painter's skill" (91), while Aragnoll's deformity defines him as "the shame of Nature" (245). But Clarion's identity as something which is framed (61), painted (90), and engraved (75) does not qualify him as one who sensitively discerns the artistry of the world. Aragnoll seems more perspicacious. When he sees Clarion, and remembers his mother's defeat, Aragnoll prepares to destroy the butterfly. He sets his "lymie snares" (429) in order that he may efface Minerva's privileged sign. His web, stretched across a cavernous space like that web spun in Mammon's den, is generated from rank poison and foul excretion (254–56).

Nominated as "th' author of confusion" (244), Aragnoll emerges as part of Spenser's demonic progeny of false poets—a devious, devising mob that includes *The Faerie Queene*'s Archimago, Duessa, Despair, and Acrasia. His art is superlative, beyond comparison with any work in silken twine (361–68). But his art is also deceptive and entrapping. Like the Arachne of Acrasia's Bower, Aragnoll spins a subtle net within a luxurious garden where Art contends with Nature. His victim, whom Spenser calls "faultles" (418) and yet who vacillates in wit and desire (161–62), enters the garden unaware of the "hatefull mansion" (246) constructed at its center. Clarion "pastures on the pleasures of each place" (176) and "casts his glutton sense to satisfie" (179). Clearly, Spenser presents him as a figure of indulgence and loose excess. But I would suggest that the poet also presents Clarion as an inadequate and bereft interpreter of the world through which he moves.[13] The butterfly, after all, surveys the workmanship of heaven and the riot of the garden with the same "curious busie eye" (171). Unable to differentiate the earthly from the divine—or the "curious networke" (368) of Aragnoll from that "wouen . . . Of *Ioues* owne hand" (236)—Clarion is a doomed reader from the start. He can interpret neither the tapestry loomed by god nor that crafted by "the foe of faire things" (244).

In *Muiopotmos,* as in Book 2 of *The Faerie Queene,* Spenser inscribes Ovid's story of Arachne within a narrative concerned with misinterpretation and miscreation alike. In each poem, Arachne's problems of representing the world in art are correlated with those of recognizing the fatal artistry of the world itself. Suggesting that writers and readers share the task of framing the tapestry, Spenser readdresses the issues of revision represented in Arachne's ancient contest with Minerva. He goes beyond a narrow reading of the myth as negative exemplum to make us aware of the important complexities of meaning in any endeavor in *textura.*

Notes

1. Don Cameron Allen offers a summary of the Christian symbolism that associates the spider with impiety, heresy, and hypocrisy, together with an overview of the moralizations of the myth by De Vitry, Giovanni del Virgilio, and Thomas Wallensis in "On Spenser's *Muiopotmos,*" *Studies in Philology* 53 (1956): 154–56.

2. My reading of the *Ovide moralisé en prose* refers to C. de Boer's edition of the fifteenth-century text (Amsterdam: North Holland Publishing Co., 1954), 187–88.

3. See D. C. Allen, "On Spenser's *Muiopotmos,*" 141–58; Judith H. Anderson, "'Nat worth a boterflye': *Muiopotmos* and *The Nun's Priest's Tale,*" *Journal of Medieval and Renaissance Studies* 1 (1971): 89–106; and Judith Dundas, "*Muioptomos:* A World of Art," *Yearbook of English Studies* 5 (1975): 30–38.

4. See the commentary of William S. Anderson, ed., *Metamorphoses, Books 6–10* (Norman: University of Oklahoma Press, 1972), 151. See also Brooks Otis, *Ovid as an epic Poet* (Cambridge: Cambridge University Press, 1966), 146–47.

5. All citations and translations from the *Metamorphoses* are from the edition and translation of Frank Justus Miller, revised by G. P. Goold, 3d ed., Loeb Classical Library (Cambridge: Harvard University Press, 1977).

6. See G. Karl Galinsky, *Ovid's Metamorphoses: An Introduction to the Basic Aspects* (Berkeley: University of California Press, 1975), 82–83.

7. Anderson, *Metamorphoses, 6–10,* commentary on lines 127–28, pages 167–68.

8. For a discussion of the wide-ranging implications of Arachne's metamorphosis, see J. Hillis Miller, "Ariadne's Thread: Repetition and Narrative Line," in *Interpretation and Narrative,* ed. Mario J. Valdes and Owen J. Miller (Toronto: University of Toronto Press, 1978), 148–66; for a feminist reading of the metamorphosis and myth see Nancy K. Miller, "Arachnologies: The Woman, the Text, and the Critic," in *The Poetics of Gender,* ed. Nancy K. Miller (New York: Columbia University Press, 1986), 270–95; see also Patricia Klindienst Joplin, "The Voice of the Shuttle Is Ours," *Stanford Literature Review* 1 (1984); 48–52.

9. All citations from the works of Edmund Spenser are from the *Poetical Works,* ed. J. C. Smith and E. de Selincourt (1912; reprint, Oxford: Oxford University Press, 1970).

10. For an extended reading of the episode as a temptation to *curiositas,* see Harry Berger, Jr., *The Allegorical Temper* (New Haven: Yale University Press, 1957). See also Humphrey Tonkin, "Discussing Spenser's Cave of Mammon," *Studies in English Literature* 13 (1973): 1–13.

11. For a discussion of Spenser's persistent representation of the fragility of the poet's art in the thinness of the spider's web, see Judith Dundas, *The Spider and the Bee: The Artistry of Spenser's Faerie Queene* (Urbana: University of Illinois Press, 1985), 5.

12. See Stephen Greenblatt, "To Fashion a Gentleman: Spenser and the Destruction of the Bower of Bliss," in *Renaissance Self-Fashioning: From More to Shakespeare* (Chicago: University of Chicago Press, 1980), 157–92; for a discussion of the near-perilous suspension of the reader within the seductive text, see also A. Leigh DeNeef, *Spenser and the Motives of Metaphor* (Durham: Duke University Press, 1982), 108–10.

13. Franklin E. Court's argument that Clarion's tragedy derives from his lack of self-knowledge would seem to support my reading. See "The Theme and Structure of Spenser's *Muiopotmos,*" *Studies in English Literature* 10 (1970): 1–15.

Living with Elizabethans; or, There Goes the Neighborhood

GEORGE GARRETT

> And this is my eternal plea
> To him that made Heaven, Earth, and Sea,
> Seeing that I must die so soon
> And want a head to dine next noon,
> Just at the strike when my veins start, and spread,
> Set on my soul an everlasting head.
> Then am I ready like a palmer fit
> To tread those blest paths which before I writ.
>
> —Sir Walter Ralegh, "The Passionate Man's Pilgrimage"

Even though I am aware that there are a considerable number of living and working American writers who write as if the Elizabethans (and many other among their ancestors) had never existed, and even though I know all too well that for large numbers of students these days (even, maybe especially, the students of creative writing) the past drops off into a primitive and simultaneous darkness somewhere in the life and times of the late Robert Lowell—the past being a constant season of chaos and old night indifferently containing the unread works of Chaucer, Spenser, Milton, Dryden, and Hart Crane—a few people seem to have managed to escape the perfect democracy of oblivion by one accident or another; for instance Louise Bogan by being a woman and working for *The New Yorker* or Virginia Woolf for being English upper-middle-class and for marrying Leonard who was not. . . . Anyway, in spite of all these depressing things (and others too sad even to mention) I find it impossible to imagine life and art, in this country and our own language, without the profound and continuing influence of the Elizabethans.

It is difficult to imagine myself as someone influenced by them and uninspired by their example. Yet to make any sense at all, to untangle the snarl of personal influence it is necessary to go back to a condition of ignorance and partial innocence and to try to trace how that influence came to be and in what sequence and with what changes it developed.

It begins appropriately with their literature, particularly the plays of Shakespeare and the poems of the Tudor and Jacobean period. Begins therefore in college. (Which gives me time and occasion to say that I like to think that, even if I had never managed to write and finish anything, purely and simply as a reader, then, I would still have been much influenced by their works and words.) Beyond that kind of guessing, though, I was greatly and eagerly influenced. In part by modernity. My college days were the salad days of the criticism of T. S. Eliot and of the Fugitives. They did not profess to be great admirers of the Elizabethan poets in general; but they were active propagandists for the Metaphysicals. And what was good enough for them was (as they kept telling me) more than good enough for the likes of me. It was later (though not very much later) that I learned by a lot of reading and a little thinking that the differences between the Metaphysicals and the mainline/mainstream Elizabethans were more a matter of emphasis than anything else and that the quarrel was basically intramural, a minor problem to be negotiated between people who shared most of the same conventions and expectations, most of the same artistic interests, and pretty much the same wide range and habits of language. A family feud.

About the same time I dropped off the back of the bandwagon of the New Criticism. Much as I admired the practice of it and some of the gifted performers. It didn't take me long in those happy sophomoric days to figure out they didn't really *know enough* to be saying what they were saying.

What were some of the things that, with a lot of help, I stumbled across, the things that were to last me from then until now and were to influence most of the writing of all kinds that I would attempt? At first these things were almost purely literary. (I knew next to nothing about the life behind and in and of the literature and, to add complexity to my native ignorance, I did not know yet that I did not know.) In the literature I was pleased to learn that gifted and inspired artists made good and often fresh use of a whole deck of conventions. That is, I was pleased to discover there could be a real and useful connection between reading and writing. Next I greatly admired their ceaseless interest in and ability to articulate characterization. Pre-Freudian, pre-Jungian, sometimes working with equally improbable and much simpler theories, they could go as deep into human beings as anyone before or since them—this included, by the way, the self-reflexive characterization of speakers and narrators.

Above all, though, I believe that then as now I was wholly overwhelmed by the range, openness, and vitality of their language, all the layers of it, from the most coarse and vulgar to the mostly highfaluting, the often indecorous joining of the vernacular with the rhetorical, all welded together somehow without any visible cracks or seams. Simultaneous with this richly various language, probably part and parcel of it, was the bringing together of an equal variety of images, of tones and moods, of subjects.

I did not know it at the time, but I was beginning to learn something about the true sophistication of culture.

(It was only much later that I would begin to perceive the truth that the Renaissance was not really the beginning of anything, not a stage along the way leading up to, of course, us; but rather the wonderful tag end of something old and fully formed.)

In any case, these notions, together with a deepening experience of reading (catching up, really, in this illiterate era), looking for and finding some of the same characteristics even in the most unlikely places and periods, these things have consciously and unconsciously influenced all my work in every form I have been able to work in ever since, poetry and prose. Including this paper. Including, yes, "Frankenstein Meets the Space Monster." Which I wouldn't have even entertained, let alone worked on if I had not been much influenced by Renaissance writers and, before that, if I had not been much challenged and influenced by a whole string of courses, undergraduate and graduate, taught by D. W. Robertson, Jr.

Next (and briefly) there are the very special problems encountered in the making of two published historical novels and one more in the works.

The relevant problem—there were many others—was seeking and finding and developing a kind of language that would do to represent and to evoke the tropes and tones of voice from the sixteenth and early seventeenth century. Not to parody the languages of those times. Nor to imitate. But rather to create, if possible, a modern equivalent.

This involved a great deal of reading, of course. Especially Elizabethan prose, Eliabethan satires, and Elizabethan translations. Translations, with all their inherent flaws, can often give us a very strong sense of the second language.

Early on I made a choice not to base my own style, or styles on any specific example, except here and there from Ralegh's *History of the World*. The way to do this was to be as vaguely familiar with as many texts and kinds of texts as possible without being directly beholden to any. With *Death of the Fox* the problem was simpler if not easier. Mostly it was handled by a conflict and contrast between two primary styles, old and new. A single passage dealing precisely and overtly with that contrast will give you the idea:*

> My son, it is the prerogative of the old to inflict upon the young a tedious celebration of the past, spent seasons, festivals, and holidays of lost time. And as the world goes, it falls the duty of the young to hear them out or to seem to; and remains the privilege of the old to practice that

*Excerpt from *The Death of the Fox* by George Garrett. Copyright (c) 1971 by George Garrett. Reprinted by permission of Doubleday, a division of Bantam, Doubleday, Dell Publishing Group, Inc.

prerogative, though the exercise serve only to prove the folly thereof. For the old hold no patent, license, or monopoly on wisdom, which, being mysterious and, all reasonable men will agree, invaluable, is beyond the possession of one man or another, one station or one age. For youth, though bound to ignorance out of inexperience, is not likewise condemned to be foolish. For if the purpose of the old be to transmit such wisdom as they deem they have come into, together with a history of themselves and their experience, judiciously framed and arranged in quiet afterthought, and thereby to preserve for the young the best of what has been, and so to defend them from the repetition of many errors and follies of the past, then their intent is surely foolish. It is doomed and fated to fail. The young will either listen, nodding assent and masking an honest indifference, thus learning chiefly the fine art of duplicity at a tender age, or they will listen truly, but without full understanding; as newly arrived in a foreign country, one listens out of courtesy, with much frowning concentration, to a strange tongue, the grammar of which is less than half mastered. Or, should a young man be fortunate enough to be free from need to listen to elders or heed the clucking of old ganders, whose chief claim to excellence is to have lived long enough to be unfit for anything except a stewing pot, he will stop his ears or walk away in insolence, leaving an old man to mutter at his own shadow by the fire.

Nonetheless, with knowledge of the vanity of my purpose and some foreknowledge of its likely failure, I would seek . . .

I would seek . . . what?

A clumsy exercise in an antiquated style, lacking the time for revision and polish; so that even if I were not to be credited for any substance whatsoever, I might win grudging approval for virtuosity.

Time will bleed away, an inward wound, until I truly bleed.

If time were blood and the executioner struck off my head now, there would be nothing left in me for a crowd to see. A drained and cured carcass only. For I have been gutted and cleaned and hung up by time like a pig in the cellar. They say—do they not?—that I have the pig's eye. Just so . . . I can find no fault now with that. What is gossip may sometimes be poetry.

"Old men are twice children," the proverb says. Perhaps he will bear with me for the sake of my second childhood.[1]

The Succession had to be much more diffuse, wide-ranging. More layers of language had to be suggested, because there were so many characters acting over such an expanse of time.

Here I moved farther away from literary reading—to letters, to Robert Carey's great autobiography, to jest books and the like. Some of the jokes in *The Succession* come directly out of jest books. Others I made up in the process of writing. Which my wife (and my most patient critic) reckons was the moment I was at last more or less at home in the times. When you can finally make a plausible joke or two in the language of ghosts, then you are at least getting there.

The most important thing I learned from studying and imagining the lives of these our ancestors (here reduced to brutal simplicity) was something close to T. S. Eliot's notion of the "dissociation of sensibility." Close, but no cigar. Over and over again I encountered . . . a sustained duplicity, a characteristic involving feelings and perceptions as much as any ideas, a capacity to entertain, simultaneously, paradoxical, indeed contradictory feelings and perceptions. That capacity stands like an ocean between us.

I have only one more point to make here: that for the making of these two novels I was much more concerned with the life of the times than the literature. But soon enough it was perfectly apparent that the only good gate leading to their lives and times was made out of words. So much else that they created and loved and lived by and for is long gone. The words—which, with a very few exceptions, they cannot possibly have taken as seriously as the wealth of vanished clothes and jewels, the lost and forgotten great houses and tombs and monuments . . . (Shakespeare was dead right: "Not marble, nor the gilded monuments of princes shall outlive this powerful rime"). Their words are not only their greatest gift to us, they are also the only true map we have to lead us to their world and safely back to our own.

Note

1. George Garrett, *The Death of the Fox* (New York: Doubleday, 1971), 516–17.

Patriarchal Fatherhood in Ben Jonson's Epigram 45

H. W. MATALENE

XLV

On My First Sonne.

Farewell, thou child of my right hand, and ioy;
 My sinne was too much hope of thee, lou'd boy,
Seuen yeeres tho'wert lent to me, and I thee pay,
 Exacted by thy fate, on the iust day.
O, could I loose all father, now. For why 5
 Will man lament the state he should enuie?
To haue so soone scap'd worlds, and fleshes rage,
 And, if no other miserie, yet age?
Rest in soft peace, and ask'd, say here doth lye
 BEN. IONSON his best piece of *poetrie*. 10
For whose sake, hence-forth, all his vowes be such,
 As what he loues may neuer like too much.

The fate of Ben Jonson, as T. S. Eliot reported in 1919, is to have suffered "the most perfect conspiracy of approval . . . damned by the praise that quenches all desire to read the book; afflicted by the imputation of the virtues which excite the least pleasure; . . . and read only by historians and antiquaries."[1] Even so, no modern reader has been able to resist Jonson's work in one small poetic genre. In an article generally hard on Jonson, for instance, E. Pearlman writes that "There is one subject [which Jonson treats best in Epigram 45] on which Jonson writes with a sensitivity and clarity unequalled in the language, and that is the death of children."[2] Indeed, most modern explanations of the power of Jonson's forty-fifth epigram, "On My First Sonne," include praise for the "sincerity" and "depth" of "the grief of the natural man" upon the death of his child, which Jonson is assumed to be expressing.[3] Even philological critics like J. Z. Kronenfeld take it for granted that the father-feeling of Epigram 45 is a "natural human affection" such as would come to any man, in any place or epoch, were he bereft of his child.[4]

But is there any "natural man"? Can we still assume, after the teachings of modern social science, that the affective impact of child mortality upon paternity is a human universal? Only W. David Kay, among recent academic interpreters of "On My First Sonne," has touched upon anthropologically oriented research in Western cultural history which suggests that our preindustrial ancestors did not feel the deaths of their children as we might today. Kay cites but makes little of the pioneer work of Philippe Ariès on the history of family life under the ancien régime.[5] And while the work which Ariès began has been continued by many other historians, its bearing on our appreciation of Jonson's forty-fifth epigram has yet to be fully explored.

For the modern reader, especially in America, problems of interpretation underlie even the monosyllabics of Ben Jonson's title. A "first son" may not mean much more to us than a slot in a chronological list of births to a nuclear couple who will eventually indicate the equal importance to them of each of their children by the practice of partible inheritance. But Elizabethan inheritance practices were different—especially in families claiming gentle or noble status. Then, as Thomas Wilson sardonically remarked in 1600, the gentleman's younger brother was probably left with "that which the cat left on the malt heap, perhaps some small annuity during his life, or what please our elder brother's worship to bestow upon us if we please him and my mistress his wife."[6] Ben Jonson, of course, had been a bricklayer's apprentice. He was not born a gentleman, though he told Drummond that his grandfather had been a gentleman under Henry VIII and that his father, who died before his birth, had been a gentleman until deprived of his estate under Queen Mary.[7] When he became an actor, Ben Jonson would have affected gentility, and when the luck of his excellent schooling and talent enabled him largely to give up the theater, and to live by his pen on aristocratic, city, and sometimes even royal patronage, Jonson might fairly have felt he had established himself as a gentleman.[8] For the poet, therefore, establishing his "first sonne" in the world could have had the feel of confirming his restoration of his patrimonial lineage to its once-proud place among the English gentry. In this case, the death of his "first sonne" would, of course, have threatened Jonson's sense of himself as the father of gentlefolk. The Marxist in us may wish to join Pearlman in scoffing at Jonson's sensitivity to the status and continuity of his lineage as a false class-consciousness with Oedipal overtones unworthy of a great poet,[9] but if we are interested in the feeling behind Epigram 45, we should perhaps resist our temptation to do so.[10]

"On My First Sonne' begins, "Farewell, thou child of my right hand, and ioy; / My sinne was too much hope of thee, lou'd boy." Like the title, the first line has a seductive plainness. Several alternative readings of the line's syntax are possible, but the simplest is that the first son is *both* the child of the poet's right hand *and* his joy. But what *is* the child of somebody's right hand? A number of modern editors and critics remark that the

Hebrew name "Benjamin" means "child of the right hand"—a metaphor that Jonson's standard editors simply assert "meant 'fortunate' or 'dexterous.'"[11] This would indicate that as Jonson does in Epigram 120, the epitaph for Salomon Pavy,[12] he is lamenting the loss of an unusually precocious child. Indeed, this must be part of Jonson's message, and certainly there is nothing at odds with modern, bourgeois father-feelings in the Herford-Simpson interpretation. We expect fathers, ideally, at least, to take an active hand in nurturing their children's individual talents. But there may be more to the metaphor of the "right hand" than mere manual dexterity.

The name "Benjamin," or "child of the right hand," first appears in the Bible at Genesis 35, verse 18; and at this point, the Anchor Bible instructs us that the name "means literally 'son of the right' (side, hand, or the like), that is, one on whom the father expects to count heavily for support and comfort; or, alternatively, one who promises good fortune, a propitious turn of events."[13] Let us therefore suggest that in line one Jonson bids farewell not only to a child of special individual dexterity, but also to a first son on whom Jonson counts, and whom the poet has specifically named to carry forward the "good fortune" to which his literary success has propitiously restored the Jonson line.

The joy of a traditional, preindustrial patriarch in the child of his right hand may not seem a very attractive sort of father-feeling to egalitarian, post-Romantic readers of poetry, who expect fathers to affect and nurture their children's development as individuals. Nevertheless, it sorts well with the observations of Lawrence Stone and Edward Shorter about family life in our culture before the massive changes of the eighteenth and nineteenth centuries. Stone remarks that

> The key to all understanding of interpersonal relationships among the propertied classes [during the sixteenth and seventeenth centuries] is a recognition of the fact that what mattered was not the individual but the family. . . . Under these circumstances the one close tie—though not necessarily one of love—which could and often did develop between parents and children among the elite was between the father and his surviving eldest son, who was designed to inherit the title, position and property.[14]

Similarly, for Shorter, the notion that families exist to help children become "individuals" is a recent idea not to be observed among our ancestors.

> In the Bad Old Days [Shorter reports] people learned who they were, and what their place in the eternal order of things was to be, by looking at the progression of generations that stretched behind them—a progression that would extend from them into a future of which one could

> say only that it would probably be like the present. People in traditional society . . . knew their names and memories would live on in the lineage of their families.[15]

In view of the translation of Benjamin as "child of the right hand" in line one of Jonson's forty-fifth epigram, then, it is worth recalling that Ben Jonson gave the name "Benjamin" to another legitimate son, and (conceivably) to an illegitimate one as well.[16] Here, we have external evidence that Jonson identified himself as the father of a lineage, as well as of a "dexterous" little boy. In the judgment of Daniel Scott Smith, an historical "shift away from parental naming . . . [helps to] illustrate the movement from a traditional lineal orientation to a modern individuated conception of children."[17] Obviously, with both (or all?) of his little Bens, Jonson exemplifies Smith's "traditional lineal orientation" toward children, and not the "modern individuated" one with which most of the poet's modern readers have likely grown up. Thus, when the poet complains in line two that his sin was too much "hope" of the loved boy, he means not only hope for the development and recognition of an individual child's special talents, but also (and, perhaps, primarily) hope for the boy on whom he and the Jonson lines are counting.

The dynastic conception of paternal "hope" also commonly turns up in the nonpoetic usage of English-speaking people in Ben Jonson's time. The study of surviving Tudor and Stuart diaries by anthropologically trained historians has just begun. Nevertheless, we do have the important work of Alan Macfarlane on the copious diary of an Essex clergyman of yeoman status, born in 1617, named Ralph Josselin. On 15 June 1673, Josselin made the following entry: "about one a clocke in the morning my eldest sonne Thomas and my most deare child ascended early hence to keep his everlasting Sabbath with his heavenly Father . . . . He was my hope, but some yeares I have feared his life."[18] Josselin's meaning for "hope" is clearly dynastic, for he applies the word to Thomas in the same context where he records not hope but fear for Thomas's personal survival. Josselin calls Thomas his "hope" not only because he feels for him as an individual with good prospects if he lives, but expressly because Thomas was his eldest son.

Let us suggest, then, that the "hope" which Ben Jonson calls a "sinne" in line two is in large part the hope that he will father a line of gentlefolk and confirm the new status to which his poetry has raised the Jonson name. It is not only a modern parent's hope for the individual talents of a particularly dexterous child. Taken together, then, lines one and two confess that the poet himself has probably called down the boy's death as God's punishment for his own familial ambition.

Such a confession, in Jonson's England, was no mere lip service to biblical warnings of visitations upon children of their fathers' sins. As Stone notes, a major official belief of the period was still "that every event in this world, including every death, is the planned result of God's inscrutable purpose. The puzzle, therefore, was to determine what sinful act, perpetrated by whom, had been the cause of the misfortune."[19] In Epigram 45, Ben Jonson makes one of many seventeenth-century attempts at working this puzzle out. Macfarlane's study shows that in the privacy of his diary Ralph Josselin puzzles over this very problem. The clergyman seems not to worry about it in advance, but like the poet, once misfortune has actually struck a member of his family, Josselin considers the chance that his own sin may have brought it on. Unlike Jonson, however, Josselin would not have held himself responsible for the death of his son in a disaster like the plague of 1603, which took at least thirty thousand other Londoners along with the poet's first son. Plagues, Josselin thought, are visited not upon individual sins, but upon national ones.[20]

An even closer analogue than Josselin's thinking to the guilt expressed in Jonson's first couplet is to be found in the autobiography of Mary, fourth countess of Warwick, cited by Stone and briefly studied by Joseph E. Illick. Illick reports that like Jonson, Lady Warwick "felt she sought too much comfort in the world, and claimed to have had"

> some inward persuasion that God would, in some way or other, punish me for my doing so. And, at last, it pleased God to send a sudden sickness on my only son, which I then doated on with great fondness. I was beyond expression struck at it; not only because of my kindness for him, but because my conscience told me it was for my back-sliding. Upon this conviction I presently retired to God; and by earnest prayer begged of Him to restore my child; and did then solemnly promise to God, if he would hear my prayer I would become a new creature.

Here, precisely as in Ben Jonson's Epigram, a parent who much affects what Lady Warwick calls the "glory of the world"[21] is convinced that the heir to her share of that glory is endangered by her own attraction to it. Like Jonson the aspiring gentleman, the noble Lady Warwick varies from the pattern of the yeoman Ralph Josselin in applying her own sense of sin to explain her family's misfortune. Josselin achieved his status and waited righteously to be struck before searching for the sin that might explain his providential punishment. But Lady Warwick, the beneficiary of ascribed status, feels guilt and anticipates the trouble justly to be expected.

A final example will indicate how pervasive in Jonson's century were patriarchal fears such as those behind the opening lines of Epigram 45. John Evelyn and Samuel Pepys spent the afternoon of 27 January 1689 examining "a young Child not 12 yeares old . . . of the most prodigious maturity of memory and knowledge." Evelyn was reminded of his own "joy," Richard, dead at "but 5 years & 3 days old [though[a prodigie for Witt & understanding."[22] So moved, Evelyn "counseled [the boy's] father, not to set his heart too much upon this Jewell, . . . as I my selfe learn'd by sad experience in my most deare child Richard many years since."[23]

In the second couplet, the fact that the poet has repaid God's loan of a right-hand man "on the iust day" after the boy has lived "Seuen yeeres" further suggests the premodern, patriarchal nature of Jonson's father-feeling. As Stone remarks, "There are plenty of examples from the seventeenth century of families being shattered by the deaths of children, especially those who lived sufficiently long for deep affective ties to develop, and who were potential male heirs to the family name and property."[24] Ben Jonson's first son may or may not have been a prodigy of dexterity, but he did meet both of these criteria for patriarchal father-feeling.

Stone notes that "The longer a child lived, the more likely it was that an affective bond would develop between it and its parents."[25] This increase of parental feeling as the child moves beyond its dreadfully perilous first year of life is explicitly recorded by Sir Simonds D'Ewes in the 1630s as well as by Mrs. Thrale in the 1770s.[26] A similar increase of feeling with the child's increasing age is suggested by Philippe Ariès's account of the criteria apparently determining (in several French parishes around 1700) whether one was to be buried in the church proper or in its less prestigious, adjacent cemetery. "The cemetery," Ariès reports, "was the domain of the poor and of [children under one year of age] regardless of whether their noble, bourgeois, or petit bourgeois parents had chosen the church for themselves and their families."[27]

That Jonson also was affected by the deaths of his children according to how long they had survived is suggested by a comparison of Epigram 45 with Jonson's twenty-second epigram, "On My First Daughter." Although a girl, "Mary, the daughter of [each her parents'] youth" was also capital on loan from heaven, duly repaid at her death. But she died "At sixe moneths end,"[28] rather than after Benjamin's "Seuen yeeres." Young (and female) as she was, the death of this daughter was an occasion for sorrow, but not for the confession, soul-searching, and new resolve that Jonson felt upon the death of his first son; for Benjamin had lived long enough for the poet not only to believe in his chances for survival, but also to invest patrilineal "hope" in him.

"Seuen yeeres" could have been the very point at which the culture of fatherhood began instructing the poet to think, actively, about his son's social future and its meaning to the Jonson lineage. In the words of Ivy Pinchbeck and Margaret Hewitt, "Of [the greatest] general importance [in determining the character of Tudor children's lives] was the consciousness that children could be used to advance family fortune." And they continue: "Conscious of the brevity of life and all too aware of the possibly disastrous consequences of leaving estates unsettled at their death, parents were eager to introduce their sons and daughters into the adult world [of service, apprenticeship, patronage, and even marriage] at the earliest possible moment, usually between the ages of seven and nine."[29] If, therefore, as most critics agree, line four means that Benjamin died on his seventh birthday, in 1603, he died just as he was old enough—and the poet successful enough—for Jonson to begin seeking a gentleman's connections for him.

Earlier in 1603, the diary of John Manningham mockingly records that "Ben Jonson the poet now lives upon one Townsend and scorns the world."[30] Moreover, the famous conversation with Drummond, in which the poet recalled the premonitory dream of his son's death, notes that Ben Jonson was in the country, at the home of Sir Robert Cotton, when the plague struck the boy.[31] Together, these references suggest that Jonson had just "arrived" when his son died, and this suggestion is born out by Professor Kay's recent reexamination of facts and problems related to the shaping of Jonson's literary career. That career was not a matter of ups and downs, as it once seemed. After the autumn of 1599, Kay reports, Jonson gains confidence in his power to lead rather than follow courtly taste; he writes manifestoes insisting on the "intellectual content" of his plays; he makes "his first datable attempts to gain patronage for his nondramatic poetry"; he decides for the first time to publish a play, and he moves to the private theater.[32] In short, the poet was sure of his audience, sure of his stature as a writer, and hopeful, now that the boy was old enough, of using his own entrèe to wealth and power in young Benjamin's behalf. Thus would the status to which his pen had restored the Jonson lineage be secured for another generation.

In line five, then, when the poet utters his anguished "O, could I loose all father, now," it is doubtful that he wishes only to be rid of what Arthur F. Marotti calls "a father's natural sorrow."[33] Illick finds "few [apparent] exceptions, at least in the upper class, to John Aubrey's observation that in [Ben Jonson's] dayes, fathers were not acquainted with their children."[34] Later in the seventeenth century, for instance, Robert Boyle recalls his own father's "perfect aversion for [his children's] fondness."[35] "Most men," Illick concludes, "chose silence, aloofness, a cold civility rather than showing emotion outwardly [toward their children]."[36] This is the patriarchal demeanor we might expect the risen Ben Jonson to try to emulate. It is not at all inconsistent with too much hope of the loved boy, since as we have seen, that "hope" could well have expressed itself not in direct, paternal nurturing, but in suits to the poet's patrons for protection of the seven-year-old's passage into the adult world of the gentry. Such aloofness is also consistent with the fact of Jonson's absence in the country at the time of the boy's death.

Various modern critics note various tonal and logical shifts between the first four lines of "On My First Sonne" and its second four.[37] But here again, it seems to me, the prayer to "loose all father" is a prayer not only to forget all fondness for Benjamin as a child of irresistible individual promise, but is also a prayer to be rid of all hope for him as inheritor of the gentleman's role and perpetuator of his father's name and social gains. Why else, lines five and six ask, but because he is thinking more as the sire of a gentle line than as a Christian, will man lament rather than envy his first son's early death? For one thing (line seven continues, illustrating), the gentle sire necessarily commits his son who survives to a lifetime of "worlds, and fleshes rage." This, again, is a seductively straightforward phrase. "Worlds, and fleshes rage," since the next line seems calculated to cover the many biological miseries that preindustrial "flesh" is heir to, would seem to indicate not physical discomforts, but *moral* miseries—or, rather, *a* moral misery, which was the gentleman's special lot. The syntax of the phrase can mean the rage of the world *with* the flesh. This would be the commonly envisioned psychological struggle—argued, for instance, in Samuel Daniel's poetic dialogue between Ulysses and the Siren—the psychomachia of the sociopolitical "world" with the appetitive "flesh." The economic freedom that defines gentility tempts the gentleman to live in idle hedonism, submitting to the drives of the flesh and squandering his estate on instant gratifications. Meanwhile, his family's honored position in the world demands that he deny the flesh and live as an example to his family, his tenants, and the nation.

In lines five through eight, then, Jonson specifically recognizes that being rid of all worldly, covetous, patriarchal father-feeling is a precondition for trying to accept the standard Christian consolation that the dead are really lucky—a consolation, incidentally, that Ralph Josselin offered his bereaved parishioners, though belief in an afterlife seldom enters into the conduct of daily affairs recorded in Josselin's diary.[38]

One further point should be made about line five before we move on to the epigrammatic climax of Jonson's last four lines. Modern editors and critics generally treat the word "l-o-o-s-e," in line five, as an old spelling of "lose." So construed, "O, could I lose all father, now" asks that the poet may *passively* have his patriarchal aspirations taken from him. But if we treat the spelling "l-o-o-s-e" as actually intended to mean "turn loose," or "let go of," Jonson is praying to be able to *act* against the sinful and self-defeating patriarchal "hope" to which he has confessed in the first four lines. In such a case, he does not see "all father" as a sinful set of "natural," instinctual, genetically programmed, biological imperatives, which he is powerless not to heed (unless, somehow, he should "lose" them). Rather, he sees fatherhood as a conventional gentleman's role, which in the future he can *choose* to play less dotingly.

And, indeed, in the last four lines of "On My First Sonne," Jonson apparently does act to turn his sinful, covetous, patrilineal ambitions "loose." The lines read as follows:

> Rest in soft peace, and ask'd, say here doth lye
> BEN. IONSON his best piece of *poetrie*.
> For whose sake, hence-forth, all his vowes be such,
> As what he loues may neuer like too much.

"Poetrie," as Jonson's Greek made him think of the word, means "making"—whether of poems or of children. Hence, in proclaiming this dead child his "best piece of *poetrie*," Jonson is resolving in lines nine and ten never again to feel that another of his children—or writings—is as good as this one. He will not invest in future heirs or poems the hope he has confessed for his first son and (by implication) for the works which brought the poet fame and patronage. And in renouncing such hope, Jonson will be renouncing the sin which the boy's death has taught him endangers the poet's restoration of his family to gentle status. L. A. Beaurline's happy resolution of the syntax of "like," in the last line, makes this renunciation plain. Beaurline cites parallel usages of "like" from Marlowe and from elsewhere in Jonson, and he concludes that "the [last] line means about the same as Martial's line [from which it is imitated]: whatever he loves may never please him too much, may never be the object of selfcongratulation."[39]

For the sake, then, of this first, right-hand son, struck down as a warning against his father's worldliness, Ben Jonson vows never again to endanger through self-congratulation his achievements as a maker of poems and families.

Perhaps it is to be regretted that even in this beloved poem Ben Jonson speaks to us across a vast historical gulf. In Epigram 45 we hear not a nurturing middle-class daddy in mourning, but a covetous partiarch in repentance. Hence, even in "On My First Sonne," Jonson is not free of the values of the preindustrial ruling class for which he spoke in his other work, and the expected attitudes of the modern literary professoriate require us to condemn him for having sanctioned the "immiseration" of millions. Still, before we do, we should pause to consider what Epigram 45 has to teach us about the limits of human competence and moral responsibility for relieving material misery that Jonson and his patrons took for granted. These were limits imposed by the ignorance of nonhuman nature, including the plague, which common sense taught them they could not choose but to accept. Only fools like Sir Politick Would-be and the founders of modern science felt that the limits of man's material competence could yet be extended, whether for profit, or for the glory of God and the relief of man's estate. But that is the story of economic modernization, which, for better and for worse, mankind is still acting out. And for now, it is another story.

Notes

1. T. S. Eliot, *Selected Essays*, New Edition (New York: Harcourt, Brace, 1932), 127.
2. E. Pearlman, "Ben Jonson: An Anatomy," *English Literary Renaissance* 9 (1979): 389.
3. R. V. Young, Jr., "Style and Structure in Jonson's Epigrams," *Criticism* 17 (1975): 205. See also T. K. Whipple, *Martial and the English Epigram from Sir Thomas Wyatt to Ben Jonson*, University of California Publications in Modern Philology, vol. 10, no. 4 (Berkeley: University of California Press, 1925), 392.
4. J. Z. Kronenfeld, "The Father Found: Consolation Achieved through Love in Ben Jonson's 'On My First Sonne,'" *Studies in Philology* 75 (1978): 65–67.
5. W. David Kay, "The Christian Wisdom of Ben Jonson's 'On My First Sonne,'" *Studies in English Literature* 11 (1971): 135–36. See Philippe Ariès, *Centuries of Childhood*, trans. Robert Baldick (1960; reprint, Harmondsworth: Penguin Books, 1973).
6. Quoted from Joan Thirsk, "Younger Sons in the Seventeenth Century," *History* 54 (1969): 360.
7. C. H. Herford and Percy and Evelyn Simpson, eds., *Ben Jonson* (Oxford: Clarendon Press, 1947), 1:139.
8. Gerald Eades Bentley, *The Profession of Dramatist in Shakespeare's Time 1590–1642* (Princeton: Princeton University Press, 1971), 30–32, 38–61.
9. Pearlman, "An Anatomy," 368–75, 382–90. Pearlman anatomizes Jonson, in part, as follows: "Caught between the classes, Jonson was immensely hostile to the bourgeoisie, among whom the new individualistic ideology appeared, [and therefore] shunned the option of a revolutionary stance, preferring to borrow from his social superiors a form of self-expression compounded of the detritus of aristocratic and feudal morality, and stressing such values as physical courage, reputation, honesty, command, status, generosity. . . . Jonson's self-awareness [thus] became detached from a tradition which might have sustained it, and split into senseless violence and free-floating egocentricity on the one hand, and creative self-dramatization and self-realization on the other" (375).
10. Don E. Wayne perceptively warns that to denigrate Jonson for "trading his power as a poet for the power represented by the eminence of his patrons . . . is to deny [him] the essential [critical] quality of his greatness which was to perceive the real basis of honour and of human relations as they bore on his own life and work." See "Poetry and Power in Ben Jonson's 'Epigrammes,'" *Renaissance and Modern Studies* 33 (1979): 101.
11. Herford, Simpson, and Simpson *Ben Jonson*, 11:9.
12. Ibid., 8:77.
13. *The Anchor Bible: Genesis*, ed. E. A. Speiser (Garden City, N. Y.: Doubleday, 1964), 274.
14. Lawrence Stone, *The Family, Sex and Marriage in England 1500–1800* (New York: Harper and Row, 1977), 112.
15. Edward Shorter, *The Making of the Modern Family* (New York: Basic Books, 1975), 8.
16. Mark Eccles, "Jonson's Marriage," *Review of English Studies* 12 (1936): 264–69, 272.
17. Cited by Joseph E. Illick, "Child-Rearing in Seventeenth-Century England and America," in *The History of Childhood*, ed. Lloyd de Mause (1974; reprint, New York: Harper Torchbooks, 1975), 325, 346.
18. Quoted from Alan Macfarlane, *The Family Life of Ralph Josselin a Seventeenth-Century Clergyman: An Essay in Historical Anthropology* (Cambridge: Cambridge University Press, 1970), 120.
19. Stone, *Family, Sex, and Marriage*, 208–9.

20. Macfarlane, *Family Life,* 174–77. See also Leslie Clarkson, *Death, Disease and Famine in Pre-Industrial England* (New York: St. Martin's Press, 1976), 71.

21. Quoted from Illick, "Child-Rearing," 315; see also Stone, *Family, Sex, and Marriage,* 210.

22. *The Diary of John Evelyn,* ed. E. S. de Beer (London: Oxford University Press, 1959), 385.

23. *Diary,* 899.

24. Stone, *Family, Sex, and Marriage,* 193.

25. Ibid., 106.

26. Ibid., 70, 106.

27. Philippe Ariès, *The Hour of Our Death,* trans. Helen Weaver (New York: Knopf, 1981), 90.

28. Herford, Simpson, and Simpson, *Ben Jonson,* 8:33. I am indebted to Professor Katharine Eisaman Maus, my fellow participant in the Jonson session at The Citadel Conference, for having been the first of several hearers of my paper to comment on the absence of young Benjamin's mother from Jonson's lament for "*my* first sonne." Maternal grief, of course, figures very prominently in "On My First Daughter." Professor Maus's own commentary on Epigram 45 in *Ben Jonson and the Roman Frame of Mind* (Princeton: Princeton University Press, 1984), 119–23, largely complements my reading of the poem. "Here," she says, "there is no hint of maternal bereavement, of collaborative authorship." Hence,

> Since Jonson thinks of the child as so completely his own, his moral situation is comewhat ambiguous. . . . Does [Jonson only realize], in retrospect, that he was unwise to stake so much on a mortal object? . . . But the line might also mean that Jonson perceives the young Benjamin's death as a kind of punishment visited upon a doting father. In this case he is directly responsible for the boy's death.

I, of course, incline to the latter reading.

29. Ivy Pinchbeck and Margaret Hewitt, *Children in English Society* (London: Routledge and Kegan Paul, 1969), 1:8.

30. Quoted from Marchette Chute, *Ben Jonson of Westminster* (1953; reprint, New York: E. P. Dutton, 1960), 112.

31. Herford, Simpson, and Simpson, *Ben Jonson,* 1:139.

32. W. David Kay, "The Shaping of Ben Jonson's Career: A Reexamination of Facts and Problems," *Modern Philology* 67 (1970): 224–37; see also Frances Teague, "Ben Jonson's Poverty," *Biography* 2 (1979): 260–65.

33. Arthur F. Marotti, "All About Jonson's Poetry," *ELH* 39 (1972): 228.

34. Illick, "Child-Rearing," 312.

35. Quoted from Illick, "Child-Rearing," 339.

36. Ibid., 315–16; see also Stone, *Family, Sex, and Marriage,* 105.

37. See especially Young, "Style and Structure," 205–6.

38. Macfarlane quotes Josselin to the effect that "the consideration of [the dead's] state in death is Honey that cureth and asswageth your griefe." *Family Life,* 166–69, 221.

39. L. A. Beaurline, "The Selective Principle in Jonson's Shorter Poems," *Criticism* 8 (1966): 68.

"Inviting a Friend to Svpper": Ben Jonson, Friendship, and the Poetics of Patronage

ROBERT C. EVANS

Perhaps more than any other writer of his time, Ben Jonson can be called a poet of patronage. Although nearly every Renaissance English author was affected in some way by the complex system of patronage relationships that pervaded Tudor-Stuart culture, the influence of patronage on Jonson's career is both obvious and obviously important. The full ramifications and subtleties of that influence remain to be explored, but there can be no denying that Jonson depended greatly on patronage, financially as well as psychologically. The support of aristocratic patrons had a determining impact not only on the way he made his living and on the way he lived his life, but also on the ways in which he conceived of himself as a poet and of his social function. The sheer number of poems he addressed explicitly to members of the English elite testifies to the important role patronage played in his career, while his long and lucrative tenure as chief masque-writer of the Jacobean court is well known. Probably the most successful patronage poet of his era, Jonson was also a patronage poet in the fullest sense of the term. Unlike other writers who depended on patronage of one sort or another but who did not define themselves exclusively as poets (Sidney, Ralegh, Spenser, and Donne, for instance), Jonson gloried in the role and helped win new respect for it among the socially influential. And unlike other writers who were affected by patronage but whose most important sources of income lay elsewhere (Shakespeare and his involvement in the public theater come to mind), Jonson relied much more fully and obviously on the financial backing of powerful people. During the height of his career as a patronage poet he abandoned play writing altogether, returning to it reluctantly only when the sources of his patronage support seemed threatened.

Important as patronage was to Jonson's life, its complex impact on his poetry has not been fully assessed. Until relatively recently, the tendency to think of patronage as social, economic, or biographical "background" to Renaissance texts remained strong. Once one realizes, however, that patronage was more than a system of economic exchange or of conventional social deference, that the patronage system reflected in practical terms some of the deepest psychological assumptions and hierarchical habits of mind of English Renaissance culture, and that no sphere of life in Tudor-Stuart England could be unaffected by these assumptions, then the significance of patronage to the tone, tactics, and complex meaning of Jonson's works begins to become apparent. For Jonson the most important audience of his works always consisted of patrons, actual or potential, since this audience could determine most significantly whether and how well he achieved his deepest aspirations as a poet. The financial importance of patronage cannot be denied, but neither should it be overemphasized; the psychological importance of patronage was, if anything, even more significant. Jonson's social esteem as well as his self-respect were both intimately bound up with the extent and quality of his patronage support, and one paradox of his competition for patronage is that the more successfully he won support, the more psychologically and financially dependent he became. Patronage was an important source of social security, but the prospect of losing it helped foster a powerful sense of insecurity and uncertainty.[1]

By the closing years of the Jacobean reign Jonson had achieved a kind of prominence in the patronage system attained by no other poet before him, but his status was always insecure, and the higher he rose, the more important maintaining that status became to him. This is why his relations with rivals and competitors are also crucial to understanding his experience as a patronage poet. Along with patrons and potential patrons, rivals and prospective rivals were the most important component of Jonson's audience. These two groups, it can be argued, were in the back of his mind whenever he sat down to write a poem, since their reactions could most powerfully determine whether or not he would achieve his most meaningful ambitions. These aspirations probably never had much to do with economic or social status per se, but neither could Jonson ever afford to forget that the process of achieving his ambitions was bound up with questions of social power and economic influence. Every poem he wrote was in some sense a performance staged for the benefit of these most important segments of his audience; every Jonsonian poem is in some sense a poem of patronage. Reading his works from a patronage perspective may thus suggest new ways of coming to grips with their semantic and aesthetic richness.

Recognizing that patrons and rivals were the most important constituents of Jonson's audience has implications not only for the poems that most obviously concern them, but even for the poems that apparently do not. His commendatory poems on other authors, for instance, or his poems on friends or friendship, were inevitably affected by some of the same issues and habits of mind that surface in the works on patrons and rivals. In these poems as in all his works, Jonson fashions a self-image that he knew would inevitably affect his status in the patronage hierarchy, an image that would either reflect favorably on him and thus promote his chances of patronage advancement, or one that could be turned against him by his antagonists. His commendatory poems, like his poems praising specific patrons, characterize the poet as well as those he commends. Often his poems to other authors call attention to qualities characteristic of Jonson's own works, and indeed, often such poems call attention to their own particular achievements or specific textual features. Inevitably Jonson's poems involved self-advertisement, and inevitably this self-promotion took place in a literary system dominated by patronage concerns and had a potential impact on the author's standing in the larger patronage system.

This is true even of those poems, addressed to friends or celebrating friendship, that often seem to define themselves in terms of their distinctness from patronage pressures and from the need to compete. A patronage perspective complicates our sense of the function and effects of these poems of friendship, just as it complicates our understanding of most of Jonson's other works. While on the one hand friendship could seem to offer a sense of refuge from the anxieties of patronage competition, a relatively secure haven from the distrust and instability inherent in the patronage system, friendships and the poems celebrating them were nonetheless themselves implicated in various ways in the poet's quest for social security. Few of Jonson's poems to friends seem simply private, nor do they simply serve larger didactic purposes. Often the friends he addresses were men whose own social standing, official positions, or unofficial connections made them valuable as allies or intermediaries, and while it would be both cynical and simplistic to suggest that Jonson's attitude toward them was grounded solely in self-interest, it would be just as simplistic to ignore the self-interest inevitably involved.[2]

Jonson's praise of his friends also serves to obligate them, to put them in his debt, just as his poems praising patrons serve much the same purpose. The issues of social power that seem latent within all of his poems to patrons are never completely absent from his works on friends or friendship. The frustrating inability to determine, once and for all, the true motives and attitudes of the other party to a social relationship, which characterizes much of Jonson's thinking about patronage and many of his poems to patrons, also plays a role in many of the poems on friendship. While the poet frequently claims to be able to distinguish clearly between the flatterer and the true friend, just as often (and frequently in the same poem) he feels forced to admit how difficult making such a distinction can sometimes prove. Flatterers, whom he attacks with the same relish, forcefulness, and dismissive contempt he uses against other satiric targets, nevertheless (like those targets) seem potent and threatening enough to need attacking.

They are threatening, first of all, because they are potential competitors. Even when Jonson himself feels confident of his own ability to tell a true friend from a false, he is usually less sure that others will be able to make the same distinction. This becomes especially important when the friend the flatterer seeks to attract is also one of the poet's patrons. And yet the threat posed by the flatterer or the false friend does more than imperil relations with social superiors; it can also infect and undermine the security of one of the poet's few alternatives to those relations. It can potentially undermine his sense of confidence in his friendships themselves. In many of his poems on friendship Jonson is forced to confront the possibility that his friends might have their own self-interests chiefly in mind, that the ideal of reciprocity that should characterize a true friendship might be illusory. And yet in celebrating that ideal Jonson himself inevitably promotes his own particular interests.

Friendship and self-promotion are important themes in "Inviting a Friend to Svpper," one of Jonson's best-known and most appealing works. Influenced by a number of the epigrams of Martial, the poem is nevertheless more than an exercise in literary emulation. While Jonson no doubt intended readers to notice his debt to his classical predecessor, "Inviting" is so convincingly English in substance and tone that one has little trouble assuming, along with the Oxford editors, that the party and guests Jonson describes are more than convenient fictions. The poem seems to have grown out of—and to have helped shape—an actual social occasion:

To night, graue sir, both my poore house, and I
    Doe equally desire your companie:
Not that we thinke vs worthy such a ghest,
    But that your worth will dignifie our feast,
With those that come; whose grace may make that seeme   5
    Something, which, else, could hope for no esteeme.
It is the faire acceptance, Sir, creates
    The entertaynment perfect: not the cates.
Yet shall you haue, to rectifie your palate,
    An oliue, capers, or some better sallade   10
Vshering the mutton; with a short-leg'd hen,
    If we can get her, full of egs, and then,
Limons, and wine for sauce: to these, a coney
    Is not to be despair'd of, for our money;
And, though fowle, now, be scarce, yet there are clarkes,   15
    The skie not falling, thinke we may haue larkes.
Ile tell you of more, and lye, so you will come:
    Of partrich, pheasant, wood-cock, of which some

May yet be there; and godwit, if we can:
    Knat, raile, and ruffe too. How so ere, my man 20
Shall reade a piece of Virgil, Tactivs,
    Livie, or of some better book to vs,
Of which wee'll speake our minds, amidst our meate;
    And Ile professe no verses to repeate:
To this, if ought appeare, which I not know of, 25
    That will the pastrie, not my paper, show of.
Digestiue cheese, and fruit there sure will bee;
    But that, which most doth take my *Muse,* and mee,
Is a pure cup of rich *Canary*-wine,
    Which is the *Mermaids,* now, but shall be mine: 30
Of which had Horace, or Anacreon tasted,
    Their liues, as doe their lines, till now had lasted.
Tabacco, Nectar, or the *Thespian* spring,
    Are all but Lvthers beere, to this I sing.
Of this we will sup free, but moderately, 35
    And we will haue no *Pooly',* or *Parrot* by;
Nor shall our cups make any guiltie men:
    But, at our parting, we will be, as when
We innocently met. No simple word,
    That shall be vtter'd at our mirthfull boord, 40
Shall make vs sad next morning: or affright
    The libertie, that wee'll enioy to night.[3]

As in a number of his satiric epigrams, Jonson demonstrates an awareness in this poem of how social gatherings can be exploited to individual advantage. In such a poem as "To Censoriovs Covrtling," for instance, he exposes the ways in which a rival, posing as a friend, used frosty praise and "weake applause" to attack his verse while pretending to commend it. In "To Covrtling" he betrays sensitivity to the power his rival enjoyed as a "chamber critic . . . / At madames table" (1.3), while the epigram "To Groom Ideot" attacks him for using his reactions to Jonson's poetry to call attention to himself. The gathering Jonson proposes in "Inviting a Friend" derives much of its charm and significance from its apparent contrast with these more competitive social encounters. And yet inevitably Jonson's own social power would be affected both by the success of his performance at dinners like this and by the opportunities they offered to make or cement profitable social connections. In fact, the opening lines of the poem evince an explicit concern with "esteeme," but any obvious or threatening sense of egocentric self-interest is minimized, partly through the poet's gracious deference to the guest and partly through the subtle good humor with which the issue is raised. The concern with "esteeme" expressed here is ostensibly of a different nature than one finds in those works in which Jonson feels his own public esteem or self-esteem threatened. In "Inviting," the unnamed friend is offered the chance to advertise his own worth; the event to which Jonson invites him affords an opportunity for self-display, yet there is no sense that that display will in any way menace Jonson. His feast, he claims, will be dignified by the guest's presence, so that the guest's acceptance of the invitation will produce mutual social profit. The importance of the poet's dinner—and thus the importance of the poet—will be enhanced, even as the guest's sense of his own social status is confirmed. The very invitation Jonson issues not only pays tribute to the guest's virtues and power but insinuates the poet's own. The gravity and graciousness he ascribes to the guest are themselves displayed in this work, with its balanced tone of composed merriment, its well-mannered intimacy. Absent is the note of arrogant self-regard that many contemporaries and later readers found unattractive in so many of Jonson's other writings. In its place is a good-humored gravity that insinuates self-containment, suggests social strength, and thus implicitly denies any desperate need for the very kinds of social connections the poem solicits. Implying self-regard and reserves of social power, the poem thereby presents Jonson to his best advantage as an attractive potential ally or friend.

Although the poem pays open tribute to the friend's character and status, it implicitly—if mildly—challenges both by reminding the friend that "It is the faire acceptance, Sir, creates / The entertaynment perfect: not the cates" (7–8). In one sense these lines merely compliment the guest, suggesting that his presence is more important to the success of the event than the food itself. In another sense, however, they pose a subtle threat: to refuse the invitation, they imply, will not only ruin the entertainment but will reflect negatively on the guest's character. Jonson's gracious invitation affords the guest an opportunity to reciprocate graciously himself—or to reveal himself incapable of a truly "faire" acceptance. Even now the resonance of the couplet is unexhausted, for the lines also suggest that a "faire acceptance" will be one in which the guest shows as much disinterest in the fare provided as the host is anxious to ensure its bountiful provision. "Faire acceptance" involves not only a formally gracious response, but one that is rightly motivated, one in which the simplest and most symbolic expression of self-interest—personal appetite—is firmly subordinated to the desire to share the company of one's friend. A fair acceptance "creates" the perfect entertainment both because it helps call the festivities into being and because the motives that prompt a "faire acceptance" are needed if the spirit of the occasion is to be sustained.

Jonson leaves deliberately vague the actual status of the banquet he promises. Again and again he describes it in conditional terms: "a short-leg'd hen, / If we can get her . . . wood-cock, of which some / May yet be there; and godwit, if we can" (11–12; 18–19). The central qualifying line, of course, is the one in which he comically admits, "Ile tell you of more, and lye, so you will come" (17). There is, however, more than humor in this admission, and the line does more, too, than simply emphasize Jonson's limited financial resources. More significantly, it raises again the question of the guest's motives. By playfully suggesting that the guest can be bribed to accept the invitation, Jonson in fact credits him with more honorable intentions. The line is funny precisely because to take it seriously would undermine both the proposed entertainment and the mood of the poem. If the guest could in fact be bribed—if the delicacies Jonson inventories were in fact important to the friend—then the character of their relationship would be wholly different from what the poem suggests. Paradoxically, Jonson's lavish catalogue of culinary attractions is, if he has correctly assessed his friend's mettle, in the strict sense superfluous—unnecessary, except insofar as it illustrates the speaker's own generosity and desire to please. His admission that the menu is at least partly fictitious is, therefore, both a testament to his friend's character and a means of subtly testing it.[4]

"Inviting a Friend" celebrates a relationship free from motives of selfish exploitation, yet a persistent awareness of the possibility of such motives informs the celebration, lending it internal tension as well as power and appeal. The "entertaynment" Jonson proposes is defined not only in opposition to the external threats referred to at the poem's conclusion, but also by contrast with the potential for internal instability. The spies Jonson mentions—and he mentions specific names—make the external threat seem plausible and authentic. Much more than Martial's poems, "Inviting" conveys a sense of the supper as a refuge from a world of power games and political machinations.[5] Yet in one sense the spies only objectify, only externally represent, a danger already inherent in the supper itself. The spies are, after all, in the simplest sense men operating with hidden agendas, with secret motives in mind. They enter into a relationship only to take advantage of the other party, and introduce into social relations a profound sense of distrust and self-consciousness. They monitor the words and behavior of others as carefully as they control their own. In short, they carry to an extreme the kind of calculating, tactical behavior that the courtly social system of Jonson's day seems to have encouraged. Thus the poem makes clear that while from one perspective the supper offers a relief from such behavior, from another it provides a possible forum for it. The mere absence of spies cannot in itself guarantee freedom from the mistrust and wariness their presence would ensure.

The occasion Jonson celebrates is one in which host and guests are ideally able to "speake [their] minds" (23)—one in which they not only need not worry about the repercussions their words might have with outside agents, but also one in which language is used for real communication and communion, in which the need for posturing, pretense, or performance is ostensibly eliminated. To speak one's mind implies a harmony between thought and word, an absence of self-censorship and intellectual inhibition, that must have been rare in a society in which being on one's guard must frequently have seemed inescapable. Jonson creates an appealing vision of a supper at which the mind is nourished as well as the body, of a feast that satisfies both flesh and intellect, of men sharing ideas as well as food as they commune with one another and with the disembodied minds of the classical past. The poem communicates and exemplifies a strong sense of art firmly rooted in real social relations, and it presents a striking blend of lofty ideals and concrete (but imagined) quotidian detail. Praising sack and good-naturedly mocking the legendary "Thespian spring" (33), Jonson presents a relaxed and appealing image of himself as poet, as a man speaking to men. Inevitably, however, the very absence of calculation and lack of self-consciousness that the poem seems to exhibit work to the poet's micropolitical advantage.

"Inviting a Friend" exalts a world—small, protected, and self-enclosed, to be sure—in which the gap between intention and expression has been abolished, one in which the freedom to be oneself encourages rather than constrains the freedom of others. Jonson is careful to distinguish this freedom of self from self-indulgence (just as he later implicitly distinguishes "libertie" from license): he will not, he professes, use the dinner as an occasion to promote himself as a poet, or even as a reader of poems. His announcement that "[his] man" will read to the guests from the Roman authors not only asserts the relative dignity of his social position—nicely balancing earlier references to his financial limitations—but also deemphasizes Jonson himself as a performer at the supper (20). To announce that he himself would read would make this dinner seem simply an occasion for pompous self-display.[6] Jonson turns the prospect of such display into a clever but understated joke in line twenty-four, when, after detailing what "[his] man" will read, he then continues, "And Ile professe. . . ." Particularly because of the metrically emphasized *Ile,* we might expect the clause to continue with a list of the subjects about which Jonson will deliver pronouncement or declarations. Instead, he playfully subverts any expectations of self-assertion by announcing that he will in fact "professe no verses to repeate"—a promised act made good in the very act of being promised.[7] Jonson's joke at his own expense—his felt need to make this comical, almost contractual declaration—only makes him seem all the more attractive, all the more genuinely modest. His willingness to "professe" his motives so openly contributes, paradoxically, to the poem's subtlety, nuance, and appealing understatement. Ironically, the humorous contract he undertakes helps emphasize the liberty, the freedom from sterile legalism, that the poem celebrates more explicitly elsewhere. Jonson's promise, like the guest's presumed acceptance of his invitation, is a social bond freely professed and embraced rather than being (as was often the case in their milieu) an obligation imposed from outside or above. Here as throughout the poem, Jonson exalts a freedom from egotism that will allow the deeper, more legitimate needs of all the assembled egos to be satisfied.[8]

In one of the epigram's more intriguing passages, Jonson indicates, while mocking, how byzantine the expressions of purely egotistical self-aggrandizement could become. After disavowing any intention to read his own poetry, he continues: "To this, if ought appeare, which I not know of, / That will the pastrie, not my paper, show of" (25–26). The lines seem to suggest an elbaorate ruse. Ian Donaldson's helpful gloss illuminates part of the statement's meaning. "[T]he cook may produce a pastry surprise," his note reads, "but Jonson will not produce a surprise reading."[9] What needs further clarifying, however, is the element of pretense to which the lines allude. Jonson imagines a situation in which a host not only surprises his guests with the unexpected circulation of his verse, but one in which he pretends to be surprised himself. The lines suggest a situation in which a host might go to elaborate lengths in order not to appear to promote himself, that being his intention all the while.

Whatever his conscious intentions concerning the present poem, the fact remains that by forswearing any such self-promotional designs, Jonson paradoxically promotes a very attractive image of himself. He has no need to perform openly at the supper, since his poetic invitation—and in a sense the entire supper as well—are themselves consummate performances. Through the poem he implicitly offers his own behavior as an ideal for his guests to emulate; as he repudiates self-aggrandizement, so, ideally, should they. In one sense simply an invitation, the poem is, from another perspective, a fully developed social contrast, its terms set—and their fulfillment exemplified—by the poet himself. Despite its celebration of an evening free from the need for self-promotion; despite its apparent embodiment of the spirit of such an occasion; although the epigram itself seems an instance of the ideal it exalts, an example of the poet freely "speaking his mind"—in spite of all this, the poem can never really achieve or participate in the innocence it extols. Inevitably it is more self-conscious, artful, and fashioned than the supper it proposes. Although Jonson disavows any intention of using the supper as a springboard to promote himself, his poetic evocation of the supper inescapably does precisely that. Indeed, since the poem so obviously invites comparison with earlier works by Martial, part of its effect must necessarily be to draw attention to Jonson's own skill and accomplishment. This would be all the more true if the poem were in fact simply a literary exercise, not intended as a real invitation to a real supper after all. If one is still willing to assume, however, that both the invitation and the supper were authentic, then the poem illustrates how inextricably self-promotion could be involved even in a context ostensibly defined by its absence.

"Inviting a Friend" celebrates a milieu from which the two sources of threat facing any patronage poet—the competitive egoism of others and anxiety in relation to superior authority—supposedly have been eliminated. And yet a pervasive awareness of both threats colors the poem throughout. The first threat is confronted in the beginning of the poem with the lines on "faire acceptance." The second is alluded to at the end, with the very specific reference to spies. No spies, the poem states, will be present, yet neither will they be necessary. The poem not only paints an attractive portrait of Jonson as a friend but also depicts him and his companions as politically trustworthy and socially reliable. Their cups will make no "guiltie men" (37), partly because the friends will commit no personally embarrassing or excessive behavior, but also because even drink cannot compromise their fundamental innocence. Yet to think of the poem simply as constructing or embodying an uncomplicated or harmonious ideal of social relations is to fail to give adequate emphasis to tensions within the work, to the awareness the poem itself betrays of the tenuousness and instability of such harmony. It is also to fail to appreciate how the poem functions not only to promote that harmony but as a weapon in the personal struggle of the poet. In "Inviting," friendship offers a satisfying but temporary refuge from social competition; the final word—"to night"—emphasizes the fleeting and fragile nature of the respite. But the poem that celebrates that friendship becomes itself another means of competing. The social ideal Jonson imagines in such works is complicated by the fact that his presentation of the ideal must necessarily function in relation to the social reality of his time. Beneath the carefully poised balances the poem exalts—balances between the interests of guests and host, between self-assertion and deference, between mundane fact and lofty ideals, between freedom and restraint—runs an unsettling but inexorable sense of tension and threat.

Thus, even such a poem as "Inviting" is on one level an exercise in power. Both the poem and the dinner it celebrates are designed to affect the poet's reputation and public "esteeme." Both the poem and the supper, for all their seeming naturalness and spontaneity, are actually carefully managed, carefully calculated; Jonson attempts to shape and control reactions to both. His modesty about the supper functions partly to anticipate and defuse any criticism, to place the meal in a context that makes its value clear, its worth obvious to any who might doubt it. And the same modest tone also protects the poem from unfriendly attack. Jonson's comic catalogue of lavish food has the serious effect of reminding us of real, genuinely lavish banquets of the sort that were increasingly common in the Jacobean period. Such banquets were intended precisely to advertise the power of those who sponsored them; their purpose was not so much fellowship as self-assertion. Obviously unable to compete on these terms, Jonson uses his poem to define new terms that seem to reject competition but that actually strengthen his competitive stance. As in his great poem "To Penshurst," his celebration here of an ideal situation free from self-promotional designs and tensions makes his work exceptionally effective as self-promotion. The epigram's apparent disinterest in and disdain for power makes it literally a more powerful work—more appealing to allies and patrons, more threatening to antagonists or competitors.

"Inviting a Friend to Svpper" is typical of Jonson's numerous poems to or about friends: few of those works can be separated completely from the social circumstances and challenges Jonson faced as a poet of patronage. However sincere his feelings about particular individuals, his public expression of those feelings—in poems circulated among an audience that included his superiors and rivals—must have been informed by an intense self-consciousness partly generated by his consciousness of significant others. Few of the friendship poems are simply private, yet neither are they didactically impersonal. Nearly all seem affected by Jonson's need to fashion an attractive (and defensible) image of himself—a need largely created and conditioned by his participation in the contemporary patronage system.[10]

Notes

1. For helpful discussions of literary patronage during the English Renaissance see, for instance, Phoebe Sheavyn, *The Literary Profession in the Elizabethan Age,* 2d ed. (New York: Barnes and Noble, 1967); Daniel Javitch, *Poetry and Courtliness in Renaissance England* (Princeton: Princeton University Press, 1978); and Patricia Thomson, "The Literature of Patronage, 1580–1630" *Essays in Criticism* 2 (1952): 267–84. For a comprehensive survey of Renaissance patronage, see *Patronage in the Renaissance,* ed. Guy Fitch Lytle and Stephen Orgel (Princeton: Princeton University Press, 1981); its notes provide a handy guide to other secondary studies. For discussions of patronage from a number of related but different perspectives, see Wallace T. MacCaffrey, "Place and Patronage in Elizabethan Politics," in *Elizabethan Government and Society: Essays Presented to Sir John Neale,* ed. S. T. Bindoff et al. (London: University of London, Athlone Press, 1961), 95–126; Linda Levy Peck, *Northampton: Patronage and Policy at the Court of James I* (London: George Allen and Unwin, 1982); G. R. Elton, "Tudor Government: Points of Contact," in his *Studies in Tudor and Stuart Politics and Government,* 3 vols. (Cambridge: Cambridge University Press, 1983), 3:3–57; Lawrence Stone, *The Crisis of the Aristocracy, 1558–1641* (Oxford: Clarendon Press, 1965), esp. 385–504; and esp. the first chapter of Conrad Russell's *Parliaments and English Politics, 1621–1629* (Oxford: Clarendon Press, 1979). On patronage, patriarchy, and Renaissance habits of mind see, for instance, Peter Laslett, *The World We Have Lost,* 2d ed. (New York: Scribner's, 1971), and Gordon J. Schochet, *Patriarchialism in Political Thought: The Authoritarian Family and Political Speculation and Attitudes Especially in Seventeenth Century England* (New York: Basic Books, 1975), esp. 54–84. Numerous sociological data are surveyed by Ann Jennalie Cook in *The Privileged Playgoers of Shakespeare's London, 1576–1642* (Princeton: Princeton University Press, 1981) and by Keith Wrightson in *English Society 1580–1680* (New Brunswick, N.J.: Rutgers University Press, 1982).

For discussions of more general issues of power and literature see, for instance, Stephen

Greenblatt, *Renaissance Self-Fashioning* (Chicago: University of Chicago Press, 1980); Jonathan Goldberg, *James I and the Politics of Literature* (Baltimore: Johns Hopkins University Press, 1983); Jonathan Dollimore, *Radical Tragedy: Religion, Ideology, and Power in the Drama of Shakespeare and His Contemporaries* (Chicago: University of Chicago Press, 1984); Eckhard Auberlen, *The Commonwealth of Wit: The Writer's Image and His Strategies of Self-Representation in Elizabethan Literature* (Tübingen: Gunter Narr Verlag, 1984); Frank Whigham, *Ambition and Privilege: The Social Tropes of Elizabethan Courtesy Theory* (Berkeley: University of California Press, 1984); Arthur Marotti, *John Donne: Courtier Poet* (Madison: University of Wisconsin Press, 1986); Graham Parry, *The Golden Age Restor'd: The Culture of the Stuart Court, 1603–42* (Manchester: Manchester University Press, 1981); and Stephen Greenblatt, ed., *The Power of Forms in the Renaissance* (Norman, Okla.: Pilgrim Books, 1982).

For helpful discussions of Jonson from a sociological perspective, see especially Richard Helgerson, *Self-Crowned Laureates: Spenser, Jonson, Milton, and the Literary System* (Berkeley: University of California Press, 1983); Don E. Wayne, *Penshurst: The Semiotics of Place and the Poetics of History* (Madison: University of Wisconsin Press, 1984); Leah S. Marcus, *The Politics of Mirth: Jonson, Herrick, Milton, Marvell, and the Defense of Old Holiday Pastimes* (Chicago: University of Chicago Press, 1986); and Annabel Patterson, *Censorship and Interpretation: The Conditions of Writing and Reading in Early Modern England* (Madison: University of Wisconsin Press, 1984). See particularly Stanley Fish, "Authors-Readers: Jonson's Community of the Same," *Representations* 7 (1984): 26–58. I discuss Jonson and patronage much more fully, and am able to cite many more secondary sources, in my book *Ben Jonson and the Poetics of Patronage* (Lewisburg, Pa.: Bucknell University Press, 1988).

Throughout this paper I use the term "patronage poet" to suggest not merely a poet who received patronage but also a poet whose whole being and mindset were shaped fundamentally by living in a system essentially rooted in hierarchical relationships. Although somewhat awkward, the term is preferable both to "patronized poet" (which suggests condescension and which emphasizes economic exchange) and to "poet dependent upon patronage" (which again stresses economics and which underlines dependency in a way that simplifies the complexities of such relationships).

2. For valuable discussions of Jonson's views and poems on friendship see, for instance, Earl Miner, *The Cavalier Mode from Jonson to Cotton* (Princeton: Princeton University Press, 1971), 250–75; Katherine Eisamen Maus, *Ben Jonson and the Roman Frame of Mind* (Princeton: Princeton University Press, 1984), 115–26; Richard Finkelstein, "Ben Jonson's Ciceronian Rhetoric of Friendship," *Journal of Medieval and Renaissance Studies* 16 (1986): 103–24; W. H. Herendeen, "Like a Circle Bounded in Itself: Jonson, Camden, and the Strategies of Praise," *Journal of Medieval and Renaissance Studies* 11 (1981): 137–67; and Sara J. van den Berg in *The Action of Ben Jonson's Poetry* (Newark: University of Delaware Press, 1987), 36–62. I discuss Jonson's poems on friendship extensively in my book *Ben Jonson and the Poetics of Patronage*.

3. For the text of the poem, see C. H. Herford and Percy and Evelyn Sympson, eds., *Ben Jonson,* 11 vols. (Oxford: Clarendon Press, 1925–52), 8:64–65. Herford and the Simpsons suggest that the "graue sir" of the first line may refer to "such a guest as Camden, to whom the reading of the classics (21–22) would appeal" (11:20). For discussion of the poem in the context of its genre, see Meredith Goulding, "A Case for the Epigram: Ben Jonson's 'Inviting a Friend to Supper,'" *Sydney Studies in English* 8 (1982–83): 16–25. Two valuable recent discussions of the poem, which appeared after my article was accepted for publication, are those by van den Berg in *The Action of Ben Jonson's Poetry,* esp. 52–62, and by Joseph Loewenstein in "The Jonsonian Corpulence; or, The Poet as Mouth piece," *ELH* 53 (1986): 491–518. Fine earlier studies include Wesley Trimpi, *Ben Jonson's Poems: A Study in the Plain Style* (Palo Alto: Stanford University Press, 1962), 185–90; Judith Kegan Gardiner, *Craftsmanship in Context: The Development of Ben Jonson's Poetry* (The Hague: Mouton, 1975), 25–31; and Alexander Leggatt, *Ben Jonson: His Vision and His Art* (London: Methuen, 1981), 115–17.

4. Jonson's penchant for using poetic catalogues is well known; for a small further illustration of his interest in lists (particularly lists of food), see my article "Ben Jonson's

Library and Marginalia: New Evidence from the Folger Collection," *Philological Quarterly* 66 (1987): 521–28.

5. For discussion of the possible personal connections between Jonson and the spies he mentions here, see Mark Eccles, "Jonson and the Spies," *Review of English Studies* 13 (1937): 385–97. In his forthcoming biography of Jonson, David Riggs intriguingly notes that "The possibility that [Jonson] was—even here—indemnifying himself against a charge of libel by alluding to spies whose names could also refer to animals (poll, parrot) only heightens the feeling of insecurity." Joseph Loewenstein also discusses this feeling, and speculates interestingly about connections between the tone of the poem and Jonson's own involvement in espionage, in "The Jonsonian Corpulence," esp. 501–3.

6. In his book *Imitation and Praise in the Poems of Ben Jonson* (New Haven: Yale University Press, 1981), Richard S. Peterson remarks that "Jonson did not always live up to his own ideal of conviviality" (144n.); he then quotes the text of a letter written by James Howell, who reported to Sir Thomas Hawkins that he "was invited yesternight to a solemne supper by *B.J.* where you were deeply remembred, there was good company, excellent chear, choice wines, and joviall wellcome; one thing interven'd which almost spoyld the relish of the rest, that *B.* began to engrosse all the discourse, to vapour extreamely of himselfe, and by vilifying others to magnifie his own *muse; T. Ca.* busd me in the eare, that though Ben had barreld up a great deale of knowledge, yet it seemes that he had not read the *Ethiques,* which among other precepts of morality forbid self commendation, declaring it to be an ill favourd solecism in good manners; It made me think upon the Lady who having a good while given her guests neat entertainment, a capon being brought upon the table, instead of a spoon she tooke a mouth full of claret and spouted it into the poope of the hollow bird; such an accident happend in this entertainment you know—*Proprio laus sordet in ore; be a mans breath never so sweet, yet it makes ones prayses stink, if he makes his owne mouth the conduit pipe of it;* But for my part I am content to dispense with the *roman* infirmity of *B.* now that time hath snowed upon his pericranium." For the full text of the letter, see the Herford and Simpson edition (11:419–20). Thomas M. Greene nicely summarizes the poem's impressively balanced tone: "The poem shows us how to be humble without servility, how to promise without promising, how to mingle playfulness with deference, how, possibly, to deflate the reverend gravity of an important acquaintance without offense to good breeding." See *The Light in Troy: Imitation and Discovery in Renaissance Poetry* (New Haven: Yale University Press, 1982), 281.

7. Syntactical complexity is increasingly being recognized as a hallmark of Jonson's verse; see, for instance, the various close readings in Gardiner's *Craftsmanship in Context;* in Stanley Fish's "Authors-Readers"; and in Richard C. Newton, "'Ben. Jonson': The Poet in the Poems," in *Two Renaissance Mythmakers: Christopher Marlowe and Ben Jonson,* ed. Alvin Kernan (Baltimore: Johns Hopkins University Press, 1977), 165–95, esp. 171–74.

8. Of course, good manners can themselves be seen as responses to social pressures, power concerns, and enlightened self-interest. They may spring from a felt need to conform to widely held and strongly enforced expectations about proper social behavior. Self-abnegation may reflect as much a preoccupation with preserving one's own social standing as a deep-seated humility or respect for others; or rather, one motive for developing such respect may precisely be an essential self-concern. Here as elsewhere, it seems wise not to exaggerate the self's autonomy. The issue seems inevitably quite complicated.

In a fine paper read at the 1987 biennial Renaissance conference at the University of Michigan at Dearborn, Michael C. Schoenfeldt interestingly discussed the connections between politics and politeness in this poem.

9. *Ben Jonson,* ed. Ian Donaldson (New York: Oxford University Press, 1985), 661. Roger Cognard offers, in one respect, a more convincing explication of these lines. "Jonson," he writes, "is referring to the common practice of using the pages of unsold books as wrappings in bakers' shops"; see "Jonson's 'Inviting a Friend to Supper,'" *Explicator* 37, no. 3 (1979): 4. But he does not deal with the idea of a surprise reading, which does seem to be implied (as Donaldson suggests) in line 26.

10. I thank the Newberry Library and the American Council of Learned Societies for fellowships in support of my research on Jonson.

Richard II, 5.3: Traditions and Subtext

DOROTHEA KEHLER

Writing of *Richard II* as *de casibus* tragedy, William Farnham observes,

> In none of the other tragedies of Shakespeare do we find such use of the form, the manner, and the conventional phrases of medieval tragical story in all its simplicity. Yet Shakespeare manages with much success to add the complexity of a psychological study to this simplicity.[1]

Although Farnham's discussion focuses on Richard, the annealing of the medieval with the psychological can be demonstrated equally well in a scene from which Richard is absent: the long denigrated act 5, scene 3. Introducing his widely used Signet edition, Kenneth Muir describes the scene, while perpetuating the received opinion:

> The situation is farcical, with York, the Duchess, and Aumerle on their knees at once, and York actually urging the excution of his son. Shakespeare must have been aware of the absurdity, but he seems to have miscalculated the effect of the scene.[2]

For the modern reader, aware that Shakespeare anticipated existentialism in his intuitive grasp of the profounder meanings of absurdity, and that as an actor-playwright he had an edge over his critics in calculating the effect of a scene,[3] other assumptions are in order. I submit that Shakespeare employs elements of the mystery and morality traditions to create a comic scene whose tragic subtext expresses the blighted psychological relationships between human beings and power.

I have found act 5, scene 3 very funny in performance but acutely disquieting upon reflection. How may this discrepancy of effect be explained? The presence of the Duchess, a comic figure, forces a temporary genre change. Comedy, female-valued, subversive of the play's darker preoccupation with power, promises that Aumerle will not be killed. But beneath the comic surface remains York's ruthless desire to end Aumerle's life, undermining our comfortable, groundless assumptions about paternal love; against the dreadful hostility of father to son, the Duchess pits herself. The scene's total effect, then, depends upon a sophisticated dramatic strategy: a surface at odds with its subtext. Within the scene are fused two medieval traditions—the shrewish wife from the Noah mysteries and the debate between the Daughters of God from the moralities. The former provides the comic characterization of the Duchess, the latter a dialectical structure. By directing his audience's associations backward in time, Shakespeare creates an implicitly bitter contrast between an idealized theological past and a corrupt psychological present. Despite our greater distance from the Middle Ages, in some measure this contrast and its corollary disillusion are accessible to us.

Although the stock character of the shrewish wife harkens back to Roman comedy, the deluge story gave England its own hugely popular, distinctively native shrew. According to the records of the Newcastle guilds, the Corpus Christi plays, if no longer performed annually during Elizabeth's reign, were nevertheless enacted as late as 1589.[4] Even if we use the more commonly cited mid-to-late 1570s as a *terminus ad quem,* the survival of the mysteries, despite the imposition and gradual domination of Protestantism in sixteenth-century England, testifies to the viability of the old dramatic tradition. The domestic dissension between Noah and his intransigent wife lay within the memories of Shakespeare and his audience, either through hearsay or direct experience.[5]

The actions of each of the shrews from three extant Noah plays in some way parallel the Duchess of York's behavior. In the York *Noah,* rather than entering the ark, the wife insists on going to town; in *Richard II* the Duchess, instead of remaining at home, vexes her husband by coming to court: "Thou frantic woman, what does thou make here?" (5.3.88). In the Towneley cycle the Wakefield Master creates an *Uxor* whose disobedience takes the form of a sit-down strike; she will not leave her loom, much as the Duchess will not rise from her knees. The wife in the Chester cycle adamantly refuses to let her gossips down, "and I may save there life."[6] Unique to this play is the wife's defiance of hierarchical precedence in marriage out of altruism rather than perversity; she revolts for her friends' sake, as the Duchess does for her son's. Whether or not Shakespeare knew any particular one of these plays, the tradition of the deluge mysteries, enlivened by the comic situation of a determined woman, invested with the authority of years and motherhood, a wife who cannot be silenced, informs act 5, scene 3.

At the appearance of the garrulous, outspoken, shrew-derived Duchess, Bolingbroke announces that "our scene is alt'red from a serious thing" (5.3.78). The Duchess provides the first bit of comedy since Aumerle's snide humor in the first nineteen lines of act 1, scene 4 and Richard's equally snide "prayer"—"Pray God we may make haste and come too late!" (1.4.64)—at its end. But whereas Aumerle callously jokes about his cousin's exile, and Richard is energized by the prospect of a tiresome—

and rich—uncle's death, her comedy is unconscious; her humor serves life and vindicates love over the ambiguous motivations that impel York to inform against his son and argue for his death. The Duchess proves herself the "unruly woman" (5.2.110) that her husband calls her, determined to countermand her husband and a council of men, however anti-hierarchical her actions; her once "Sweet York" (5.3.90) becomes "my sour husband, my hardhearted lord" (5.3.120), and with her pointed reference to "His weary joints" (5.3.104), she pays him back for his cruel synecdoche, "Shall thy old dugs once more a traitor rear?" (5.3.89). Warmed by her spirit, in the theater we choose to believe that the rift between husband and wife is somehow mendable, that for all the dangerous and uncertain currents of political change, this one family will remain intact.[7] The scene plays well: in David Giles's BBC production the Duchess (Wendy Hiller) exuberantly upstaged York (Charles Gray), a testy but not inhumane *senex*. As an intervention almost as sentimental as farcical, the scene provides a welcome release of tension from the heretofore merciless power struggle.

The Duchess's insistence on mercy is an element of the structural *topos* underlying act 5, scene 3 that can be traced as far back as the morality play *The Castle of Perseverance* (ca. 1425), i.e., the debate between the Four Daughters of God, drawn from Psalm 85:10: "Mercy and truth are met together; righteousness and peace have kissed each other." In *Castle*, the Four Daughters of God approach his scaffold; Mercy and Peace plead for Mankind, while Truth and Righteousness unsuccessfully oppose his salvation, for God wills that

> To make my blysse perfyth
> I menge [mix] wyth my most myth,
> Alle pes, sum treuth, and sum ryth,
>   And most of my mercy.[8]

This pattern is reflected in the successful pleas of the Duchess (Mercy/Peace) for her son's life and the pleas of York (Righteousness/Truth) against Aumerle (Mankind), in fact thrice forgiven by Henry IV (God).

Lest this last identification seem to smack of sacrilege, consider that as the morality plays became politicized there emerged a variant on the Four Daughters' debate. The religious ideals expressed in *The Castle of Perseverance* could not withstand the form and pressure of the Tudor age. The new pattern is exemplified by *Respublica,* attributed to Nicholas Udall and written in 1553, the first year of Mary Tudor's reign. A subgenre of the morality and predecessor of the chronicle play, the "moral interlude" *Respublica* concludes with a debate *topos* that parallels Shakespeare's scene even more closely than does *Castle*'s. By 1553 Misericordia wins only a limited victory over her sisters Justicia and Veritas. Of the four

Vices who have imposed on widow Respublica, only one, Adulacion, is saved from the stern judgment of the goddess Nemesis, God's agent. Significantly, what Adulacion is saved from is imprisonment and trial by law, not damnation. The setting is no longer heaven but earth, where Nemesis, as the prologue asserts, is an allegorical representation of the queen—"She [Mary] is our most wise / and most worthie Nemesis. . . ."[9] This politicized agon, in which the power of Mercy is weaker and the monarch is explicitly given divine status is analogous to the action of act 5, scene 3, in that the Duchess (Misericordia) saves Aumerle (a minor Vice), but Henry IV (Nemesis), who has already sentenced and executed Bushy and Greene,[10] now vows to destroy Aumerle's fellow conspirators (Vices); Henry's right stands unchallenged because, like *Respublica*'s Mary, he is "a god on earth" (5.3.135).

This is not to say that Shakespeare or his audience was familiar with either of these two moral plays; more likely not, since *The Castle of Perseverance* is one of the oldest moralities, and *Respublica,* performed as far as is known only once under Mary, would have been regarded as heterodox by Elizabeth's Protestant government. We may assume, however, an acquaintance with the opposition between Mercy and Righteousness as a theological concept and probably as a dramatic convention. (Marlowe, for example, writing within the same decade, incorporates the morality-derived Good and Bad Angels,[11] the Seven Deadly Sins, and Mephistophilis, Lucifer, and Belzebub into *Doctor Faustus.*) We may also assume the Elizabethan awareness of Mercy's decline in sixteenth-century drama, as the morality play gave way to retributive interludes and early tragedies in which malefactors are punished in an increasingly pitiless universe.

Yet another medieval dramatic element found in act 5, scene 3 is rhyme. Significantly, Swinburne borrows Marlowe's phrase to damn Shakespeare's couplets, especially in this scene, for to Swinburne the "jigging vein" bespeaks a relapse into the earlier native tradition.[12] And, indeed, throughout the play the high incidence of rhymed verse evokes an older time. For an audience and author too sophisticated to accept with interest the old mystery and morality formulas of the shrewish wife and the triumph or partial triumph of Mercy over Justice, the generic conventions required modification. If the audience could be alerted to the conventions on which the playwright was to ring changes, the scene would gain historical resonance. May we not construe the rhyming speeches of 5.3 as deliberate allusions to medieval drama? The use of rhyme not only brings the past to mind but also accomplishes a prosodic finesse: by lightening both the Duchess's *sententiae* and her desperate pleas for the son whose life she believes is forfeit, rhyme induces a spectator mood change without changing the somber direction of the play. In the gestalt of text and subtext, the opposition between medieval manner and psychological matter creates a comedic moment that is yet disturbing.

Shakespeare's handling of these medieval materials calls for our attention. While we may note that theatrically the conflict between the Duchess and York not only provides humor but builds tension in a scene which had seemingly climaxed with Bolingbroke's pardon of Aumerle at line 34 and again at lines 64–65, our chief critical concern is with the conceptual uses to which Shakespeare put the older traditions, with the contrasts he draws between past and present in a play so largely concerned with past and present. The present, that is, the psychological concerns of 5.3 that preclude a simplistic interpretation, is found in its subtext. To illustrate: perhaps the most memorable scene in Kafka's "Metamorphosis" is where Gregor's father shies apples at his son, now changed into a man-sized but still vulnerable insect; just before fainting from the pain of an apple embedded in his back, Gregor sees his mother, in deshabille, run stumblingly toward his father to embrace him and beg for her son's life. Gregor's body, loathsome yet befitting the life he had led; the open hostility of the father toward a son whose existence threatens and shames him; the apples suggesting a lost Eden; the sexuality of the mother's loosened clothing—all come together to form an archetypal image that haunts us with its potential to unlock vast segments of human experience. How different is *Richard II,* 5.3? An only son[13] begs an authority figure for his life, his frantic mother defies her husband by pleading for their son's forgiveness, and the father who informed against his son now insists on his death.

The "absurdity" that Muir sees in this situation lies above all in the unnatural action of the Duke of York, "actually urging the execution of his son." What Muir overlooks but Kafka and Shakespeare knew was that absurdity is the point, that the darkest truths about human nature are irrational and alien: Abraham, to prove his love to God, was willing to sacrifice Isaac; Laius, to protect his own life, tried to kill Oedipus, his infant son; and within a decade of *Richard II* Shakespeare will show an infuriated Gloucester promising a reward to the man who brings his son Edgar to the stake. In *Richard II,* which begins with the murder of an uncle by a nephew and concludes with the murder of a cousin by a cousin, for York to seek his son's death is neither dramatically inappropriate nor any less absurd than for him to see God's surrogate in a usurping politician, to attempt to save his honor by an act that ineluctably blemishes that honor, or to safeguard his life by destroying the life of the son who ensures his earthly immortality. The world of the play reflects the ultimate absurdity: that for man, the social animal, to live in society, he must license the exercise of authority that corrupts the powerful and the powerless alike.

Act 5, scene 3 clarifies these terrifying truths. In the theater they may pass us by; the comic tone of the surface relieves and satisfies; we accept a simplified and immediately comprehensible aesthetic experience. But after leaving the theater, as the scene works upon our unconscious minds, we become aware of the subtext. As our deeper imaginative participation fills up the interstices in characterization and action, allowing us to interpret more perceptively, we discover that the scene has *not* "alt'red from a serious thing." However farcical the surface (and farce itself is a savage genre, precariously skirting the ontological implications of brutality), the subtext is in deadly earnest, presenting a morality scene of moral perversity.

The major morphological difference between Kafka's scene and act 5, scene 3 is Shakespeare's inclusion of an external authority figure, a feature of the moralities' Daughters of God debate. The presence of the king enlarges Shakespeare's scene so that it deals not only with the dynamics of authority within York's family but also within the state. For the Elizabethans, linking family and state is the theological-political premise that king and father are, by God's ordination and the theory of correspondences, lesser versions of divine authority.[14] But as we might expect in a play whose main action is usurpation, the person in whom God's authority is vested is unclear. "Where is the king?" exclaims Aumerle wildly, entering the King's council chamber at Windsor (5.3.23). Aumerle's distraction aside, figuratively the question expresses his political and ethical confusion, in which England shares; and it suggests that Bolingbroke, notwithstanding the unholy, discordant coronation intended to sanitize his military coup, is not yet a self-evident, acknowledged king. The remaining action of the play must be considered in light of Aumerle's implied question: *Who* is the king?

Bolingbroke's real coronation, his first full and conscious savoring of power, takes place over the bodies of his kneeling relations. First Bolingbroke watches Aumerle's character crumble under the touch of power that translates precoronation fealty to postcoronation treason. No mean flatterer with his life at stake, Aumerle obsequiously uses Bolingbroke's royal titles three times in two lines: "God save *your grace!* I do beseech *your Majesty* / To have some conference with *your grace* alone" (5.3.25–26; my italics). Nor does the man who wept for Richard (3.3.159) balk at the casuistry already associated with villainy in Shakespeare:[15] "My heart is not confederate with my hand" (5.3.52). The "daring tongue [that] / Scornst to unsay what once it hath delivered" (4.1.8–9) now unsays his love and loyalty to Richard. Although Bolingbroke pardons "This deadly blot in thy [York's] disgressing son" (5.3.65), the blot and digression that the text calls conspiracy against Bolingbroke, the subtext calls betrayal of Richard. Unlike *Castle*'s Mankind, Aumerle does not save his soul; rather, like *Respublica*'s Adulacion, he must be content to save his skin, for love of life makes a turncoat of Aumerle as it does of his father.

In the old Duke, Bolingbroke's authority brings out something far more monstrous than political betrayal, an all-engulfing, relentlessly destructive id. In hot pursuit of Aumerle, York cries, "Open the door, secure, foolhardy king! / Shall I for love speak treason to thy face?" (5.3.42–43). For love of what? The surface says for love of Bolingbroke, of honor, of country. Yet the father as implacable enemy is so explosive an image—despite its being partially defused for generic reasons by Bolingbroke's pardon of Aumerle before York's arrival—that the subtext remains activated, and we question further. Does Aumerle's loyalty to Richard, a loyalty that lasted longer and involved greater risks than York's, shame the Duke into domestic tyranny? Or is the "boy" (5.2.69) so much a moral fool that his life threatens York's "calm contents" (5.2.38)? Kneeling to plead for his son's death, he inverts a standard emblem of pity[16] into a Kafkaesque image of the unbridled hostility of father to son, of age to youth, of one self to an encroaching other. Even after York is assured of both Bolingbroke's safety and his own—"O loyal father of a treacherous son!" (5.3.59)—he persists in demanding Aumerle's death. His wife, too, comes under the lash. She is to blame, he is exonerated; Aumerle is the child of *her* dugs, and she is old, too old to allure him into pity. In his metaphors, pity becomes a serpent—"Forget to pity him, lest thy pity prove / A serpent that will sting thee to the heart" (5.3.56–57)—and virtue a pimp—"So shall my virtue be his vice's bawd . . ." (5.3.66). What unleashes the demon in York, the savagely insistent "I," is the tribute the powerless must pay to power.

But it is finally the Duchess who gives Bolingbroke a greater prize than the abasement and betrayal of their better selves that Aumerle and York undergo. The Duchess is a tarnished reification of Mercy, having urged that the assassination conspiracy against Bolingbroke be allowed to go forward without Aumerle: "We'll keep him here. Then what is that to him?" (5.2.100). Her indifference to murder, so long as her son is safe, converts altruism to self-interest and vitiates her praise of pity before the king. If a less than satisfactory personification of mercy, the Duchess is also a less than satisfactory wife, a shrew to the husband whose authority she challenges. But to her nephew she comes as a self-declared "beggar" (5.3.77), and is the only woman with whom we see Bolingbroke interact.

Shown with neither wife nor mother,[17] Bolingbroke's encounter with the Duchess of York becomes for us perforce the sum of his relations with women and reveals him as a commanding male presence. On the surface he plays the role of indulgent uncle to a childish inferior; kingship allows him to reverse their ages and family roles, benignly granting his gracious pardon. As he did with Richard, the silent king scores off the compulsive chatterer. But the pardon he grants has already been granted. Why does he toy with the terrified woman, seeming to withhold what he has, unknown to her, already promised, allowing her to reiterate her "prayers"—she uses inflectional forms of *prayer* seven times between lines 100 and 109—while replying to her only with admonitions to rise? Does he relish the kneeling tableau? Does he wish Aumerle to be less certain of pardon, more fearful and therefore more likely to serve him well? Is he inflating the value of Aumerle's pardon that it may weigh more heavily as the price of his own divine pardon? Or does he sense that "sick for fear" (5.3.132) this mother is ready to proffer more than the obsequiousness that gives zest to a conquered kingdom, that Woman—neither dominating nor faithless—in the person of the Duchess will utter the shibboleth and confer the final crown on the successful politician and unsuccessful father: divinity? "A god on earth thou art" (5.3.135) is the Duchess's gift. Her "old son" is to be made "new" (5.3.145) under the new dispensation. For all that it may have been "normal Tudor doctrine"[18] to speak of kings as gods on earth, here Shakespeare demurs. As Bolingbroke's frightened tool, Aumerle, not Hal, becomes the king's new son, thereby corrupting the father-son, king-subject, and God-man relationships. The too grateful Duchess has answered Aumerle's implied question: Who is the king? He whose power can corrupt the powerless into slavish idolatry.

How does the new god on earth celebrate his deification? With cold sarcasm he passes the sentence of death on "our trusty brother-in-law" (5.3.136), then vents his anger on the Abbot of Westminster and "all the rest of that consorted crew" (5.3.137), who had no chance to beg for mercy and whose lives are of less value to Bolingbroke than that of the heir of York. Shakespeare ironically depicts the abuse of the theory of correspondences by graceless, immoral kings, for the title of god on earth for one who openly plans to kill both a relative and a churchman sits as absurdly on Bolingbroke as Richard's likening himself to Christ sits on the murderer of his uncle. Neither divine omniscience nor mercy informs Bolingbroke's words: "They shall not live within this world, I swear, / But I will have them *if* I once know where" (5.3.141–42; my italics). Bolingbroke must first discover where the conspirators are hidden; he does not know. Only then can his "destruction straight . . . dog them at the heels" (5.3.138); the self-reflexive animal imagery evokes a creature not godlike but less than human. A politician, not a god, lets York save face by asking his assistance in rounding up the traitors; the old Duke, still smarting from his wife's victory, nevertheless still holds a place in a man's world, the battlefield and the chambers of the great. Bolingbroke, the wily politician, knows that efficient control is based on allegiance won with a minimum of bloodshed and the conservation of such potential resources as York and Aumerle.[19] A politician, not a god, orders Richard's assassination with a shifty duplicity even more cowardly than King John's attempted subornation of Hubert de Burgh.

Bolingbroke's writ on Richard's life comes as no surprise to those alert to the subtext. It is prepared for when the king says, "I pardon him as God shall pardon me" (5.3.130). Ostensibly the stock phrase expresses generosity and piety. But beneath the surface lies Bolingbroke's attempt, probably unconscious, to corrupt God—to strike a bargain with God that will allow the king to carry out his further vicious purpose. As Bolingbroke asked Aumerle, so we ask Bolingbroke, "Intended, or committed, was this fault?" (5.3.32). For what fault does Bolingbroke seek pardon? For the execution of Bushy, Greene, and Wiltshire? For Richard's deposition? Or is it rather for the intended assassination? The intention may have been conceived as early as act 5, scene 1, when Richard was sent not to the tower but to Pomfret, as remote from aid as Calais, to which he sent his uncle Gloucester. Doubtless, the assassination is intended now as Bolingbroke realizes that while the ex-king lives, he gives hope to his partisans and presents a perpetual danger to the new king. A god on earth speaks the scene's last line: "Your mother well hath prayed . . ." (5.3.144); a god on earth has a special understanding with his maker.

" 'Have I no friend will rid me of this living fear' " (5.4.2), says Sir Pierce of Exton, quoting Bolingbroke. If we recall that the only act and scene divisions for any of the early editions of *Richard II* appear in the Folio where 5.3 and 5.4 are printed as a single scene, implying a single situation,[20] the link between the deification of Bolingbroke, Shakespeare's Nemesis, and the words he speaks to Exton is unmistakable. It is not merely the conspiracy against Bolingbroke that costs Richard his life. Richard dies because the new god on earth, drunk with power, beyond good and evil, need accept no constraints. Only when publicly confronted with Richard's coffin, like a thief caught red-handed, does Bolingbroke stammer out an equivocal renunciation of intent that convinces no one, not even himself. Yet his projected "voyage to the Holy Land" (5.6.49) still implies his belief that for a price a god on earth can buy salvation despite regicide.

The old allegory was pure. Justice and Mercy were disinterested, not discredited, their only motive to realize themselves before an omnibenevolent God. Shakespeare, however, takes as his province the rubbing of humanity against its finest ideals. Thus the verses of the psalmist and the message of Christ are parodied by the action. By the close of *Richard II* the genuine religious values of the Middle Ages lie shattered; Righteousness is self-serving and savage; Mercy, cowed into a will to worship, feeds power; God the Father is displaced by a false god free to butcher at will. What is diagrammatic in the moralities has taken on the multiple shadings of reality. The allegorical moral schemata survive, if veiled, thanks to a broader vision of liminally Freudian personalities playing for blood at Hobbesian politics. Shakespeare's overtly farcical, covertly tragical recension of the mystery and morality *topoi* situates act 5, scene 3 in both the medieval and psychological worlds. Drawing on a complex, innovative perspective of old and new, of text and subtext, Shakespeare represents the psychic corruption bred of power.

Notes

1. *The Medieval Heritage of Elizabethan Tragedy* (1936; reprint, Oxford: Blackwell, 1963), 415.
2. "Introduction," *The Tragedy of King Richard II*, in *The Complete Signet Classic Shakespeare*, ed. Sylvan Barnet (New York: Harcourt, 1972), 438. All citations to Shakespeare will be taken from this text.
3. I have tried to confine my discussion to lines 73–135, the "scene" to which Muir objects, but from time to time the logic of the play's development has required expanding these artificial limits in order to understand more fully the passage in question.
4. The records of the Newcastle shipwrights' guild, producers of the ark play, have been lost, but comparable records of Newcastle millers, carpenters, masons, and joiners testify to this date; see Norman Davis, ed., *Non-Cycle Plays and Fragments*, EETS, s.s., no. 1 (London: Oxford University Press, 1970), xlii–xliii.
5. Hal's referring to Falstaff as "that reverend vice, that gray iniquity" (*1 Henry IV* 2.4.458) and Hamlet's complaint against bombastic acting that "out-herods Herod" (*Hamlet* 3.2.14) are perhaps the most familiar examples of Shakespeare's acquaintance with medieval drama.
6. R. M. Lumiansky and David Mills, *The Chester Mystery Cycle*, EETS, s.s., no. 3 (London: Oxford University Press, 1974), 50, line 204.
7. In contrast, Gaunt loses a son to enforced exile as Bolingbroke loses his "unthrifty son" (5.3.1) to self-chosen exile; and both Isabel and the Duchess of Gloucester lose a husband to arrest and death.
8. *The Macro Plays: The Castle of Perseverance, Wisdom, Mankind*, ed. Mark Eccles, EETS, o.s., no. 262 (London: Oxford University Press, 1969), 108, lines 3570–73.
9. *Respublica: An Interlude for Christmas 1553*, re-ed. W. W. Greg, EETS, o.s., no. 226 (London: Oxford University Press, 1952 [for 1946]), 3, line 53.
10. E. M. W. Tillyard identifies Richard's flatterers with the morality Vices: "Bushy, Green, and Bagot, however, remain very plainly Morality figures and were probably marked in some way by their dress as abstract vices." See *Shakespeare's History Plays* (1946; reprint, New York: Collier, 1962), 298.
11. In at least one morality, *Mankind* (ca. 1470), Mercy played yet another forensic role, appearing as the Good Angel opposed by the Vices and the devil Titivillus.
12. Algernon Charles Swinburne, *A Study of Shakespeare* (1879; reprint, New York: AMS, 1965), 40.
13. Since York's other son, Richard of Cambridge, appears in *Henry V*, Shakespeare has apparently chosen to intensify the psychological horror by treating Aumerle as an only son—"Have we more sons? Or are we like to have?" (5.2.90).
14. Within the scene York and Bolingbroke, as frustrated fathers, are in effect doubles. York compares Aumerle to "thriftless sons" (5.3.68) who spend their father's gold [honor], echoing Bolingbroke's complaint about Hal, his "unthriftly son." Shakespeare's predilection for creating fusion in division here transforms politically endorsed theology into psychological complexity.
15. Compare Richard's speech convincing his father to be forsworn (*3 Henry VI* 1.2.22–27) and the soliloquy in which Proteus attempts to rationalize his betrayal to Julia (*Two Gentlemen of Verona* 2.6.11–13).

16. Anne Pasternak Slater, *Shakespeare the Director* (Totowa, N.J.: Barnes & Noble, 1982), 71–76.

17. The only mother he mentions is his country: "Then, England's ground, farewell; sweet soil, adieu; / My mother and my nurse that bears me yet!" (1.3.305–6). The only loving relationship we see Bolingbroke participate in is with his father at the end of act 1, scene 3. Nevertheless, Bolingbroke's return from exile would have been abhorrent to Gaunt. Although Bolingbroke's return to England after Gaunt's death makes possible Richard's confiscation of the Lancastrian estates, his ostensible motive should not obscure the inner release from Gaunt's loyalist creed afforded by the death of his father.

18. Peter Ure, ed., *King Richard II*, 5th ed., The Arden Edition of the Works of William Shakespeare (London: Methuen, 1961), 166 n. 134.

19. Aumerle is saved to die for Bolingbroke's "unthrifty son" at Agincourt.

20. The break signaled by the *exeunt* and appearance of new characters does not strike me as overriding the cohesive quality of the action.

Nightingales That Roar: The Language of *A Midsummer Night's Dream*

JAY L. HALIO

In an essay called "On the Value of *Hamlet,*" Stephen Booth has shown how that play simultaneously frustrates and fulfills audience expectations and otherwise presents contradictions that belie or bedevil the attempts of many a reductionist critic to demonstrate a coherent thematic pattern in Shakespeare's masterpiece. Booth's commentary is particularly directed to the language and action of act 1 which, from the very outset, arouse in the audience a "sensation of being unexpectedly and very slightly out of step" with the drama that the players unfold. "In *Hamlet,*" Booth says, "the audience does not so much shift its focus as come to find its focus shifted."[1] The end result, though initially disturbing, is not finally so: "People see *Hamlet* and tolerate inconsistencies that it does not seem they could bear. . . . Truth is bigger than any one system for knowing it, and *Hamlet* is bigger than any of the frames of reference it inhabits. *Hamlet* allows us to comprehend—to hold on to—all of the contradictions it contains."[2]

The kind of linguistic and dramatic complexity that Booth describes, while preeminently demonstrable in *Hamlet,* is by no means limited to that play. It is far more prevalent than perhaps has been recognized, although several critics before and since Booth's essay have tried to show similar situations in other plays. David Bevington, for example, has shown how in *A Midsummer Night's Dream* the debate between Oberon and Puck in act 3, scene 2 "reflects a fundamental tension in the play between comic reassurance and the suggestion of something dark and threatening."[3] In "Titania and the Ass's Head" Jan Kott argued that *A Midsummer Night's Dream* is "the most erotic of Shakespeare's plays" and nowhere else is the eroticism "expressed so brutally."[4] Kott's focus is largely upon the animal imagery and erotic symbolism. The metaphors in Helena's speech to Demetrius in which she proclaims herself his "spaniel," his "dog" (2.1.203–10), Kott regards as "almost masochistic." Contrary to the romantic tradition, reinforced by Mendelssohn's music, the forest in *Dream* represents anything but a version of Arcadia, inhabited as it is by "devils and lamias, in which witches and sorceresses can easily find everything required for their practices."[5] Titania caressing the monster with the head of an ass is closer to the fearful visions of Hieronymous Bosch, in Kott's view, than to the gentler depictions of Chagall and countless other illustrators of Shakespeare's dream play.

Like Bevington, we need not go as far as Kott does. We need not imagine Titania's court consisting of toothless old men and shaking hags, "their mouths wet with saliva" as they, sniggering, "procure a monster for their mistress."[6] But there is a good deal more going on beneath the play's surface than many have been willing to notice, or have deliberately been persuaded (or lulled) into not noticing. This surely was the point, in part, of Peter Brook's 1970 production: to shake us out of complacency. In much of the poetry, indeed in some of the most celebrated passages, there is a repeated undercutting of the tenor by the vehicle Shakespeare chooses, or a subverting of the overall tone by the actual sense of the language employed. Although this point is related to Kott's, it is, I think, a more general one and characterizes similar phenomena in other plays.

As so often in Shakespearean drama, the first clues come early, in the very opening speeches. Theseus tells Hippolyta that their nuptial hour approaches and he is, like any bridegroom, impatient for the event. But the specific language suggests a crass motive and includes images that are otherwise scarcely flattering to his bride, who is, like Theseus, somewhat advanced in years:

> Four happy days bring in
> Another moon—but O, methinks how slow
> This old moon wanes! She lingers my desires,
> Like to a stepdame or a dowager
> Long withering out a young man's revenue.
>
> (1.1.2–6)[7]

Hippolyta's response, meant to be reassuring, yet includes the simile of a "silver bow / New-bent in heaven" that reminds Theseus in his turn how he wooed her with his sword and won her love by doing her injuries. He promises to wed her in "another key," but suggestions of discord have already been sounded, and many more will follow before Oberon's final benediction and Puck's epilogue—and their interesting peculiarities.

One such discord occurs immediately with the entrance of Egeus, Hermia, and her two suitors. It is a situation not unlike the opening scenes of *Othello,* and Egeus's complaints against Lysander are similar to Brabantio's accusations of the Moor: the young man has "bewitched" the old man's daughter with rhymes and presents, "messengers / Of strong prevailment in unhardened youth" (34–35). As the dialogue develops, however, it is clear that if any bewitching has so far occurred—some will certainly occur later—it has been Hermia who has enchanted the affections of both young men. Nevertheless, Egeus's determination to have his way, or his daughter's death, is more than a little disconcerting. It is Theseus—not Egeus—who recalls a third alternative that he makes sound, in this dramatic context, less attractive than a more orthodox view requires. Hermia, after all, can become a nun:

> Therefore, fair Hermia, question your desires,
> Know of your youth, examine well your blood,
> Whether, if you yield not to your father's choice,
> You can endure the livery of a nun,
> For aye to be in shady cloister mewed,
> To live a barren sister all your life,
> Chanting faint hymns to the cold fruitless moon.
> Thrice-blessèd they that master so their blood
> To undergo such maiden pilgrimage;
> But earthlier happy is the rose distilled
> Than that which, withering on the virgin thorn,
> Grows, lives, and dies in single blessedness.
>
> (67–78)

Anachronisms apart, Theseus's description of a "thrice-blessèd" life is shall we admit, rather forbidding. The whole conception of devotion—filial, religious, amorous—is further subverted a few lines later when Lysander mentions Helena's love for Demetrius, who has jilted her:

> she, sweet lady, dotes
> Devoutly dotes, dotes in idolatry
> Upon this spotted and inconstant man.
>
> (108–10)

And, strangely enough, Theseus sets his own wedding day as the date on which Hermia must make her fateful decision:

> Take time to pause, and by the next new moon—
> The sealing day between my love and me
> For everlasting bond of fellowship—
> Upon *that* day either prepare to die
> For disobedience to your father's will,
> Or else to wed Demetrius, as he would,
> Or on Diana's altar to protest
> For aye austerity and single life.
>
> (83–90; my italics)

Left with the three alternatives that Theseus enumerates, the lovers look for consolation from each other. Lysander tries to comfort Hermia with a disquisition upon the theme, "The course of true love never did run smooth." The stichomythia in which they then engage reveals only the most obvious way Lysander's words of "comfort" are undercut: "O cross! . . . O spite! . . . O hell!" begins each of Hermia's comments. She eventually allows herself to be persuaded by the lesson Lysander seems to be emphasizing—"Then let us teach our trial patience"—only to discover, contrary to his explicit assent, that this is not what he really has in mind at all. His "therefore" (156) leads in quite a different direction, wherever his earlier logic might have been pointing, as he presents to Hermia his plan to elope.

Hermia's ready agreement to the plan concludes with what is, again given the dramatic context, a most curious set of oaths. It begins conventionally enough, but then something happens to the conventions, or rather some oddly inappropriate ones intrude:

> I swear to thee by Cupid's strongest bow,
> By his best arrow with the golden head,
> By the simplicity of Venus' doves,
> By that which knitteth souls and prospers loves,
> And by that fire which burned the Carthage queen
> When the false Trojan under sail was seen,
> By all the vows that ever men have broke—
> In number more than ever women spoke,—
> In that same place thou hast appointed me
> Tomorrow truly will I meet with thee.
>
> (169–78)

Hermia may be merely teasing her lover, so sure she is of him, as Alexander Leggatt says, and the joking does no harm.[8] But teasing always contains a barb, and (not only in light of what comes later) the allusions to male infidelity are ominous, to say the least. In any event, the rhetoric of the first eight lines is neatly undercut by the final couplet, whose jingling and prosaic simplicity collapses the soaring quality of what precedes it. This may all be part of the comic effect intended, and Lysander's flat "Keep promise, love," while confirming the anticlimactic effect, at the same time suggests by its peremptoriness that he may be caught a little off balance by Hermia. But before we can ponder this exchange further, Helena enters with paradoxes of her own.

Consider her lines on love and the imagination. Although earlier she laments how Demetrius is misled in large part by Hermia's external beauty, here Helena complains of the transforming power of the imagination under the influence of love:

> Things base and vile, holding no quantity,
> Love can transpose to form and dignity.
> Love looks not with the eyes, but with the mind,
> And therefore is winged Cupid painted blind.

Nor hath love's mind of any judgement taste;
Wings and no eyes figure unheedy haste.
And therefore is love said to be a child
Because in choice he is so oft beguiled.

(232–39)

Throughout her speech Helena shows remarkable maturity of insight, except of course that all of her insight helps not a jot to correct her own love's folly. She errs as badly as Demetrius, by her own admission. Nor is she correct about visual susceptibility. As much of the central action of the play demonstrates, the eyes decidedly lead—or mislead—lovers. The capacity for transposing "things base and vile" to "form and dignity" is not in the imagination, or "mind," but in the fancy, which as she indicates is devoid of judgment. Shakespeare shows the relation between eyesight and fancy (or love) in a song from *The Merchant of Venice:*

Tell me where is fancy bred,
Or in the heart or in the head?
How begot, how nourished?
Reply, reply.
It is engendered in the eyes,
With gazing fed; and fancy dies
In the cradle where it lies.

(3.2.63–69)

Later, in a speech notable for its dramatic irony, Lysander justifies his sudden passion for Helena by an appeal to his reason, which he claims has led his will, or desire (2.2.121–23). But like others in the Athenian forest, he is led by his eyes, influenced by Puck's misapplied herb juice, which has engendered his fancy. And it will be through his eyes also that his fancy, his infatuation for Helena, will die. Although the terms were often used interchangeably by Shakespeare and his contemporaries, the power of the imagination *could* be distinguished from the fancy, as some Elizabethans knew two centuries before Coleridge's *Biographia Literaria.* It is, moreover, this power, fancy (or phantasy), that Theseus unfortunately calls "imagination" in his famous fifth act speech, which connects the lunatic, the lover, and the poet.[9]

The frequent malapropisms of the rude mechanicals' dialogue also add to our growing sense of linguistic (and other) disorder. Here Bottom is the most notorious, because the most pretentious; but he is not the only one. Wanting the role of Lion, as well as the roles of Pyramus *and* Thisbe—and Ercles, too, if that "part to tear a cat in" could somehow be worked into the play—he pleads that he will use moderation in his roaring so as not to frighten the ladies in the audience:

> But I will aggravate my voice so that I will roar you as gently as any sucking dove. I will roar you an 'twere any nightingale.
>
> (1.2.76–78)

Peter Quince, the stalwart impresario, also gets tangled up in his language, not only in failing to stand upon his points in the Prologue, but earlier, speaking more accurately than he realizes, when he explains how moonlight can be provided for their play. As an alternative to leaving the casement window open, he suggests "one must come in with a bush of thorns and a lantern and say he comes to *disfigure* or to present the person of Moonshine" (3.1.53–55; my italics). When it is finally staged before the court, the "*most lamentable comedy . . . Pyramus and Thisbe*" will function on various levels of significance well prepared for by the kinds of linguistic subversion that appear elsewhere in the play.

The sense of disorder that characterizes much of *A Midsummer Night's Dream* is, in one way, explained by the conflict between Oberon and Titania. These adept lovers, when they meet in act 2, upbraid one another with accusations of jealousy, philandering, insubordination, and downright meanness. As a result of their quarrel, Titania complains that everything in nature has turned topsy-turvy (2.1.81–117). The vagaries of love have power, apparently, in these supernatural beings to make the seasons alter:

> . . . hoary-headed frosts
> Fall in the fresh lap of the crimson rose,
> And on old Hiems' thin and icy crown
> An odorous chaplet of sweet summer buds
> Is as in mockery set.
>
> (107–11)

But the disorder is conveyed in other, more subtle ways than in this image of old Hiems and his fragrant chaplet. Immediately after Oberon vows to "torment" his queen for her injurious behavior, he calls upon his "gentle" Puck. Again, as he describes hearing a mermaid on a dolphin's back "uttering such dulcet and harmonious breath / That the rude sea grew civil at her song," he notes that at the same time "certain stars shot madly from their spheres / To hear the sea-maid's music" (2.1.150–54). How can it happen both ways: the rude sea grows civil, but certain stars go mad in the firmament? The subsequent magnificent passage describing the "fair vestal throned by the west" concludes with the sad plight of the once milk-white flower, love-in-idleness, stained purple, which will provide Oberon with the magic he needs for his plot against Titania. The epitome of this kind of doublespeak occurs in the famous passage where Oberon describes his plan in detail:

> I know a bank where the wild thyme blows,
> Where oxlips and the nodding violet grows,
> Quite overcanopied with luscious woodbine,
> With sweet muskroses and with eglantine.
> There sleeps Titania some time of the night,
> Lulled in these flowers with dances and delight.
> And there the snake throws her enamelled skin,
> Weed wide enough to wrap a fairy in.
> And with the juice of this I'll streak her eyes,
> And make her full of hateful fantasies.
>
> (2.1.249–58)

As Harold Brooks remarks, the lines are "famous for their melody, as well as for their imagery, which is no less lyrical."[10] The mellifluousness of the verse, the lulling rhythms of the end-stopped lines, but especially the beauty of the images combine to hide for the reader or spectator almost entirely the edge of Oberon's real malice. If the image of the snake is hardly an image here that repels, its appearance is at least problematical—whatever generic relation it may have to Hermia's dream of the crawling serpent on her breast after Lysander deserts her in the next scene. Jan Kott has noted a parallel in the fairies' lullaby in act 2 where the linguistic effect is reversed:

> You spotted snakes with double tongue,
> Thorny hedgehogs, be not seen.
> Newts and blindworms, do no wrong,
> Come not near our Fairy Queen.
> Philomel with melody
> Sing in our sweet lullaby,
> Lulla, lulla, lullaby; lulla, lulla, lullaby.
> Never harm
> Nor spell nor charm
> Come our lovely lady nigh.
> So good night, with lullaby.
> Weaving spiders, come not here;
> Hence, you longlegged spinners, hence!
> Beetles black, approach not near,
> Worm nor snail, do no offence.
> Philomel with melody. . . .
>
> (2.2.9–24)

Despite its invocation to Philomel in the refrain, this is not the sort of lullaby to forecast or inspire pleasant dreams. But the harmonies of sound, especially enhanced by music (as in many lullabies), do everything—or almost everything—to hide from us the actual horrors. The same point can be illustrated where Titania explains her opposition to Oberon's demand for the changeling Indian boy:

> His mother was a votress of my order,
> And in the spicèd Indian air by night
> Full often hath she gossiped by my side,
> And sat with me on Neptune's yellow sands,
> Marking th'embarkèd traders on the flood,
> When we have laughed to see the sails conceive
> And grow big-bellied with the wanton wind;
> Which she with pretty and with swimming gait
> Following—her womb then rich with my young squire—
> Would imitate, and sail upon the land
> To fetch me trifles, and return again
> As from a voyage, rich with merchandise.
> And she, being mortal, of that boy did die,
> And for her sake do I rear up her boy;
> And for her sake I will not part with him.
>
> (2.1.123–37)

The beauty of the passage—"spiced Indian air," the imagery of conception, and the mocking gait of the pregnant young woman—bears the full emphasis, and the serious point of the speech—the mother's childbirth death, leaving her son an orphan—becomes almost anticlimactic, certainly less emphatic, though to Shakespeare's audience the dangers of childbirth were quite real.

Bottom's meeting with Titania also offers some surprising paradoxes. Can Oberon really mean to have himself cuckolded by an asinine country bumpkin? We may laugh, and are surely meant to do so, when Titania greets Bottom's rustic song: "What angel wakes me from my flowery bed?" (3.1.122). But Bottom goes on, providing some interesting clues to what actually is about to happen:

> The finch, the sparrow, and the lark,
> The plainsong cuckoo grey,
> Whose note full many a man doth mark
> And dares not answer "Nay"—
> for, indeed, who would set his wit to so foolish a bird? Who would give a bird the lie, though he cry "cuckoo" never so?
>
> (123–129)

Cuckoos and cuckolds—need one remark?—traditionally have a strong association, which modern audiences may miss, but Shakespeare's would not. Oberon plans to punish Titania and succeeds—not without some cost to himself, however, which he may ignore or perhaps relish ("This falls out better than I could devise!" he says to Puck at 3.2.35). But Bottom's song and comment point to what the cost actually is.[11]

These linguistic and dramatic complexities and contradictions serve, as Stephen Booth has said about *Hamlet,* to keep us from simplistic reductions of experienced situations, specifically the play's mirrored experiences of reality, to say nothing of its own reality. As such, they force us out of, rather than into, an artificial prison that R. P. Blackmur has (in another connection) described as a tendency to set artistic unity as a chief criterion of excellence.[12] Coherence, existentially considered, is more, much more, than rhetorical cohesiveness, though to some extent that kind of coherence is also necessary. But however necessary, it is not a sufficient condition of great art, such as Shakespeare's. The point can be illustrated as well by examples from the great literature of music, such as the late Beethoven quartets. But (to remain with Shakespeare) let me expand the reference to other plays of the same period as *A Midsummer Night's Dream*.

In an essay on "Shakespeare and the Limits of Language," Anne Barton some years ago contrasted Richard II's verbal adeptness with Bolingbroke's political skill to show how, despite his manifold successes, Shakespeare did not allow language, the efficacy of the word, an "unexamined triumph."[13] In the deposition scene, for example, Barton shows how it is the weak king who insists upon inventing a rite, creating a litany that will, through words, invest the transference of power with meaning. The speech she specifically cites uses the well metaphor as its controlling device:

> Here, cousin, seize the crown.
> On this side my hand, and on that side thine.
> Now is this golden crown like a deep well
> That owes two buckets, filling one another:
> The emptier ever dancing in the air,
> The other down, unseen, and full of water.
> That bucket down and full of tears am I,
> Drinking my griefs, whilst you mount up on high.
> (4.1.181–88)

As Barton says, Bolingbroke's submission is "oddly qualified"; he reaches out his hand, but verbally he will not cooperate; his blunt inquiry—"I thought you had been willing to resign"—tears through and destroys the validity of the metaphor.[14] Or does it? We can see Bolingbroke containing himself in patience while Richard goes through his ceremonies of self-debasement, for Bolingbroke fully understands the political might he now controls. Richard's wit is keener than Bolingbroke suspects, or lets on.

The well metaphor, like much else in this scene, carries more than an acknowledgment of Richard's defeat and Bolingbroke's success. Richard, the heavier bucket, down and unseen, is also fuller, weightier; Bolingbroke, the high bucket, is also lighter, emptier, frolicking in the air as in a dance. The word, as Richard delivers it then, in this speech as in others, is hardly impotent. Its triumph is not an unqualified one, but neither is Bolingbroke's. Many of Shakespeare's plays make the same point.

In the last act of *The Merchant of Venice* the equations appear reversed. Some of the same verbal inconsistencies that analysis of *A Midsummer Night's Dream* revealed occur in the opening speeches between Lorenzo and Jessica, creating the initial tension that leads indirectly to the tensions created by the ring trick that Portia and Nerissa have played upon their husbands. Or are all of these tensions, as Jonathan Miller's production (with Laurence Olivier as Shylock) seemed to argue, actually the result, or aftermath, of those generated in the previous act, where Shylock learns the meaning of justice as taught him by Portia and Antonio and the rest?

Lorenzo and Jessica are sitting outside Portia's house in Belmont. Lorenzo speaks:

> The moon shines bright. In such a night as this,
> When the sweet wind did gently kiss the trees
> And they did make no noise, in such a night
> Troilus methinks mounted the Troyan walls
> And sighed his soul toward the Grecian tents,
> Where Cressid lay that night.
>
> (5.1.1–6)

The first three lines set both the scene and time and prepare for the lovely passage fifty lines later that begins, "How sweet the moonlight sleeps upon this bank!" But here as later a discordant note slips in, even as the mellifluousness of the lines, the soft alliterations and rhythm beguile the listener—the less attentive audience, at any rate—but not Jessica. She follows Lorenzo's allusion to the tragedy of Troilus and Cressida with:

> In such a night
> Did Thisbe fearfully o'ertrip the dew,
> And saw the lion's shadow ere himself
> And ran dismayed away.
>
> (6–9)

And so on, back and forth, through Dido and Medea until Lorenzo openly teases Jessica about stealing away with him to Belmont, and she retorts in kind. Only the entrance of a messenger apparently halts the contest; but later, as they await Portia's return and Lorenzo describes the music of the spheres, Jessica feels compelled to say: "I am never merry when I hear sweet music" (69). And so on, again, throughout the scene concords find discords, discords concord, in a seemingly unending series. Although the overall tone is joyful and the teasing playful, Shakespeare does not let us forget the more somber aspects of human relationships, which can and do intrude.

The same kind of linguistic and dramatic strategy is at work in the final act of *A Midsummer Night's Dream*. Philostrate's list of possible wedding entertainments is an odd one, beginning as it does with "The battle with the Centaurs, to be sung / By an Athenian eunuch to the harp" (5.1.44–45). His fourth possibility brings us to

> "A tedious brief scene of young Pyramus
> And his love Thisbe; very tragical mirth."
>
> (56–57)

Theseus's reaction summarizes ours:

> Merry and tragical? Tedious and brief?
> That is, hot ice and wondrous strange snow.
> How shall we find the concord of this discord?
>
> (58–60)

Philostrate's condescending reply to the question does not probe deeply enough, of course: How indeed shall we find the "concord of this discord"? Not, I submit, by simply acquiescing in the general merriment of the stage spectators while the playlet is in progress, beginning with the "tangled chain" of Quince's Prologue. Even if we grant that the play was first performed at an actual wedding celebration, with fun and laughter very much in the spirit of the occasion, we cannot stop there. However well things may turn out for Theseus and Hippolyta, Lysander and Hermia, Demetrius and Helena, Oberon and Titania, there is still one couple whose fortunes do not end happily. Within the happy framework of this celebration, the solemn notes of tragedy still intrude, all but obliterated by peals of mirth that the simple rustics inspire, but nonetheless there.

Critics have been at some pains to show how Shakespeare "brilliantly reconciles opposites"[15] in his dream-play. The usual reference is to the passages on Theseus's hounds in act 4, scene 1, lines 109–26, specifically to "So musical a discord, such sweet thunder" that their baying offers. Not remarked often enough, perhaps, is the providential role that characters like Oberon and Theseus enact in bringing about the concord between the jarring couples in the play. (Shakespeare as playwright is of course the relevant analogy here.) But my purpose has been to show that the concords exist at only one level, and that one not the most profound. The thunder may be "sweet," but it is still thunder. Oberson overmasters Titania, reduces her to tears, and has his way finally. Theseus suavely ignores the law Egeus and he himself have invoked in act 1 to enable the young couples to be married, and Egeus (with whatever silent, grudging acceptance) goes along: Theseus quite frankly tells him "I will overbear your will" (4.1.178). Shakespeare is hardly as direct, but in effect he overbears ours as well, lulling or beguiling us into an acceptance of concord and amity, however achieved, through the artistry of his verse and the adeptness of his comic genius. But he has left sufficient pointers (for those willing to recognize them) that this is artifice, after all; that a benevolent providence does not always or inevitably enter into human affairs to make things right. His most significant indication of that fact is in the play-within-the-play, where no providential solution to Pyramus and Thisbe's plight appears. The "thunder" there may be nearly drowned out by laughter and jollity, but it still rumbles. And what the thunder says is *not* a message of concord or reconciliation of opposing wills.

Of this situation Marjorie Garber has commented that the play-within-the-play is "ultimately nothing less than a countermyth for the whole of *A Midsummer Night's Dream,* setting out the larger play's terms in a new and revealing light."[16] If the playlet "absorbs and disarms" the tragic alternative to the happy outcome that the other couples have experienced, it is nevertheless present to remind us of what we all know but usually prefer to ignore or forget, especially on such occasions as this. By framing the images of nightmare terrors in "an illusion within an illusion," as James Calderwood has said, Shakespeare here dissolves their threat in laughter. But the laughter is generated, Calderwood continues, at least in part by the act of self-recognition that follows from the transformation of "subjective vagueness" into the "objective clarity" of dramatic form.[17]

As "the iron tongue of midnight" summons the couples to bed, with Theseus's anticipation of yet a fortnight of "nightly revels and new jollity," Puck steals in and reminds us that

> Now the hungry lion roars
> And the wolf behowls the moon,
> Whilst the heavy plowman snores
> All with weary task foredone.
>
> (5.1.361–64)

Not that the fairies' work is done, and Puck is "sent with broom before / To sweep the dust behind the door" (379–80). Perhaps that is the best image for Shakespeare's strategy in this play. As every housewife knows, sweeping the dust behind the door, or under the rug, may hide it for awhile, but does not get rid of it. In *A Midsummer Night's Dream* Shakespeare, like Puck, is busy with his broom, but we do not altogether lose sight of his, or the world's, dust.

Notes

1. In *Reinterpretations of Elizabethan Drama*, ed. Norman Rabkin (New York: Columbia University Press, 1969), 143.

2. Booth, "Value of *Hamlet*," 175.

3. "But We Are Spirits of Another Sort: The Dark Side of Love and Magic in *A Midsummer Night's Dream*," *Medieval and Renaissance Studies* 7 (1975): 81.

4. *Shakespeare Our Contemporary*, trans. Boleslaw Taborski (Garden City, N.Y.: Doubleday, 1964), 212.

5. Ibid., 218.

6. Ibid., 219.

7. Quotations are from the New Penguin Shakespeare, ed. Stanley Wells (Harmondsworth, England: Penguin, 1967).

8. *Shakespeare's Comedy of Love* (London: Methuen, 1974), 95. The New Arden editor, Harold Brooks, also refers to Hermia's "tender teasing."

9. See David P. Young, *Something of Great Constancy* (New Haven: Yale University Press, 1964), 126–41. For an acute analysis of Helena's speech, cf. Ruth Nevo, *Comic Transformations in Shakespeare* (London: Methuen, 1980), 98–99.

10. Introduction to *A Midsummer Night's Dream*, New Arden ed. (London: Methuen, 1979), cxxx. Cf. Leggatt, *Comedy of Love*, 96, on the experiences of the Athenian lovers in the forest: "Over and over, the violence of the ideas is lightened by jingling rhythm and rhyme."

11. On the other hand, as Bevington notes, these gods "make a sport of inconstancy." Out of her love for Theseus, Titania has helped him to ravish Perigouna, break faith with Aegles and with others; while Oberon has made love with Aurora as well as, apparently, with Hippolyta. "This is the sort of mysterious affection," Bevington says, "that only a god could practice or understand." See "Spirits of Another Sort," 90.

12. *Form and Value in Modern Poetry* (New York: Doubleday, 1957), 83. Cf. Stanley Wells's comments on the theme of concord in his introduction to *A Midsummer Night's Dream*, 31. He says that the baying of Theseus's hounds is "a symbol of the possibility of a unity that is not sameness, an agreement that can include disagreement." Cf. Young, *Great Constancy*, 86.

13. In *Shakespeare Survey* 24 (Cambridge: Cambridge University Press, 1971), 20.

14. Barton, "Limits of Language," 22.

15. Wells, introd. to *A Midsummer Night's Dream*, 28. Cf. Leggatt, *Comedy of Love*, 114: "But the artistic vision itself, which draws these disparate experiences together, is also limited."

16. *Dream in Shakespeare* (New Haven: Yale University Press, 1974), 81.

17. "*A Midsummer Night's Dream:* The Illusion of Drama," *Modern Language Quarterly* 26 (1965): 522. Cf. Madeleine Doran, *Shakespeare's Dramatic Language* (Madison: University of Wisconsin Press, 1976), 16, on *Pyramus and Thisbe* as a suitable antimasque for the wedding ceremony.

Thomas Heywood's *A Woman Killed with Kindness* as Domestic Morality

MICHAEL WENTWORTH

A. M. Kinghorn in a brief but perceptive study of medieval drama claims that "the primary aim of [such] drama was to show man the path to Redemption, and it did so by teaching . . . the doctrine of Repentance, which was the key to salvation in a society believing in Original Sin."[1] Speaking more specifically of the morality tradition in English drama, Robert Potter similarly observes: "The morality plays have a common theme and a practical (if theologically complex) moral: sin is inevitable; repentance is always possible."[2] Whether Thomas Heywood was directly familiar with the morality tradition is impossible to establish. Nevertheless, *A Woman Killed with Kindness,* generally regarded as Heywood's masterpiece, reflects the same instructive impulse, the same emphasis upon the inevitability of sin and the possibility of repentance typical of such morality plays as *Everymen, Mankind,* and *The Castle of Perseverance*. In fact, the play, which has been variously described as a domestic tragedy, a middle-class drama, a tearful comedy, an Elizabethan problem play, and a sentimental comedy, might be equally—if not even more appropriately—described as a repentance play or a domestic morality, for, no less than the medieval morality, *A Woman Killed with Kindness* provides a dramatic reenactment of the process of repentance. Unlike the conventional morality, however, the focus of such a reenactment is not some generic prototype or allegorical representative of mankind but Anne Frankford, the wife of a prominent middle-class landowner. Initially viewed as a woman of unexcelled virtue, Anne, victimized as much by her naiveté and innocence as by any flaw of moral character, commits adultery and, acting upon her husband's startling and highly unconventional judgment, leaves his household, whereupon she enacts, interestingly enough in an informal religous context, the stages of repentance and then, prior to her death, is forgiven by and reconciled to her husband. This basic morality paradigm of fall and redemption, together with the typical morality emphasis upon the complementary relationship between repentance and forgiveness, not only organizes the structural and thematic movement of the play but clarifies various problematic aspects of the play that have frequently perplexed critics—most notably, the abruptness of Anne's fall and the questionable nature of Frankford's response to that fall.[3]

In the opening scene of the play, during the course of celebrating Anne's marriage to Frankford, numerous characters call attention to Anne's many assets, including her exemplary moral character. Charles Mountford congratulates Frankford on his choice of brides by noting the nobility of Anne's birth, the quality of her education, and her linguistic facility and virtuosity as a musician, and concludes:

> To end her many praises in one word,
> She's beauty and perfection's eldest daughter,
> Only found by yours, though many a heart hath sought her.
> (22–24)[4]

Anne's brother, Francis Acton, describes her in equally idealistic terms as "a perfect wife already, meek and patient" (37). The wedding guests credit Frankford's assets as no less remarkable than his wife's, leading Mountford to observe:

> . . . There's equality
> In this fair combination; you are both scholars,
> Both young, both being descended nobly.
> There's music in this sympathy, it carries
> Consort and expectations of much joy,
> Which God bestow on you, from this first day
> Until your dissolution—that's for aye.
> (66–72)

But the focus throughout the wedding celebration is upon Anne who, according to the testimony of her admirers, would appear to be nothing less than a paragon of virtue: "beauty and perfection's eldest daughter"; "a perfect wife already, meek and patient."[5] That Heywood's play opens with the marriage of the principal characters—that is, where many stage comedies of the period end—would not have passed unnoticed by his audience and most likely would have invoked a sense of tragic foreboding. Similarly, Heywood's audience—most likely familiar with the medieval notion of Fortune and the precariousness of human prosperity and happiness[6]—would have viewed the pronounced felicity of the opening scene and the equally pronounced emphasis upon Anne's perfection as suspect and potentially ironic. Although there is no reason at the outset of the play to doubt Anne's virtue, she, nonetheless, is naive, innocent, inexperienced; her virtue as yet has been untested. As a result, the early claims for her perfection, though appropriate to the epithalamic occasion, are premature and, in fact, within the short space of three scenes, her initial status as the most excellent of women and the most perfect of wives is drastically qualified. Beyond her own inexperience, the primary cause of Anne's fall is Wendoll, whose willful commission of sin and obdurate persistence in that sin provide a revealing contrast to Anne's own fall and ultimate redemption.

Shortly following the festivity of the opening scene, Frankford prefers Wendoll, on the basis, it would seem, of little more than his affability and "many good deserts" to "second place" in the Frankford household (4.26–35).[7] Wendoll himself will later regret his preferment, since it places him, unnegotiably in his estimation, in harm's way, for, much in the vein of popular television drama, he has the misfortune to fall in love with his employer's wife. When he first becomes aware of his feelings, Wendoll vindicates Frankford's earlier estimate of his character by reproaching himself with ingratitude, treachery, and the even more serious moral consequence of being "damn'd without redemption" (6.3). In a series of soliloquies remarkable in their similarity to those of Marlowe's Faustus—and as the editor and possible revisor of Marlowe's *Jew of Malta,* Heywood was in all likelihood familiar with *Doctor Faustus*—Wendoll attempts to control his infatuation. He initially determines to "drive away this passion with a song" but is unsuccessful. He then determines to pray to God, but is again frustrated since, as he observes in a typically Faustian sequence of moral incapability, "Why, prayers are meditations, / And when I meditate—O God, forgive me— / It is on her divine perfections" (6.9–11). He finally resolves, "I will forget her," but his resolution is ultimately ineffectual, and he is forced to powerlessly conclude, "O God, O God! With what a violence / I'm hurry'd to my own destruction" (6.17–18). He expects such destruction at the hands of a punitive, indignant "God of thunder" though he pleads that God stay those "thoughts of vengeance and of wrath" that would, of necessity, exact his "speedy execution." Wendoll's self-debate in this and the soliloquies and asides that immediately follow recalls the morality dramatist's allegorization of the conflict within the human soul between what Sidney later specifies in his *Defense of Poesie* as man's "erected wit" and his "infected will." Such a conflict in Wendoll's case is, of course, directly and literally voiced by Wendoll himself; however, the moral alternatives that shape and define that conflict are so categorically opposed and formalistically drawn that Wendoll's extended self-contention may be viewed as implicitly allegorical. If Wendoll's articulation of his moral conflict is essentially medieval in form, the conclusions he reaches are directly opposed to conventional medieval theology. His apparently helpless surrender to his passion and his accompanying inability to repent deny a medieval emphasis upon free will and the ever present possibility of repentance. Such a deterministic attitude contrasts directly with Anne's eventual understanding of the cleansing and restorative effect of penance and forgiveness. Wendoll's perception of God as an agent of "vengeance" and "wrath" is equally significant since it recalls the Old Testament law of fear and retribution and thus provides a dramatic contrast to the New Testament law of love and mercy signified by Christ and ultimately enacted by Frankford in his unconventional judgment of his wife's infidelity.

Following one final, tortured aside (6.90–99), Wendoll submits to the "fury" that "pricks" him on and, fully conscious of the destructive consequences of his passion, openly confesses his love to Anne. Understandably startled by Wendoll's confession, Anne is amazed not so much by the fact that she is the object of Wendoll's misplaced affection as by his disloyalty and ingratitude to her husband. Anne's immediate concern with the injury to her husband reveals her basic naiveté and inexperience. Anne's own relationship to Frankford has been based on faith, trust, and a voluntary submission to his authority and care. She thus finds it difficult to imagine or accept the violation of trust implicit in Wendoll's present confession, for Wendoll, like Anne herself, has been the recipient of Frankford's generosity and high regard and, ironically, is even appointed as a "present Frankford" in her husband's "absence" (6.79). Significantly, Anne does nothing at this point to discourage Wendoll since she has no intention, nor does she even consider the possibility, if only to reject it, of returning Wendoll's affection.

Wendoll plays upon Anne's amazement, as well as her innocence and weakness as a woman, by fixing the responsibility for his passion and accompanying disloyalty not, as previously, upon some impersonal agency such as "fury" (6.100) or the "swift Fates" (6.101) but upon Anne herself, directly and primarily implicating her as an accessory to his fall:

> Go, tell your husband; he will turn me off,
> And I am then undone. I care not, I—
> 'Twas for your sake. Perchance, in rage he'll kill me.
> I care not—'twas for you. Say I incur
> The general name of villain through the world,
> Of traitor to my friend—I care not, I.
> Beggary, shame, death, scandal, and reproach—
> For you I'll hazard all; why, what care I?
> For you I'll live, and in your love I'll die.
>
> (6.131–39)

Compared to the hyperbole and calculated equivocation of Wendoll's declaration, Anne's response is simple, brief, direct: "You move me, sir, to passion and to pity; / The love I bear my husband is as precious / As my soul's health" (6.140–42). That Anne fails to provide a more decisive coordination of the independent constructions comprising her response signals her related inability to coordinate her loyalty to her husband and her compassion for Wendoll. If naively moved by Wendoll's speech, Anne nonetheless recognizes and explains that her spiritual well-being is directly associated with and defined in terms of her love for her husband, a realization that she will ultimately deny. When Wendoll informs her that he loves her husband no less than before and then reassures her that he intends to use every cautionary discretion, she responds with typical candor and simplicity: "What shall I say? / My soul is wand'ring and hath lost her way. / O Master Wendoll, O" (6.150–52).[8] Overwhelmed by the apparent selflessness, the persistence, and the artfulness of Wendoll's rhetoric, Anne is quite simply at a loss for words. Her sense of impotence is equally evident in her next speech when she remarks:

> . . . O Master Wendoll,
> Pray God I be not born to curse your tongue,
> That hath enchanted me. This maze I am in
> I fear will prove the labyrinth of sin.
>
> (6.158–61)

Critics, however enthusiastic their endorsement of *A Woman Killed with Kindness,* have frequently faulted Heywood for the ease and apparent lack of motivation in Anne's fall. However, Anne herself, at least partially, if not altogether convincingly by more sophisticated standards of human motivation and behavior, explains her capitulation. If not in fact, she has been ravished, or "enchanted," by the artful rhetoric of Wendoll's "tongue."[9] Moreover, she is disadvantaged by the unexpectedness of Wendoll's proposal—for, indeed, he is proposing a second, if illicit, marriage—and is further disadvantaged by her very innocence, which to this point has never been threatened by the possibility of compromise. She is no match, then, for Wendoll's rhetorical virtuosity and insistent passion nor, unlike Wendoll, does she enjoy the advantage of premeditation and extended self-debate.[10] On the other hand, although Anne's fall provides a provocative focus for critical speculation, the plausibility of her fall becomes a null point if one assumes that Heywood was not so much interested in how Anne fell as he was with the necessity that she fall.

For again, no less than the medieval miracle cycle or the morality play, the focus in *A Woman Killed with Kindness* is upon the inevitability of sin and the subsequent rehabilitation of the individual sinner. The means by which such a rehabilitation is effected is, of course, repentance. But the very possibility of repentance presupposes some sinful act on the part of the protagonist. No doubt, for Heywood's purposes, then, it was simply sufficient that Anne fall.

Whatever the tragic inevitability and the questionable motivation of her fall, Anne remains an essentially sympathetic figure and though she does, in fact, enter that very "labyrinth of sin" she had earlier predicted, she does so, it would seem, against her will. Later, for example, when Frankford feigns business in town to confirm his servant Nicholas's report of Anne's infidelity, she pleads, "I hope your business craves no such dispatch / That you must ride to-night" (11.57–58). When Frankford persists in his intentions, Anne requests that Wendoll accompany him. Wendoll, however, is to remain behind, no longer as mere master but as husband in Frankford's absence, a situation that leads Anne to reflect:

> Oh, what a clog unto the soul is sin.
> We pale offenders are still full of fear;
> Every suspicious eye brings danger near,
> When they whose clear hearts from offence are free,
> Despise report, base scandals do outface,
> And stand at mere defiance with disgrace.
>
> (11.103–8)

If Anne is a sinner, she is obviously a reluctant sinner, and her paranoia and emphasis upon the deterministic and irrevocable momentum of sin poignantly underscore the helplessness of her situation. When Wendoll reproaches her for talking "too like a Puritan," Anne further betrays the confused and involuntary nature of her actions, which even now she fails to completely understand:

> You have tempted me to mischief, Master Wendoll;
> I have done I know not what. Well, you plead custom;
> That which for want of wit I granted erst
> I now must yield through fear. Come, come, let's in.
> Once o'er shoes, we are straight o'er head in sin.
>
> (11.110–14)

Anne, initially victimized by her compassion for Wendoll and a corresponding "want of wit," or understanding, still lacks the intellectual resources and the moral insight to discern any solution to her predicament. She can hardly expect assistance from Wendoll, who, completely motivated by self-interest, merely ignores Anne's sense of desperation by observing: "My jocund soul is joyful above measure; / I'll be profuse in Frankford's richest treasure" (11.115–16).

Intimidated by Wendoll and fearful of the consequences should their adultery be discovered, Anne never considers the possibility of turning to her husband. But, ironically, it is finally her injured husband Frankford who saves her. In the typical morality, the protagonist, who has willfully turned his back on God and, instead, has freely chosen a life of profligate indulgence, is ultimately called to account for his sins. Following such a reckoning scene, the protagonist, through the intervention and ministration of appropriate allegorical agents (e.g., Mercy, Knowledge, Confession) is led to reevaluate his life and to recognize, openly admit, and repent his sins, whereupon he is reinstated in God's favor. This pattern of repentance provides the structural and thematic pivot in *A Woman Killed with Kindness,* though the pattern is enacted within an essentially secular or, even more precisely, a domestic context: a context, moreover, within which the traditionally separate roles of agent of reckoning, judge, and agent of ministration are all subsumed by Frankford. In Book 4 of *Paradise Lost,* Milton draws a distinction between the sexes whereby he assigns to Adam "valor" and "contemplation" and to Eve "softness" and "sweet attractive grace." Heywood would no doubt have been sympathetic with such a distinction, and it is fitting, in this respect, that Frankford, given his heightened understanding and his authoritative role as husband, should serve as the primary agent of Anne's moral rehabilitation. However, when he first discovers Anne and Wendoll "lying / Close in each other's arms," he nearly responds with the same impulsive recklessness typical of most of the other principal characters in the play.[11] Outraged by his discovery of the guilty couple, Frankford chases the awakened Wendoll about the stage with drawn sword but is ultimately restrained by a maid whose "angel's hand" prevents his intended "bloody sacrifice." Hereafter, however, Frankford conducts himself with remarkable reserve and reason. He waives the prerogative of bloody revenge to which he is legally entitled and very much like Christ assumes and shares Anne's sin and shame, as he instructs her: "Spare thou thy tears, for I will weep for thee; / And keep thy countenance, for I'll blush for thee" (13.84–85). Frankford's restraint and moral authority are further reflected when he reassures Anne: "I will do nothing rashly. / I will retire awhile into my study, / And thou shalt hear thy sentence presently" (13.129–31). Thus, unlike the conventional morality, in which God passes judgment directly upon an allegorical representative of mankind, Anne is to be judged by her husband. The precise nature of that judgment is soon made explicit when he returns and informs her:

> My words are regist'red in Heaven already;
> With patience hear me: I'll not martyr thee
> Nor mark thee for a strumpet, but with usage
> Of more humility torment thy soul,
> And kill thee even with kindness.
>
> (13.152–56)

The ambiguity of Frankford's proposed "kindness" is clarified when he explains that Anne is to be banished from the household and to be denied any further contact with either himself or their children. Instead she is to live in isolation in a nearby lodging.

Critics have often regarded Frankford's kindness as problematic and, even more extremely, as cruel and excessive,[12] and, of course, from a modern perspective that diminishes the legalistic distance between husband and wife, Frankford's judgment does seem excessive. But Frankford is acting not out of malice, perverseness, revenge, or personal injury but out of a concern for his wife's spiritual welfare. He thus invokes Anne's concurrence with his sentence, "as thou hop'st for Heaven . . . [and] believ'st / Thy name's recorded in the Book of Life" (13.172–73), and Anne herself describes her husband's judgment as "mild" and more than she deserves. The leniency and "humility" of Frankford's judgment is intended to allow Anne sufficient opportunity to negotiate her spiritual salvation by reenacting the ritual of repentance. Had he simply killed her, her soul would have been forfeit, for following the discovery scene she still lacks a proper understanding of her sin and guilt and the necessary means of recovery. In fact, when she first confronts her injured husband, she dismisses the very possibility of her husband's—and, by implication, God's—"pardon":

> O by what word, what title, or what name,
> Shall I entreat your pardon? Pardon! O
> I am as far from hoping such sweet grace
> As Lucifer from Heaven.
>
> (13.78–81)

Overwhelmed by the supposed enormity of her sin and a corresponding sense of shame, Anne, no less than Everyman, Marlowe's Faustus, or Spenser's Redcrosse Knight, is overpowered by a false sense of pride and perceives no other alternative to her situation than despair. Utterly desperate, she thus observes, prior to Frankford's withdrawal to consider her sentence:

> . . . O to redeem my honour,
> I would have this hand cut off, these my breasts sear'd,
> Be rack'd, strappado'd, put to any torment;
> Nay, to whip but this scandal out, I would hazard
> The rich and dear redemption of my soul.
> He cannot be so base as to forgive me,
> Nor I so shameless to accept his pardon.
>
> (13.134–40)[13]

This is a crucial speech since it once again demonstrates the extent of Anne's moral confusion and her inability, in her present state, to effect her spiritual recovery. The honor of which she speaks, though hardly inconsiderable, is essentially a superficial matter of reputation, for the reclamation of which she, without recognizing the paradox of her statement, is willing to sacrifice the "rich and dear redemption" of her soul. Equally revealing is the fact that the essentially mechanical devices of physical torture—more appropriate to Jacobean revenge tragedy than to domestic drama—which Anne proposes as a means of retribution are the very devices Frankford rejects in his sentence. The "kindness" of that sentence, however, consists not in his rejection of physical violence but in his consideration of Anne's spiritual welfare, a consideration that she, at the moment, is incapable of.

That Anne does ultimately recognize and understand her sin within a proper Christian context of repentance and forgiveness is largely due to Frankford's imposed exile, and there are actually precedents for the intended effect of his decision. Christ himself voluntarily withdraws from society prior to his crucifixion and spends forty days in the desert. Early Christian saints such as St. Basil and St. Anthony also voluntarily withdrew from society for purposes of contemplation, mortification, and penance. The beneficial effects of voluntary exile, not the least of which is an enhanced state of moral perception, provide the rationale for various monastic orders as well as various forms of religious meditation that developed during the Middle Ages and the Renaissance. The advantages of solitude are further reflected in those medieval theologians, philosophers, and poets who believed that the surest means of avoiding the moral distractions of worldly pleasure was a complete disassociation from the world. Such an attitude is voiced by Anne herself in the scene immediately following Frankford's judgment when, enroute to her new lodging, she announces to an attendant servant her "farewell / To all earthly joys" (16.73–74). This determination is anticipated earlier in the same scene when she refuses the coach provided by Frankford to carry herself and her belongings; she prefers instead to walk, "being hurl'd," as she says in an appropriate medieval turn of thought, "so low down by the hand of fate" (16.2). Even more revealing than Anne's renunciation of the world is her supplication of her attendants' tears "to wash my spotted sins" (16.30). The intended effect of Frankford's judgment becomes fully apparent here. Compared to her earlier histrionics, Anne's thought and actions are now marked by a measure of composure and self-control suggestive of Frankford himself. More importantly, Anne's previous sense of despair has been replaced by a genuine sense of guilt and the possibility of expiation. The most remarkable development in the present scene, however, is Anne's resolution not only to renounce the world but to leave it altogether by starving herself to death, following the announcement of which she concludes: "But when my tears have wash'd my black soul white, / Sweet Saviour, to Thy hands I yield my sprite" (16.105–6). Anne's invocation of Christ at this point is entirely appropriate since it is accompanied and, in fact, effected by her clarified perception of the possibility of forgiveness. Such a realization, which provides a dramatic contrast to her earlier moral confusion and desperate sense of helplessness, is immediately reinforced when she suddenly discovers Wendoll, who had been following her at a distance:

> . . . O for God's sake fly!
> The Devil doth come to tempt me ere I die.
> My coach! This sin that with an angel's face
> Courted mine honour till he sought my wrack,
> In my repentant eyes seems ugly black.
>
> (16.107–11)

Whereas her vision was previously impaired by her inexperience and, paradoxically, by her very innocence, now, by virtue of her "repentant eyes," Anne perceives the true nature of Wendoll and her sin and directly confronts her conscience. On the other hand, Wendoll, though he feels remorse that he has "divorc'd the truest turtles / That ever liv'd together" (16.47–48), chooses, unlike Anne, to flee the moral consequences of his sin and "to wander, like a Cain / In foreign countries and remoted climes" (16.126–27). As earlier, however, Wendoll, regardless of his remorse, is still essentially motivated by self-interest, for once "these rumors" of his ingratitude have subsided, he intends to return to England where, he speculates, "My worth and parts being by some great man prais'd, / . . . I may in court be rais'd" (16.135–36). This final meeting between Anne and Wendoll bears an obvious relation to the earlier seduction scene. Had Anne known then what she knows now, she of course would have been more than equal to Wendoll's seductive rhetoric. But her present knowledge, no less than that proceeding from the clarified vision of Everyman or any morality protagonist, is made possible only through and as a result of her fall in the first place.

The ultimate effect of Anne's rehabilitation is dramatically demonstrated in the final scene of the play. As the scene opens, Anne, near the point of death, is visited by family and friends, including her brother Sir Francis Acton, who, startled by his sister's transformation, observes:

> I came to chide you, but my words of hate
> Are turn'd to pity and compassionate grief;
> I came to rate you, but my brawls, you see,
> Melt into tears, and I must weep by thee.
>
> (17.63–66)

Frankford himself, moved, as Malby informs Anne, by "your sorrow and your penitence" (17.48), arrives shortly after. Anne's primary concern, upon her husband's arrival, is to secure his pardon, the very possibility of which had earlier seemed out of the question:

O good man,
And father to my children, pardon me.
Pardon, O pardon me! My fault so heinous is
That if you in this world forgive it not,
Heaven will not clear it in the world to come.
Faintness hath so usurp'd upon my knees
That kneel I cannot; but on my heart's knees
My prostrate soul lies thrown down at your feet
To beg your gracious pardon. Pardon, O pardon me!
(17.84–92)

The extended reiteration of "pardon" in the present speech clearly emphasizes the quality and extent of Anne's repentance and recalls her earlier despairing resignation: "He cannot be so base as to forgive me, / Nor I so shameless to accept his pardon" (13.139–40). Frankford compassionately complies with Anne's request, observing that even as he himself hopes "for pardon at that day / When the Great Judge of Heaven in scarlet sits, / So be thou pardon'd" (17.105–7). He then concludes: "Though thy rash offence / Divorc'd our bodies, thy repentant tears / Unite our souls" (17.107–9). Much like the formal sacrament of penance, Frankford's pardon certifies the constructive effect of Anne's rehabilitation—he significantly notes, in this regard, her "repentant tears," which contrast with her more theatrical, though no doubt no less genuine, tears of shame and self-pity following the earlier discovery scene. His pardon also signifies the formal conclusion of that process of repentance reenacted over the preceding scene, for the logical end of repentance is forgiveness. Thus, immediately following Frankford's pardon, Mountford reassures Anne: "Then comfort, Mistress Frankford; / You see your husband hath forgiven your fall" (17.109–10). The timing, then, of Frankford's pardon is not only dramatically effective but theologically appropriate; for Frankford's pardon, had it been administered earlier, would have been premature and ineffectual in his wife's rehabilitation. Rather, Frankford allows Anne the opportunity to earnestly entreat his pardon, and the constructive result of such a strategy is noted by Acton, who had previously censured Frankford's sentence as too lenient (see 17.16–22):

Brother, had you with threats and usage bad
Punish'd her sin, the grief of her offence
Had not with such true sorrow touch'd her heart.
(17.133–35)

The genuineness and pathos of Anne's sorrow are such that not only Frankford but the others in attendance wish to die with her, and it is fitting that, fully absolved of her sin, Anne is reunited to her husband in a renewal of their wedding vows, as Frankford informs her:

> My wife, the mother to my pretty babes,
> Both those lost names I do restore thee back.
> And with this kiss I wed thee once again.
> Though thou are wounded in thy honour'd name,
> And with that grief upon thy death bed liest,
> Honest in heart, upon my soul, thou diest.
>
> (17.115–20)

Circumstances have come full circle. Even as the play opens with the celebration of the Frankfords' marriage, so it concludes with a reaffirmation, though obviously under much different circumstances, of the marriage contract. Similarly, the play ends with a general approbation of those very assets of Anne's character that were praised at the outset. Opening testimonials of Anne's virtue are, of course, mistaken and premature since her virtue, as yet, has been untested. Ironically, it is only through her fall, through Frankford's strategic intervention, and through her own subsequent repentance—or more generally through Heywood's domestication of the fall-repentance paradigm of the medieval morality—that Anne vindicates the admiration and encomiastic praise of the wedding guests in the opening scene and thereby becomes, if only in death, a "perfect wife . . ., meek and patient."

Notes

1. A. M. Kinghorn, *Medieval Drama,* Literature in Perspective (London: Evans Brothers, 1968), 20.
2. Robert Potter, *The English Morality Play: Origins, History and Influence of a Dramatic Tradition* (London and Boston: Routledge & Kegan Paul, 1975), 16.
3. Though the focus in this paper is upon the main plot in *A Woman Killed with Kindness,* the subplot, involving the disgrace and dishonor of Sir Charles Mountford, also incorporates a number of distinctive morality elements, the most notable of which are Mountford's repentance of his reckless murder of Sir Francis Acton's huntsman and falconer; Mountford's fall from fortune and his acquiescence in his resulting "mean estate"; Mountford's mistaken dependence, like Everyman's upon the charity of friends and family; and Acton's own repentance of his persecution of Mountford as a result of his love for Mountford's sister.
4. Thomas Heywood, *A Woman Killed with Kindness,* ed. R. W. Van Fossen, The Revels Plays (London: Methuen, 1961). Subsequent scene and line references in *A Woman Killed with Kindness* are based on this edition.
5. At the outset of scene 4, Frankford himself reconfirms the general estimate of Anne's character, describing her as "a fair, a chaste, and loving wife, / Perfection all, all truth, all ornament" (4.11–12). Later, when informed of her infidelity, Frankford reiterates Anne's many assets, only to conclude, "Is all this seeming gold plain copper?" (7.101).
6. Heywood's play may be instructively viewed in this regard as a domestication of the *de casibus* tradition that informs many popular works of the period, the most notable of which is the *Mirror for Magistrates* which enjoyed seven sixteenth-century editions, the last appearing in 1587. The opening scene, of course, also provides a structural contrast to a second, and more meaningful, exchange of wedding vows by Anne and Frankford at the end of the play.
7. Like the wedding guests' opening assessment of Anne's character, Frankford's assessment of Wendoll eventually proves ironic. In fact, most of the assumptions through the early part of the play are ultimately ironic.

8. Anne's reference to Wendoll as "Master" at this point (she has previously referred to him as "sir") signifies the almost imperceptible but nonetheless decisive change in their relationship and underscores the persuasive effect of Wendoll's rhetoric and Anne's own emotional vulnerability.

9. Anne's brother Sir Francis Acton thus appropriately observes, when informed of his sister's disgrace: "O that same villain Wendoll! 'Twas his tongue / That did corrupt her; she was of herself / Chaste and devoted well" (17.12–14).

10. Various critics have attempted to explain the apparent ease of Anne's fall in more general terms. For example, Hardin Craig feels that Anne's fall is entirely consistent with the common Renaissance view of woman as "strong in passion [and] weak in reason." See *The Enchanted Glass: The Elizabethan Mind in Literature* (New York: Oxford University Press, 1936), 128–36. Hallett Smith similarly contends that Heywood's characterization of Anne was modeled after the fallen woman in the sixteenth-century complaint tradition and that the problematic nature of her fall is satisfactorily resolved in terms of that tradition. See *"A Woman Killed with Kindness," PMLA* 53 (1938): 138–47.

11. Anne and Wendoll are, of course, the most obvious examples of such reckless behavior, though Sir Charles Mountford is equally reckless in killing Sir Francis Acton's huntsman and falconer, an act of rashness that serves as the occasion both for Sir Charles's fall and his own subsequent repentance and moral rehabilitation.

12. For example, see John Canuteson, "The Theme of Forgiveness in the Plot and Subplot of *A Woman Killed with Kindness*," *Renaissance Drama,* n.s. 2 (1969): 123–41; Robert Ornstein, "Bourgeois Morality and Dramatic Convention in *A Woman Killed with Kindness*," in *English Renaissance Drama: Essays in Honor of Madeleine Doran & Mark Eccles*, ed. Standish Henning, Robert Kimbrough, and Richard Knowles (Carbondale and Edwardsville: Southern Illinois University Press, 1976), 128–41; and Howard Felperin, *Shakespearean Representation: Mimesis and Modernity in Elizabethan Tragedy* (Princeton: Princeton University Press, 1977), 151–57.

13. Anne in this speech contradicts her earlier injunction that Frankford defer the use of such violence: ". . . mark not my face / Nor hack me with your sword, but let me go / Perfect and undeformed to my tomb" (13.98–100). In both speeches Anne fails to perceive the actual nature of her moral offense and the proper Christian means of retribution.

The Tragedy of Annabella in *'Tis Pity She's a Whore*

NATHANIEL STROUT

That the most interesting figure in John Ford's *'Tis Pity She's a Whore* is male has become something of an unexamined critical assumption. We have been told, for example, not only that Giovanni is the play's tragic hero, but that the structural importance of the female characters lies in their relation to him, instead of to each other.[1] Even an excellent recent study of the tested woman plot throughout Ford's drama looks less at the consequences for Annabella of being tested than at the way Giovanni adopts the male roles of her tempter, wooer, husband, punisher, and avenger.[2] Yet in responding to the brutal consequences of Giovanni's single-minded desire to unify figurative language with literal action, to make the deed fit the word no matter what the cost, we are surely moved less by what Giovanni says about himself than by what he has done to his sister. That heart on his dagger at the end of the play is hers, after all, not just an embodied figure of speech.

Giovanni's hyperbolic rhetoric, his rebellion against social convention, and the simple fact that he speaks more lines and appears in more scenes than any other character invites our critical attention. But of all the characters in the play, Annabella speaks most often (140 times to her brother's 129). She has fewer lines than her brother, though, because her usual mode of verbal expression is the short phrase of interjection, a response to what others say to her; Giovanni, in contrast, usually talks at length about what he wants. In her first scene (1.2), for instance, twenty-five of the thirty-four times Annabella speaks are one full line or less in length. Of the twenty-six times Giovanni speaks in the same scene, only seven are that short. In fact, no male character comes close to matching Annabella's high proportion of short utterances except for a minor servant.[3] For most of the play, Annabella is a woman more spoken to than speaking.

This relative silence, I suggest, reflects Annabella's social position, not a low level of dramatic importance. Annabella listens to others rather than asserts her opinions, that is, because in Annabella's Parma, as in Ford's England, marriageable daughters were expected to follow the lead of men, especially their fathers and the husbands those fathers approved of. Having been brought up to defer to male authority, Annabella tries throughout the play to please all the men in her life at once—not only her father and her husband, but her brother and her confessor, Friar Bonaventura. As we shall see, her efforts to live up to their conflicting notions of what she should be like are the key to her character and to what happens to her.

Annabella calls what happens a "wretched woeful woman's tragedy" (5.1.8).[4] But to Giovanni, the events are triumphant rather than tragic. And to a character like Richardetto, the drama is one of revenge and divine justice. The multiplicity of generic perspectives makes tempting the apparent clarity of a neo-Brechtian reading like that argued by Jonathan Dollimore for Webster's *The White Devil*:[5] Annabella's being killed despite—or because of—her repeated deference to men reveals the inherent contradictions in the dynamics of the gender hierarchy. Yet such an analysis would not give fair attention to the emotional responses, the imaginative involvement, that even Brecht's plays arouse in performance. I propose, therefore, to investigate the general questions raised by Annabella's personal statement: In what sense is her life tragic? To what degree does the tragedy, if there is one, depend on her gender? "Ford's tragic power," T. J. B. Spencer has suggestively remarked, "often seems to be directed to the women more than to the men. There is a deep sympathy with their emotions."[6] In essence, my goal is to show that in the case of Annabella our sympathy places her and not her brother at the *tragic* center of *'Tis Pity*. Further, I will argue that Annabella's tragedy, perhaps more directly than those of women in other Renaissance plays, results from the expectations placed on her as a woman. It may be worth mentioning here that my use of the plural in discussing the play's effect is not intended to be a male imposition. Responding to *'Tis Pity* as Annabella's tragedy is possible, I believe, for both men and women. But if Annabella is true only to Ford's male fantasies about womanhood, if the shape of the play reflects the limitations of Ford's male imagination, then my similarly limited commentary may be taken as fittingly gender-specific.[7]

Many critics have noted in passing that *'Tis Pity She's a Whore* differs from Ford's other independently composed plays in not being set at court. Indeed, as Nicholas Brooke points out, distinctions of social rank are simply not stressed, especially in comparison with plays by Middleton and Webster.[8] The result is a clearer focus on gender distinctions than would otherwise obtain. A court setting complicates the hierarchy of gender that, along with the political hierarchy, had official cultural status in Ford's day. At court, women can, if their rank is high enough, have authority over men, as do the sisters, cousins, and daughters of the princes, dukes, and kings in Ford's *The Lover's Melancholy, The Broken Heart,* and *Love's*

Sacrifice. But as the Homily on Obedience reminds us, the social status of wives officially paralleled that of children, or servants, or subjects, the status of husbands that of fathers, or masters, or kings:

> Every degree of people in their vocation, calling, and office hath appointed to them, their duty and order. Some are in high degree, some in low, some kings and princes, some inferiors and subjects, priests and laymen, masters and servants, fathers and children, husbands and wives, rich and poor.[9]

According to the Homily on Marriage, the hierarchy should produce reciprocity: the willing submission of the wife should be matched by the forgiveness and forbearance of the husband. One of Sir John Harington's many anecdotes about his life suggests how this dynamic might actually work. Harington says that his wife told Queen Elizabeth "she had confidence in her husband's understanding and courage, well founded on her own stedfastness not to offend or thwart but to cherish and obey; hereby did she persuade her husband of her more affection and in so doing did command his."[10] By obeying, Harrington's wife gains the authority to "command" her husband's love, yet even this mutual exchange of power is based on male recognition of an obligation to an inferior. In the words of the Homily on Marriage, the husband "ought to be the leader and author of love, in cherishing and increasing concord, which then shall take place, if he will use moderation and not tyranny, and if he yield some thing to the woman." Unfortunately, the Homily must acknowledge, "the common sort of men doeth judge, that such moderation should not become a man: for they say that it is a token of womanish cowardness, and therefore they think that it is a man's part to fume in anger, to fight with fist and staff." The result is that "few matrimonies there be without chidings, brawlings, tauntings, repentings, bitter cursings, and fightings." Significantly, although the Homily argues at length that men should not treat their wives with manly violence, it urges women to remain patiently submissive even when husbands beat them.

The Homilies, of course, are merely prominent presentations of a traditional view, also put forth in the many sixteenth- and seventeenth-century domestic conduct books, that informs such "character" writing as Patrick Hannay's poem, *A Happy Husband; or, Directions for a Maid to Choose Her Mate* (1622) and such "domestic" tragedies as *A Woman Killed with Kindness*.[11] Like Heywood, Ford saw the potential for dramatic conflict in a hierarchical model of human interaction, but his more complex analysis dramatizes women's responses to the conflicting authority of male expectations in general, not of husbands in particular. *The Broken Heart*, for example, gets much of its odd power from the multiple loyalties of Penthea—to the man she thinks of as her ideal mate in marriage, to the brother who arranged she marry someone else, and to the jealous husband she does not care for—loyalties that, as Peter Ure has argued, have affinities to husband/wife relations in domestic drama.[12] Penthea rejects adultery:

> I profess,
> By all the laws of ceremonious wedlock,
> I have not given admittance to one thought
> Of female change since cruelty enforced
> Divorce betwixt my body and my heart.
>
> (2.3.53–57)

But the impassioned pleas of Orgilus, her familial affection for Ithocles, and the wifely loyalty she owes to Bassanes drive her mad enough to starve herself to death. In *Love's Sacrifice,* Bianca too is caught between the moral values of her society and her personal desires, only she actively pursues her love for Fernando despite being married to the Duke: "Why should the laws, / The iron laws of ceremony, bar / Mutual embraces?" (5.1.5–7)[13] When first declaring her passion, Bianca juxtaposes the idea of hierarchy with the power of desire:

> Since first mine eyes beheld you, in my heart
> You have been only king; if there can be
> A violence in love, then I have felt
> That tyranny.
>
> (2.4.18–21)

The outcome of the play reflects Ford's practice of portraying the literal consequences of lovers' metaphors: Bianca feels the tyranny of her husband's affection when the Duke kills her. In Ford's drama, love is not so much mutual as hierarchical, women not so much objects of male desire as subjected, willingly or unwillingly, to it. And for Ford, to be a subject is to be potentially a victim.

Whereas Bianca places her personal desires above her society's moral values and Penthea refuses to devalue either her love for Orgilus or her moral obligations, Annabella seems to act with great inconsistency, appearing to be, in Eliot's withering phrase, "virtually a moral defective."[14] First, she commits incest, uniting body and heart while divorcing herself from society. Yet she remains concerned about what others will think: "I would not have it known for all the world" (2.1.50). Then, after she attempts, apparently repentant, to fulfill social expectations by following Friar Bonaventura's advice to marry, she refuses to obey her husband and continues to see Giovanni. Finally, she returns to conventional modes of behavior by repenting the sexual side of her love for her brother. However impatient we become with Annabella, whether for her early moral obtuseness or her later moral conventionality, we should see the dramatic necessity of her double repentance. For her to have completely followed the Friar's directives from the first would have turned the play into melodrama. The conversion from incestuous lover of Giovanni to faithful wife of Soranzo would have been too rapid to be emotionally credible, and the violence at the end of the play would have become gratuitous sensationalism.

Just because *'Tis Pity* is not a melodrama does not, of course, make it a tragedy. Indeed, like most plays written in the shadow of Beaumont and Fletcher, it is not fully explicable in Aristotelian terms. Thus, critics have felt the need either to expand the concept of tragedy to cover not only an individual character but a society at large or to claim "that *'Tis Pity* is essentially a realist play."[15] Nevertheless, the Aristotelian notion that the experience of tragedy involves a combination of pity for someone who suffers undeserved misfortune and fear that what is happening could happen to us helps us understand the importance of Annabella's final self-judgment to the overall effect of the play. For us to feel that characters are like ourselves requires that they judge themselves, at least in part, as we would. The self-awareness can be immediate, continuous, and paralyzing (Hamlet), delayed, concluding, and decisive (Othello), or increasingly frequent and determinedly ignored (Macbeth or Faustus). Without a moment of self-recognition by the tragic figure, though, we can all too easily set ourselves complacently above the drama. We can scorn as foolish blindness what we should pity. We can rest secure in our differences from rather than be made fearful by our similarities to.

The closest Giovanni comes to judging himself as we might is to assert late in the play the primacy of emotional truths over both socially defined and privately held standards of moral judgment:

> If ever after-times should hear
> Of our fast-knit affections, though perhaps
> The laws of conscience and of civil use
> May justly blame us, yet when they but know
> Our loves, that love will wipe away that rigour
> Which would in other incests be abhorred.
>
> (5.5.68–73)

Given a surrounding society corrupted by worldly self-interest, the love between brother and sister, as has often been noted, has an attractive air of innocence about it.

Yet we should not therefore be prepared fully to link ourselves imaginatively with Giovanni. For one thing, like Marlowe's Tamburlaine he repeatedly declares how different he is from everyone else, defying us to feel as he does. For another, he indulges too often in the self-justifying rhetoric of Marlowe's Faustus without voicing Faustus's haunting doubts about his course of action.[16] Most important, the distorted logic of his feelings for Annabella equates mutual sufficiency in love with a solipsistic self-reliance. On the surface, this makes him sound at times rather like the speakers of Donne's lyrics:

> Are we not therefore each to other bound
> So much the more by nature? by the links
> Of blood, of reason? nay, if you will have 't,
> Even of religion, to be ever one,
> One soul, one flesh, one love, one heart, one all.
>
> (1.1.30–34)

> But we will have a way more liberal,
> Than changing hearts, to join them, so we shall
> Be one, and one another's all.
>
> ("Lover's Infiniteness," 31–33)[17]

> O, the glory
> Of two united hearts like hers and mine!
> Let poring book-men dream of other worlds,
> My world, and all of happiness, is here.
>
> (5.3.11–15)

> Let sea-discoverers to new worlds have gone,
> Let maps to others, worlds on worlds have shown,
> Let us possess one world, each hath one, and is one.
>
> ("The Good Morrow," 12–14)

Donne's poems, though, address a woman or women who do not take the hyperbole seriously.[18] Giovanni woos a sister encouraged by ties of familial affection to believe what he says. Donne's poems display not simple masculine self-centeredness, but an inclusive vision: not *I* and *me,* but *we* and *us.* Giovanni, in contrast, ultimately excludes even his sister from "*my* world": "When thou art dead / I'll give my reasons for 't" (5.5.87–88), he tells her before killing her, an act he claims brings him "the fame / Of a most glorious executioner" (5.6.31–33). "There is," in Roger Stilling's words, "no romantic double suicide here."[19] By the end of the play Annabella is not Giovanni's equal in love but the victim of what her brother proudly calls his "rape of life and beauty" (5.6.19).

The end of *'Tis Pity,* therefore, does not have the same effect on us as that of *Romeo and Juliet,* the play often said to have given Ford the models of Annabella's garrulous "tutress" Putana, the friar who tries to help Giovanni, and the young couple in love against parental wishes.[20] The difference in effect, however, results not just from the ways the couples die. Their relationships differ in tone as well. When Juliet wishes Romeo would go "no farther than a wanton's bird, / That lets it hop a little from her hand" (2.2.178–79), Romeo accepts the implicit subordination of his freedom to her control: "I would I were thy bird" (2.2.183).[21] Giovanni's radical redefinition of appropriate behavior does not extend to the relative status of men and women. His language assumes his sister's subjection to his desires: "I envy not the mightiest man alive, / But hold myself in being king of thee / More great, than were I king of all the world" (2.1.18–20). Giovanni may be at the center of the play's action, but he is not at the center of our sympathy. He excites horrified fascination, not compassion.

Giovanni sees the world in terms of himself: what he thinks is right is right. Annabella sees the world in terms of figures of authority: what they wish her to do she tries to do. In this regard, it is important to note that male authority dominates the world of *'Tis Pity* more completely than that of Shakespeare's earlier play. Shakespeare gives Juliet, and Romeo, too, for that matter, both a father and a mother as he sets the affections of the young against the prejudices of the old. Giovanni and Annabella's mother, in contrast, is dead, and Annabella herself, as Putana delightedly exclaims, is at the center of masculine violence rather than familial attention: "here's threatening, challenging, quarreling, and fighting, on every side, and all for your sake" (1.2.63–65). Ford's play, that is, presents not feuding families but feuding suitors, presents a world ruled not by a generation of parents, but by a sex, by fathers, brothers, uncles, and husbands.

In this male-dominated world, Annabella's responses are framed by those of the adulterous, assertive Hippolita, who tries to do what she wants, and the almost utterly silent Philotis, who always does as she is told. Meekly submitting to her uncle Richardetto's plan that she marry the foolish Bergetto and, after Bergetto is killed, to his plan that she enter a nunnery, Philotis represents an extreme of feminine passivity and obedience. Richardetto's wife, Hippolita, in contrast, speaks forcefully and at length about her desires, and her actions match her verbal energy. Appropriately, she first appears on stage having forced her way into her lover Soranzo's private room, unwanted, unwelcome, and undaunted, claiming she is not subject to masculine power:

> know Soranzo,
> I have a spirit doth as much distaste
> The slavery of fearing thee, as thou
> Dost loathe the memory of what hath passed.
> (2.2.42–45)

Appropriately, having been rejected by Soranzo, tricked out of her revenge, and poisoned by his servant Vasques, she dies unrepentant: "Take here my curse amongst you" (4.1.94). The more deferential Annabella dies *praying* for her murderer: "Forgive him, Heaven—and me my sins"

(5.5.91). And she enters the play quietly "above" (1.2.30, stage direction) the action rather than as immediately part of it.

Putana's charge, however, is not as passively obedient to masculine authority as Richardetto's niece. Like Hippolita, Annabella acts to fulfill her sexual desires, albeit with a brother, winning her tutress's enthusiastic, amoral approval: "Your brother's a man I hope, and I say still, if a young wench feel the fit upon her, let her take anybody, father or brother, all is one" (2.1.47–50). And Annabella has some Hippolita-like moments of self-assertion and passion, notably her defiance of Soranzo after they are married: "I dare thee to the worst: strike, and strike home" (4.3.70). But as with Hippolita, Annabella cannot just "take" who or what she wants. As with Hippolita, her assertiveness cannot keep her from becoming a victim of masculine violence. Annabella may defy conventional morality by committing incest, but she is eventually killed by her brother. She may defy her husband, but only by urging him to carry out his threat to "rip up" her heart (4.3.53). Even her defiance—"strike, and strike home"—echoes Giovanni's earlier demonstration of his sincerity:

> And here's my breast, *strike home,*
> Rip up my bosom, there thou shalt behold
> A heart in which is writ the truth I speak.
>
> (1.2.205–7)

Even in defiance, Annabella speaks in a way already associated with accepting the potential violence of another.

In Ford's *Honour Triumphant,* that youthful presentation of courtly, Neoplatonic commonplaces, lovers get the usual advice to "let him, then, subject himselfe to her wil."[22] Giovanni's phrasing, however, is not so much submissive as self-dramatizing. The power he briefly grants his sister depends not on her but on him—on his initiative, on his rhetorical stance. At first, Annabella reacts to Giovanni's rhetoric of desire with disbelief and dismay: "Are you earnest?" (1.2.212); "Forbid it, my just fears; / If this be true, 'twere fitter I were dead" (1.2.220). Not until her brother authorizes thinking about incest by claiming that both "wise Nature" (1.2.236) and "holy Church" (1.2.241) approve does she tell him how she feels:

> what thou hast urged,
> My captive heart had long ago resolved.
> I blush to tell thee—but I'll tell thee now—
> For every sigh that thou hast spent for me,
> I have sighed ten; for every tear shed twenty:
> And not so much for that I loved, as that
> I durst not say I loved; nor scarcely think it.
>
> (1.2.245–51)

Annabella rejects the authority of conventional morality, in other words, by substituting for it the authority of her brother. Not surprisingly, even after the two swear mutual love, she continues to defer to him, answering "What you will" when he asks, "What must we now do?" (1.2.261).

The answer, it seems to me, suggests both Annabella's deference and the eager sensuality her brother has just brought to the surface. But possibly, Annabella is more flirtatious here than submissive, more a leader than a follower.[23] Her deference to male authority, though, is evident throughout the play, not merely with her brother. In fact, Annabella is even deferential toward the female authority of Putana—"Would you would leave me" (1.2.70); "Pray do not talk so much" (1.2.74)—until her brother asks to speak with her privately and she directly commands Putana to withdraw (1.2.172). More tellingly, because she does not know that her father prefers she marry Soranzo—indeed, Florio urges her to send Bergetto a ring promised in her mother's will to her future husband—she asks her father for "freedom" (2.6.46) to speak her mind before forthrightly rejecting Donado's suit on behalf of his foolish nephew: "In short, I'm sure I sha'not be his wife" (2.6.52). That she does not also plainly reject Soranzo has been taken to indicate her contempt for him:[24]

> As ever virtue lived within your mind,
> As ever noble causes were your guide,
> As ever you would have me know you loved me,
> Let not my father know hereof by you:
> If I hereafter find that I must marry,
> It shall be you or none.
>
> (3.2.57–62)

Yet Soranzo does not think her contemptuous here, even though earlier in the scene he recognizes Annabella's mockery: "'Tis plain, she laughs at me!" (3.2.38). Instead of contempt, I would argue, the indirectness of the rejection is one more example of Annabella's impulse to defer to male authority. Annabella, after all, has now been told by her father: "Soranzo is the man I only like: / Look on him" (2.6.127–28). If Soranzo cannot be certain whether he has been accepted or rejected (as is the case, see 3.2.84), and if Annabella's father does not know either (thus Annabella's otherwise odd request to Soranzo to "let not my father know by you"), the prolonged courtship will permit Annabella partially to please three men at once—the father eager for marriage, the suitor anxious for an answer, the brother jealous of her loyalty.

In a later scene, which vividly portrays the potential for violence between husband and wife noted by the Homily on Marriage, Annabella demonstrates a similar pattern of rebellion followed by partial submission to what she thinks Soranzo wishes. Discovering that the wife he expects to be a virgin carries another's child, Soranzo angrily and violently insists on knowing who the father is: "Thus will I pull thy hair, and thus I'll drag / Thy lust be-lepered body through the dust. / Yet tell his name" (4.3.60–62). Faced with his wife's repeated refusal, he ultimately, on the advice of Vasques, dissembles his anger:

> Forgive me, Annabella: though thy youth
> Hath tempted thee above thy strength to folly,
> Yet will not I forget what I should be,
> And what I am, a husband; in that name
> Is hid divinity. If I do find
> That thou wilt yet be true, here I remit
> All former faults, and take thee to my bosom.
> (4.3.133–39)

In response, Annabella prepares once again to be submissive—"Sir, on my knees" (4.3.141)—offering to kneel before the man who claims to be the ideal forgiving, forbearing husband just as she kneels with Giovanni to swear her love in act 1—"On my knees, / Brother" (1.2.253–54)—and kneels before the Friar seeking forgiveness and guidance in act 3 (see 3.6, stage direction). The repeated action underscores the confused hierarchy of Annabella's deference: it is impossible for her to enact the ideal woman for all three men at once. To please the husband, she must betray the brother. To please the brother, she must refuse to obey the husband. To please the Friar, she must stop loving Giovanni and follow his advice to marry.

That she agrees to marry Soranzo is not, however, further evidence of the moral shallowness critics like Eliot accuse her of. Stunned by her pregnancy, she characteristically lets a man in authority tell her what to do. In the scene with the Friar, she kneels, whispers, weeps, wrings her hands, listens, and acquiesces. The Friar talks for most of the forty-odd lines; Annabella says little: "Wretched creature!" (3.6.6); "Mercy, O Mercy!" (3.6.24); "Is there no way left to redeem my miseries?" (3.6.33); "Ay me!" (3.6.39); "I am" (3.6.42). Ronald Huebert has argued that Annabella's character can be explained in terms of her efforts "to reconcile two contrary impulses—her constant devotion to Giovanni even in death, and her conviction that he has led her into a life of sin."[25] But, as we have seen, Annabella agrees to incest on Giovanni's authority, and she accepts here, at least in part, the Friar's ideas on what to do about her sinfulness. Her actions, in other words, are based not on devotion and conviction, but on a deeper impulse to defer to men who ought to be thinking of her best interests—her brother and her confessor.

Not until the fifth act, when, "barred of all company" (5.1.49) by her husband, she is removed from the immediate expectations of others, when she is alone on stage for the first and only time, does Annabella finally judge her past and plan her future for herself. At this point, her third act concern for "*my* miseries" becomes an unselfish concern for Giovanni:

> My conscience now stands up against my lust
> With depositions charactered in guilt,
> And tells me I am lost: . . .
> O, would the scourge due to my black offence
> Might pass from thee, that I alone might feel
> The torment of an uncontrolled flame.
>
> (5.1.9–11, 21–23)

Here, Annabella puts in a conventional, Christian context the imagery her brother uses to describe his unconventional sexual passion: "I have too long suppressed the hidden flames / That almost have consumed me" (1.2.222–23; and see 2.1.4–5). Here, she chooses her course of action, however hopeless, on her own. Rather than wringing her hands helplessly, she writes her brother a letter "double-lined with tears and blood" (5.1.34), a letter at once an emblem of the strength of her penitence for violating conventional values, of the emotional cost to her in adopting them, and of her willingness to sacrifice herself for a man she loves.

On the one hand, Annabella's self-sacrificing self-awareness is dramatically important because it enables us to take Annabella seriously. Her self-awareness means we cannot condemn her for errors we see and she does not. Her self-sacrifice means that we can sympathize with her in ways we cannot with her selfishly self-assertive brother. On the other hand, Annabella's repentance in part merely rephrases her love for Giovanni in the socially approved terms of "that man, that blessed friar" (5.1.24), in part subordinates her yet again to her brother. This final instance of a play-long subordination of self to the wishes and values of others may appear today to be oppressively self-negating. We may well think a play like Webster's *Duchess of Malfi* a better tragedy about a woman.[26] Widowed, remarried, not only childbearing but childrearing, the Duchess is both older and more independent of male authority than Annabella. Where one accedes to her brother's desire to submit to incest, the other disobeys her brothers' injunctions against remarriage. Where one defers to her father's ideas about suitors, her brother's about love, the Friar's about repentance, the other has a strong sense of self: "know, whether I am doom'd to live, or die, / I can do both like a prince" (3.2.70–71); "I am Duchess of Malfi still" (4.2.139).[27] We may wish that Annabella ruled, instead of merely lived in, Parma.

Yet for an author and an audience to whom feminine deference and Christian morality were part of the official culture, Annabella's life can be tragic precisely because of her submissiveness to men. The tragedies of male characters in English Renaissance drama arise out of the tension between the responsibilities for action imposed by their public positions—king, prince, general, important scholar—and their decisive acts, based on private desires and emotions, that disrupt the social order. Even the more sinned against than sinning Lear is, as Kent well knows, a figure with authority. Even Giovanni declares himself king of Annabella and her love. Similarly, the tragedy of Webster's Duchess depends on her being not just a sister and a wife, but a ruler too: "I am Duchess of Malfi still." As such, she makes plans, initiates action, adopts, as she and others are aware, conventionally male patterns of behavior (as in her wooing of Antonio). Like the Duchess, Annabella finds that what society expects of her powerfully conflicts with what she actually desires to do. But unlike the Duchess, she is sister, wife, daughter, and penitent—all roles from which her society, and Ford's, expected passivity and self-sacrifice rather than self-assertion. Even when pregnant, she never acts like a mother-to-be, a role that might have given her a degree of psychological independence.[28]

That Giovanni displays his sister's heart impaled on a dagger, having first "ripped" her open from the womb up off stage (5.6.59), can seem so theatrically extravagant as to invite what a critic has termed "horrid laughter."[29] Yet our earlier witnessing of Annabella's murder prevents even such laughter, should it arise, from devaluing our sympathy for her. Even the Cardinal at the very end of the play sees wasted potential and conventional immorality: "Of one so young, so rich in Nature's store, / Who could not say, 'Tis pity she's a whore?" (5.6.159).[30] But the audience can see more deeply, can see that in death, as in life, Annabella is subjected to masculine ideas, including the Cardinal's, about her value. In *Love's Sacrifice,* because the Duke stabs Bianca, mistakenly thinking her affair with Fernando has been consummated, we feel something like sympathy for a wronged innocent despite Bianca's refusal to repent. In *'Tis Pity She's a Whore,* Annabella arouses pity because she does repent and yet that final repentance—felt so strongly that she writes it out in her own blood—does not, as even today we half hope it might, as might in fact have happened in a didactic melodrama by a lesser playwright, save her from being killed by a man she loves. The fear aroused, in turn, is that like her we can neither live up to the demands and expectations of our society, its ideals, and the authority figures we have been brought up to respect, nor live out our private desires, without significant suffering. Fifty years ago, Joan Sargeaunt argued that between Annabella and Giovanni, Annabella is "the better man of the two."[31] I have sought to show that our responses to Annabella—and hers to what happens to her—depend on her being different from her brother in kind rather than just in degree. Even if our responses do not make Annabella a truly tragic figure, in its treatment of her, *'Tis Pity She's a Whore* gives us a drama about a woman that is particularly appropriate to its historical context, a play shaped by the potential for violence against women inherent in the social ideal of feminine deference to even willful masculine authority.

Notes

1. See A. P. Hogan, "'*Tis Pity She's a Whore:* The Overall Design," *Studies in English Literature* 17 (1977): 303–16; also Richard Levin, *The Multiple Plot in English Renaissance Drama* (Chicago: University of Chicago Press, 1971), 86. The critical emphasis on Giovanni is most obvious, of course, in essays like Kenneth A. Requa's " 'Music in the Ear': Giovanni as Tragic Hero in Ford's '*Tis Pity She's a Whore,*" *Papers on Literature and Language* 7 (1971): 13–25. But Giovanni is given pride of place in most studies of the play; see, among many, G. F. Sensabaugh, *The Tragic Muse of John Ford* (Stanford: Stanford University Press, 1944); H. J. Oliver, *The Problem of John Ford* (London: Cambridge University Press, 1955); Clifford Leech, *John Ford and the Drama of His Time* (London: Chatto & Windus, 1957); R. J. Kaufmann, "Ford's Tragic Perspective," *Texas Studies in Literature and Language* 1 (1960): 522–37; Robert Ornstein, *The Moral Vision of Jacobean Tragedy* (Madison: University of Wisconsin Press, 1960); Mark Stavig, *John Ford and the Traditional Moral Order* (Madison: University of Wisconsin Press, 1968); Dorothy M. Farr, *John Ford and the Caroline Theatre* (London: Macmillan, 1979).

2. Lois E. Bueler, "Role Playing and Reintegration: The Tested Woman Plot in Ford," *Studies in English Literature* 20 (1980): 325–44.

3. The claims in this paragraph are based on my counts of speech prefixes and lines in the Revels edition of '*Tis Pity,* ed. Derek Roper (Manchester: Manchester University Press, 1975). I have not included characters who speak fewer than five times, and I have counted Annabella's fifth-act soliloquy (interrupted twice by the Friar's asides) as a single utterance. For the play as a whole, Annabella speaks for one line or less 69 percent of the time (97/140), Giovanni ony 42 percent (54/129). The only characters who approach Annabella's ratio are the servant Poggio, the only male over 60 percent, at 69 percent (18 of 26), and Philotis, the only other woman over 60 percent, at 71 percent (12 of 17). Both, of course, are in extremely subordinate positions socially.

4. All quotations from the play are taken from Roper's edition, except that all italics represent my emphasis.

5. *Radical Tragedy: Religion, Ideology and Power in the Drama of Shakespeare and his Contemporaries* (Chicago: University of Chicago Press, 1984), esp. 246.

6. See his introduction to the Revels edition of *The Broken Heart* (Manchester: Manchester University Press, 1980), 49. See also Leech's comment that "if we take Ford's drama as a whole, it is his women rather than his men that remain in our minds" (64), an insight that Leech does not develop in his analysis of '*Tis Pity*. The quotation from *The Broken Heart* below is from Spencer's edition.

7. In *Still Harping on Daughters: Women and Drama in the Age of Shakespeare* (Totowa. N.J.: Barnes and Noble, 1983), although she says little about the play (just enough to get Annabella's name wrong [133]), Lisa Jardine makes the related objection that women in the drama of Ford's time are essentially constructs of dramatic conventions, not insightful representations of female psychology. One might also object, as Roper does at times in his introduction, that the play reflects Ford's attention to local effects at the expense of overall coherence. As spectators/readers, however, we habitually seek to impose coherence, to draw connections to our lives, to believe that plays and characters make sense. Authors may try to disrupt our expectations of coherence, but there is no evidence that Ford is doing so.

8. *Horrid Laughter in Jacobean Tragedy* (New York: Barnes and Noble, 1979), 112.

9. Quotations from the Homilies are based on the facsimile edition prepared by Mary Ellen Rickey and Thomas B. Stroup (Gainesville: Scholars' Facsimiles and Reprints, 1968). For consistency, I have modernized spelling.

10. *Nugae Antiquae* (1804), ed. Thomas Park, quoted by J. V. Cunningham in *In Shakespeare's Day* (New York: Fawcett, 1970), 67. The major study of familial relations in this

period is Lawrence Stone, *The Family, Sex and Marriage in England, 1500–1800* (New York: Harper and Row, 1977); see esp. 180–91, 195–202.

11. For discussions of the conduct books, see C. L. Powell, *English Domestic Relations, 1487–1653* (New York: Columbia University Press, 1917) and Louis B. Wright, *Middle-Class Culture in Elizabethan England* (Chapel Hill: University of North Carolina Press, 1935), 201–27. In *English Domestic or Homiletic Tragedy, 1575–1642* (New York: Columbia University Press, 1943), H. H. Adams, who discusses *'Tis Pity* on pp. 177–83, looks at domestic drama in terms of theological and ethical issues rather than in terms of gender relations.

12. "Marriage and the Domestic Drama in Heywood and Ford," *English Studies* 32 (1951): 200–216. Because Ure does not extend his analysis to the broader dynamic of women's relations with men in general, he dismisses comparing domestic drama to *'Tis Pity.*

13. Quotations from *Love's Sacrifice* are from vol. 2 of *The Works of John Ford,* ed. William Gifford and revised by Rev. Alexander Dyce (London: James Toovey, 1869), an unlineated edition. I have added the line numbers.

14. "John Ford," *Elizabethan Essays* (London: Faber & Faber, 1934), 142.

15. For the first, see Larry S. Champion, "Ford's *'Tis Pity She's a Whore* and the Jacobean Tragic Perspective," *PMLA* 90 (1975): 78–87. For the second, see Brian Morris's introduction to the New Mermaids edition of the play (London: Benn, 1968). In the introduction to the Regents Renaissance Drama edition of the play (Lincoln: University of Nebraska Press, 1966), N. W. Bawcutt argues that the play is the joint tragedy of brother and sister. But the two are never a couple in the way Romeo and Juliet are; see my comments below.

16. Thus, Stavig is reduced to claiming that Giovanni "subconsciously knows" he is in the wrong. See his *John Ford,* 117. On the similarities and crucial differences between Faustus and Giovanni, see Cyrus Hoy, " 'Ignorance in Knowledge': Marlowe's Faustus and Ford's Giovanni," *Modern Philology* 57 (1960): 145–54.

17. Quotations of Donne's poems are from *The Complete English Poems,* ed. A. J. Smith (Harmondsworth: Penguin, 1971). Hoy notes the similarities, though not the differences, between Giovanni and Donne's speaker. See his " 'Ignorance in Knowledge,' " 151.

18. See Ilona Bell's excellent "The Role of the Lady in Donne's *Songs and Sonnets*" *Studies in English Literature* 23 (1983): 113–29.

19. *Love and Death in Renaissance Tragedy* (Baton Rouge: Louisiana State University Press, 1976), 271.

20. The most sensible discussion of the obvious parallels and the important differences between the plays is to be found in Ronald Huebert's *John Ford: Baroque English Dramatist* (Montreal: McGill–Queen's University Press, 1977), 79–90.

21. Quotations are from *The Complete Pelican Shakespeare* (Baltimore: Penguin, 1969).

22. *Honour Triumphant; and A Line of Life* (London: Shakespeare Society, 1843), 32.

23. Apparently, several modern productions of the play have presented Annabella as such a character; see Roper, lx–lxi.

24. Roper, 61n.

25. Huebert, *John Ford,* 142. Huebert's analysis, in contrast to mine, stresses psychological rather than social factors. The best account of the difference in values between Giovanni and the Friar, and of the consequences for Giovanni, is now Bruce Brehrer, " 'Nice Philosophy': *'Tis Pity She's a Whore* and the Two Books of God," *Studies in English Literature* 24 (1984): 355–71.

26. This is especially true for feminist critics. See, for example, the admiration for the Duchess in Simon Shepherd, *Amazons and Warrior Women: Varieties of Feminism in Seventeenth-Century Drama* (New York: St. Martin's Press, 1981), 116–18; and Linda Woodbridge, *Women and the English Renaissance: Literature and the Nature of Womankind, 1540–1620* (Urbana: University of Illinois Press, 1984), 259–61.

27. Quotations are from the New Mermaid edition of the play, ed. Elizabeth Brennan (New York: Hill and Wang, 1965).

28. For a brief discussion of Annabella's failure to adopt the role of mother-to-be, see Claudine Defaye, "Annabella's Unborn Baby: The Heart in the Womb in *'Tis Pity She's a Whore,*" *Cahiers Elizabethains* 15 (1979): 35–42.

29. Brooke, *Horrid Laughter,* 124.

30. For the ironies in the Cardinal's final words, see Stavig, *John Ford,* 120, and Brehrer, " 'Nice Philosophy,' " 371.

31. *John Ford* (Oxford: Basil Blackwell, 1934), 186.

Woman on the Jacobean Stage: Type and Antitype

CHARLOTTE SPIVACK

Portrayals of women in medieval and Elizabethan drama tend to be simplistic and polarized, Mary and Mary Magdalene, chaste maid and foul whore. By the Jacobean period, however, female characters become complex, strong, even heroic, such as the comic "Roaring Girls" and the tragic Duchess of Malfi. How and why this change came about has been studied largely in terms of the influence on drama of social and economic factors. I wish to suggest that the significant role of the theater in Jacobean society was in itself a major influence on the perception of women in that period. Just as medieval mystery plays, performed by the guilds under the auspices of the church, ritualistically confirmed the scriptural position on women, so Renaissance dramatic performance in public theaters by professional writers and actors also functioned ritualistically but in secular terms for the society as a whole. With its tremendous popularity the theater, somewhat like modern television, was able to offer a meaningful social and psychological experience for mass audiences. Playwrights were thus able either to confirm or to invert socially sanctioned behavior. Jacobean dramatists began to offer a marginal and even subversive image of women that inverted structural norms without mocking or rejecting them, thus functioning as what Victor Turner has called an "anti-structure," ritualistically reversing accepted social structure. These images of women as acting outside of social norms are presented with both sympathy and admiration, thus functioning as what I wish to call the "antitype."

Turner theorized that culture is a product of the interplay between officially affirmed and officially proscribed cultural patterns. "The normative structure represents the working equilibrium, the anti-structure represents the latent system of potential alternatives from which novelty will arise when contingencies in the normative system require it."[1] Elizabethan drama had clearly affirmed the dominant cultural pattern in its normative structure. Dramatic structure reflected the established doctrine of a divinely sanctioned hierarchical and analogical order. Comedy typically ended in wedding, confirming the sacrament of marriage, and tragedy ended with the restoration of political and moral order. The final speech was delivered by the ranking person in keeping with the principle of hierarchy. Most plays included a negative figure—an outsider or antitype—who was either totally rejected or totally transformed at the end so as no longer to be a threat to the society. To cite a familiar example, Prince Hal *had* to reject Falstaff. The young prince might be merely admonished but ultimately excused for his temporary and playful comradeship with the beguiling fat knight, provided that from the moment he becomes king he recognize the serious moral danger in this relationship. Theft and drunkenness are aberrations that cannot be condoned even as play on the part of a responsible, anointed king.

Although this conservative doctrine had been asserted by the Tudor dynasty as the anchor of their own temporal and spiritual power, it no longer applied to the changing realities of London life at the beginning of the Stuart reign. England, as historians like Lawrence Stone have shown, was in a state of flux. London suffered from the problems of overpopulation, inflation, unemployment, crime, poverty, disease, and juvenile deliqquency. At about this time a subtle displacement begins to take shape in dramatic structure. Over the next two decades, as theatergoers flock by the thousands to see plays, they will find that socially acceptable behavior is no longer depicted with unquestioning affirmation, and that the outsider figure, the antitype, becomes more and more sympathetic. One outstanding example is the prostitute Bellafront, protagonist of Thomas Dekker's *The Honest Whore* I and II, who is presented as morally superior to most of the citizenry and whose career on the streets is infinitely preferable to her marriage. Another example is Moll, the protagonist in Thomas Middleton's *The Roaring Girl,* who outrageously defies social norms but is not rejected for her rebellious behavior. By the time of Moll, the outsider has moved to center stage; Jacobean drama has begun to negate the accepted cultural patterns of Jacobean society.

There had of course always been a certain antagonism between the theater and the civil authorities. By definition actors challenge the established order. Boys pretend to be women; men of low degree dress up and pretend to be princes or nobles. But in order for the drama to function as anti-structure in the anthropological sense, i.e., a marginal social experience that inverts the structural norms, the theater itself must affect a large audience with the impact of significant ritual. In Jacobean London, although most of the public theaters were still outside of the city limits and in spite of a flood of antitheatrical pamphlets, playgoers crowded the theaters at the rate of approximately fifteen thousand a week, with performances on six days for ten months of the year. The collective experience of these thousands was profoundly ritualistic. To all evidence, these audiences found the passionate involvement in the play as moving and meaningful as the divine service, usually more so. Henry Crosse writes in 1603 that

> plays do not only feed the ear with sweet words, equally balanced, the eye with variable delight, but also with great alacrity both swiftly run over in two hours' space, the doings of many years, galloping from one country to another, whereby the mind is drawn into expectation of the sequel, and carried from one thing to another with changeable motions, that although he were unacquainted with the matter before, yet the cunning he seeth in the conveyance maketh him patiently attend the catastrophe; when as at a lecture and holy exercises, all the senses are mortified and possessed with drowsiness.[2]

The theater, then, in its dynamic presentation of a negative cultural pattern, converted that pattern into a meaningful reality for the majority of the London population. Thus the theater did not merely *reflect* change but helped *create* change.

I suggest therefore a closer interaction than has been hitherto recognized between the theater and society in Jacobean London. The players on the stage articulated the ambiguities and contradictions, the shifting attitudes of their society. The statements in the Tudor tracts and homilies about the nature of women and the relationships between the sexes are often totally inverted in the portrayal of women on the Jacobean stage, and *not* for purposes of mocking the inversion. The traditional formula of "chaste, silent, and obedient" as feminine ideal simply no longer applies to women in Jacobean drama. Since the inherited models were no longer rigidly accepted, the ritualistic experience of stage plays liberated the imagination by offering alternative models, thus making cultural innovation possible. In some cases inverted status becomes the structural norm.[3]

One major social type very popular in stage representation was the prostitute. In medieval drama Mary Magdalene represented the mythic paradigm. The fullest dramatic treatments of this important figure were in the late fifteenth-century morality play, the Digby Mary Magdalene, and the early sixteenth-century play, *The Life and Repentance of Mary Magdalene,* by Lewis Wager. Both of these versions didactically demonstrate the fall into sin of the youthful protagonist followed by her mature repentance and salvation. The moral is clear and unequivocal. The whore is wretched and damned, but the penitent whore is happy and saved. Mary Magdalene is thus the "type" of the penitent prostitute. There were over a hundred stage prostitutes in Elizabethan and Jacobean drama. Many reflected the ideal type, while many others simply reflected the social stereotype of the outcast fallen woman. Some are vicious even beyond the demands of the stereotype, like John Marston's Franceschina in *The Dutch Courtezan*. A strong example of the antitype, as she emerges in the Jacobean era, is the portrayal of Bellafront in Thomas Dekker's two-part play *The Honest Whore* (1604, 1608).[4] A complex, dynamic, and sympathetic character, she is not the simplistic type of a reformed whore. Her conversion to honesty does *not* make her happy. Instead the conversion serves to indict the society that categorically, and hypocritically, condemns prostitution and honors marriage, however corrupt.

Bellafront is introduced as a blithe, thriving, successful prostitute, a role that would have been unthinkable a generation earlier on the stage. Singing and chatting with friends and servants in racy, jovial language, ordering wine, donning her complexion from boxes of red and white, she boasts, "I am in bonds to no man" (2.1.328). Her manner and appearance lack propriety, but not vitality. Her cheerful mien is shattered, however, by a visit from a young gentleman named Hippolito, who persuades her with his powerful rhetoric that her profession is vile, that she is "base as any beast" (458), "the miserablest creature breathing" (486). Smitten by this handsome aristocrat, she confesses that she has always wanted to "single out that one man whose love could follow" her (2.1.363–64), and she is stirred to repentance by his smooth-tongued address. She rejects her stunned servants and vows to become honest again. The conventional moral formula would call for her to be rewarded with a happy marriage based on mutual love, preferably with Hippolito, but such is by no means the case. Instead Part I ends with Bellafront's marriage to Matheo, the gallant who had been her first lover. In conventional generic terms the wedding should represent a happy ending, but it clearly does not. Matheo is not an ideal bridegroom. He regards the marriage as entrapment, protesting, "must I sail in your flie-boat / Because I helpt to rear your mane-mast first?" (5.2.512–13) Bellafront does not declare her love for him, asserting rather her scorn for the man who first made her dishonest. The ritual comic ending is thus ironic in its inversion, typical of the anti-structure, reversing audience expectations.

In Part II things go from bad to worse. Already a drunk and a gambler, Matheo becomes a thief and a murderer. He mistreats his wife shamefully in every kind of way, even selling the clothes off her back. When Lodovico, who had known Bellafront earlier, visits her he is shocked at her changed appearance. "I scarce know her for the beauty of her cheek hath, like the moon, suff'red strange eclipses since I beheld it" (1.1.126–29). Furthermore the same self-righteous Hippolito, who made Bellafront reform through his virtuous rhetoric, reappears and hypocritically tries to seduce her back into the trade. Bellafront's proud assertion that she was "new born" on that day when he converted her becomes a hollow mockery.

Matheo, too, is reborn, but in an equally ironic way. When he is released from prison for his crimes, Bellafront asks "wert thou in thy grave and art alive again?" (2.1.1–2), but his freedom suggests to him only an opportunity to "fly high" once more, resuming his old dissolute life. Bellafront generously attributes his unregenerate nature to the prison system: "He's spoiled by prison, he's half damned comes there" (2.1.58). Matheo's profligate ways leave his wife not only bereft of clothing but near starvation. He wears satin while she lacks bread to eat. In her suffering she maintains her honest path, rocky and barren though it is, not as mere patient Griselda; for her spirited nature is not subdued but intensified through adversity:

> That cunning bawd, Necessity, night and day
> Plots to undo me, drive that hag away,
> Lest being at lowest ebb, as now I am,
> I sink for ever.
>
> (4.1.173–76)

Part II ends as ironically as Part I. Matheo is saved from the gallows (doubtless to the disappointment of most viewers and readers) and Bellafront faces a wretched future with him. One is haunted by the disturbing image of her as a carefree whore, engaged in light-hearted banter with her appreciative customers, and cannot but wonder whether her moral conversion has only rendered her unfit to survive in an immoral world. Neither despised nor despicable, Bellafront is sympathetic and heroic, a far cry from the stereotyped prostitute. Significantly she is sympathetic from the start and becomes heroic not because of her reformation but in spite of it. She is thus also a far cry from the type of blissful penitent. At the end of the play, when her father Orlando asks her a series of biting questions about her marriage ("Has he not beaten thee, kick'd thee, trod on thee; and dost thou fawn on him like a spaniel? Has he not pawned thee to thy petticoat, sold thee to thy smock, made ye leap at a crust, . . . ?" [5.2.555–60]), the faithful wife still begs mercy for her errant husband. But the pat ending, abrupt as it is ironic, does not convince the reader that this marriage is a valid sacrament. In pragmatic terms, Bellafront was much better off on the streets; in ethical terms, she in her paradoxical virtue calls into question the moral fabric of the society about her, epitomized in the hypocritical reformer-seducer and the brutal husband. Prostitution is a product of this society, in the context of which the faithful wife as type pales before the energetic whore as antitype. The final scenes of these two plays, set in Bedlam and Bridewell, confirm this judgment through their deliberate anti-structure. The resolution of conflict is parodically imaged through madness and criminality in a mad and criminal society, which convicts and confines its most vital members.[5]

Other examples of prostitutes who function as antitypes within the context of the social world of the play are Frank Gullman in Thomas Middleton's *A Mad World, My Masters,*[6] and the courtesan Jane in his *A Trick to Catch the Old One*.[7] Frank Gullman both exploits and exposes the hypocrisy of her society, which cares only about property. The audience is on her side as she takes advantage of the prevalent vice and greed to further her own ends. When she is finally admitted to "decent" society by becoming "honest," she is then justifiably fulfilling her own name. "What I have been is past," she demurely—and winkingly—asserts, as her tricked bridegroom cheerfully allows that she is "as good a cup of nectar as any bachelor needs to sip at" (5.2.265). Similarly, the courtesan in *A Trick to Catch the Old One* is essentally more honest in the ethic of her profession than is the materialistic world about her. Her repentance becomes totally ironic as lip service to institutionalized fraud. Her marriage to old Hoard only convinces the audience that she is really too good for him.

Not a prostitute by profession, Vittoria Corombona in John Webster's *The White Devil*[8] is a whore as mistress of the married Duke Brachiano. As the title suggests, her role is not only complex but also ambivalent. When she is brought to trial on charges of murder, the evidence against her is but circumstantial. As a result the trial scene serves as a vehicle to reveal her character and also to condemn her accusers. A woman of courage and high spirits, she defies hypocrisy, injustice, and cant. She insists at first that her case not be heard in Latin, but then finds the legal jargon even worse. As she remarks, "This is Welch to Latin" (3.2.48). She throws her accusations back in the faces of her smug accusers and does not hesitate to point out that their *wives* should be on trial as well as she. In her final defense she claims, "Sum up my faults, I pray, and you shall find / That beauty and gay clothes, a merry heart, / And a good stomach to a feast are all, / All the poor crimes that you can charge me with" (3.2.206–9). The play is a tragedy, and Vittoria dies, not by court sentence but as victim of her villainous brother. She dies heroically, however, asserting in her last breath, "I'll tell thee what, / I will not in my death shed one base tear; / Or, if look pale, for want of blood, not fear" (5.6.267–69). Although Vittoria is not a totally admirable figure (unlike her tragic sister the Duchess of Malfi), the major thrust of her role is positive. Energy, courage, and emotional honesty set her apart from the decadent, cynical world that condemns her. Her ringing rebuke to the hypocritical wives whose dishonest behavior is condoned by virtue of their marital status makes its point with the audience in an unforgettable way.

My next example of a new sympathetic revisioning of the social outcast is neither prostitute nor whore, but a much maligned and suffering figure, the old woman accused of witchcraft. *The Witch of Edmonton*[9] by Thomas Dekker and John Ford is based on the actual trial of Elizabeth Sawyer, who was executed for witchcraft. In the play she is depicted as a poverty-stricken woman, alone and defenseless against the cruelty of a society which scorns her. Her first soliloquy (2.1.1–14), more didactic than poetically subtle, is clearly designed to evoke sympathy:

> And why on me? Why should the envious world
> Throw all their scandalous malice upon me?

> 'Cause I am poor, deform'd, and ignorant,
> And like a bow buckled and bent together,
> By some more strong in mischiefs than myself,
> Must I for that be made a common sink
> For all the filth and rubbish of mens tongues
> To fall and run into? Some call me witch,
> And being ignorant of myself, they go
> About to teach me how to be one; urging,
> That my bad tongue (by their bad usage made so)
> Forespeaks their cattle, doth bewitch their corn,
> Themselves, their servants, and their babes at nurse.
> This they enforce upon me; and in part
> Make me to credit it.
>
> (2.1.1–15)

Her accusation is promptly confirmed by the entrance of a country gentleman who orders her to drop the "few rotten sticks" she has been gathering to warm her. When she angrily rebuffs him, he beats her, driving her away without her much needed firewood. In outrage and frustration she wishes she could indeed become the witch she is repeatedly accused of being. Although she is at yet ignorant of the ways of witchcraft, she muses " 'Tis all one, / To be a witch as to be counted one" (2.1.151–52). Not surprisingly the devil then appears to her in the shape of a black dog, offering to become her "familiar."

Later in the play we see the townspeople and country folk in a growing state of hysteria because of certain complaints and problems which they attribute to their scapegoat, the witch. When the fiddler cannot tune his instrument, when the corn does not thrash properly, when the horse becomes sick, all are the result of being bewitched. They set fire to the thatch on her hovel to "prove" the old woman a witch. A justice appears on the scene, offering a few rational words, suggesting that "instead of turning her / Into a witch, you'll prove yourselves stark fools" (4.1.60–61). He tries to speak gently with the irate old woman who denies the charge of witchcraft, but adds "if every poor old woman, / Be trod on thus by slaves, revil'd, kick'd, beaten, / As I am daily, she to be reveng'd / Had need turn witch" (4.1.104–7). "Mother" Sawyer eventually becomes guilty of their charges because of their persecution. She enters into a pact with the demonic dog because she has been driven to desperation by the cruelty of the people about her. Ultimately she is led off to execution, but by then the reader or viewer has learned to blame her poverty and age, along with the brutality of her neighbors, for her unhappy fate.

My concluding example is also taken from real life, but neither rejected like the prostitute nor maligned like the witch. This dynamic female protagonist takes up the cudgel of freedom where Bellafront, Frank Gullman, and Vittoria, bending to social pressure, put it down in favor either of meaningless marriage or the ostracized status of mistress. Whereas Bellafront's lively spirit led her to the trade of prostitution, the somewhat similar personality of Moll Cutpurse in Middleton's *The Roaring Girl*[10] leads her also to the streets, not for hire, but in flagrant male garb. Moll, in complete defiance of social norms, dresses and behaves like a man. The character Moll is based on the actual figure of Mary Frith, who had achieved notoriety in the first decade of the seventeenth century. Born in 1584, even as a child Mary (who came to be known as Moll) had rejected sewing, wishing to exchange her needle and thimble for a sword and dagger. As an adult she refused to go into domestic service, as one of her class was expected to do, and made her way in the world by more enterprising activities such as fortune-telling and picking pockets. She dressed as a man, wore a sword and used it, and is said to have been the first woman who smoked. Once when she was forced to do public penance for some offense, she appeared at St. Paul's tearful and seemingly contrite. It was soon discovered, however, that she had just tippled off three quarts of sack before coming to repent. She lived to a ripe old age, dying about 1660, and it is said that she attended the theatrical performance of the play called *The Roaring Girl,* which is about her.

In the play Moll is portrayed in a wholly positive light. Although the authorities, ecclesiastical and civil alike, deplored the custom of women dressed in male clothing, and although King James had personally forbidden its practice, the playwrights saw fit to present the most notorious example on stage in a favorable way. Moll is portrayed as madcap and merry but chaste. One character affectionately describes her: "Sh'as a bold spirit that mingles with mankind, / . . . and oftentimes / Through her apparrell somewhat shames her birth; / But she is loose in nothing but in mirth" (2.2.174–78). On occasion Moll has to deal with some tough gallants, whom she handles in her own inimitable way. She accepts assignations with them, only to challenge them to a duel at the trysting place, a duel that she always wins. In one scene, when she defends herself with a sword against a particularly ardent wooer, she proclaims rousingly:

> . . . thou art one of those
> That thinks each woman thy fond flexible whore:
> . . . .
> In thee I defy all men, their worst hates,
> And their best flatteries, all their golden witchcrafts
> With which they entangle the poor spirits of fools.
> . . . .
> I'm given to sport. I'm often merry, jest:
> Has mirth no kindred in the world but lust?
> Oh, shame take all her friends then: but howe'er
> Thou and the baser world censure my life,
> I'll send 'em word by thee, and write so much

Upon thy breast, 'cause thou shalt bear't in mind:
Tell them 'twere base to yield, where I have conquered.
I scorn to prostitute myself to a man,
I that can prostitute a man to me.

(3.1.70–71, 90–92, 102–10)

By the end of the play, which is a good-natured, realistic romp through Jacobean London, Moll has awed her associates, aided several young people in distress, saved a few city husbands from blackmail and city wives from lustful gallants, and scared the hell out of her own would-be seducers. But at the end of the play, she is still the outsider. The comedy ends, as comedy must, in marriage, but not Moll's. Another young woman named Mary weds, to provide the necessary ritualistic ending. But Moll rejects marriage for herself:

My spirit shall be mistress of this house,
As long as I have time in't.

(3.1.139–40)

Moll has won the respect of those who came to know her, and she will, one feels, go on doing outrageous things, either in the name of virtue or just for fun, but she will not be entirely accepted by society because she does not have a definite role in that society. She is neither a bride-to-be nor a nun-to-be, not even an aristocrat with an estate to manage. As a free-wheeling young woman of the lower middle class, she makes her living running a tavern. She does not *need* to be a prostitute. Young and able-bodied, she also does not *need* to turn to witchcraft. Yet she does not fit what remains of hierarchical values in 1610. Instead she is very busy undermining those values. If the real Mary Frith were in that audience, she must have felt vindicated. Her image is not held up to scorn but to admiration.

In their sympathy for the prostitute, the witch, and the roaring girl, the Jacobean playwrights not only defended but actually exalted the social outcast. Furthermore, in their dynamic and sensitive presentation of female roles that had been traditionally scorned, they helped to convert those roles into an acceptable reality for the majority of the London population of their time. In plays that functioned as anti-structures, they ritualistically inverted the norms of female behavior. The Jacobean theater therefore was not merely a reflection of social change but an instrument of that change.

Notes

1. Victor W. Turner, *The Ritual Process: Structure and Anti-Structure* (Chicago: Aldine, 1969). My use of "type" and "antitype" is directly analogous to Turner's "structure" and "anti-structure." It differs therefore from the same terms as used in Protestant typology. I am

indebted for this application of Turner's theories to Louis Montrose, "The Purpose of Playing: Reflections on a Shakespearian Anthropology," *Helios* 7 (1980): 51–74.

2. Quoted from Muriel Bradbrook, *The Rise of the Common Player* (Cambridge: Harvard University Press, 1962), 125. The interaction between the stage and the culture in Stuart England has been of concern to many recent critics. I cite the following as representatives of the view I offer here: Steven Mullaney, "Brothers and Others, or The Art of Alienation," in *Cannibals, Witches, and Divorce: Estranging the Renaissance,* ed. Marjorie Garber (Baltimore: Johns Hopkins University Press, 1987), 67–89. "I would suggest," writes Mullaney, "that the Renaissance stage did not merely reflect the larger civilizing process of its times. The destabilizing dialectic between self and other, audience and play, social and psychological constitutions of the subject, which defined the complex theatrical transaction we know as Elizabethan and Jacobean drama, was itself an influential forum."

3. See Turner, *Ritual Process,* 177, 184, and passim concerning status reversal. Montrose argues that the public stage became a site for such challenges to orthodoxies through status reversals.

4. Thomas Dekker, *The Honest Whore* 1 and 2, in *Elizabethan Plays,* ed. Hazelton Spencer (Boston: D. C. Heath, 1933).

5. See my article on this subject: "Bedlam and Bridewell: Ironic Design in Thomas Dekker's 'The Honest Whore' 1 and 2," *Komos* 3 (1973): 10–24.

6. Thomas Middleton, *A Mad World, My Masters,* ed. Standish Henning (Lincoln: University of Nebraska Press, 1965).

7. Thomas Middleton, *A Trick to Catch the Old One,* ed. Charles Barber (Berkeley and Los Angeles: University of California Press, 1968).

8. John Webster, *The White Devil,* ed. J. R. Mulryne (Lincoln: University of Nebraska Press, 1970).

9. Thomas Dekker and John Ford, *The Witch of Edmonton,* in *Stuart Plays,* ed. Arthur Nethercot, Charles Baskervill, and Virgil Heltzel (New York: Holt, Rinehart & Winston, 1961).

10. Thomas Middleton and Thomas Dekker, *The Roaring Girl,* ed. Andor Gomme (London: Ernest Benn, 1976).

The Temptation of Eve

DEBORA K. SHUGER

In his final speeches in *Paradise Lost,* Adam describes his sin as seeking "Forbidd'n knowledge by forbidd'n means" (12.279) and the "folly" of aspiring to more knowledge than "this Vessel can contain" (12.558–60).[1] Now, on the face of it, Adam here refers not (or at least not exclusively) to his sin of eating the apple out of a misguided love for Eve, but to his astronomical *curiositas.* Perplexed by Eve's question whether the stars serve any purpose besides lighting the earth for people (4.657–58), he brings up the subject in his conversation with Raphael. To this the Archangel replies first by offering various theories of celestial motion and then by a stern warning against indulging in the pursuit of useless and forbidden knowledge: "Heav'n is for thee too nigh / To know what passes there; be lowly wise: / Think only what concerns thee and thy being" (8.172–74). The Archangel Michael, Adam's interlocutor in Book 12, confirms this connection between Adamic folly and the desire to grasp the *arcana naturae* in his reply to Adam: "This having learnt, thou hast attain'd the sum / Of wisdom; hope no higher, though all the Stars / Thou knew'st by name. . . . / . . . only add / Deeds to thy knowledge answerable" (12.575–77, 581–82). As in Book 8, astronomical inquiry is juxtaposed to practical goodness and piety. Obviously, this thematic juxtaposition is Milton's addition to the biblical text, but it is not obviously related to his treatment of the Fall in Book 9. How does the desire to know good and evil—to say nothing of uxoriousness—pertain to the desire to understand the workings of the physical heavens?

Milton criticism, on the whole, has not explored this relation. On the question of forbidden knowledge, scholars have pointed out that Adam and Eve's interest in heavenly mechanics inclines toward the sin of intellectual curiosity and thus falls under the commonplace Renaissance prohibition of seeking abstruse and irrelevant information instead of a knowledge useful for daily life and the exercise of virtue. A. O. Lovejoy thus characterizes Milton's position as "pragmatic, in the most vulgar sense of that ambiguous term, the sense in which it designated an obscurantist utilitarianism hostile to all disinterested intellectual curiosity and to all inquiry into unsolved problems about the physical world."[2]

Subsequent critics have tempered this harsh conclusion, claiming that Milton does not condemn astronomy or natural science, but merely the desire for useless knowledge. According to Dennis Burden, "God is forbidding Man that sort of knowledge which turns out to be (for him) uncertain, fruitless, and which does not forward human happiness."[3] Similarly, Howard Schultz finds Raphael's comments to be "an orthodox caution against trivial speculation,"[4] and Joseph Summers observes that "there is more evidence here that Raphael is warning against the pursuit of overly 'curious' philosophical and theological knowledge than that he is warning against a too anxious devotion to scientific inquiry."[5]

Yet this does not explain why Adam and Eve's interest in astronomical matters—an interest manifested while they remain "yet sinless" and one not overtly connected to the eating of the apple in Book 9—should occupy such a prominent place in the poem, by the end intrinsic to the longing for "forbidd'n knowledge" that constitutes the essence of sin.

A clue to the relationship between the temptation and astronomy is suggested in Carlo Ginzburg's "High and Low: The Theme of Forbidden Knowledge in the Sixteenth and Seventeenth Centuries." Ginzburg notes that the prohibition against searching into the *arcana naturae,* symbolized by astronomy, remains closely intertwined with the prohibition against searching into the *arcana Dei:* knowledge of "high" things is forbidden knowledge.[6] That is, as Raphael says, Adam's curiosity about the stars is misguided not only because such knowledge is useless but because "Heav'n is for thee too high" (8.172). So Satan tells Eve that by eating the forbidden fruit he had learned "to trace the ways / Of highest Agents" (9.682–83). The desire to know about the physical heavens relates to the desire to "be as Gods" (9.708) inasmuch as both are attempts to gain knowledge of that which is "too high" for man.[7]

What is this "high" knowledge? One answer is suggested by an apparent similarity between Milton's depiction of the temptation of Eve and Aristotle's account of the genesis of philosophy in the *Metaphysics.* If this similarity is more than accidental, it would seem to imply that "high" knowledge, forbidden knowledge, is the divinizing wisdom Aristotle, like Plato before him, holds out as the goal and justification of the ancient philosophic enterprise. Aristotle discusses this divinizing wisdom in connection with his treatment of the origins of philosophizing in the second chapter of the *Metaphysics.* We can begin by setting out this argument and then examine its relation to the temptation of Eve.

Wisdom, Aristotle writes, is the "science that investigates the first principles and causes" (982b10) and "God is thought to be among the causes of all things and to be a first principle" (983a10).[8] It begins with wonder, for "it is owing to their wonder that men both now begin and at first began to philosophize" (982b12). They started by wondering about "obvious difficulties" (982b12), for example, "automatic marionettes" (983a15), and "then advanced little by little and stated difficulties about the greater matters, that is, about the phenomena of the moon and those of the sun and stars" (982b15–16), and finally about "the genesis of the universe" (982b17). Such people pursued this knowledge "in order to know, and not for any utilitarian end" (982b21). Since this knowledge is "beyond human power" it might be thought that the "divine power" would be jealous of men who strove to attain wisdom; but "the divine power cannot be jealous." Yet "this science alone is, in two ways, most divine. For the science which it would be most meet for God to have is a divine science, and so is any science that deals with divine objects" (982b30–983a7). In the *Nicomachaean Ethics,* Aristotle expands upon this final point: in itself, the contemplative or philosophic life

> would be too high for man; for it is not in so far as he is man that he will live so, but in so far as something divine is present in him. . . . But we must not follow those who advise us, being men, to think of human things, and being mortal, of mortal things, but must, so far as we can, *make ourselves immortal,* and strain every nerve to live in accordance with the best thing in us (10.7.1177b25–35; my italics).

For the sake of convenience, we may distinguish seven points here. Wisdom is (1) the knowledge of causes and first principles, including God; (2) it begins with small questions, like that about some sort of mechanical puppet; (3) and progresses to questions about astronomical phenomena; (4) and the genesis of the universe; (5) it is not utilitarian; (6) the gods or God is not jealous of human wisdom; (7) but such wisdom is divine and divinizes its practitioners. Now, of these seven points, all but the third and fifth, that is, those concerning astronomy and useful knowledge, occur prominently in Satan's temptation of Eve in Book 9. The two omitted there are precisely those that constitute the discussion of "high" knowledge in the conversation between Raphael and Adam in Book 8. But these issues belong to the same Aristotelian matrix as those operative in the temptation scene.

Let us now look more closely at that episode. At the beginning of his temptation, Satan addresses Eve: "Wonder not, sovran Mistress" (9.532). The term *wonder* is crucial here. For Milton uses the word in two nearly opposite senses to denote the relationship of the perceiving creature to the divine creation. On the one hand, wonder is identical to religious awe, the perception of the Creator in and behind the universe. Milton thus speaks of "wonder" throughout *Paradise Lost* to signify the correct response both of men and angels to God and his works.[9] On the other hand, the repetition of "wonder" and related terms during Eve's temptation suggests something quite different. Milton insists upon Eve's wonder at the serpent's voice; she remarks "such wonder claims attention due" (9.566); she is "much marvelling" (9.551), "not unamaz'd" (9.552), "more amaz'd" (9.614). This is Aristotelian wonder, a wonder born of ignorance that initiates the process of questioning—whether about "automatic marionettes" or talking snakes. Calvin explicitly connects "wonder" in this second sense to Eve's reaction to the serpent: "Eve perceived it [the serpent's speech] to be extraordinary, and on that account received with the greater avidity what she admired."[10] In fact, as Summers notes, Milton himself employs almost the same pun in the dialogue on astronomy in Book 8.[11] Adam tells Raphael that when he beholds how all the stars seem to serve no other purpose than to light the earth, "reasoning I oft *admire,* / How nature wise and frugal could commit / Such disproportions" (8.25–27; italics mine). The angel replies, "that such matters "the great Architect / Did wisely to conceal, and not divulge / His secrets to be scann'd by them who ought / Rather *admire*" (8.72–75; italics mine). Admiration (or wonder), as Adam uses it and as it is used in the temptation scene, springs from a deficiency of insight into the reason or nature of an event. Whereas in Raphael's sense admiration accompanies awe, in this Aristotelian sense it gives birth to curiosity.

The psychology of wonder in the *Metaphysics* corresponds to Eve's wonder at the serpent, which Satan utilizes to entice her into the more difficult questions of God's justice and goodness. Her wonder is in this sense her baptism into the philosophic quest, whose goal, both for Aristotle and our first parents, is divinization through wisdom. By line 650, Eve has already adopted a distinctly philosophical vocabulary; the fruit is "Wondrous indeed, if cause of such effects." This concern for causation reappears in the crucial passage in which Satan makes explicit the *kind* of knowledge bestowed by the forbidden fruit.

> O Sacred, Wise, and Wisdom-giving Plant,
> Mother of Science, Now I feel thy Power
> Within me clear, not only to discern
> Things in thir Causes, but to trace the ways
> Of highest Agents, deem'd however wise.
>
> (9.679–83)

Satan's description of wisdom as the knowledge of causes and highest agents corresponds to Aristotle's definition of the same as knowledge of "the first principles [which include God] and causes." Furthermore, while the definition of wisdom as knowledge of divine things is a commonplace in the Renaissance and before, the inclusion of knowledge of causes seems to have been distinctively Aristotelian.[12]

After Eve has wondered about her talking serpent, Satan leads her on to more difficult matters. There may be a brief reference to the Aristotelian topics of astronomy and utility in 9.602–5, where Satan tells Eve that after eating the apple, "Thenceforth to Speculations high or deep / I turn'd my thoughts, and with capacious mind / Consider'd all things visible in Heav'n, . . ." Such speculations are not the lowly wisdom Raphael commends to Adam but resemble Aristotle's knowledge desired for its own sake rather than for any practical purpose. The "things visible in Heav'n," in turn, suggests astronomical topics. But Satan then leads Eve to consider Aristotle's final difficulty: the genesis of the universe and particularly her own origins.

> The Gods are first, and that advantage use
> On our belief, that all from them proceeds;
> I question it, for this fair Earth I see,
> Warm'd by the Sun, producing every kind,
> Them nothing.
>
> (9.718–22)

Once Satan has insinuated that the cause and first principle of the universe is not divine but natural, he proceeds to the next Aristotelian topic—the jealousy of God.

Like Aristotle, Milton's Satan rejects the notion that God or the gods will envy man's self-acquired knowledge: "Or is it envy, and can envy dwell / In heav'nly breasts?" (9.729–30). In fact, Satan attempts to have it both ways, for he earlier insinuates that God does envy human happiness and excellence and is therefore not worthy of being obeyed: "Why then was this forbid? Why but to awe, / Why but to keep ye low and ignorant, / His worshippers" (9.703–5). God might be thought to be envious, for, like Aristotle's divine science, the knowledge of good and evil (Satan claims) makes it possible to "be as Gods." Nowhere do the deliberate differences between the Greek and Protestant views of reason appear more strikingly than in Milton's transformation of the goal of classical philosophy—the divinization of man through knowledge—into the primary impulse behind human sin. Eve, like Aristotle, associates wisdom with deification; she eats with "expectation high / Of knowledge, nor was God-head from her thought" (9.789–90). Or as she tells Adam, the forbidden fruit is "of Divine effect / To open Eyes, and make them Gods who taste" (9.865–66). The question for Milton—both here and in Adam's dialogue with Raphael—as well as for Aristotle, is whether or not man should seek a knowledge appropriate to his creaturely status, or whether, by seeking a knowledge of highest things, strive ultimately to be conformed to the object of his quest. Both understand that the knowledge philosophy offers is not quite suitable for mortals. Aristotle insists that the happiest and best human life centers on the contemplative search for divine and divinizing science. Michael, in his final speech to Adam, scorns the attempt to acquire such wisdom (12.575–81); and even before the Fall, Raphael insists that it is largely unsuitable for man, whose virtue is to remain content with the knowledge appropriate to human life and its obligations. Immediately following Adam's fall, Milton explicitly links the biblical temptation to be as God with this Greek effort to wrest divinity through knowledge by a brief allusion to the Platonic image of man's ascent: "They swim in mirth, and fancy that they feel / Divinity within them breeding wings" (9.1009–10).

While Milton adheres to the language of Scripture, he nevertheless incorporates into the temptation of Eve most of the major topics Aristotle treats in his definition of metaphysics: the role of wonder in stimulating curiosity, the inclusion of a knowledge of causes as part of the highest wisdom, the possibility that the gods could envy man such knowledge, and the end of philosophy as transformation into "Gods, or Angels Demigods" (9.937). The other Aristotelian topics, astronomy and utility, also occur in *Paradise Lost,* but in the earlier conversation between Adam and Raphael. These issues are intimately related to the temptation, for both pertain to the critique of the divinizing wisdom that forms the justification for classical philosophy. For Aristotle, the stars are divine, and astronomy is thus not so much a branch of physical science as a stage in the journey of the mind to divinity; as he writes in *The Parts of Animals,*

> Of substances constituted by nature some are ungenerated, imperishable, and eternal, while others are subject to generation and decay. The former are excellent and divine, but less accessible to knowledge. . . . [But] the scanty conceptions to which we can attain of celestial things give us, from their excellence, more pleasure than all our knowledge of the world in which we live.[13]

Milton's apparent dismissal of astronomy in *Paradise Lost* has far less to do with his attitude toward natural science than his criticism of the classical ideal of the mind's contemplative ascent to the divine—as opposed to the descent of God to man in revelation.[14]

But the matter is too complex to be left here. In the remainder of this paper I want first to traverse briefly the two millenia between Aristotle and Milton in order to indicate the antecedents and implications of Milton's rejection of classical philosophy, and second to suggest that the antinomies in *Paradise Lost* are not so simple as my argument thus far would allow.

The significance of forbidden knowledge in Milton is sharply etched in the contrast between classical and Protestant anthropology. Classical philosophy emerges from the acute consciousness of human longing and unrest. To that longing the Greeks gave the name Eros, explaining that man possessed a composite nature—an earthly and hence evil body imprisoning a spark of the divine being. This spark or spirit yearns to return to its heavenly home, and this yearning or love is its Eros.[15] This philosophic eros expresses itself initially as wonder or questioning about the source (*archē*) of reality and specifically of one's own being, for in becoming conscious, man becomes aware that he is not *causa sui*.[16] Classical man "discovers his specific humanity as that of a questioner."[17] Thus for Aristotle, wonder and the desire to know characterize all men, each to the degree that his inner divine nature becomes luminous as an urgent mysterious force that moves him to question and search. For Plato and Aristotle, this longing unrest in search of knowledge contains within itself its own comforting answer: man is moved to seek for his origin by the divine origin of which he is in search, for man's longing is precisely his response to the magnetic attraction of the divine, which, as Aristotle said, moves by being loved. Philosophy in the classical sense is "man's responsive pursuit of his questioning unrest to the divine source that has aroused it."[18]

As Anders Nygren showed many years ago, the classical doctrine of the philosophic Eros was imported through Augustine into the mainstream of Catholic thought. For Augustine, the Christian way *to* God is Eros; that is, the ascent of the soul fired by love to the divine. And while grace is necessary for man to ascend on "the wings of Caritas," the end remains "the ascent of Caritas to God."[19] The Augustinian notion of grace as the infused love that makes our ascent possible—the former existing for the sake of the latter—constitutes the basis of Catholic soteriology. And it is this notion of man's ascent to God through love that was so vehemently rejected by the reformers as inimical to the Christian's passive and trusting reliance upon God's good will.

The source of Milton's identification of metaphysics (which Aristotle terms theology) with original sin lies in the writings of the reformers. Luther sharply criticizes Aristotle for minimizing the total corruption of fallen man or, in his words, "the whole of Aristotle is to theology as darkness to light."[20] In his commentary on Genesis, Luther concedes that philosophers may discover the formal and material causes of things, but human wisdom is unable to penetrate either efficient or final causes; hence, Aristotelian teleology is nonsense.[21] But if final and efficient causes lie hidden from reason, then the whole classical project—which arises from the awareness of one's ignorance of the "whence" and "whither" of existence—becomes impossible. For Luther, natural theology is a wasted enterprise and inherently sinful; it is "the practical wisdom of the flesh which is hostile to God."[22] And by philosophy Luther does not mean abstruse scholasticism but qutie simply reason's judgment of what seems right and good. For once reason presumes the authority to seek what it thinks good, it rejects God's revealed judgment in order to find salvation in its own wisdom. In this desire to trust in reason rather than revelation lies the source of all rebellion against God.[23] In his own analysis of the Fall, Luther remarks that idolatry is simply the individual's worship of what appears good or holy to him.[24] When Adam and Eve were not satisfied with the knowledge they had been granted, but longed to know God outside his self-disclosure, they fell. Reason itself in its characteristic function of aspiring to all knowledge and all power (for individuals think they ought to do what reason dictates) rebels against God.

Even more clearly than in Luther, right and wrong for Calvin reduce to obedience versus reason. The tree of knowledge, Calvin writes, was prohibited so that man "might not seek to be wiser than became him, nor by trusting to his own understanding, cast off the yoke of God, and constitute himself an arbiter and judge of good and evil."[25] Man becomes "wise only by his obedience."[26] The devil succeeds in corrupting Eve by encouraging her to seek the cause of the prohibition; that is, Satan makes man fall by insinuating that God need not be obeyed except insofar as the reason of his command is understood.[27]

To claim that either Milton or Protestant tradition in general flatly identified philosophy with Satan would, however, be as gross an oversimplification as the reduction of Milton's concept of forbidden knowledge to astronomical trivia. In both, a profound tension exists between the vertical impulse native to all Eros-based philosophies and the horizontal, social virtues emphasized by the reformers. In Milton these tensions appear most visibly in Raphael's conversation with the unfallen Adam. On the one hand, the angel insists that the proper use of reason lies in obedient virtue and the proper use of love in domestic happiness. Yet juxtaposed to this antimetaphysical stance, one sees that Milton takes pains to insist that Adam *can* ascend to the vision of God both through contemplation of his works and through Eros. Adam thus thanks Raphael for showing him "the scale of Nature . . . whereon / In contemplation of created things / By steps we may ascend to God" (5.510–12). In Book 8 Adam responds to the angel: "love thou say'st / leads up to Heav'n, is both the way and guide" (8.612–13). Both with respect to knowledge and love, one notes the conflicting pulls of a vertical against a horizontal ideal. These tensions, however, belong exclusively to the prelapsarian state; once Adam and Eve fall, all talk of man's ascent to God—by merit, knowledge, or love—ceases.

These contrary estimates of human nature and destiny also occur in the effort of the reformers to find a place for the classical ideal of humanity within a Christian universe. Unable to dismiss the Greek's assertion of the dignity of human nature properly exercised in the schools of virtue and knowledge, Luther and Calvin identify this *homo classicus* with prelapsarian man. Unfallen man becomes a classical philosopher. Before the Fall, Calvin argues, man mounted up even to God and eternal bliss; but "hence the great obscurity faced by the [classical] philosophers, for they were seeking in a ruin for a building."[28]

The incongruity between the old moral drawn from Adam's fall, "*Noli altum sapere,*" and the hellenization of the state of innocence imparts a real sadness to these discussions, including Milton's, of prelapsarian man. On the one hand, man's upward potential is so great, on the other, this urge to self-divinization precipitates his fall. Raphael's speech to Adam has posed so many critical problems precisely because it is not unambiguous, as the Protestant tradition of the state of innocence is not.

For it was one of Luther's fundamental insights that the best in man could lead him to hell as effectively as the worst; and with that insight he cut the links between man's innate desires and their supernatural fulfillment. That is, for the classical and Catholic philosophers, man's longing for knowledge is the response of his Eros to the divine; insofar as all men desire happiness, they desire God. There exists an ontological bond between our innate yearnings and their divine ground, as if God were pulling us up to himself by a chain. Once this chain breaks, as it does in Protestant thought, human desire becomes inherently neutral; or, to put it another way, the *same* desires become good or bad insofar as they are performed out of obedience to God or to self. This is a difficult idea, but essential for grasping the extraordinary variation Milton plays on the temptation motif in Adam's retelling of his initial memories of his own creation.

In exploring the similarities between the *Metaphysics* and Satan's temptation of Eve, we noted the progress from an initial wonder to a search for knowledge of first principles and causes, especially the causes of one's own being, and thence to a divine science that attempts to understand the ways of highest Agents. Wonder, investigation of causes, and theology mark both the stages of the ascent to metaphysics and of Eve's descent into infidelity, self-reliance, and disobedience. It is remarkable, then, to discover that this same triple movement can be readily discerned in Adam's account of his creation:

> Straight toward Heav'n my wond'ring Eyes I turn'd,
> And gaz'd a while the ample Sky. . . .
> . . . .
> But who I was, or where, or from what cause,
> Knew not. . . .
> . . . .
> . . . Thou Sun, said I, fair Light,
> And thou enlight'n'd Earth, so fresh and gay,
> Ye Hills and Dales, ye Rivers, Woods, and Plains
> And ye that live and move, fair Creatures, tell,
> Tell, if ye saw, how came I thus, how here?
> Not of myself; by some great Maker then,

> In goodness and in power preeminent;
> Tell me, how may I know him, how adore,
> From whom I have that thus I move and live,
> And feel that I am happier than I know.
>
> (8.257–58, 270–71, 273–82)[29]

What Adam describes here is the classical experience of reason. For Adam the wondering spirit seeks to know God in order to adore Him; Eve will seek the same knowledge to become His equal. Yet this obvious ethical difference in some ways is not as significant as the fact that Milton chooses to portray both experiences as structurally the same, a sameness underlined by a curious verbal echo: immediately after the lines quoted above, Adam falls asleep and dreams that a divine being leads him to Paradise, where he sees trees that, laden with "fairest Fruit, that hung to the Eye / Tempting, stirr'd in me sudden appetite / To pluck and eat; whereat I wak'd . . ." (8.307–9), the sequence "Tempting," "pluck," "eat" proleptically representing Eve's fatal act: "she pluck'd, she eat" (9.781). The verbal and thematic connections between Adam's awakening and Eve's transgression suggest some psychological and/or ontological likeness between original worship and original sin. The next question, then, concerns the implications of this similarity. What does it mean to say that the classical experience of reason lies behind our first consciousness and love of God and behind our rebellion against Him?

In medieval theology, the classical experience of reason reappears in the concept of the *synteresis,* "an inextinguishable spark of goodness . . . a natural point at which every man, even if he did not consciously choose to be so, was conformed to God. Here was a residue of man's prefallen . . . purity—now experienced as pangs of conscience and an irrepressible desire for truth and goodness."[30] Classical reason and the medieval *synteresis* are both inherently theological; they imply that man by nature desires God above all else.

In Luther and Calvin the doctrine of the *synteresis* becomes profoundly ambiguous, for in both this innate love of truth and goodness becomes the psychological ground of man's perdition as well as his salvation. Both are aware, as is Milton, that it is the best in us, our highest faculties and aspirations, that damn us—not just our animal nature. In an early sermon Luther thus agrees that the *synteresis* makes man's redemption possible, but adds that precisely this innate desire for God also leads men into damnation, for "the wisdom of the flesh, following the *synteresis,* can erect a contrary means of salvation."[31] "Is it not ironic," Luther comments, "that sinners are punished by their very will for salvation and fear of damnation, that is, by that very will in which they are conformed to God?"[32] It follows that true religion rests only on obedience to God's commandments. Calvin likewise denies that Man's innate love of God has any necessary connection with redemption. Since the Fall, our love is not a response of the divine within us to the Divinity without, but natural man's groping efforts to assuage his fears by projecting a Being to authorize his vanity and presumption.[33] The old indwelling divinities, Ideas, sparks have departed and with them the guarantee that the object of our spiritual longing bears any relation to the true God. Thus in Milton's Eve we see a desire for basically good and spiritual things perverted into original sin. Milton emphasizes the overriding importance of obedience by paralleling Adam's discovery of his Maker with Eve's rejection of hers. Both are expressions of the *synteresis,* but that desire, not coupled with adherence to the Word, precipitates her into idolatry.

This awareness of the ambiguities in human reason lies behind Milton's "anti-intellectualism." Like Luther and Calvin, he knows the seductive appeal of the contemplative ideal where through love and knowledge man ascends to God. In Raphael's discourse and Adam's creation, Milton honors the classical (and medieval) notion of reason as the road by which human love and wonder reach their heavenly fulfillment. Yet Raphael and Michael will also emphatically restrict human aspiration to the merely useful and confine heavenly wisdom to revelation. And in Eve's fall one sees the Satanic potential of man's thirst for knowledge, in Adam's the perversion of the amorous ascent from marital love to divinization. In both instances the moral ambiguity of the experiences themselves—there is nothing wrong with desiring wisdom or loving one's spouse—emphasize that Protestant sense of the isolation of the psyche from participation in the divine life and the concomitant centrality of literal adherence to the Word. Hence, in *Paradise Lost* classical philosophy becomes forbidden knowledge because it replaces trust in the Word with trust in one's own reason, and even in the state of innocence, reason can carry man both to God and the devil.[34]

Notes

1. All quotations from *Paradise Lost* are taken from *John Milton: Complete Poems and Major Prose,* ed. Merritt Y. Hughes (New York: Odyssey Press, 1957).

2. Arthur O. Lovejoy, "Milton's Dialogue on Astronomy," in *Reason and the Imagination: Studies in the History of Ideas, 1600–1800,* ed. J. A. Mazzeo (New York: Columbia University Press, 1962), 142. Lovejoy also argues that Milton "violently introduced" the astronomical passages for theological reasons: "It was a derivative of the same primitive conception of a 'jealous' deity, fearful lest his human creatures should, through *hybris,* become forgetful of their inferiority and seek to exercise powers reserved for himself" (141).

3. Dennis H. Burden, *The Logical Epic: A Study of the Argument of Paradise Lost* (Cambridge: Harvard University Press, 1967), 121.

4. Howard Schultz, *Milton and Forbidden Knowledge,* MLA Revolving Fund Series, 17 (New York: Modern Language Association, 1955), 176.

5. Joseph H. Summers, *The Muse's Method: An Introduction to Paradise Lost* (Cambridge: Harvard University Press, 1962), 175. See also Irene Samuel, *Plato and Milton,* Cornell Studies in English, 35 (Ithaca: Cornell University Press, 1947), 110.

6. Carlo Ginzburg, "High and Low: Forbidden Knowledge in the Sixteenth and Seventeenth Centuries," *Past and Present* 73 (1976): 32.

7. Eve's dream thus conjoins spatial "highness" and the temptation to be "a Goddess, not to Earth confin'd, / But sometimes in the Air, as wee, sometimes / Ascend to Heav'n . . ." (5.78–80). So she dreams that she "Could not but taste," and then immediately "up to the Clouds / With him I flew . . ." (5.86–87).

8. Aristotle, *Metaphysics*, trans. W. D. Ross, in *The Complete Works of Aristotle: The Revised Oxford Translation,* ed. Jonathan Barnes, Bollingen Series 71.2 (Princeton: Princeton University Press, 1984).

9. For such use of "wonder" and "amazement" in *Paradise Lost* see 3.271–73, 7.70–71, 8.10–11, 12.468. According to the *OED,* in Renaissance usage, "wonder," "amazement," and "admiration" all possess a similar range of meaning. On the one hand they signify surprise, confusion, and bewilderment (i.e., Aristotelian wonder), on the other, a profound awe and marveling (religious wonder).

10. John Calvin, *Commentaries on the First Book of Moses Called Genesis,* trans. John King (Grand Rapids: Eerdmans, 1948), 1:145.

11. Summers, *Muse's Method,* 157.

12. In the temptation of Adam and Eve, wonder is repeatedly associated with the knowledge of causes (e.g., 9.650, 865). See also Eugene F. Rice, *The Renaissance Idea of Wisdom* (Cambridge: Harvard University Press, 1958), 14–17, 89–90.

13. Aristotle, *Parts of Animals,* in *The Complete Works of Aristotle,* 1.5.664b.

14. In his *Seventh Prolusion,* the young Milton gives a splendid and enthusiastic account of this divinization via astronomy:

> This eternal life . . . is to be found in contemplation alone, by which the mind is uplifted, without the aid of the body, and gathered within itself so that it attains, to its inexpressible joy, a life akin to that of the immortal gods. . . . God would indeed seem to have endowed us to no purpose, or even to our distress, with this soul which is capable and indeed insatiably desirous of the highest wisdom, if he had not intended us to strive with all our might toward the lofty understanding of those things, for which he had at our creation instilled so great a longing into the human mind. . . . Can we indeed believe, my hearers, that the vast spaces of boundless air are illuminated and adorned with everlasting lights, that these are endowed with such rapidity of motion and pass through such intricate revolutions, merely to serve as a lantern for base and slothful men, and to light the path of the idle and the sluggard here below? . . . What a thing it is to grasp the nature of the whole firmament and of its stars, all the movements and changes of the atmosphere, whether it strikes terror into ignorant minds by the majestic roll of thunder or by fiery comets, or whether it freezes into snow or hail. . . . So at length, my hearers, when universal learning has once completed its cycle, the spirit of man, no longer confined within this dark prison-house, will reach out far and wide, till it fills the whole world and the space far beyond with the expansion of its divine greatness. (*Prolusions [1628–32],* trans. Phyllis B. Tillyard, notes and preface by Kathryn A. McEuen, in *The Complete Prose Works of John Milton,* ed. Don M. Wolfe [New Haven: Yale University Press, 1953], 1:291–96).

15. See Eric Voegelin, "Reason: The Classic Experience," in *Anamnesis,* trans. Gerhart Niemeyer (Notre Dame: University of Notre Dame Press, 1978), 92–103; Anders Nygren, *Agape and Eros,* trans. Philip Watson (London: SPCK, 1939), 2:121–27.

16. One remembers Satan's effort to convince himself (and Eve) that he is indeed self-caused (e.g., 9.719–22).

17. Voegelin, "Reason," 92–93.

18. Ibid., 96.

19. Nygren, *Agape,* 2:248–49, 264–66, 294, 309.

20. Quoted in Steven Ozment, "Luther and the Late Middle Ages: The Formation of Reformation Thought," in *Transition and Revolution,* ed. Robert Kingdon (Minneapolis: Burgess, 1974), 152. Milton's own *A Treatise on Christian Doctrine compiled from the Holy Scriptures Alone,* trans. Charles R. Sumner, (Boston: Cummings, Hilliard, 1825), 1:9, 12, 19, 24, 389, consistently, as the title suggests, opposes reason to revelation, philosophy to Scripture.

21. Martin Luther, *Lectures on Genesis, Chapters 1–5,* ed. Jaroslav Pelikan, in *Luther's Works,* ed. Pelikan (St. Louis: Concordia, 1958), 1:124.

22. Martin Luther, "The Disputation Concerning Man," ed. Lewis Spitz, in *Luther's Works,* ed. Jaroslav Pelikan (Philadelphia: Fortress Press, 1960), 34:144.

23. Rice, *Renaissance Idea of Wisdom,* 139–40.

24. Luther, *Genesis,* 1:154, 161.

25. Calvin, *Genesis,* 1:118. See also John Calvin, *Commentary on the Epistles of Paul to the Corinthians I,* trans. W. Pringle (Grand Rapids: Eerdmans, 1948), 74.

26. Calvin, *Genesis,* 1:118, 147; Milton, *Christian Doctrine,* 1:24, 389.

27. The association of sin and philosophic wisdom occurs not only in the magisterial reformers and their adherents but also among those who shared Milton's Arminianism. Of particular interest here is the fact that one of Milton's sources, the *Adamus Exul* (1601) by the Dutch Arminian, Hugo Grotius, makes this association explicit. In Grotius's temptation scene, Satan openly seduces Eve with classical philosophy. Unlike Milton's, Grotius's Satan shows considerable eclecticism; he begins in a Stoic vein, denying that Eve can die, "for the Fates control all things. / We merely do that which has been ordain'd, and suffer / That which comes down from Heav'n. Writ by the Hand divine, Decrees endure forever. . . ." He then switches into the language of Pythagoras: "Death itself is nothing but / An everlasting chain of metamorphoses." The devil then tries Aristotelian teleology: "For thou canst surely die / To live in higher state; this is a law of bodies, / Ever to be drawn on towards a more perfect lot." He reinforces this argument with commonplaces drawn from the Platonic doctrine of the natural immortality of the soul: ". . . No parts hath the soul, Nor can it suffer any loss by Time's delays. / Subsisting in itself, its own sole principle, / It seeks not otherwhere the life that it contributes." None of these arguments convinces Eve. She finally yields, however, when Satan turns Epicurean: "Desire, wisely placed / Within the mind, leads on to its own proper end. / All that delights thee by its odor, sight, or taste, / Is Nature's friend"; see *Adamus Exul,* reprinted in *The Celestial Cycle: The Themes of Paradise Lost in World Literature, with Translations of the Major Analogues,* ed. Watson Kirkconnell (Toronto: University of Toronto Press, 1952), 161–71. For Grotius, classical philosophy proves ignorant both of God and man—ignorant of God's power, omniscience, wrath, and paternal authority and likewise of man's personal moral responsibility. Grotius, like Milton an Arminian, is deeply conscious of the inadequacy of man's reason when confronted by the mysteries of God's nature and providence and he, like Milton, uses the errors of the Greek philosophers as a symbol for that consciousness. In the Dutchman, Milton would have found a precedent for viewing the Fall as the rebellion of natural reason. On Milton's use of Grotius, see Marjorie Curry Woods, "Milton's Interruption of Genesis: A Note on the Structure of Books VII and VIII of *Paradise Lost,*" *Notes and Queries,* n.s. 28 (1981): 205–7.

28. John Calvin, *Institutes of the Christian Religion,* ed. J. T. McNeill, trans. F. L. Battles, Library of Christian Classics (Philadelphia: Westminster Press, 1960), 1:192–96. See also Luther, *Genesis* 1.46, p. 142.

29. The beginnings of the Aristotelian ladder occur also in Eve's creation. She first awakens, ". . . much wond'ring where / And what I was, whence thither brought and how" (4.451–52), but since she is distracted by her own narcissisism, this initial wonder does not attain its religious fruition.

30. Ozment, "Luther and the Late Middle Ages," 125.

31. Ibid., 136–37.

32. Ibid., 140.

33. Calvin, *Institutes,* 1:43, 47, 263–64, 277.

34. Significantly, Milton rarely uses "love," with its evocation of the Platonic Eros, to refer to man's relation to God. "Love" in *Paradise Lost* almost always refers to God's love for man, or marital love. Indeed Milton speaks of man's "love" for God on only four occasions, and on two of these only with qualification. Thus Adam is told to "love" God "whom to love is to obey" (8.633–34) and later Adam says he will "love with fear the only God" (12.561). The unqualified uses of the term occur at 3.550 and 8.592.

Narcissus in *Paradise Lost* and *Upon Appleton House:* Disenchanting the Renaissance Lyric

KATHLEEN KELLY

It is generally recognized that the love lyric was one significant casualty of the shift in English poetic sensibility from the Renaissance to the Restoration.[1] Various cultural factors are cited to explain this shift: religious controversy and civil war, a new rationalism and a distrust of enthusiasm, and a considerably expanded reading public.[2] But can we explain more precisely why the Renaissance metaphysical lyrics, which could convincingly celebrate love, were displaced by the disenchanted Restoration lyrics of the Court Wits?[3] A comparison of pre- and post-Restoration lyrics reveals this disenchantment, but I propose that two longer, narrative poems best explain the logic behind that disenchantment.

Standing between the Renaissance and the Restoration, *Paradise Lost* and *Upon Appleton House* comprehend and in large part affirm the ideals of the Renaissance love lyric, and yet they paradoxically prepare the way for the deflation that characterizes the Restoration lyric. Each of these poems uses the image of Narcissus to describe the birth of what appears to be an ideal, transcendent, "metaphysical" love, but the poems then go on to expose the severe limitations of that love. In doing so, they circumscribe the lyric moment with consideration of reason and worldly circumstances, and thereby "disenchant" the ideal upon which the Renaissance lyric depended.

i

In mentioning the ideal of the Renaissance love lyric and a love which the Renaissance lyric convincingly celebrated, I am referring to the Neoplatonic *furor amoris* that takes the soul out of itself, beyond time and reason, and unites it with a higher good, a truer Self. Although Neoplatonism may have been looked upon with suspicion by the English, and its influence on English poetry perhaps overrated, the Italians did provide the English with a quandary fruitful for love poetry.[4] Neoplatonic theorists describe the ideal love as the desire to unite oneself with the good, the souls of the lovers joining to make a perfect union. In such a union, a *furor amoris,* the soul leaves the body in an ecstasy analogous to the ecstasy of Divine Contemplation.[5] The critical feature of this furor is that it is not available to mere human reason, but that beauty inspires an ecstasy beyond reason's reach. Such an ecstasy thus raises the question whether this sanctifies a physical as well as a spiritual union. Ficino, who is conservative when compared with later Petrarchists such as Leone Ebreo and Giordano Bruno, remains ambiguous about the value of sensual experience, but not about the value of the furor. This ambiguity permits a sensual love poetry with metaphysical significance.

Ficino represents the ambiguity of the soul's situation with the myth of Narcissus. Because all beauty is a reflection of the divine Beauty and therefore love of beauty is the means to God, Narcissus in love with his own image may be admired for loving to distraction what is beautiful. For Ficino, insofar as Narcissus is attached to the beauty of his own image and is overcome by Amor, his desire is good. His problem is a misplaced concreteness. The Beauty of the body is good, but it is "fragile and like running water." What the soul actually wants is not the body itself but its own beauty reflected in the body.[6]

What is remarkable about Ficinian love theory, then, is that the same Narcissus loving his own beauty represents the possibility for either kind of love. He has a choice between two ecstasies, the ecstasy through love of matter which leads to captivity, or the ecstasy through love of the divine Beauty reflected in matter, which leads to heaven. Beauty's ecstasy may enslave us to passion or perfect us beyond the reach and need of moralizing reason. Thus as long as such an ecstasy beyond the power of reason is conceivable, love poetry could convincingly celebrate a sensuous rapture and sanctify the ecstasy of human, sexual love.

This Ficinian ambiguity is directly exploited in Donne's "The Extasie," Chapman's "Ovids Banquet of Sense," and Davies's *Orchestra.*[7] Each of these poems is so carefully ambiguous as to encompass the double possibilities of a rapturous experience. Each describes events that may be interpreted as occasions either for transcending oneself or for self-deception and debauch.

Of course not all Renaissance love lyrics directly entertain the moral ambiguity Narcissus represents, and the earlier English Renaissance lyric remained skeptical about yoking physical desire with anything sacred. Spenser could celebrate a sensual married love only after it is carefully distinguished from lust, and if it approaches heavenly love only by analogy.[8] But by the seventeenth century the lyric found the means to avoid the carnal, lustful connotations of sensuous experience while at the same time intensifying the rapturous sensuality of love. John Donne and Robert

Herrick, for example, although in very different ways, use religious language to transform sensual experience into something sacred. And Herrick, Edmund Waller, and Andrew Marvell use pastoral language to link the sensuality of love with the innocence and infinite richness of nature.[9] Although exemplifying only one of a number of possible ways poets could celebrate rapture, Thomas Carew's "Ask Me No More" suggests how the ideal can inform love poetry. In the first four stanzas, Carew's speaker claims that the roses, sunbeams, stars, and nightingales all find their source and end in the mistress's beauty. In the final stanza he makes the same statement about the phoenix:

> Aske me no more where East or West,
> The Phoenix builds her spicy nest:
> For unto you at last shee flies,
> And in your fragrant bosome dies.[10]

The phoenix, a traditional symbol both for Christ and for the lover who dies to himself to be reborn in the beloved, perishes in the mistress's bosom in a rapture that is at once sensuous and transforming, a union with the source and end of life, a power that recreates the lover. By referring to an innocent, sensuous nature and to the mystical phoenix to suggest rapture, Carew can avoid conjuring moral restraint at the same time that he suggests sensuous indulgence outside the bounds of reason.

This is not by any means to say that most Renaissance love lyrics celebrated this ideal of romantic love; it was rejected or ridiculed at least as often as it was celebrated. But even here the poetry relies on the romantic ideal against which to define itself. Religious poets, for example, diminished the mistress's power in order better to praise the power of God. We can cite a stanza from George Herbert's verse, for example:

> My God, where is that ancient heat toward thee,
> Wherewith whole showls of Martyrs once did burn,
> Besides their other flames? Doth Poetry
> Wear Venus Livery? Only serve her turn?
> Why are not Sonnets made of thee?[11]

And Cavalier poets often diminished beauty's power, not to praise God, but to celebrate their own appetites. A stanza from a John Suckling sonnet begins, "There's no such thing as that we beauty call":

> If I a fancy take
> To black and blue,
> That fancy doth it beauty make.[12]

But it is not such clearly partisan attacks on love's promise that break the spell on the Renaissance love lyric and bring it into the domain of neoclassical sensibility. These lyrics use polemics to strike a pose or assert a feeling that is powerful but obviously incomplete. That very exaggeration and partiality leaves ideal love essentially unscathed by the arguments. Instead, it is the much fuller, more sympathetic treatment of love's promise in the context of Milton's and Marvell's narrative poems that qualifies love's power. Each of these poems uses the figure of Narcissus to present a sympathetic version of ideal love, a *furor amoris*, but then each goes on to expose the limitations of that love, and to exorcise its furor.

ii

It is fitting that both Milton and Marvell initiate an extended exploration of the *furor amoris* with allusions to the figure of Narcissus, for as we have seen, Narcissus was an emblem for the ambiguous possibilities of rapturous love. Medieval poets used the Narcissus figure as the emblem for "the birth of self-consciousness through love" and for the central problem of the courtly lover: whether the beautiful lady genuinely reflects his ideal perfection or is merely the creation of his own desire.[13] In *Paradise Lost* Milton not only alludes to Narcissus to describe the birth of Eve's love for Adam, but his figure is the background against which we are asked to judge Adam and Eve's love and their fall from grace.[14]

In *Paradise Lost* the most conspicuous allusion to Narcissus occurs when Eve describes her first awakening, when she sees a reflection in the pool returning her looks with "answering looks / Of sympathy and love."[15] Yet for all the precise similarities between Eve and Narcissus, what is most remarkable is how unlike Narcissus Eve actually is.[16] Before recognizing the identity of the image she is, like Narcissus, enchanted, unaware of herself. But Narcissus, even before he realizes the figure in the lake is himself, suffers extremely that such a thin veil of water can separate him from his beloved. And when he discovers the reflection to be himself, he wants to be parted from his own body, to die, so that he might be united with that other self. Eve, on the other hand, experiences the awakening of desire more felicitously. No sooner does she experience desire than a voice at once points out to her the folly of loving a watery image, and at the same time brings her to one who can satisfy her, not by outward beauty but by "manly grace and wisdom." Eve experiences no unquenchable longing and her desire to be united with a sympathetic image is satisfied immediately and completely by Adam. The only reference to passion and desire is hypothetical: "there I had fixt / Mine eyes till now, and pin'd with vain desire, / Had not a voice thus warn'd me" (4.465–67) But even in this speculation it is not that Eve feels overcome by some outside force. The location of the power and choice are within herself: "*I* had fix't / Mine eyes." And rather than being possessed by Amor, she is straightforwardly led to her mate, whose highest recommendation is his self-possession, his reason. Thus Milton, while invoking the Ficinian emblem for an inspired desire, restricts the power of desire so that there is no suggestion of its being overwhelming. There is no tension in a longing for unearthly beauty, and the lover feels no ecstasy, whether divine or sensual, other than that which is self-possessed.

This rejection of a desire beyond the power of reason is even more explicit in the depiction of Adam. For although Eve looking into the pool most explicitly suggests Narcissus, Adam is the more susceptible to Narcissus's passion for loving his resemblance.[17] Recognizing his own incompleteness, Adam requests a companion "By conversation with his like to help, / Or solace his defects" (8.418–19) and with whom to "beget / Like of his like, his Image multipli'd" (8.423–24). This version of desire for one's own image the poem sanctions: God gives him Eve, "Thy likeness, thy fit help, thy other self" (8.450). Eve's likeness is not a simple replication, but a complement, both more and less than Adam.

But although, like Eve, Adam suffers no severe pertubations as he recognizes his desire and is satisfied, he speaks of Eve in the traditional lyric language of Beauty's overwhelming power:

> transported I behold,
> Transported touch. . . .
> . . . .
> . . . when I approach
> Her loveliness, so absolute she seems
> And in herself complete, so well to know
> Her own, that what she wills to do or say,
> Seems wisest, virtuousest, discreetest, best;
> All higher knowledge in her presence falls
> Degraded, Wisdom in discourse with her
> Loses discount'nanc't, and like folly shows;
> Authority and Reason on her wait,
> As one intended first, not after made
> Occasionally; and to consummate all,
> Greatness of mind and nobleness thir seat
> Build in her loveliest, and create an awe
> About her, as a guard Angelic plac't.
>
> (8.529–30, 546–59)

We are reminded of the lyric praise of the mistress's beauty and the power of love to take the soul out of itself in an ecstasy beyond human understanding.[18] In the language Adam uses here, Knowledge, Wisdom, Authority, and Reason are not located within him and under his control, but instead are personified agents that surrender their autonomy to Eve's beauty, as if he were a field upon which this capitulation takes place. He is availing himself of the Renaissance "language of passion" precisely as described by George L. Dillon in explaining the shift from the Renaissance to the Restoration theory and language of passion.[19] In typical Elizabethan passion metaphor—for example, "Love bids me speak," or "Expectation whirl me around"—the *I* involved becomes a field or battleground where autonomous forces play themselves out, the self becoming the victim of powers outside its control.

Milton does allow us to see Eve's beauty seeming actually to do what Adam claims for it—to ennoble her admirer—and in the process Milton may seem for the moment to be endorsing Adam's Renaissance view. For Eve overcomes no less a power than Satan's:

> her every Air
> Of gesture or least action overaw'd
> His Malice, and with rapine sweet bereav'd
> His fierceness of the fierce intent it brought:
> That space the Evil one abstracted stood
> From his own evil, and for the time remain'd
> Stupidly good, of enmity disarm'd,
> Of guile, of hate, of envy, of revenge.
>
> (9.459–66)

Yet if we look at the language describing Eve's power here, we must note its contrast with Adam's. Here no autonomy is given to the power of beauty. All verbs are ascribable to persons: *her* gesture overawes, and what she overawes is *his* malice, *his* fierceness; it is not Enmity that is disarmed, but *his* enmity. Dillon shows that Restoration style, as revealed for example in revisions of Shakespeare, exhibits precisely this tendency to eliminate metaphors which make passions autonomous agents or causes, and to increase the emphasis on the *I* in the processes. The effect is to contain or limit the passions to the soul or the self, and thus to emphasize the inwardness and self-scrutiny of characters, no longer allowing us to conceive of passions as fatal forces. It is precisely this limitation of the power of passion that Raphael demands Adam recognize, and Adam, "half abash't," immediately acknowledges: "[I] still free / Approve the best, and follow what I approve" (8.610–11). As for Satan, he quickly resumes his guile, his hate, his envy, and revenge. Thus Beauty has power only momentarily to stun us, to make us "stupid" and therefore capable neither of good nor of evil. Whatever ennobling action may ensue from beauty's inspiration must be determined and sustained by reason and "self-esteem, grounded on just and right / Well manag'd" (8.572–73).

When Adam later urges Eve not to work alone, he tells her that "I from the influence of thy looks receive / Access in every Virtue" (9.309–10), but as subsequent events prove, access is not possession. For the poem does not leave us merely with this hypothetical and stylistic qualification of lyric rapture; it demonstrates it dramatically. Eve and Adam come to grief precisely because they succumb to the powerful and sympathetic lure of beauty.[20] Satan promises Eve that by eating the apple she will have the power Adam had ascribed to her. She will feel what Satan describes himself feeling as he addresses the Tree of Knowledge:

> I feel thy Power
> Within me clear, not only to discern
> Things in thir Causes, but to trace the ways
> Of highest Agents, deem'd however wise.
>
> (9.680–83)

He seems to promise Eve that Knowledge, Wisdom, Authority, and Reason will indeed "on her wait." And yet the narrative shows that the moment she believes this, Sin and Death, that narcissistic and incestuous pair, enter the world.

Thus Eve falls by believing she can genuinely be the fulfillment Adam ascribed to her, the fulfillment Narcissus's watery image seemed to promise him. Adam, on the other hand, justifies his turning away from God by saying, Narcissus-like, that he cannot relinquish the image of himself in Eve:

> I feel
> The Bond of Nature draw me to my own,
> My own in thee, for what thou art is mine;
> Our State cannot be sever'd, we are one,
> One Flesh; to lose thee were to lose myself.
>
> (9.955–59)

Ironically, to justify his being overcome by female charm Adam uses not the Elizabethan but the Restoration language of passion. While the "Bond of Nature" does at least have the autonomy to "draw" him, its effect is firmly located within himself, and while he is reporting that he is overcome, he sounds entirely self-possessed. Although he invokes the familiar lyric rapture that makes two souls one in a divine union, the context makes clear that his choice leads directly away from anything divine. And finally when, after eating the apple, Adam and Eve feel "Divinity within them breeding wings / Wherewith to scorn the Earth" (9.1009–10), such desire the narrator explicitly labels the product of "fancy," "lust," and "carnal" desire. It is exactly the intoxication in hell that Sin feels in intuitive sympathy with Satan's victory on earth: "Methinks I feel new strength within me rise / Wings growing, and Dominion giv'n me large / Beyond this Deep" (10.243–45).

Thus in *Paradise Lost* Milton lets Adam describe the lyric moment—"transported I behold, transported touch"—primarily in order to expose its inadequacy. While Adam seems transported, in fact his reason and will are in command. And when he reasons falsely, far from being liberated in a divine rapture, he is enslaved to death. While Milton has not, as had the religious lyric, rejected the subject of romantic love, nor, as had some cavalier lyrics, reduced it to a discussion of the appetites, he has, by insisting on reason and self-control, so carefully qualified the notion of divine rapture that there can no longer be much confidence in a *furor amoris.* Instead, beauty and love are presented as fragile and precariously dependent for their ennobling effects on self-possessed lovers.

iii

In a very different but no less fatal way, Andrew Marvell rejects the lyric rapture of love. Rather than, as *Paradise Lost* does, exposing as a narcissistic illusion any rapture that raises us above our intellect, Marvell's *Upon Appleton House* presents two versions of Narcissus that together define genuine rapture. But paradoxically these raptures have little to do with sexual love, and in fact, these are raptures that sexual love destroys.

In *Upon Appleton House,* the poet or narrator walks through the Fairfax estate—through the convent ruins, the gardens, the meadows, and the woods—and as he progresses, he gradually loses his critical distance as observer until, in the woods, he succumbs to nature's enchantment.[21] In the woods he feels completely, sensuously gratified, his spirit released in union with nature. Subject-object dualism disappears and in languorous ecstasy he becomes one with nature. He is a bird, or a tree, and he speaks their languages:

> Give me but wings as they, and I
> Straight floating on the air shall fly:
> Or turn me but and you shall see
> I was but an inverted tree.
>
> . . . .
>
> And where I language want, my signs
> The bird upon the bough divines;
>
> . . . .
>
> No leaf does tremble in the wind
> Which I returning cannot find.
>
> (566–69; 571–72; 575–76)[22]

Here we have the classic lyric rapture—the soul is taken out of itself and united with powers greater than itself. Except in this case it all happens with no woman. Woman has become superfluous. Marvell seems to be suggesting that the essentials for a lyric rapture exist outside of sexual love.[23]

He reinforces this exclusion by making the description of his situation analogous to that of Narcissus before Narcissus has recognized himself to be the reflection in the water, in fact, before he even sees himself at all.

According to Ovid, Narcissus's trouble begins because, though very beautiful, he spurned all lovers, causing one love-sick boy to curse him: "So may he himself love and not gain the thing he loves!"[24] But before that curse, Narcissus remained entirely satisfied alone and looked on love as entrapment. When he spurned Echo, for example, he cried, "Hands off! embrace me not! May I die before I give you power o'er me!" Like Narcissus, Marvell's narrator spurns love too, rejoicing that these woods make him immune to love:

> Where Beauty, aiming at the heart,
> Bends in some tree its useless dart;
> And where the world no certain shot
> Can make, or me it toucheth not.
>
> (603–6)

Rather than be embraced by a woman, the narrator wants to be tied down by the river—"There at the evening stake me down" (624)—enjoying nature's innocence, where the river is "among the weeds the only snake" (632):

> See in what wanton harmless folds
> Its everywhere the meadow holds;
> And its yet muddy back doth lick,
> Till as a crystal mirror slick;
> Where all things gaze themselves, and doubt
> If they be in it or without.
> And for this shade which therein shines,
> Narcissus-like, the sun too pines.
>
> (633–40)

In the river, the sun and all things can lose the burden of their identities, mesmerized and will-less.

Thus what Marvell seems to suggest in this novel permutation of the Narcissus myth is that Narcissus's great error lay not at all in a callous refusal to love anyone, nor in self-love. Rather, his great error lay in coming to self-awareness at all. When Narcissus was born Tiresias prophesied that Narcissus would live long only "If he never know himself." Whereas other poetry drawing on that myth had taken the prophecy to be richly ambiguous[25]—when he dies, does Narcissus really know himself at all?—Marvell here seems to be taking it quite literally. Self-awareness is the beginning of a subject-object dualism that only destroys our original sensuous identification with all things. Here, staked down on the bank of the Fairfax river, then, is a playful Marvellian version of the lyric ecstasy of love. Reduced to its essentials, no "love," at least not between two people, is necessary.

But Marvell doesn't rest with this version of love. Just when the narrator seems about to slide into the river in a blissful ecstasy, a second Narcissus figure enters, the young Maria, who puts an end to the narrator's indulgent ecstasy:

> But now away my hooks, my quills,
> And angles, idle utensils.
> The young Maria walks tonight:
> Hide, trifling youth, thy pleasures slight.
>
> (649–52)

With Maria, the ecstatic relation between the lover and the woods is reversed: the woods and stream, to which the narrator would give himself, actually rely on Maria for their gratifying sensuousness. While the narrator would give himself up to nature as the supreme power, nature is giving itself to Maria. She becomes the mirror in which all things see themselves. But unlike the mirror of Narcissus, which reflects only an insubstantial image, in the mirror of Maria's beauty, all things find perfection and repose, and an escape from the ruin of time. Reflected in Maria, things are glassed into permanence: "by her flames, in heaven tried, / Nature is wholly vitrified" (687–88). And they are made ideal:

> 'Tis she that to these gardens gave
> That wondrous beauty which they have;
> She straightness on the woods bestows;
> To her the meadow sweetness owes;
> Nothing could make the river be
> So crystal pure but only she;
> She yet more pure, sweet, straight, and fair,
> Than gardens, woods, meads, rivers are.
>
> (689–96)

In gratitude for that perfection, nature reflects its perfection back upon Maria: "Therefore what first she on them spent, / They gratefully again present" (697–98).

Thus in an endless series of reflections, Maria provides nature with the best image of itself, and nature in return reflects Maria's virtue. But paradoxically this Narcissus, who in the river and woods receives a truly substantial reflection of her beauty's virtue, disdains that reflection, looking for a higher beauty beyond herself. Maria disdains the very thing from which the narrator derived so much sensuous gratification—the consubstantiality of herself and nature. She does not speak in the language of sensuous immediacy that the narrator in the woods had learned; instead

> She counts her beauty to converse
> In all the languages as hers;
> Nor yet in those herself employs

But for the wisdom, not the noise;
Nor yet that wisdom would affect,
But as 'tis heaven's dialect.

(707–12)

The higher beauty beyond herself is not the sensuous beauty of the garden, but neither is it the beauty of romantic love which the original Narcissus disdained. For she, too, avoids love: "Knowing where this ambush lay, / She scaped the safe, but roughest way" (719–20). For the moment at least, Marvell seems to be rejecting the image of the sensuous "green" love the narrator had represented,[26] in favor of an innocent, but sacred and spiritual, love that knows no self-indulgence. Through ascetic study Maria has become the pure vessel through which the heavenly and ideal forms of things are translated to earth.

This description of Maria is the lyric praise of the mistress taken to its full extreme, seeming essentially to confirm the lyric's praise of woman. The difference in *Upon Appleton House,* however, is that while praising the mistress so fully for the moment, Marvell greatly qualifies her powers in time. For he makes clear at the end of the poem that though Maria's beauty mesmerizes all things into their ideal selves, her power is fleeting, secure only for a season. Her innocence depends on her youth, her vigilant parents, and the estate's peaceful, orderly avenues. The narrator explains the "rough way" by which she has so far escaped the world:

This 'tis to have been from the first
In a domestic heaven nurst,
Under the discipline severe
Of Fairfax, and the starry Vere;
Where not one object can come nigh
But pure, and spotless on the eye;
And goodness doth itself entail
On females, if there want a male.

(721–28)

Maria is a conduit of heavenly influences because she is protected, pure and innocent. At some point, however, she will have to enter into the world of experience that made Narcissus suffer so. And while, as the narrator suggests, she can surely handle the darts of love, she will no longer be the spiritual source for all green things. She too will have to grow and bear fruit in the dark soil of the world. In the language of the poem, this bud will be cut:

Hence she with graces more divine
Supplies beyond her sex the line;
And, like a sprig of mistletoe
On the Fairfacian oak doth grow;

Whence, for some universal good,
The priest shall cut the sacred bud;
While her glad parents most rejoice,
And make their destiny their choice.

(737–44)

Like the indulgent narrator who would live in a child-world of gratifying sensuous pleasure, then, the ascetic Maria too gives us only a temporary vision of a filfilled self, a self which is stopped short by the endless business of the world, a self unrecoverable.

Thus Marvell's vision of the ecstasy that brings together earthly and heavenly delights is very much removed from the traditional lyric ecstasy of love. He has denied the source of sensuous gratification to be any particular beauty, and while he affirms in the young Maria that beauty may converse in the "languages" of heaven, hers is the innocent language of a child. Time looms ominous around such inspirations as Maria, and makes them only temporary; they are momentary visions of possibilities we can never wholly possess, visions that must inevitably be mixed in time and change.

iv

Before Milton and Marvell, the lyric ideal claimed that love of the beautiful took us out of ourselves in an ecstatic and divine union. In serious love poetry, lovers could be possessed by the beauty of the beloved and taken out of themselves to become a new, divine being in the ecstasy of passion. Some lyrics reacted against this ideal: religious lyrics found God's love to be the true source of beauty, and cavalier lyrics claimed that the power of beauty derived from the lover's appetites. But Milton and Marvell do something more fatal to the lyric ideal than anything these frontal attacks by the religious and cavalier lyrics could. They affirm the lyric model, but in a context that so qualifies its powers that love's passion no longer so securely redeems us of our limitation. Instead of taking us out of ourselves and above human reason and intellect, the *furor amoris* must be controlled and contained by reason. With the power of love thus circumscribed, it is not a long step to the Restoration's disenchanted lyrics. For as the Restoration became skeptical of that reason, which alone was left to protect love, love easily declined into the "ostentatious profligacy" with which the Court Wits expressed dismay at the determinism they were left with.[27]

Critics of the English Renaissance love lyric observe in its development a tendency to become more realistic: the lovers recognize their control in love, their choice to love whom they choose and not to be overwhelmed by any madness, whether divine or sensual.[28] In a sense, *Paradise Lost* and

Upon Appleton House are eloquent and reluctant admissions that that is indeed so. The Narcissus of these poems finally does come "to know himself." But as a result, these poems bring an end to the holy raptures of love, and at the same time to a paradox that Narcissus had so faithfully been called upon to represent.

Notes

1. Earl Miner makes this observation in "The Private Mode," a chapter in *The Metaphysical Mode from Donne to Cowley* (Princeton: Princeton University Press, 1969).
2. Paul J. Korshin, in *From Concord to Dissent: Major Themes in English Poetic Theory 1640–1700* (Menston, Yorkshire: Scolar Press, 1973), 1–10, distinguishes long-term, medium-term, and short-run precipitants of this change.
3. K. E. Robinson, in "The Disenchanted Lyric in the Restoration Period," *Durham University Journal* 73 (1980): 67–73, catalogues this disenchantment.
4. See J. W. Lever's introduction in *The Elizabethan Love Sonnet* (1956; reprint, London: Methuen, 1966) for his account of the English lyric's only gradual adjustment to the continental ideas of love. Earl Miner, in "Love," a chapter in *The Cavalier Mode from Jonson to Cotton* (Princeton: Princeton University Press, 1971), observes that Neoplatonism in English love poetry was no doubt desirable, but exceedingly difficult to discover; he sees more evidence for a Horatian movement inward.
5. For an account of the Neoplatonic theories of ecstasy, see A. J. Smith, "The Metaphysic of Love," *Review of English Studies* 9 (1958): 362–75; and John Huntington, "Philosophical Seduction in Chapman, Davies, and Donne," *ELH* 44 (1977): 40–59.
6. Louise Vinge, in *The Narcissus Theme in Western European Literature up to the Early 19th Century,* trans. Robert Dewsnap and Nigel Reeves (Lund: Gleerups, 1967), 123–27, explains Ficino's distinctive use of the Narcissus myth.
7. This is the thesis of Huntington's very fine article.
8. In an interesting analysis Calvin R. Edwards, in "The Narcissus Myth in Spenser's Poetry," *Studies in Philology* 74 (1977): 63–88, shows that while Spenser celebrates married love, he also uses the Narcissus figure to suggest that our desire can never be truly satisfied; we long for the impossible. (See especially pp. 70–75.)
9. H. R. Swardson, in *Poetry and the Fountain of Light: Observations on the Conflict between Christian and Classical Traditions in Seventeenth-Century Poetry* (Columbia: University of Missouri Press, 1962), demonstrates Herrick's and Marvell's use of the pastoral for this effect.
10. *The Poems of Thomas Carew,* ed. Rhodes Dunlap (1949; reprint, Oxford: Clarendon Press, 1957).
11. This Herbert stanza is quoted by Swardson; he cites several such examples of poets rejecting "lewd layes of lighter loves," as Barnabe Barnes, also cited by Swardson, puts it.
12. *The Works of Sir John Suckling: The Non-Dramatic Works,* ed. Thomas Clayton (Oxford: Clarendon Press, 1971).
13. Frederick Goldin, *The Mirror of Narcissus in the Courtly Love Lyric* (Ithaca: Cornell University Press, 1967), 22, 37.
14. Jean Hagstrum, in *Sex and Sensibility: Ideal and Erotic Love from Milton to Mozart* (Chicago: University of Chicago Press, 1980), 41–46, discusses "The Narcissistic Sins" in *Paradise Lost,* including references to the Divine Trinity and the Satanic one.
15. Quotations are from *John Milton: Complete Poems and Major Prose,* ed. Merritt Y. Hughes (New York: Odyssey Press, 1957).
16. Hagstrum (*Sex and Sensibility,* 44) argues that Eve is undergoing a real temptation here, but I agree with Stanley Fish that in evoking the Narcissus myth, Milton wants to raise up the thought that Eve's later sin can somehow be explained by an innate vanity only in order to exorcise it. Thus it is the difference between Eve and Narcissus that is most evident. For a brief history of this critical controversy over Eve, as well as for his own opinion, see Stanley Fish, *Surprised by Sin: The Reader in Paradise Lost* (New York: St. Martin's Press,

1967), 216–32. While not including the myth of Narcissus, Diane McColley, in "Shapes of Things Divine: Eve and Myth in *Paradise Lose*," *Sixteenth Century Journal* 9 (1978): 47–55, makes this same argument about Eve's difference from all the other mythological personages to which she is compared.

17. Hagstrum says of Adam, "The primary attraction, the emotion he feels more strongly than any other, is that of consubstantiality—not carnal contrast but carnal similitude" (*Sex and Sensibility*, 42).

18. We may even consider these lines a kind of submerged lyric within the epic. As A. K. Nardo, in "The Submerged Sonnet as Lyric Moment in Miltonic Epic," *Genre* 9 (1977): 21–35, points out, for several Renaissance theorists the epic was considered encyclopedic, containing all genres, including the lyric.

19. "The Seventeenth-Century Shift in the Theory and Language of Passion," *Language and Style* 4 (1974): 121–43.

20. John M. Steadman, in "The Critique of *Amor*," a chapter in *Milton and the Renaissance Epic* (Oxford: Clarendon Press, 1967), 108–36, argues that while Eve's power to arouse admiration and wonder serves the essential end of heroic poetry, through her Milton criticizes the epic's and romance's ideal of romantic love by making beauty subservient to masculine dominance.

21. David Evett, in " 'Paradise's Only Map': The *Topos* of the *Locus Amoenus* and the Structure of Marvell's *Upon Appleton House*," *PMLA* 85 (1970): 504–13, writes a fine analysis of the stages in our relation to nature that the narrator's walk through the estate represents.

22. Quotations are from *Andrew Marvel: The Complete English Poems*, ed. Elizabeth Story Donno (New York: St. Martin's Press, 1974).

23. This is also suggested in a few of Marvell's lyrics, notably "The Garden."

24. Quotations are from Ovid, *The Metamorphoses*, ed. and trans. Frank Justus Miller, rev. G. P. Goold, 3d ed., The Loeb Classical Library (Cambridge: Harvard University Press, 1977).

25. See Goldin, *Mirror of Narcissus*, passim.

26. See Swardson's discussion of Marvell's presexual eroticism in his chapter "Marvell: A New Pastoralism," in *Poetry and the Fountain of Light*, 83–103.

27. Hagstrum notes that "Miltonic love, unprotected as it is by ascetic prohibition, stoic indifference, or Platonic denigration, is precisely the kind that might easily drive on toward lust" (*Sex and Sensibility*, 41). For a highly readable dissertation on several ways a distrust of reason manifests itself in Restoration love poetry, see Richard E. Quaintance, Jr., "Passion and Reason in Restoration Love Poetry," Yale 1962, abstracted in *DAI*, 1981 June; 41(12): 5111A. It is Robinson's argument that what critics of the Restoration lyric see as "ostentatious profligacy" is actually the Court Wits' expression of dismay; they are "cast adrift from a traditional teleology but without a substitute for it."

28. See especially H. M. Richmond's conclusions in *The School of Love: The Evolution of the Stuart Love Lyric* (Princeton: Princeton University Press, 1964), particularly "New Attitudes."

Herbert's Reciprocal Writing: Poetry as Sacred Pun

HARRIET KRAMER LINKIN

George Herbert uses his poetry to build a bridge to God in *The Temple,* defining verse in "The Quidditie" as "that which while I use / I am with thee."[1] Like many seventeenth-century thinkers, Herbert hopes to bypass the inherent limitations that arose in language when mankind fell;[2] though Adam once named the animals (Gen. 2 : 19–20), his linguistic gift fractured into endless signs long before God smote the tower of Babel. Because mankind's redemption through Christ extended the potential salvation of language, seventeenth-century grammarians believed they might reintegrate the scattered Word into a linguistic form capable of reaching God's infinitude. Herbert follows the spirit of his times in trying to speak to God in language that restores what he considers the prelapsarian Adam's ease in moving from earth to heaven. In "The H. Communion," he describes the time before original sin as one when

> A fervent sigh might well have blown
> Our innocent earth to heaven.
>
> For sure when Adam did not know
> To sinne, or sinne to smother
> He might to heav'n from Paradise go,
> As from one room t'another.
>
> (31–36)

Although humanity loses direct intercourse with God through the fall, the poem ends by reminding us how Christ's sacrifice "restor'd to us this ease / By this thy heav'nly bloud" (37–38); "The H. Communion" celebrates the Eucharist's ability to impart temporary transcendence through the medium of Christ's blood. Recognizing how the Eucharist provides humanity's one sanctioned mode of achieving communion, Herbert models his poetry on what he defines as the dualistic nature of the Holy Communion. Just as the Eucharist manifests a kind of sacred pun in presenting Christ's body and blood as bread and wine, Herbert approximates the duality of the Eucharist in a poetry composed of sacred puns and hieroglyphic verse. Offering praise in poetic forms that embody the twofoldness of the Christ in whom "two natures met to be thy cure" ("An Offering," 6), Herbert attempts to devise a language of transcendence that will gain God's hearing. Once in God's hearing, Herbert would request reciprocal writing, wherein Christ finally responds to the poet's Eucharistic words of praise by engraving a new dispensation on his heart.

The Eucharist establishes a model of duality for Herbert's poetry by revealing the paradox of Christ's divinity and humanity. Throughout *The Temple,* Herbert ecstatically demarcates the sacred pun inherent in a Eucharist composed of body and blood as bread and wine: "The Agonie" exclaims, "Love is that liquor sweet and most divine, / Which my God feels as bloude; but I as wine" (17–18). "The Bunch of Grapes" asks:

> But can he want the grape, who hath the wine?
> I have their fruit and more.
> Blessed be God, who prosper'd *Noahs* vine,
> And made it bring forth grapes good store.
> But much more him I must adore,
> Who of the laws sowre juice sweet wine did make,
> Ev'n God himself, being pressed for my sake.
>
> (22–28)

"The Invitation" urges readers to

> Come ye hither all, whom wine
> Doth define,
> Naming you not to your good:
> Weep what ye have drunk amisse,
> And drink this,
> Which before ye drink is bloud.
>
> (7–12)

And "The Banquet" declares, "God took bloud, and needs would be / Spilt with me, / And so found me on the ground. / Having rais'd me to look up, / In a cup / Sweetly he doth meet my taste" (34–39). By focusing on the combinative structure of the Eucharist, Herbert enables the essentially secular nature of the pun to perform a sacred purpose: the language of puns in "The Church" attempts to reach God through poetry that speaks in God's own voice.

Herbert himself justifies the use of puns to evoke a sacred language in his poem "The Sonne."[3] In this sonnet, he not only celebrates the capacity of English to capture two senses at once, but also notes the grace with which language identifies Christ's doubleness:

> Let forrain nations of their language boast,
> What fine varietie each tongue affords:

I like our language, as our men and coast:
Who cannot dress it well, want wit, not words.
How neatly doe we give one onely name 5
To parents issue and the sunnes bright starre!
A sonne is light and fruit; a fruitful flame
Chasing the fathers dimnesse, carri'd farre
From the first man in th'East, to fresh and new
Western discoveries of posteritie. 10
So in one word our Lords humilitie
We turn upon him in a sense most true:
For what Christ once in humblenesse began,
We him in glorie call, *The Sonne of Man*.

Because English embodies the multivalence evident in Christ's Eucharist, it offers the possibility of extending appropriate praise: though Christ humbly calls himself the son of man, language reveals the glory of his divinity by homophonically echoing the sun's bright star. The neatness language demonstrates in using a single word for two meanings echoes the neatness of the world at large; just as the sound "sun" signifies both "parents issue and the sunnes bright starre," single objects connote a variety of meanings and uses. In "Man" Herbert puzzles out several definitions for water, discriminating function through location: "Each thing is full of dutie: / Waters united are our navigation; / Distinguished, our habitation; / Below, our drink; above, our meat, / Both are our cleanlinesse" (37–41). Herbert ends his classification of water with a question: "Hath one such beautie? / Then how are all things neat?" (41–42). The poem answers the question by suggesting a higher order of neatness in the dualistic range of both language and the world. The beauty of the creation lies not in singularity, but in a way single objects or words such as *water* or *sun* incorporate multiplicity. Like many language philosophers of the seventeenth century, Herbert believes in a world of resemblances where signifiers point to other signifiers;[4] puns capture the intrinsic duality of a universe laid out in correspondent signs.

In "Providence" Herbert lists series of riddle puns to categorize the diversity of God's creation, suggesting such doubleness as a precedent for the form humanity's praise should take. Calling man the secretary of God's praise, Herbert provides a semiotic description of the world:

. . . The Indian nut alone
Is clothing, meat and trencher, drink and kan,
Boat, cable, sail and needle, all in one.

Most herbs that grow in brooks, are hot and dry.
Cold fruits warm kernells help against the winde.

The lemmons juice and rinde cure mutually.
The whey of milk doth loose, the milk doth binde.

. . . .

Frogs marry fish and flesh; bats, bird and beast;
Sponges, non-sense and sense; mines th'earth & plants.

. . . .

I give thee praise
In all my other hymnes, but in this twice.

Each thing that is, although in use and name
It go for one, hath many wayes in store
To honour thee; and so each hymne thy fame
Extolleth many wayes, yet this one more.
(126–32; 135–36; 147–52)

Herbert adopts the principle he notes in the world as a means of formulating praise: by listing the puns of God's creation, he exalts God's fame in binary language. Like the animals in "Humilitie," told to bring "double gifts" for the "Vertues," Herbert gives double praise to God through puns, as he strongly urges in "Mans Medley": "Happie is he, whose heart / Hath found the art / To turn his double pains to double praise" (34–36). "Mans Medley," "Humilitie," and "The Sonne" underscore the explicit message of "Providence": puns mimetically express the doubleness humanity should praise in both God and creation.

In offering praise, Herbert expands the sacred pun of the Eucharist into a larger metaphor that frequently describes the crucifixion as an act of sacred writing. Heather Asals similarly notices what she labels the "chirograph" in *Equivocal Predication,* implying more than "handwriting" in her term by gently punning on the graphic relationship between "chiro" (or hand) and "Christ."[5] Like Asals, I believe Herbert represents the crucifixion as an act of writing in order to justify the possibility of his reaching God through language. *The Temple* repeatedly demonstrates how Christ's death on the cross inks the letters of the new dispensation. In "The Sacrifice" Christ equates his death with language by defining blood as the only adequate measure of his words: "my hearts deare treasure / Drops bloud (the onely beads) my words to measure" (21–22). "The Thanksgiving" provides a more painful description of the crucifixion as writing when a speaker despairs of ever measuring Christ's grief in poetic stanzas:

Shall thy strokes be my stroking? thorns, my flower?
Thy rod, my posie? crosse, my bower?

> But how then shall I imitate thee, and
> Copie thy fair, though bloudie hand?
>
> (13–16)

The strokes, thorns, posie, bower, copy, and hand of "The Thanksgiving" form a discrete pattern evoking the writer's world. Sometimes Herbert uses commercial metaphors to image Christ's death on the cross as sacrificial writing. God defines the sacrifice as an "account" in "Dialogue"; the speaker of "Sunday" calls the crucifixion "Th'indorsement of supreme delight / Writ by a friend, and with his bloud" (3–4); "Conscience" names the Eucharist a "receit"; and "Redemption" presents Christ's death as co-requisite with his granting of a "new small-rented lease" (4). By associating the crucifixion with language and presenting the Eucharist itself as a sacred pun, Herbert establishes a strong precedent for his own Eucharistic offering.

Although there are many kinds of puns offering special praise to God in *The Temple,* Herbert's hieroglyphic forms are notable in possessing a visual dimension. The visual-verbal puns in poems such as "The Altar" or "Love-joy" imitate the Eucharist by enforcing duality through sight and sound. As Joseph Summers suggests in his classic work on Herbert, hieroglyphic form encompasses more than shaped verse. He writes "there is one true anagram (labelled as such), one echo poem, one 'hidden acrostic,' one poem based on a syllabic pun, and 'Paradise,' which can only be described as a 'pruning poem.' "[6] Summers makes a point of saying Herbert never repeats himself. While I agree to an extent, I think the hieroglyphic poems group together under larger categories: there are the word games of "Anagram," "Coloss. 3.3," "Paradise," or "JESU," the distorted or special rhyme schemes of "Home" or "Deniall," the magical formulas or liturgical refrains of "A Wreath" or "Trinitie Sunday," the diversified line lengths of "The Collar," the mixed stanzaic patterns of "Easter" or "An Offering," and, of course, the shaped verse. All the hieroglyphic poems serve the same sacred purpose: attempting to address God through a dual offering that emulates the model of Christ's Eucharist. In his poem "An Offering," Herbert uses hieroglyphic form to delineate the larger pattern of *The Temple* by providing a short overview of the way humanity extends appropriate praise. Explaining how Christ's blood cleanses the wounds inflicted by sin, Herbert radically shifts line lengths and meter midway through to underline the hieroglyphic or dualistic nature of the thanks we offer:

> There is a balsome, or indeed a bloud,
> Dropping from heav'n, which doth both cleanse and close
> All sorts of wounds; of such strange force it is.
> Seek out this All-heal, and seek no repose,

Untill thou finde and use it to thy good:
Then bring thy gift, and let thy hymne be this;
Since my sadnesse
Into gladnesse
Lord thou dost convert,
O accept
What thou hast kept,
As thy due desert.
Had I many,
Had I any,
(For this heart is none)
All were thine
And none of mine:
Surely thine alone.
Yet thy favour
May give savour
To this poore oblation;
And it raise
To be thy praise,
And be my salvation.

(19–42)

By setting aside his offering from the rest of the poem through a change in shape, Herbert exploits the properties of written language to present hieroglyphic praise in "An Offering."[7]

The hieroglyphic forms and sacred puns with which Herbert structures *The Temple* are only the means he adopts for a greater end: achieving reciprocal writing. *The Temple* dedicates sacred poetry to God as a way of inviting a new chirograph, engraved upon the poet's heart. Herbert spells out the concept of reciprocal writing in "Good Friday," a lyric that incorporates sacred puns in hieroglyphic form. The first half of the poem delineates a familiar concern in associating the crucifixion with writing; however, "Good Friday" agonizes over the possibility of finding transcendent language to describe Christ's sacrifice:

O my chief good,
How shall I measure out thy bloud?
How shall I count what thee befell?
And each grief tell?

(1–4)

The second half of the poem reveals a dramatic metrical transformation in begging Christ to write in blood upon the poet's heart:[8]

Since bloud is fittest, Lord, to write
Thy sorrows in, and bloudie fight;

My heart hath store, write there where in
One box doth lie both ink and sinne:

(21–24)

"Good Friday" explicitly connects Herbert's equation of writing and blood with his hope for a response from Christ; in "Obedience" he similarly invokes a new writing from Christ by offering poetry inked in blood:

My God, if writings may
Convey a Lordship either way
Whither the buyer and the seller please;
Let it not thee displease,
If this poore paper do as much as they.

On it my heart doth bleed
As many lines as there doth need
To passe it self and all it hath to thee.
To which I do agree,
And here present it as my speciall deed.

(1–10)

Like "Good Friday" and "Obedience," many other poems in *The Temple* voice the desire for Christ's writing. In "The Sinner" a speaker declares "Remember that thou once didst write in stone" (14), wrongfully reminding God of the old dispensation; in "Unkindnese" a friend requests God's writing in brass, exclaiming "O write in brasse, *My God upon a tree / His bloud did spill*" (22–23). Even the recalcitrant speaker of "Nature" pleads for an engraving upon his heart: "O smooth my rugged heart, and there / Engrave thy rev'rend law and fear; / Or make a new one, since the old / Is saplesse grown" (13–16). In asking for reciprocal writing, Herbert makes the general argument of *The Temple* come full circle. Expanding the sacred pun inherent in Christ's Eucharist into his larger depiction of the crucifixion as sacred writing, he establishes a linguistic model for his offering; that offering invokes Christ's grace through a new "sweetnesse readie penn'd" ("Jordan II," 17) upon the poet's heart.

Although he hopes God will accept his Eucharistic offering, Herbert simultaneously fears that language constructs too fragile a bridge to God: we walk upon it in great peril, knowing that at any moment the bridge might shatter into Babelistic fragments. Poem after poem lists the intrinsic danger language poses in resurrecting the tower of Babel. In "Frailtie," a speaker has already chosen God's "regiment" over the secular world but expresses apprehension at the temptations offered by the world's "brave language": "It may a Babel prove / Commodious to conquer heav'n and thee / Planted in me" (22–24). As "The Flower" suggests, the Babelistic tendencies of language inhibit Herbert's efforts to reach God through verse;

> Many a spring I shoot up fair,
> Offring at heav'n, growing and groning thither:
> . . . .
>
> But while I grow in a straight line,
> Still upwards bent, as if heav'n were mine own,
> Thy anger comes, and I decline.
>
> (24–25; 29–31)

Herbert identifies the Babelistic heritage of language in "Sinnes Round" by describing the three stanzas of the poem as sins ascending three stories high: "My hands to joyn to finish the inventions: / And so my sinnes ascend three stories high, / As Babel grew before there were dissentions" (13–15). "Sinnes Round" linguistically represents the speaker locked within a cycle of sin by beginning each stanza with the preceding one's final line; the identical first and last lines highlight the lyric's claustrophobic form through further enclosure: "Sorrie I am, my God, sorrie I am." The chilling Babel image defines how ambivalent hieroglyphic structures can be: though Herbert tries to reintegrate the broken pieces of fallen language into a crown of praise, buildings too easily degenerate into corrupt towers.

Herbert agonizes over the limitations language imposes, but longs to surpass them by offering the special praise that might invoke new writing. Throughout *The Temple* Herbert's goal centers on ways of spelling God's word in the hope that God will reciprocate in kind. In both "JESU" and "Love-joy" he writes out the very letters of Christ's name, attempting to manifest what he declares impossible in "The Flower": "Thy word is all, if we could spell" (21). *The Temple* charts Herbert's struggle with the potential and boundaries of language, ranging from the deep despair of "Longing" to the real anticipation of "Heaven." By modeling his poetry on a logocentric view of Christ, Herbert strengthens his chances of using puns and hieroglyphic forms to speak in transcendent language. Once in God's hearing, Herbert seeks a new divine handwriting inscribed upon his heart. The cry of the hard heart offering praise on the broken altar of human speech opens "The Church" and resounds through all Herbert's lyrics: "O let thy blessed SACRIFICE be mine, / And sanctifie this ALTAR to be thine" ("The Altar," 15–16).

Notes

1. George Herbert, "The Quidditie," *The English Poems of George Herbert*, ed. C. A. Patrides (Totowa, N.J.: Rowman and Littlefield, 1974), lines 1–12. All references to Herbert's poetry will be taken from this edition.

2. For an excellent discussion of linguistic theory in the seventeenth century see Murray Cohen, *Sensible Words: Linguistic Practice in England 1640–1785* (Baltimore: Johns Hopkins University Press, 1977). Martin Elsky has written on how Herbert's hieroglyphic poetry fits into the seventeenth century's larger conception of materiality in language; see his "George Herbert's Pattern Poems and the Materiality of Language: A New Approach to Renaissance Hieroglyphs," *ELH* 50 (1983): 245–60.

3. Mary Ellen Rickey similarly discusses how Herbert's lyric "The Sonne" provides a general justification of his poetic technique in *The Utmost Art: Complexity in the Verse of George Herbert* (Lexington: University Press of Kentucky, 1966). I support her larger conception of the pun as a literary device containing a wide range of verbal ambiguities, serving "as the most compact conceivable means of pointing up the sense of analogy, or, as frequently, of painful discrepancy between what is and what should be, which is the genesis of most of Herbert's meditations: one word is made the nexus of two imagerial systems" (90).

4. In her discussion of the correspondences and resemblances that mark seventeenth-century thought, Sharon Cadmon Seelig points to the words of Jacob Boehme in her *The Shadow of Eternity: Belief and Structure in Herbert, Vaughan, and Traherne* (Lexington: University Press of Kentucky, 1981): "When I take up a stone or clod of earth and look upon it; then I see that which is above, and that which is below, yea the whole world therein" (2).

5. Heather Asals, *Equivocal Predication: George Herbert's Way to God* (Toronto: University of Toronto Press, 1980), 18–21 and passim.

6. Joseph H. Summers, *George Herbert: Religion and Art* (1954; reprint, Cambridge: Harvard University Press, 1968), 138.

7. It is ironic that "An Offering" follows "Praise II" in *The Temple;* although the poetic voice in "Praise II" tries to offer appropriate praise, the poem fails to present the offering that appears hieroglyphically in "An Offering."

8. "Good Friday" represents a mixed stanzaic form in part because Herbert revises an earlier poem, "Prayer" (lines 25–40 of "Good Friday"). Because Herbert deliberately chooses to change meter, he makes the poem into a hieroglyph.

Resonance in the Poetry of Robert Herrick

ROBERT W. HALLI, JR.

In a 1969 article, William V. Spanos discusses one special type of the relation of classical (usually Latinate) and English elements in Ben Jonson's poetry. He notes that Jonson frequently creates either a classical or an English context of some duration and then injects into it an apparently incompatible element of the other sort. In "An Ode, To himselfe," for instance, the classical equilibrium of "*Aonian* springs" and the city of "*Thespia*" is disturbed by British "Chattring Pies." Similarly, after Jonson establishes the real English setting of "To Penshurst," we find the estate enjoyed both by real English men and women and by Greco-Roman mythological figures.[1] Spanos argues that this technique charges a poem with a tension which transfigures our apprehension of it, and that we must rethink such a poem in light of the intrusive element. Having done so, we should find the value of the poem greatly enhanced by this tension's effect, which Spanos calls "resonance."

Importantly, resonance has potential as a highly effective and widely useful critical tool for analysis, evaluation, and discussion of the poetry of Ben Jonson and his followers. There are, however, a number of limitations to Spanos's arguments. First, although he searches hard for one, he is unable to locate any statement by Jonson to the effect that the poet uses, or advocates the use of, the effect called resonance. Second, Spanos restricts his field of investigation to classical and English elements, surely one of the most important areas of resonance in the poetry of Jonson and his contemporaries, but not the only one. Lastly, although Spanos suggests that resonance can be caused by the appearance of elements of diction or technique incompatible with the established contexts into which they intrude, he dwells almost exclusively on resonance created by intrusive elements of subject matter or detail.

In fact, the poetry of Robert Herrick provides a more rewarding body of writing for treatment in terms of resonance. Jonson's chief lyric disciple achieves this effect in many more ways than does his mentor. Herrick not only employs resonance in the construction of hundreds of the verses of *Hesperides,* but he also treats it didactically in at least a dozen poems, most notably in "*The Lilly in a Christal.*" In its first two stanzas, aesthetic contexts are clearly established, apparently incompatible elements are introduced into them, and the effects of vitalizing resonance are thereby created:

> You have beheld a smiling *Rose*
> When Virgins hands have drawn
> O'r it a Cobweb-Lawne:
> And here, you see, this Lilly shows,
> Tomb'd in a *Christal* stone,
> More faire in this transparent case,
> Then when it grew alone;
> And had but single grace.
>
> You see how *Creame* but naked is;
> Nor daunces in the eye
> Without a Strawberrie:
> Or some fine tincture, like to this,
> Which draws the sight thereto,
> More by that wantoning with it;
> Then when the paler hieu
> No mixture did admit.[2]

Although a diaphanous lawn and a rose are both lovely, placing the rose beneath the lawn's context causes it to "smile," and creates "more" beauty than the mere sum of the separate beauties of lawn and rose. The same is true of placing the "Lilly" (or "Grapes" and "Cherries" in the fourth stanza) within the context of the *"Christal"* bell jar. Likewise, although the bowl of cream is lovely in its pure whiteness, it is, as Achsah Guibbory has noted, "aesthetically uninteresting,"[3] as is the strawberry, for that matter. But when the red fruit is inserted into the "naked" cream, element and context establish a more beautiful, actively resonant ("wantoning") relationship. In the third stanza Herrick reinforces this point with an image of amber placed in water. The aesthetic value created by such imposition is "more faire" than "single grace." Especially active in its effect, this resonance "draws" or "stroaks the sight" and "daunces in the eye" of its viewer. These "dynamics of voyeurism"[4] are designed, as Herrick tells us in the fifth stanza, "to juggle with the sense."

I define resonance, then, more broadly than does Spanos. It is an active relationship between a disturbing element of detail or of language and the established context into which that element is introduced. By sharpening our perception of element and of context, resonance both increases the aesthetic worth of each and also creates a new whole, whose aesthetic value is greater than the sum of the individual values of the element and the context.

One of the commonest sorts of resonance of detail in the poetry of both

Jonson and Herrick is that created by the intrusion of modern, English, or nonclassical details into an essentially Greco-Roman classical atmosphere. Interestingly, both authors employ such resonance in their adaptations of Catullus's fifth song, *"Vivamus, mea Lesbia,"* in which the persona asks his mistress for hundreds and thousands of kisses.[5] Jonson's translation, "To the Same [Celia]" (no. 6 in *The Forrest*), is very faithful to the original until its speaker asks the woman to continue kissing "Till you equall with the store" of kisses

> All the grasse that *Rumney* yeelds,
> Or the sands in *Chelsey* fields,
> Or the drops in silver *Thames,*
> Or the starres, that guild his streames. . . .[6]

Spanos correctly notes that "the ideal classical world has suddenly become seventeenth-century England; the Catullian lover, a Londoner; and his conventionally urbane tone, more sharply ironic and intimate."[7] Herrick, too, introduces material not present in the original into his translation of Catullus. But where Jonson's resonant details do not change the purpose of the catalogue of kisses, Herrick's, in "*To* Anthea," propel the poem in a new direction after the oscular enumeration:

> But yet, though Love likes well such Scenes as these,
> There is an Act that will more fully please:
> Kissing and glancing, soothing, all make way
> But to the acting of this private Play:
> Name it I would; but being blushing red,
> The rest Ile speak, when we meet both in bed.
>
> (24)

Gordon Braden has noted that while "Catullus's kisses are clearly synechdoche for full sexuality," Herrick's seem to be "an alternative kind of sexuality that threatens . . . to displace actual coition."[8] Thus, in Herrick's poem, the English speaker's mode of seduction is both more and less forthright than that of his model. He must make his desires clear, and the prospect of sexual intercourse attractive, while not overly embarrassing either Anthea or himself (he is already "blushing red"). In part he sneakily does this by arguing not for his own gratification, but for that of "Love" who "makes me write" and who "likes well such Scenes" as their kissing but is "more fully pleased" by the "acts" that constitute "this private Play." This resonant shift of detail radically changes the effect of the catalogue of kisses from endgame to foreplay.

Again like Jonson, Herrick frequently achieves resonance of detail by introducing classical elements into an English setting. He presents "*A New-yeares gift sent to Sir* Simeon Steward" as an artful catalogue of

English holiday foods and entertainments, saturated with the joys of the rural peasantry. But a foreign guest appears late in the poem:

> Sit crown'd with Rose-buds, and carouse,
> Till *Liber Pater* twirles the house
> About your eares. . . .
>
> (127)

The introduction of Bacchus in the Latin *"Liber Pater"* resonates back through the poem, re-creating our perception of its rustic sports in terms of Roman festivity, or of an inspired revel like that described in the familiar *"When he would have his verses read"* and in many other poems in *Hesperides*. Herrick links the English holiday with classical rites that emphasize particularly the discarding of the old year and the acceptance of the new with its coming spring of fertility and rebirth. Thus, by the resonant effect of this one Latin phrase, Herrick lifts his poem from merely local reference to participation in the mythic cycle of the natural year.

Unlike Jonson, Herrick sometimes uses a Christian detail to create resonance within a "pagan" classical context, as in the concluding line of the exuberantly bacchanalian drinking song, *"The May-pole":*

> A health to my Girles
> Whose husbands may Earles
> Or Lords be, (granting my wishes)
> And when that ye wed
> To the Bridall Bed,
> Then multiply all, like to Fishes.
>
> (239)

In this context the reference to God's Edenic command to increase and multiply and to Christ's miracle of the loaves and fishes is strikingly incongruous. But Herrick's invocation of both paganism and Christianity in his blessing of human fertility emphasizes the supreme importance of the principle of rebirth, which could not be so exalted within either tradition alone, nor within both traditions separately. Like most good jokes, the poem's conclusion resonates with seriousness: the licensed sexual play may well produce children, and responsibility.

Although many of Herrick's best-known poems in the *carpe diem* tradition, such as *"To the Virgins"* or *"To Blossoms,"* begin with an argument from mortality, others first establish a carefree context of youth, beauty, and joy. In each of these latter poems, the delayed introduction of the *memento mori* creates a resonance of detail that recasts our perception of the entire poem. Much of the overall effect of "Corinna'*s going a May-*

ing," for example, depends on this resonance of death within life, and, in smaller scope, "*To* Dianeme" resonates just as powerfully:

> Sweet, be not proud of those two eyes,
> Which Star-like sparkle in their skies:
> Nor be you proud, that you can see
> All hearts your captives; yours, yet free:
> Be you not proud of that rich haire,
> Which wantons with the Love-sick aire:
> When as that *Rubie,* which you weare,
> Sunk from the tip of your soft eare,
> Will last to be a precious stone,
> When all your world of Beautie's gone.
>
> (61)

Sidney Musgrove correctly notes that "the clue to the poem lies in its final phrase: 'your world of beauty.' She is, quite literally, a microcosm of all beauty that anywhere exists."[9] Allied with the two purest elements, the fire in her eyes and the airy wantoning of her hair, Dianeme rejoices in perfect freedom while capturing the hearts of all others. But that stone, that bit of red earth, mocks humanity's "world of beauty" that must die, leaving behind only its mementoes to carry as grimly resonant a lesson of death as John Donne's "bracelet of bright haire about the bone."[10]

Our second sort of resonance, resonance of language, is created by the introduction into a poem of a word or phrase which, in itself and apart from the reality to which it refers, seems incompatible with the context of diction already established. Herrick activates this sort of resonance in *Hesperides* most frequently and most famously by introducing a sophisticated word into a poem otherwise composed of simple words. Consider, for example, *"Poetry perpetuates the Poet":*

> Here I my selfe might likewise die,
> And utterly forgotten lye,
> But that eternall Poetrie
> Repullulation gives me here
> Unto the thirtieth thousand yeere,
> When all the dead shall re-appeare.
>
> (265)

Through the very sound of its *u*'s and *l*'s, "Repullulation" suggests repetition more strongly than would the more common word "regeneration," which would also fit the meter. Because "Repullulation" specifically refers to resprouting or rebudding *(OED),* the rebirth of nature in the spring, Roger B. Rollin has argued cogently that the word "combines Herrick's pastoral sense of the affinity between man and nature and his faith in the eternizing power of verse: like nature's blossoms, the poet dies only temporarily."[11] In fact, "Repullulation" suggests that not only is Herrick kept "alive" by the life of his book, but that he is also born anew in every new reader who takes up *Hesperides*. Thus, the term from biology resonates strongly with the simpler words to vitalize the concept of poetic immortality.

Another type of resonance of language resides in Herrick's use of diminutives, as in *"The Rock of Rubies: and the quarrie of Pearls":*

> Some ask'd me where the *Rubies* grew?
> And nothing I did say:
> But with my finger pointed to
> The lips of *Julia.*
> Some ask'd how *Pearls* did grow, and where?
> Then spoke I to my Girle,
> To part her lips, and shew'd them there
> The Quarelets of Pearl.
>
> (24)

The only difficulty in the poem itself emanates from the last line's seeming diminutive of the title's *"quarrie":* "Quarelets" is plural and Julia's mouth can only be compared to a single quarry. But, as the diminutive of "Quarrel" (a "square . . . pane of glass" or "square tile"), "Quarelets" also means "small squares" *(OED),* the perfect shape of Julia's teeth, which are as white and hard as *"Pearls."* Problems remain with that title, however. *"Pearls,"* like teeth, indeed "grow" (line 5), but not in quarries. *"Rubies,"* moreover, do not "grow" (line 1), not are Julia's lips a *"Rock."* The phrase "*Rubies* grew," however, animates the stones and prepares for their metaphorical application to the color of Julia's lips. Thus, the seemingly inappropriate use of "Quarelets" sets up a resonance that particularizes strikingly the beautiful lips and teeth of the inestimable Julia.

The introduction of a humorous word into a serious context, or of a serious word into a humorous one can also produce a resonance of language. As A. Leigh DeNeef has noted, Herrick couches his verse, "*To* Jos: *Lo: Bishop of* Exeter," "in the latter's own ecclesiastical language and uses that language to elevate and 'sanctifie' both the patron and the poem."[12] Herrick commends his verses to the bishop and maintains at least a facade of seriousness until the last line, in which he says that if his ecclesiastical superior approves of any poem "'Tis Good Confirm'd; for you have Bishop't it" (64). Humor resides in the redundancy of "Confirm'd" and "Bishop't" referring to the Anglican sacrament, and the latter word carried specifically jocular connotations in the seventeenth century *(OED).* The humor resonates back through the poem to infuse the seemingly merely correct formal relationship of Herrick and his bishop with light-hearted friendship. The *"Diocesan"* of Exeter probably enjoyed the bantering, for he was that Joseph Hall who, in his younger days, had been an excellent satirist and humorist.

Herrick uses a serious word to create resonance in an otherwise humorous and light-hearted poem in *"To his Mistresses."* Here the aged persona calls "To my pretty *Witchcrafts* all" for *"Magicks, Spels, and Charmes"* in order "to beget / In my limbs their former heat," and he urges the women to "Find that *Medicine* (if you can) / For your drie-decrepid man" (10). The very sound of that last phrase insists upon the speaker's declining physical condition, and the poem closes in a much quieter and more resigned manner than that of its beginning. The dry decrepitude of the old speaker resonates back through his earlier jovial commands. He can toy with his decline, but that decline is real.

Throughout *Hesperides,* in more works and ways than we have accounted for here, Robert Herrick disturbs his poems' established contexts by introducing into them discordant elements of detail or language. Each dynamic relationship thus created vitally animates its poem, sharpens our perception of the poem's implications, and renders the combined aesthetic value of the context and element greater than the sum of their separate values. The effect of resonance is akin to that of binary opposition, as described by Jonathan Culler, which forces the reader "to explore qualitative similarities and differences, to make a connection so as to derive meaning from the disjunction."[13] But in the case of resonance we note a disjunction so as to derive new meaning from a connection.[14]

Notes

1. "The Real Toad in the Jonsonian Garden: Resonance in the Non-Dramatic Poetry," *Journal of English and Germanic Philology* 68 (1969): 7–8.

2. *The Poetical Works of Robert Herrick,* ed. L. C. Martin (Oxford: Clarendon Press, 1956), 75. All citations of Herrick's poems are taken from this edition; page numbers will be given in the text of the essay. Herrick evidently considered *"The Lilly in a Christal"* important. He refers to very few of his poems in other pieces, but in *"His Age"* he singles out for praise "that flowre of mine / Enclos'd within a christall shrine" (135). Other poems in *Hesperides* that treat resonance explicitly include *"Upon the Nipples of Julia's Breast," "To* Julia, *in her Dawn, or Day-breake," "The Amber Bead,"* and *"Upon a Flie."*

3. "*'No lust theres like to Poetry':* Herrick's Passion for Poetry," in *"Trust to Good Verses": Herrick Tercentenary Essays,* ed. Roger B. Rollin and J. Max Patrick (Pittsburgh: University of Pittsburgh Press, 1978), 81.

4. Paul R. Jenkins, "Rethinking What Moderation Means to Robert Herrick," *ELH* 39 (1972): 64.

5. *Catullus: A Critical Edition,* ed. D. F. S. Thomson (Chapel Hill: University of North Carolina Press, 1978), 77.

6. In *Ben Jonson,* ed. C. H. Herford, Percy and Evelyn Simpson (Oxford: Clarendon Press, 1947), 8:103.

7. Spanos, "The Real Toad," 8.

8. *The Classics and English Renaissance Poetry* (New Haven: Yale University Press, 1978), 178, 229.

9. *The Universe of Robert Herrick* (Auckland: Auckland University College Bull. 38, English ser. 4, 1950), 8.
10. "The Relique," in *John Donne: The Elegies and The Songs and Sonnets,* ed. Helen Gardner (Oxford: Clarendon Press, 1965), 89.
11. *Robert Herrick* (New York: Twayne, 1966), 202.
12. *"This Poetick Liturgie": Robert Herrick's Ceremonial Mode* (Durham, N.C.: Duke University Press, 1974), 103.
13. *Structuralist Poetics: Structuralism, Linguistics, and the Study of Literature* (Ithaca, N.Y.: Cornell University Press, 1975), 15.
14. I wish to acknowledge my gratitude to the Research Grants Committee of The University of Alabama for financial assistance that enabled me to complete the research for this article.

Victim Criminalized: Iconographic Traditions and Peacham's Ganymede

LORRAYNE Y. BAIRD-LANGE
(With the assistance of Hildegard Schnuttgen)

In his *Minerva Britanna* of 1612,[1] Henry Peacham presents an unusual emblematic version of the Ganymede myth, hitherto unnoticed either in Ganymede studies or in Peacham scholarship. The emblem (see fig. 1) shows Ganymede riding a cock in midair, and as the verses below explain, carrying in his left hand Circe's wand as well as a cup of poison, and in his right, false coins and medallions made of base metals—details which, except for the cock, seem not to have been thus connected with Ganymede prior to Peacham. While representing a radical departure from Ganymede traditions, this emblem nevertheless reveals Peacham's familiarity with both the ancient forms and the neoplatonic allegorizations of the myth current in Peacham's day. Only in light of these varied traditions can Peacham's exploitations and perversions of the material be understood.

Although the myth of Γανυμήδης appears in Cretan, Phrygian, and Lydian traditions, it is not clear where the myth had its origins or when, but it probably antedated Homer.[2] A passage in the *Iliad* gives us a point of departure. In a flyting match with Achilles, Aeneas, as part of his own genealogy, outlines the main features of the myth, relating that Ganymede, son of the Trojan king Tros and brother of Ilos and Assarakos [Aeneas's progenitor] was the "handsomest of mortals, whom the gods caught up to pour out drink for Zeus and live amid immortals for his beauty's sake" (20.232–37).[3] Later writers added that in compensation for the young son swept up by a whirlwind while he was herding sheep on Mount Ida, Zeus gave Ganymede's father a golden vine or, more frequently, four immortal horses to draw his chariot.[4] In the earlier accounts of male attachments, male love took the form of friendship rather than homosexuality,[5] and in its earliest form the myth of Ganymede has none of the homosexual or pederastic implications which as early as the sixth century B.C. became attached to the story,[6] so that the name *Ganymede* became a catchword for Παιδοφίλεω ("to love boys") among the Greeks, and *Catamite,* the Latin distortion of the name, signified the same thing among the Romans.

Crimina gravißima. 48

VPON a Cock, heere *Ganimede* doth ſit,
Who erſt rode mounted on *IOVES* Eagles back,
One hand holdes *Circes* wand, and ioind with it,
A cup top-fil'd with poiſon, deadly black:
The other Meddals, of baſe mettals wrought,
With ſundry moneyes, counterfeit and nought.

Theſe be thoſe crimes, abhorr'd of God and man,
Which Iuſtice ſhould correct, with lawes ſevere,
In * *Ganimed*, the foule Sodomitan:
Within the Cock, vile inceſt doth appeare:
Witchcraft, and murder, by that cup and wand,
And by the reſt, falſe coine you vnderſtand.

* O fuge te teneræ puerorum credere turbæ, Nam causam iniusti ſemper amoris habent. Tibullus.

Iſta a te puniantur (ô Rex) ne tu pro illis puniaris. Ciprian. de vtilitate Pœnitentiæ.

Fig. 1. Emblem 48 from Henry Peacham, *Minerva Britanna*, London, 1612. (Bodleian Library, Mal. 748, fol. 48.)

In Crete, where pederasty was highly cultivated and refined, the primitive ruler of the island, Minos, replaced Zeus as ravisher, but elsewhere the boy was said to be carried off by Zeus or his eagle, the Dorians especially emphasizing the divine kidnapper's homosexual passion for the youth.[7] This myth is but a part of a pattern of erotic associations of the gods with men in the fifth century B.C., when Apollo, for example, is himself thus presented with Hyacinthus and others of his "darlings."[8] Although like the Kore maiden archetype represented by Persephone, who was similarly abducted, Ganymede also became associated with vegetation myths, the chief emphasis among the Greeks and Romans was upon the pederastic implications of the rape, the attitudes of the writers varying with the moral climate of their day or with their own moral persuasions and sexual preferences.[9]

Frankly celebrating the fashionable homosexual attachments of Greek and Roman life, the *Musa puerilis* of the *Greek Anthology*,[10] with which Peacham was familiar, presents some pretty conceits in verses on homosexual passion, comparing Zeus's affair with Ganymede unfavorably with the poets' own love affairs (nos. 133, 194, and 254), or expressing the fear that Zeus has carried off or will soon swoop down on the poet's own lover (nos. 65, 67, 68, 69, and 70). Here as in other post-Homeric mentions of Ganymede, the abductor has become the eagle of Zeus, or Zeus in eagle form, a detail amusingly alluded to in number 70 by Meleager, epigrammatist of the first century B.C.: "I will stand up even against Zeus if he would snatch thee from me, Myiscus. . . . And yet Zeus often told me himself, 'What dost thou dread? I will not smite thee with jealousy . . .' but I, if even a fly [not an eagle] buzz past, am in dread lest Zeus prove a liar. . . ." The divine passion was expressed by Ovid: "Something was found which even Jupiter would rather be than what he was,"[11] or, alternatively, "One day the very king of all the gods / Took fire when he looked at Ganymede. / Then, O, he wished himself less masculine. . . ."[12] Less enraptured by the pederasty associated with the myth, Plato four centuries earlier, holding homosexuality and lesbianism to be major crimes, accused the Cretans of making gods in their own image: "they were so firmly convinced that their laws came from Zeus that they saddled him with this [the Ganymede] fable, in order to have a divine 'precedent' when enjoying that particular pleasure" (*Leges* 1.636c).[13] Likewise, Cicero held that the principal poems and songs about Ganymede reveal the homosexuality of the writers, blaming Homer for giving the gods the imperfections of men.[14]

Greek and Roman writers always present Ganymede as the innocent young victim, surprised and frightened, or at least passive, when seized, as for example in Hermes' speech in Lucian's Judgment of the Goddesses:

> I myself spent some time on Ida when Zeus was in love with his Phrygian lad, and I often came here when he sent me down to watch the boy. Indeed, when he was in the eagle, I flew beside him and helped him to lift the pretty fellow, and if my memory serves me, it was from this rock just here that Zeus caught him up. You see, he chanced to be piping to his flock then, and Zeus, flying down behind him, grasped him very delicately in his talons, held in his beak the pointed [shepherd's] cap which was on the boy's head, and bore him on high, terrified and staring at him with his head turned backwards. So then I took the syrinx, for he had let it fall in his fright.[15]

Lucian further emphasizes the youth and innocence of the victim by representing him in Olympia as a homesick child, pouting and asking Zeus, "When I want to play, who will be my playmate?" Zeus answers, "You may have Eros as playmate and play at astragal [dice] as much as you wish."[16] Ganymede's association with Eros preceded Lucian, especially in vase paintings, where the two are indistinguishable, except for Eros's wings.[17]

Ganymede was a favorite of Greek vase painters, who added to the myth the motif of Zeus's homosexual pursuit prior to the abduction of the fleeing boy. The iconography of Zeus is always the same: dressed in a long robe, bearded and crowned with a love wreath in the typical fashion of the ἐραστής (older homosexual lover), carrying a scepter in his right hand, running, he reaches out with his left hand to grab Ganymede. Likewise, the iconography of Ganymede makes him also easily recognizable: a beardless youth or ἐρωμένη, sometimes nude, sometimes dressed, Ganymede is typically shown on vase paintings—either alone (fig. 2),[18] or followed by Zeus—running at full speed toward the left, with his right hand trundling a hoop with a stick, while carrying a cock in his left hand stretched out as far away as possible from Zeus, at whom he glances fearfully with his head turned backward.[19] On certain vases depicting the pursuit appears the inscription KALOS HO ΠAIS or HO ΠAIS KALOS ("the beautiful boy"), an unmistakable reference to Ganymede.[20]

Like certain other small animals, the cock was a traditional love gift from the *erastes* to the *eromene,* also apparently a phallic symbol or a symbol of the act of love.[21] Thus, I believe that the Ganymede shown fleeing with the cock held as far away as possible from Zeus is the virgin or uninitiated Ganymede, as for example, in the hydria of Nola in the Georgian Museum of the Vatican.[22] One vase, a Vienna amphora, shows Ganymede with the cock on his right hand extended backward toward Zeus, who is reaching out to grab either Ganymede or the cock (fig. 3).[23] The oldest of the Ganymede vases which has come to my attention, an amphora of the sixth or fifth century B.C., now in Munich, demonstrates these ideas fully. Now in Olympus, an almost nude Ganymede facing a

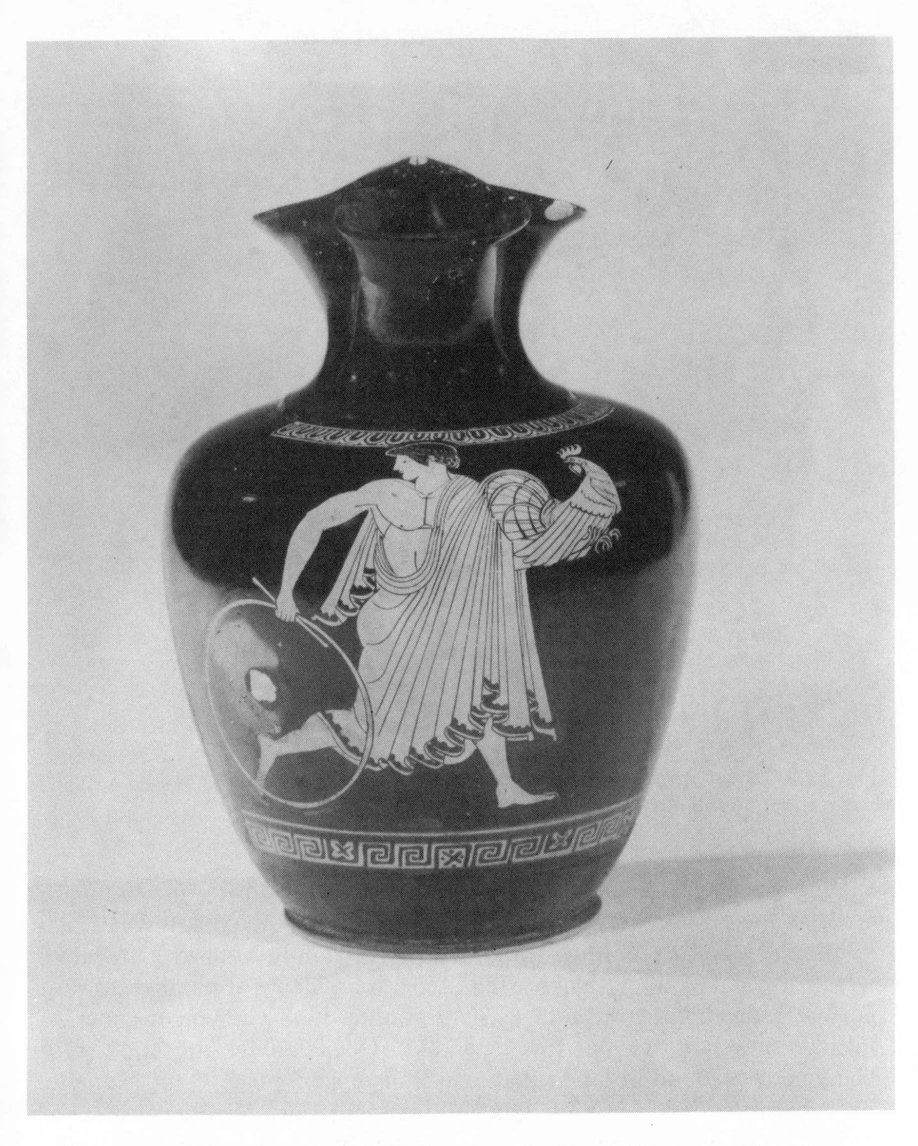

Fig. 2. Rf. Oinochoe, 23.160.55 (attributed to The Pan Painter, ca. 470–460 B.C.). (The Metropolitan Museum of Art, Rogers Fund, 1923.)

Fig. 3. Rf. Attic Amphora, AS Inv. Nr. IV 652. (Kunsthistorisches Museum, Antikensammlung, Vienna.)

smiling Zeus, gesticulates with outstretched hand downward toward a cock on the ground between them, as if presenting the cock to Zeus. An attendant standing behind Ganymede is crowning him with the love wreath typical of the *erastes,* while Zeus in an identical parallel upward gesture indicates the wreath, as if presenting it to Ganymede, now an initiate into homosexual love (fig. 4).[24] Occasionally the cock with Ganymede is found in other media, in Roman sarcophagi,[25] for example, but most remarkably in an Olympian ornamental or votive terra cotta of 475–470 B.C., which depicts a smiling Zeus in human form bodily carrying off a passive or complaisant Ganymede who still holds the cock between him and Zeus.[26] After the Greek and early Roman period, the cock appears very rarely in Ganymede iconography. Peacham may have studied the early iconography; certainly he knew the popular ideas about cocks and cock-riders in his own day. Among Peacham's near predecessors and contemporaries, the eagle, not the cock, was the bird associated with Ganymede.

It was perhaps the *pikanterie* or scandal of these earlier human representations of the homosexual god that was responsible for the iconographic metamorphosis of Zeus into the eagle. Artistic decorum militating against the use of the eagle in the pursuit scenes where he would have looked ridiculous, the eagle abduction typically shows the boy either at the moment of being seized or during his aerial transport toward Olympus, held by eagle claws and beak. The most famous early representation of Ganymede with the eagle, the inspired ethereal marble of Leochares, fourth century B.C., presents an aerial quality in the upward movement of the lines, while Ganymede's posture and expression suggest spiritual rapture at the moment when both eagle and youth are poised for flight, while the shepherd boy's forlorn little dog howls upward after his disappearing master.[27] After Leochares, the eagle was standard in art in both the abduction and the cup-bearer scenes.

While the homosexual pursuit was dropped in favor of the abduction by the eagle, Ganymede's level of terror is increased, as is depicted in the third century B.C. Sicilian mosaic of ancient Morgantina, described by Kyle M. Phillips as follows:

> Ganymede with his red cap, chlamys, and boots, is a vigorous Phrygian boy approaching puberty. His body is curiously hard and virile even though his skin is pure white. The contrast between masculine form and feminine color indicates a rather sensitive understanding of a compli-

Fig. 4. Sf. Amphora, Vas. N. I. 6009 (834), KM 3075 (6–5th c.). Staatl. Antikensammlungen (München. Inv. Nr. 6009. Etr.-sf. Amphora. [Negativ Museum]).

> cated subject matter. The position of Ganymede expresses the nature of the action. Not yet completely recovered from the initial shock of being seized, Ganymede gazes at his abductor. The position of the arms and legs, resembling that of a struggling child at the moment it is picked up from a rapid run, emphasizes the fright of Ganymede and his attempt to escape. His right arm stretches forth to fend off the eagle's wing, the right leg is cocked ready to sprint, the left leg violently thrusts to the side in an abortive jump. In this wild flurry, Ganymede has discarded the right half of his shepherd's flute but holds tight in his left hand the remaining part, an action which stresses his swift abduction.[28]

This mosaic is one of several almost identical works belonging to the pre-Christian Roman era.[29] Similarly, on Roman sarcophagi of the same era, where the beautiful youth guarantees the immortality of the honored dead, the abduction scene shows him trying to ward off the attack of the eagle.[30]

The violence of the rape, with Ganymede terrified or resisting, was, however, largely abandoned in the later iconography of the abduction: even Leochares' early Ganymede does not show terror, but rather rapture. Like the cup-bearer motif, which also typically shows Zeus as eagle, the eagle abduction permitted and invited idealizations. A symbol of immortality,[31] the eagle is superbly appropriate as the carrier of a mortal to Olympus, where he will be made immortal; thus, the introduction of the eagle into Ganymede iconography made it possible to convert the euhemerized myth into something of its primal innocence and moreover to idealize it through a rich tradition of allegorization not possible so long as the anthropomorphic Zeus in overt homosexual pursuit prevailed as the abductor. The "otherness" of the myth can be demonstrated as far back as the late Hellenistic and early Christian era; in the late Middle Ages and in the Renaissance, allegorizations of the myth reached their fullest development.

The cupbearer motif gave rise to late Hellenistic and Roman accounts of Ganymede as waterbearer: as the Greek Ὑδροχοεύς (Hydrocheus) or the Roman Aquarius set in the heavens as an astrological sign, Ganymede was recognized as a genius of the Nile, presiding over its fertilizing headwaters.[32] In this tradition, Philo Judaeus makes Ganymede an "image of the divine Logos," presented as a fountain, and an "outpouring from God, a continuous flow which brings constant order to all creation"; God's grace, an "intoxicating draught," he compares to the nectar and ambrosia of the Olympians."[33] On an early fourth-century Christian sarcophagus, tomb of a Christian martyr, connected with the Memoria Apostolorum ad Catacumbas in San Sebastiano, Ganymede appears offering a cup to the eagle, a scene interpreted to represent the Eucharist,[34] and a similar design also appears on a Vatican sarcophagus. The astral myth was accepted by Hyginus and Aratus, medieval writers on astronomy, and by Le

Maire de Belges[35] in the sixteenth century; emblematists, sometimes invoking Xenophontian etymology, as explained below, preferred Philo's interpretation: Bocchius, for example, compares the pleasure of the true knowledge and worship of God to the enjoyment of the ambrosia of Olympia: VERA IN COGNITIONE DEI, CVLTQVE VOLVPTAS. SIC FRVIMVR DVLCI NECTARE, ET AMBROSIA.[36] The mystic possibilities of the cupbearer motif inform the famous Rubens *Ganymede,* in which Ganymede as transported soul still resting on the wings of the eagle receives the cup from the hand of Hebe,[37] a work produced between 1611 and 1617, roughly contemporaneous with Peacham's emblem book, but very different in conception from Peacham's Ganymede.

The carrying off or rape of Ganymede offered even richer possibilities for the allegorists. As early as the fourth century B.C. when Plato was explaining the myth euhemeristically, Xenophon quite to the contrary explained it as a moral allegory of the ascendancy of the mind over the body. Deriving the name from γάνυσθαι ("to enjoy") and μήδεα ("intelligence"), he argues that the beauty of the mind, rather than of the body, wins the love of the gods and confers immortality.[38] In Christian thought appears the same ambivalence. Interpreted euhemeristically, the abduction myth was used by the Christian Fathers in their invectives against paganism, Saint Augustine, for example, referring to the scandal of it;[39] yet on the other hand, earlier than Augustine, in the first century A.D., when Christian art syncretizes Christian and pagan motifs—as is clear in the Roman basilica at Porta Maggiore, where pagan mythological characters are infused with Christian Truth[40]—the Ganymede myth begins to appear on Christian sarcophagi, where it is believed to represent the personal apotheosis of the commemorated dead, or the "ascent of the soul to immortality."[41] What has been referred to as an "incompatibility of medieval Christianity and Classicism"[42] (in light of pagan ambivalence, this is really a deeper incompatibility inherent in human sexuality and morality) produced a dilemma or feeling of unease among Christians who admired pagan mythology and were not, like Milton, willing simplistically to dispose of all pagan gods by turning them into devils. Idealized Christian versions of Ganymede transcended the moral plane of Xenophon, reaching into spiritual, metaphysical, or mystical realms. Writing in the late fourteenth century, Francesco da Buti interprets the eagle as *la divina charita* ("divine love"); Mount Ida, whence Ganymede was abducted, reminds us, he says, that penitent hermits in the woods are better candidates for salvation than others.[43]

Christian writers invoked the principle of figurism, the notion that pagan myths anticipated, or prefigured, scriptural motifs. In this spirit the Middle Ages allegorized Ovid's *Metamorphoses* and *Ars amatoria,* which were read, according to Seznec, even by nuns in the thirteenth century.[44]

In the late medieval moralizations of Ovid, Ganymede is seen as a prefiguration of John the Evangelist, who was often represented as an eagle, of course, among the four apostles; and the eagle in this scheme is a symbol of Christ or of that divine inspiration and insight that enabled the prophet to be drawn upward and thus to reveal the divine mysteries or secrets of heaven.[45] Adopting this interpretation, Claudius Minos (Mignault) in the sixteenth century explains that the eagle *(aquila,* supposedly from *acumen)* was the attribute of Saint John, *ut eius in divinis rebus acumen longe perspicax et oculatum, ut ita dicum, ostenderent* (so that to him difficult matters were made clear and plain, i.e., revealed).[46]

Dealing with the difficult matter of pagan eroticism, Renaissance Neoplatonists either distinguished moralistically between Ἀντέρως and Ἔρως,[47] or by converting eroticism to Christian doctrine, emphasizing the spiritual within the material. The winged Cupid, for example, became the angel of the annunciation; the Infant Jesus took over Cupid's arrows to pierce human hearts with his love.[48] In this intellectual climate, Cristoforo Landino in his famous Dante commentary (1529) sees Ganymede as an image of the *mens* ("mind") or highest faculty of the human soul beloved by Jupiter, Supreme Deity: *Sia adunque Ganimede l'humana mente la quale Gioue, idest el sommo Idio ama.* He further explains that the shepherd companions of Ganymede (often seen in art) stood for lower faculties of the soul, the vegetal and sensory, left behind as Jupiter transports the mind to heaven, where being separated from the body *(rimossa dal corpo),* the mind contemplates heavenly mysteries.[49] Other contemporary humanists, both writers and painters, invoked this Neoplatonic doctrine of the *furor divinus* (divine inspiration, passion, or madness) in presenting Ganymede. Whether Michelangelo's famous *Ganymede* (1532) was intended to represent the *furor amoris* of his passion for Tommaso Cavalieri,[50] or whether it was meant to represent the *furor divinus,* the latter interpretation was accepted by Michelangelo's followers and imitators. The drawing shows Ganymede in a state of trance or enraptured passivity, his arms resting on the wings of the eagle and his legs grasped by the talons, the expression on his face suggesting a soul *rimossa dal corpo.* This drawing is often compared with another in similar style and technique, the *Tityus,* which depicts the torture of Tityus—an eagle perpetually tearing out his liver—for having assaulted Apollo's mother, Latona. This allegory of the "tortures caused by immoderate love" Panofsky sees as Michelangelo's version of *amor profano* as opposed to the Ganymede allegory representing *amor sacro.*[51] Whatever Michelangelo's intention, many Neoplatonic artists imitated this *Ganymede,*[52] including the copper engraver, Giulio Bonasone, in an illustration (1555) for the Ganymede emblem of A. Bocchius, captioned VERA IN COGNITIONE DEI,

CVLTVQ. VOLVPTAS ("delight in the true knowledge and worship of God").[53]

Predecessors of Bocchius in this emblematic tradition translated Ganymede's abduction by Zeus as the *sursum corda* or elevation of heart, mind, or soul, or joy and rapture in God or the love of God. Among these epigrammatists cited as sources or influences by Peacham in his address "To the Reader" prefacing *Minerva Britanna,* the most famous, Alciatus, an anthologer of epigrams, shows Ganymede as a small child, not *rimossa dal corpo,* but fully in charge of his steed, an eagle in midair, his arm flung upward toward the heavens (fig. 5) as an allegory of the innocent soul enraptured by God. Above emblems of this type collected by Alciatus appears the caption IN DEO LAETANDUM ("rejoicing in God"), and typically beneath these woodcuts appears a Latin poem (fig. 5), which I have rendered rather freely as follows:

> Behold how excellently an artist has shown
> Jove's Trojan boy carried up to starry heights!
> Who does not know that Jove was touched by love
> As Homer, the ancient bard, has sung so well?
> Whoever woos God with heart and mind and soul
> Ascends in rapture to God in realms on high.[54]

Variations on the motif appear in the emblems: Conti says that the wise man through love of God rises to his divine nature;[55] Rollenhagen emphasizes the desire for the eternal: NON EST MORTALE QUOD OPTO; and Bocchius interprets Leochares' Ganymede as the soul distinguished from the body: SCULPTORIB. IAM NUNC GANYMEDEM CERNE LEOCRAE PACATI EMBLEMA HOC CORPORIS, ATQ. ANIMA EST.[56]

Emblematists and other Renaissance artists sometimes represented Ganymede as a child, and like Minos, invoked Christ's order to the apostles: *Sinite parvuli ad me veniant* ("Suffer the little children to come unto me"); or they were reminded of the scriptural saying that one must become as a little child to enter into the kingdom of heaven (*nisi efficiamur sicut parvuli,* etc.).[57] Major sixteenth-century painters represented Ganymede as a young man or half-grown boy;[58] others show him much younger. Nicolaes Maes in the 1670s produced a number of personal portraits for his patrons, showing their infants or small children as Ganymedes either riding on an eagle or clinging to his neck.[59] Cherubino Alberti represents Zeus in human form on Olympus, embracing Ganymede, a charming toddler with a water pitcher.[60] Well-meaning interpretations devolved into sentimentality and, as Panofsky notes, became more objectionable to the Church than the original pagan myths themselves,[61] a fact which perhaps illuminates Ganymede parodies such as

IN DEO LAETANDVM

Aſpice ut egregium puerum Iouis alite pictor
Fecerit Iliacum ſumma per aſtra uehi.
Quis ne Iouem tactum puerili credat amore?
Dic hæc Mæonius finxerit unde ſenex.
Conſilium mens atq; dei cui gaudia præſtant,
Creditur is ſummo raptus adeſſe Iouis.

Fig. 5. Emblem from Alciatus, *Emblematum liber* (1531), B6, Held no. 42.

Peacham's, but more remarkably the later *Rape of Ganymede* (1635) by Rembrandt. Rembrandt shows the abducted Ganymede as a fat, ugly, unwieldy baby with contorted face, shrieking and urinating in terror in the claws of an upward straining eagle, his beak hitching up the baby's dress to reveal his heavy buttocks prominently in center field to emphasize the pederastic intention of the abductor.[62] Laughably calling attention to the improbability that an eagle could, in fact, carry off a grown young man, this de-allegorization more importantly serves as a "drastic renunciation of the deification of Beauty,"[63] and makes ridiculous the Neoplatonic tradition. (In our own century, Rembrandt's *Ganymede* has itself been parodied in the playful, enigmatic *Canyon* by Rauschenberg, who makes the rapist a taxidermist's stuffed eagle jutting out frontward from the composition, while Ganymede has been reduced to a pair of buttocks represented only by a stuffed pillow divided in the middle by a cord and dangling below the lower edge of the collage.)[64]

Earlier than Rembrandt's *Ganymede* by more than two decades, Peacham's emblem is perhaps the first in revolt against the Neoplatonic tradition.

Addressed to Henry, Prince of Wales and oldest son of James I, the *Minerva Britanna*—the first totally original and completely illustrated emblem book in the English language—grew out of Peacham's efforts beginning in 1603 to convert into emblem form the substance of *Basilikon Doron* ("King's Gift") written by James I himself for his five-year-old son Henry in 1599, while the father was still on the throne of Scotland as James VI. Of august lineage, this mirror for princes is an impressive treatise dealing with the ruler's proper relationship to God (Bk. 1) and his subjects in his office as king (Bk. 2) and with his everyday social and public demeanor (Bk. 3). Before his first printed edition, Peacham produced three earlier manuscripts (1603, 1604, 1610)—the 1604 version dedicated to James, the other two, like the printed edition, addressed to Henry, each version containing more epigrams than the one preceding and reflecting the political climate of the year in which it was produced.[65] In the year 1612—sadly the year in which the eighteen-year-old dedicatee, Henry of Wales, died—appeared the *Minerva Britanna* in its first printed edition, containing 206 emblems, including those of earlier manuscripts, interspersed with others "newly invented," for "the fashioning of a vertuous mind," as Peacham explains.

Entitled "Crimina gravissima," the Ganymede emblem, number 48, is Peacham's version of the unpardonable crimes listed by King James in Book 2 of his *Basilikon Doron:* "horrible crimes that ye are bound in conscience neuer to forgiue: such as Witch-craft, wilfull murther, Incest (especially within the degrees of consanguinitie), Sodomy, Poysoning, and false coine"[66]—a list both ironic and prophetic in light of James's own notorious career.[67]

Clearly parodying Ganymede emblems of the type collected by Alciatus, Peacham depicts Ganymede astride a cock (not an eagle) in the ancient fashion of Eros or Amor, sometimes shown mounted upon the cock as steed. Always a symbol of the libido, whether directed heterosexually or homosexually, and associated with the venerable fertility deities of antiquity,[68] the cock by the late Middle Ages had become a symbol of unbridled lust, whoredom, adultery, and incest, as well as of sodomy. In his *Confessio Amantis* Gower compares one guilty of incest to "a cock among the Hennes,"[69] and Peacham himself repeats the idea in Emblem 118: the cock "most deseru'd to die, / For that contrarie vnto Natures Law, / His kindred he abus'd incestuously: / His Mother, Sisters. . . ." An avid student of the emblem tradition, Peacham very likely knew the emblematic "cock-rider" cuckold tradition of the Germans;[70] he may have also seen contemporary woodcuts associating the cock with brothels;[71] and the generality of the emblem suggests that he also knew that the cock by the late Middle Ages had become associated with witchcraft and the demonic.[72]

Astride the cock, Ganymede seems to float languorously through the air, not looking toward heaven and rejoicing in God, but glancing downward, his hands not flung heavenward in rapturous gesture, but holding symbols obnoxious to heaven. In his left hand, the rod with which he had trundled his hoop in primordial innocence has been metamorphosed into a witch's symbol, Circe's wand, which he holds together with the cup—the cup once filled with ambrosial nectar and then with the grace of God—now filled with the murderer's poison. In his right hand Ganymede now holds a scepter, topped with a crown roughly similar to Zeus's scepter and King James's.[73] Mounted on the scepter appear three "Meddals, of base mettals wrought," crudely decorated with puzzling figures, perhaps, but not clearly, suggestive of phallic symbols, such as those which appear on medieval leaden medals in the Foregias collection.[74] The left hand also holds beneath the scepter what appears to be a box (money box?) decorated with a curious diamond-shaped design, somewhat similar to certain pictorial representations of the jewel of the Mirror of Great Britain, made in 1604 to symbolize the union of Scotland and England under James, and typically worn by the king on his royal headdress.[75] Above and behind the box, we can see that Ganymede holds such a leather pouch or purse as was typical in the iconography of fertility deities such as Hermes or Priapus.[76] The ancient equation of sex and money (or fertility and monetary increase) prevails in Chaucer's reference to the treadfowl Monk: "no lussheburghes [spurious coin] payen ye!"[77] In Peacham's day impotence or unfruitful sexual activity was expressed in the image of the counterfeit coin, as in John Webster's *The White Devil* (1608, 1612),[78] where an impotent male is referred to as a "counterfeit diamond." Also, the term was used to signify the insincere convert.[79]

Peacham's Ganymede not only stands convicted as the agent of sodomy, of which he was traditionally the unwilling, or at least the passive, victim, but he also subsumes in his being all the other unpardonable crimes listed in James's *Basilikon Doron*. Beyond that unjust and cowardly, but instinctive, urge common to the human race to put the blame for a crime on the victim (who being weaker and more vulnerable than the aggressor is considered of less value to society and less of a threat to the accuser), what can be a firmer rationale for such an inversion of tradition?

A few artistic representations of Ganymede show ambivalence about his role in the affair with Zeus. A Carthaginian marble group of the fourth or fifth century A.D. presents a nude Ganymede in languorous pose looking seductively into the eyes of an eagle half his size, his limp-wristed arm draped lovingly around the eagle's neck,[80] and various other representations show Ganymede looking seductive, dwarfing the eagle, or demonstrating affection for him.[81] Through thorough grounding in the classics, Peacham obviously knew the early literary traditions of Ganymede, but there is no guarantee that he had ever seen any of these representations in art: certainly he did not know the Carthaginian Ganymede, which was thrown into a cistern along with other sixth-century debris, to be unearthed only in 1977 or shortly thereafter by a team of archaeologists from the University of Michigan. Peacham may also have known contemporary Ganymedes: the Ganymede in Spenser's *Faerie Queene* (3.11.34) on the tapestries in the Castle of Busirane depicting the history of lust; the Ganymede in Marlowe's *The Tragedie of Dido* (2.1), where Jupiter dandles his favorite like a bedecked queen upon his knee, offering him gifts of jewels, promising to make fools of other gods and goddesses for Ganymede's amusement; the Ganymede in the same author's *Hero and Leander* (1.144–48), where in Venus's Temple, gods were "committing headdie ryots, incest, rapes . . . Jove, slylie stealing from his sisters bed, / To dallie with Idalian Ganimed"; or the Ganymede in Marlowe's *Edward II* (1.4.180–81), where queen Isabella compares Edward's love for Gaveston to Jove's for Ganymede: "For never doted Jove on Ganimed, / So much as he on cursed Gaveston." Far worse than these, Peacham's Ganymede comes closer to one he could not have known: Milton's cupbearer to Satan (*Paradise Regained,* 2.350–53).

Peacham's sceptered Ganymede appears to be his own original creation, and the complexity and integrity of the interlocking iconographic details suggest not a lazy emblematic economy but a deliberate one.

Is Peacham making a statement about the character weaknesses of James, or worse, about the critical disorders endemic in his youthful

Scottish reign under powerful regents, who were his homosexual bedfellows? Does Peacham's sceptered Ganymede represent, in particular, James's first favorite, the French cousin twenty-four years his senior, the handsome Esmé Stuart, seigneur d'Aubigny, for whom the impressionable and love-starved thirteen-year-old James conceived a powerful (and in a sense "incestuous") romantic passion? Beyond the obvious fraudulence of spurious currency, does Peacham's "false coine" suggest the dissimulation of this pro-Vatican double agent under the pay of the French Duke of Guise in a plot to reestablish on the Scottish throne James's exiled mother, Mary Queen of Scots, the central figure and rallying point of Catholic forces? Certainly a religious "counterfeit coin," Esmé feigned a gradual conversion to the young king's Calvinistic Reform persuasions, through long hours of intimate conversation with the learned young king, "punctuated by wine and embraces behind closed doors,"[82] so that reports of his conversion exerted a countervailing force against the suspicions of the leaders of the Reform as Esmé assumed an obvious ascendancy over the young king. Promoting Esmé by giving him Arboath, the richest abbey in Scotland, and making him earl of Lennox in 1580, and soon thereafter by giving him the governorship of Dumbarton Castle and making him a member of the Privy Council and lord chamberlain, James thereby made his unscrupulous and opportunistic cousin, his "First Gentleman of the Bedchamber," the most powerful man in Scotland and himself Esmé's thrall. After his meteoric rise, Esmé, undestimating the strength of the Reform, and, forcibly separated from James, went back to France, where he died in 1583. The official cause of his death was dysentery and gonorrhea; the rumor was poison.

Could it be then that in this emblem Peacham is holding up the king's own mirror to the king's own face? Two Latin quotations in the margins of the emblem lend some credibility to this conjecture: from Tibullus, *O fuge te tenerae puerorum credere turbae, Nam causam iniusti semper amoris habent* (O flee the foolish effeminacy of boys, who as trusting a whirling top, always have passions for an unjust cause);[83] from Ciprian, *Ista a te puniantur (o Rex) ne tu pro illis puniaris* (By that vice which you do not correct you will be punished, O King).[84]

Notes

1. *Minerva Brittana; or, A Garden of Heroical Deuises, Furnished, and Adorned with Emblemes and Impresas of Sundry Natures, Newly Devised, Moralized, and Published* (London, 1612; New York: Da Capo Press, 1971), no. 48. For extensive treatments of Ganymede with bibliographies, see Hellmut Sichtermann, *Ganymed: Mythos und Gestalt in der antiken Kunst* (Berlin: Mann, 1953) and Gerda Kempter, *Ganymed: Studien zur Typologie, Ikonographie, und Ikonologie* (Vienna: Böhlau Verlag, 1980). [These two fundamental works will be cited hereafter as Sichtermann and Kempter.] See also Emil Kunze, "Zeus und Ganymed," in *100. Winckelmannsprogramm der Archäologie* (Berlin: Gesellschaft zu

Berlin, 1940), 27–50; Georg Lippold, "Leda und Ganymedes," *Sitzungsberichte der Bayerischen Akademie der Wissenschaften* (Munich) 3 (1954): 5–12; A. Pigler, *Barockthemen: Eine Auswahl von Verzeichnissen zur Ikonographie des 17. und 18. Jahrhunderts,* 2d enl. ed. (Budapest: Akadémiai Kiadó, 1974), 2:93–95; and Erwin Panofsky, *Studies in Iconology* (New York: Harper, 1962), 213–23. None of these standard works recognizes Peacham's Ganymede, likewise ignored in Eric Smith, *A Dictionary of Classical Reference in English Poetry* (Cambridge: D. S. Brewer, 1984), 99, where Ganymede passages are listed for Browning, Chaucer, G. Fletcher, Keats, Marlowe, Milton, Noyes, Shakespeare, Shelley, Spenser, Tennyson, and Wordsworth.

2. Sichtermann, 13–20; Kempter, chap. 1, esp. 5–18.

3. Trans. Robert Fitzgerald (Garden City, N.Y.: Anchor, 1975), 480.

4. Sichtermann, 18–20; Kempter, 5–18; and Herbert Hunger, *Lexikon der griechischen und römischen Mythologie* (Vienna: Hollinek, 1959), s.v. "Ganymed."

5. L. P. Wilkinson, "From the Point of View of Antiquity: Classical Approaches, IV: Homosexuality," *Encounter* (London) 51, no. 3 (September 1978): 20–31; Sichtermann, 13.

6. Sichtermann, 19. On an etymological explanation of μεδεα (from Γανυμή́δης[?]) as "männliche Genitalien," see Kempter, 7.

7. *Encyclopaedia Britannica* (London: Benton, 1970), s.v. "Ganymede"; Robert E. Bell, *Dictionary of Classical Mythology* (Oxford: ABC/CLIO, 1982), 119. Plautus seems to have originated the term *Catamite.*

8. Sichtermann, 13.

9. Sichtermann, 14–15. The vegetation myth is central to the Ganymede poems of Goethe (1774) and Hölderlin (1804).

10. *The Greek Anthology,* trans. W. R. Paton (London: Loeb Classical Library, 1918). On Peacham's familiarity with *The Greek Anthology* see Robert Ralston Cawley, *Henry Peacham: His Contribution to English Poetry* (University Park: Pennsylvania State University Press, 1971), 45.

11. *Metamorphoses* 10.155–57, trans. Horace Gregory (New York: Viking, 1958), 274–75.

12. *Mythology: An Illustrated Encyclopedia,* trans. Richard Cavendish (New York: Rizzoli, 1980), 137.

13. *Plato: The Laws,* trans. Trevor J. Saunders (Baltimore: Penguin, 1970), 61–62.

14. *Tusculan Disputations* 4.33; 1.26, trans. C. D. Yonge (New York: Harper, 1877), 37, 157.

15. *Dialogi deorum* 20.6, in *Lucian,* trans. A. M. Harmon (Cambridge: Harvard University Press, 1947), 3:393.

16. *Dialogi deorum* 4.3ff. See Bernhard Neutsch, "Spiel mit dem Astragal," in *Ganymed: Heidelberger Beiträge zur antiken Kunstgeschichte,* ed. Reinhard Herbig (Heidelberg: F. H. Kerle, 1949), 18–28. Dice playing belongs to the art of love, according to Ovid's *De arte amandi.* See Robert Nares, *A Glossary of Words Phrases Names and Allusions in the Works of English Authors Particularly of Shakespeare and His Contemporaries* (London: Routledge, 1905), s.v. "cockal."

17. Ch. Lenormant and J. De Witte, *Élite des monuments céramographiques* (Paris: Leleux, Librairie-Éditeur, 1857), 4:179 and pl. 49.

18. Museum photo, permission of the Metropolitan Museum of Art, New York (Rogers Fund, 1923). Similar is the Ganymede on an Attic red-figured Krater (ca. 480–470) of the Berlin Painter, reproduced in Ludovico Ragghianti, *Louvre, Paris,* Great Museums of the World (Milan: Arnoldo Mondadori, 1967), 54–55.

19. Sichtermann, 76–78, lists twenty-nine vase paintings of the *Verfolgung;* see also 21–28 and pls. 1,3, 2,2, and 2,4, and the hydria of Nola in Lenormant and De Witte, *Élite des monuments,* 1:35–36, 316, and pl. 18.

20. Lenormant and De Witte, *Élite des monuments,* 2:119.

21. On the erotic significance of the cock, see my article, "*Priapus Gallinaceus:* The Role of the Cock in Fertility and Eroticism in Classical Antiquity and the Middle Ages," *Studies in Iconography* 7–8 (1981–82): 81–111; Sichtermann, 24–31.

22. Lenormant and De Witte, *Élite des monuments,* 1:35–36, 316 n. 6, and pl. 18.

23. Museum photo, permission of Kunsthistorisches Museum, Vienna.

24. Museum photo, permission of Staatliche Antikensammlungen und Glyptothek,

Munich. Staatl. Antikensammlungen München. Inv. Nr. 6009. Etr.-sf. Amphora. (Negativ Museum).

25. Konrad Schauenburg, "Ganymed und Hahnenkämpfe auf Römischen Sarkophagen," *Archäologischer Anzeiger* 3 (1972), 501–16; Kempter, 41ff.; and Panofsky, *Studies in Iconology,* 171, 214.

26. Kunze, "Zeus und Ganymed," 27–50; Gisela M. A. Richter, *Greek Art,* 6th ed. (New York: Phaidon, 1969), 93–94; Sichtermann, 28–31.

27. Walter Copland Perry, *Greek and Roman Sculptures* (London: Longmans, 1882), 462–64; Sichtermann, 39ff. and pl. 3; Kempter, pl. 1.

28. "Subject and Technique in Hellenistic-Roman Mosaics: A Ganymede Mosaic from Sicily," *Art Bulletin* 42 (December 1960): 254.

29. Phillips, "Subject and Technique," 243–62; Louis Foucher, "L'enlèvement de Ganymède," *Revue archéologique,* n.s. 1 (1979): 25–28; Georg Lippold, *Leda und Ganymedes* (Munich: Verlag der Bayerischen Akademie der Wissenschaften, 1954), 10 and Taf. 1,1.

30. Schauenburg, "Ganymed und Hahnenkämpfe," 508, and pls. 503–6; Panofsky, *Studies in Iconology,* 171, 184.

31. Schauenburg, "Ganymed und Hahnenkämpfe," 508; L. Charbonneau-Lassay, *Le Bestiarie du Christ* (Bruges: Desclée, de Brouwer, 1940), 71–85. On the iconography of the cupbearer motif, see Reinhard Herbig, "Ganymed und der Alder," in *Ganymed: Heidelberger Beiträge,* ed. Herbig, 1–9.

32. Panofsky, *Studies in Iconology,* 214; *Meyers Enzyklopädisches Lexikon,* s.v. "Ganymed"; Hunger, *Lexikon,* 140–41.

33. John Dillon, "Ganymede as the Logos," *Classical Quarterly,* n.s. 31 (1981): 183–85. Ganymede is not mentioned, but the myth is obviously in Philo's mind.

34. Hellmut Sichtermann, "Der Ganymed-Sarkophag von San Sebastiano," *Archäologischer Anzeiger* 3 (1977): 462–70, esp. 463. Schauenburg notes that the sarcophagus in the courtyard of the Palazzo Venezia, depicting Ganymede, is used as a fountain; see "Ganymed und Hahnenkämpfe," 501.

35. Panofsky, *Studies in Iconology,* 214 n. 137; Kempter, 34–41 and pls. 12–16; Ann Moss, *Poetry & Fable: Studies in Mythological Narrative in Sixteenth-Century France* (London: Cambridge University Press, 1984), 17, 46–47.

36. Panofsky, *Studies in Iconology,* p. 215. For emblems invoking Xenophon, see Kempter, pls. 62–64; Svetlana Alpers, "Manner and Meaning in Some Rubens Mythologies," *JWCI* 30 (1967): pl. 32 b and c. See also my fig. 4, and Sichtermann, 3–36 for early allegorizations.

37. Alpers, "Manner and Meaning," 272–95; John Rupert Martin, *Rubens before 1620* (Princeton: Princeton University Press, 1972), 4, 17, 20–21.

38. *Symposium* 8.30. See Panofsky, *Studies in Iconology,* 215.

39. *De civitate Dei* 7.26 and 18.13. See Panofsky, *Studies in Iconology,* 214.

40. Jean Seznec, *The Survival of the Pagan Gods,* trans. Barbara F. Sessions, Bollingen Series, no. 38 (New York: Pantheon, 1953), 105.

41. Kempter, 41–45; Seznec, *Survival of the Pagan Gods,* 105. The Ganymede apotheosis motif has also been identified on a silk of the twelfth or thirteenth century found in a tomb at Château de Quedlinbourg, according to M.-Th. Picard-Schmitter, "Scènes d'apothéose sur des soieries provenant de Raiy," *Artibus Asiae* 14 (1951): 306–8.

42. Panofsky, *Studies in Iconology,* 177.

43. Ibid., 215.

44. Seznec, *Survival of the Pagan Gods,* 104. On Ganymede in the *Ovide moralisé,* see Kempter, 27–33.

45. Thomas Walleis, *Metamorphosis Ovidiana moraliter . . . explanata* (Paris, 1515), fol. 82. See Panofsky, *Studies in Iconology,* 213–14.

46. Panofsky, *Studies in Iconology,* 213 n.130. On the medieval comparisons of Ganymede with Christ, see Kempter, 29, and Elaine K. Gazda, "Ganymede and the Eagle: A Marble Group from Carthage," *Archaeology* 34 (July/August 1981): 60.

47. Seznec, *Survival of the Pagan Gods,* 103.

48. Ibid., 103–5.

49. *Commedia di Dante Alighieri . . . con l'espositione di Cristoforo Landino* (Venice, 1529), fol. 156. See Panofsky, *Studies in Iconology,* 215 n.140 for text.

50. Baruch D. Kirschenbaum, "Reflections on Michelangelo's Drawings for Cavalieri," *Gazette des Beaux Arts,* 6th ser., 38 (1951, pub. 1960): 99–110.

51. Panofsky, *Studies in Iconology,* 213–18; Kempter, 85–90; British Museum, *Drawings by Michelangelo in the Collection of Her Majesty the Queen at Windsor Castle, the Ashmolean Museum, the British Museum, and Other English Collections* (British Museum Publications, 1975), 104–5; Alpers, "Manner and Meaning," 275; F. M. Godfrey, "Paintings of the Legend of Jove, Part 1," *Apollo* 44 (November 1951): 124.

52. Michelangelo's *Ganymede* is lost, but a copy, made by Giulio Clovio (1601–8) and retouched by Rubens, is represented in Michael Jaffé, *Rubens and Italy* (Ithaca, N.Y.: Cornell University Press, 1977), 22 and pl. 30. For other imitations see Alpers, "Manner and Meaning," 275 and pl. 32; Kempter, pls. 87–90, 92, 95.

53. Kempter, 93 and pl. 88; Alpers, "Manner and Meaning," 275 and pl. 32; *Emblemata: Handbuch zur Sinnbildkunst des XVI, und XVII. Jahrhunderts,* ed. Arthur Henkel und Albrecht Schöne (Stuttgart: J. B. Metzlersche Verlagsbuchhandlung, 1967), col. 1726, including the Ganymede emblem of Alciati (1531), which Peacham apparently knew. On Alciati's influence on Peacham, see Alan R. Young, *Henry Peacham* (Boston: Twayne, 1979), 35, 42, 48, and 55.

54. Reproduced by permission of Georg Olms Verlag, Hildesheim, West Germany and J. B. Metzlersche Verlagsbuchhandlung und Carl Ernst Poeschal Verlag, Stuttgart. See *Emblemata,* col. 1726. On the Ganymede emblematic tradition, see Kempter, 62–71, 70–82.

55. Panofsky, *Studies in Iconology,* 215–16 n. 143; Alpers, "Manner and Meaning," 274 n. 10.

56. Achille Bocchi, *Symbolicae quaestiones* (Bologna, 1574), 166, nos. 78, 79; reproduced in *Emblemata,* col. 1727. See also Kempter, 93 and pl. 89.

57. Mark 10:14; Luke 18:16. John 13:33 give the first passage; Luke 18:17 and Mark 10:15 give the second. See Panofsky, *Studies in Iconology,* 213; Seznec, *Survival of the Pagan Gods,* 101.

58. Rubens, Michelangelo, Correggio, Girolamo da Carpi (Kempter, pl. 29), and Baldassare Peruzzi (Kempter, pl. 28), among others.

59. Kempter, 82–84, and pls. 80, 81, 82. In the sixteenth century many drawings and paintings show Ganymede using the eagle as steed. See Kempter, pls. 56, 57, 62–68, 75, 76, and 78.

60. Kempter, pls. 43, 48. Cf. also pls. 44, 49.

61. Panofsky, *Studies in Iconology,* 213.

62. Kempter, pl. 116.

63. *Der Grosse Brockhaus,* 16th rev. ed. (Wiesbaden: F. A. Brockhaus, 1954), vol. 4, s.v. "Ganymed"; Tewin Copplestone, *Rembrandt* (New York: Paul Hamlyn, 1967), 39; Kempter, 127ff.

64. Kenneth Bendiner, "Robert Rauschenberg's 'Canyon,'" *Arts Magazine,* June 1982, 57–59; *Robert Rauschenberg* (Washington, D.C.: Smithsonian Institution, 1976), 13. For a color plate of "Canyon," see Andrew Forge, *Rauschenberg* (New York, n.d.), 189.

65. Young, *Henry Peacham,* 38–41.

66. *The Basilicon Doron of King James VI,* ed. James Craigie, Scottish Text Society, ser. 3. no. 16 (London: Blackwood, 1944), 1:65.

67. Homosexuality was notorious not only in the royal circle around James, but also in the contemporary court of France. On James's belief and involvement in witchcraft, see William McElwee, *The Wisest Fool in Christendom* (New York: Harcourt, Brace, 1958), 70–73; Otto J. Scott, *James I* (New York: Mason, 1976), 210, 330, 345. Among famous poisonings in James's reign are included those of Overbury (discussed in Scott, 343), possibly Esmé Stuart, James's favorite (Scott, 124), and even James himself (Scott, 407). James's son, Prince Henry of Wales, agreed entirely with the principles in *Basilikon Doron,* a fact that ironically caused his estrangement from his father, once he was old enough to perceive the disparity between his father's precepts and practices.

68. See *"Priapus Gallinaceus,"* note 21 above.

69. *Confessio Amantis* (3d recension), 8.159.

70. Herman Wäscher, *Das deutsche illustrierte Flugblatt* (Veb Verlag der Kunst, 1955), 88, 93.

71. See, for example, a woodcut (ca. 1566), depicting a cock and a bull as emblems over a bawdy house, in Arthur F. Kinney, ed., *Rogues, Vagabonds & Sturdy Beggars* (Barre, Mass.: Imprint Society, 1973), 108.

72. Treated in my unpublished paper, "The Cock as God, Demon, and Fool in the Middle Ages," presented at the Eighth American Imagery Conference, sponsored by the International Imagery Association, New York City, 11 November 1984.

73. See the simple scepter of Zeus in Sichtermann, pl. 2,2 or in Lenormant and De Witte, *Élite des monuments,* vol. 1, pl. 18. James's simple scepter is represented in Lady Antonia Fraser, *King James* (New York: Knopf, 1975), 111, 119, 144. Compare the elaborate scepter of Charles V of France in *The American Heritage Dictionary of the English Language* (Boston: Houghton Mifflin, 1969), illustration s.v. "scepter."

74. Thomas Wright, *The Worship of the Generative Powers During the Middle Ages of Western Europe* (1866), vol. 2 of Richard Payne Knight and Thomas Wright, *Sexual Symbolism* (New York: Julian, 1957), 59–63 and pl. 9. On the proverb "Every medal has its reverse," see Florio, *Essayes of Montaigne* (1603), 3.3.293: "to show the reverse of the medal, viz., for one to shew his breech," noted in Morris Palmer Tilley, *A Dictionary of the Proverbs in England in the Sixteenth and Seventeenth Centuries* (Ann Arbor: University of Michigan Press, 1950), 455.

75. Fraser, *King James,* frontispiece and 75, 93, 105, 144, and 213.

76. See, for example, Michael Grant and Antonia Mulas, *Eros a Pompei: Il Gabinetto Segreto del Museo di Napoli* (Milan: Arnoldo Mondadori Editore, 1974), 134, and my *"Priapus Gallinaceus,"* 93 and n. 135.

77. *The Prologue of the Monk's Tale,* in *The Riverside Chaucer,* ed. Larry D. Benson (Boston: Houghton Mifflin, 1987), VII.1962. A Pompeian painting in Grant and Mulas, *Eros a Pompei,* 53, shows a priapic figure balancing his phallus with a bag of money on a scale, an equation also known in the Middle Ages, and possibly informing an illumination in a French *Ovide moralisé* (Kempter, pl. 8) showing Zeus encircled by a rainbow showering coins on a copulating couple on the earth below, while the eagle approaches with Ganymede in its claws.

78. See also James T. Henke, *Courtesans and Cuckolds: A Glossary of Renaissance Dramatic Bawdy Exclusive of Shakespeare* (New York: Garland, 1979), 55.

79. Nares (note 16 above), 196, s.v. "counterfait."

80. Gazda (note 46 above), 56–60; color photo, p. 56.

81. For examples of the seductive or willing Ganymede, see Kempter, pls. 29, 31, 37, 38, 39, 104, 106, 110; Sichtermann, pls. 6,2; 7,3; 8,1; 14,1; 14,3; and *Brockhaus Enzyklopädie* (1968), s.v. "Ganymed."

82. Scott, *James I,* 100.

83. James's effeminacy was recognized in a contemporary saying: *Rex fuit Elizabeth: nunc est Jacobus Regina* ("Elizabeth was king; now James has become queen"), noted in E. J. Burford, *Bawds and Lodgings: A History of the London Bankside Brothels* (London: Peter Owen, 1976), 164.

84. I am grateful to Youngstown State University for a Research Professorship providing release time for the writing of this article and to Hildegard Schnuttgen for her support in taking the initiative in search and procurement of materials, in interlibrary loan service, and in aid with translations.

King George of England Meets Samuel Johnson the Great Cham of Literature: The End of Courtly Letters and the Beginning of Modern Literature

ALVIN B. KERNAN

Literature, as we use the word at the present time, refers primarily to a group of texts sharing a number of characteristics such as fictionality, structure, and the intensive use of certain tropes like metaphor and irony. But literature also exists, both objectively and subjectively, in the day-to-day world as an extensive social system of letters that includes, for example, a set of established literary roles such as poet, critic, scholar, teacher, student, editor, reviewer, and so forth. Literature's reality in the social world is also substantiated by a corpus of secondary writings—the poetic texts being primary—such as criticism, literary history, biographies of writers, bibliographies, carefully edited texts and concordances, all of which give objective existence to literature, define it, organize it, and impute to it an importance to the culture that requires this kind of careful preservation and intricate interpretation. Literature is visibly real in the world's great libraries where it is shelved and ordered in a classification system that differentiates it from other categories of knowledge, such as philosophy and history, that are also recognized and made real by the library. The status of a mode of knowledge conferred on literature by the library is extended and hardened by the place literature occupies in the educational system, which further establishes its epistemological *bona fides* by giving it a faculty of specialists, departmental and curricular structures, and a degree certifying competence in this field and the right to profess it. And, like any other social reality, literature exists throughout society, shaping and shaped by glancing interactions with other institutions, such as its encounters with wealth through patronage, the state through censorship, the law through libel and pornography statutes, and

---

Alvin Kernan, *Printing Technology, Letters & Samuel Johnson*. Copyright (c) 1987 by Princeton University Press. Chap. I adapted with permission of Princeton University Press. Reprinted by permission of Princeton University Press.

the marketplace through publishers, printers, and audiences. The Massachusetts legislature has, for example, recently passed a statute forbidding the owners of paintings and statues to change them in any way without the permission of the artist, giving the force of law to the view that art is more sacred than property. At the same time in a theater in Cambridge, a director is defending his right to adapt *Endgame* against Beckett's view that he as author controls all productions.

Letters, to give a name to the full-scale social institution of literature I have been outlining, is a socially constructed reality, like a family, the state, the law, or religion, made up of a loosely coordinated set of activities, texts, theories, educational arrangements, histories, library collections, roles, critical writings, and on and on. Letters is not a fixed *thing*, an absolute, unchangeable, given fact of culture or nature, but a social activity always in movement, always changing its colors and adjusting its component parts to one another and to the rest of the social world. Fundamental structural rearrangements of literary systems occur, however, only at points in time when the entire society is also changing in a radical way. Literary history divides, usually on the basis of style, Western literature up into a number of distinct periods—medieval, renaissance, neoclassical, romantic, modern—but there have been only three major social systems of letters in postclassical Western society. (1) The oral poetry of scop, bard and jongleur that celebrated in formulaic verse heroic exploits and tribal virtues in the mead hall and before the feudal lord; (2) an oral-scribal system of polite or courtly letters that began with Dante's appearance in *The Divine Comedy* as a new type of spiritualized poet and flourished as an art of aristocratic amateurs in the Renaissance courts of Italian princes and European sun kings; and (3) the romantic literary system of print and universalized creative self-expression extending from the late eighteenth century to the present, passing through a succession of modes such as high romanticism, symbolism, modernism, and now, we are frequently told, a last "deconstructive" phase, which is sometimes said to mark the "death of literature," though not, presumably, the disappearance, though it is a possibility, of some kind of system of letters.

Obviously, the literary system is always related to the dominant political and economic systems and to the mode of communication in the society of which it is a part in ways that can be illustrated by reference to the system of letters that I shall henceforth call courtly or polite letters, extending, roughly, from the time of Dante to that of Samuel Johnson, from the birth of humanism to the end of the Enlightenment, centering on the court and supporting its hierarchical world view. The characteristics of courtly letters are so well known that brief reference to a few major elements will sketch the outlines of a social system of letters that centered politically on the ruler and his court and aesthetically on the classical texts of Greece and Rome. On the social level, crown censorship and patronage controlled the work of writers who were, or pretended to be, gentlemen amateurs, avoiding print in favor of manuscript circulation among a small group of friends—"fit audience though few"—and writing in an elegant style about such aristocratic subjects as love or chivalry. On the level of poetics, arrangements were equally hierarchical: idealized classics in elite languages providing genre models for imitation, set standards of tightly controlled structure (the unities), decorum (the high, middle, and low styles), and a hierarchy of meaning (literal, allegorical, moral, and anagogic). Print finally destroyed this old system of courtly letters in the eighteenth century and replaced it at first with Grub Street, transforming writers from gentlemen into paid hacks, the idealized classical texts of polite letters into print commodities, and the literary audience from the small genteel private group of friends with shared tastes that Dryden shows us in the *Essay of Dramatic Poesy,* into the common reader and reading public. This print-forced change in the old courtly order of letters is chronicled ironically in Swift's *Battle of the Books* (1704) and apocalyptically in Pope's *Dunciad* (1728–43), but a famous meeting of Samuel Johnson, a heroic figure of the new type of print writer, with his king, marks, in my view, the true historical end of courtly letters. Because the scene includes all the major elements of the literary *ancien régime* that was ending, and the social and literary forces that were replacing it, it can serve as a model for understanding what courtly letters was and what the dynamics of the literary system that replaced it were.

On 10 February, a Tuesday, in 1767, Samuel Johnson went, as he often did, to read in the King's Library, a collection of fine books and manuscripts assembled by that dedicated royal collector, King George III, after his accession to the English throne. The library was located in the private royal residence then known as the Queen's House, originally Buckingham House, on the site where Buckingham Palace was later erected by John Nash. Richard Dalton was then the librarian, but Johnson's friend, Frederick Augusta Barnard, a royal godson and a member of the family that had been royal pages for three generations, became the librarian in 1774 and was the person most responsible for building the collection on which several thousand pounds a year was spent to make it reflect, like the king's palaces and his art collections, royal taste, power, and patronage of the arts. Johnson himself, in a letter of 1768, advised Barnard, departing on a continental book-buying expedition, on how to go about procuring only the best books, first editions, perfect copies, the finest printings needed as "the great ornaments of a Library furnished for Magnificence as well as use."[1] Ultimately the library contained more than 65,000 volumes plus many pamphlets and manuscripts covering all areas of what was then called "literature," or "polite letters": classical learning, religion, philosophy, poetry, geography, history, mathematics, law, and many other subjects. The romantic sense of the term "literature" as an *universalpoesie* consisting of all the works of the creative imagination from all places and times had not yet become current. The king's policy was one of liberally admitting scholars to his library, but he still considered his books not a national library, open to all, but a personal possession of the monarch. When the politically radical chemist Joseph Priestely applied to use it in 1779, the king grudgingly agreed that it should be open to him as to other scholars, but did not wish himself, he told Lord North regally, to give personal permission: "I can't think [Priestley's] character as a Politician or Divine deserves my appearing at all in it."[2] But Johnson was welcome, for by 1767, with his dictionary more than ten years behind him, he was the most distinguished man of letters in England, and when he visited what Boswell calls "those splendid rooms and noble collections of books," Barnard "took care that he should have every accommodation that could contribute to his ease and convenience."[3] So great in fact was his reputation that the king had expressed a desire to meet him, and on being notified on this day that Johnson had arrived and was reading at a table before the fire, George III, still according to Boswell, left his own affairs and went graciously to the great literary authority to question him about the state of letters in his kingdom. There then ensued a polite literary conversation, with many exchanges of graceful compliments, in which Johnson gave the king his views on such matters as the comparative states of the Oxford and Cambridge libraries, the writings of Warburton, Lyttelton, and Aaron Hill, and the quality of several literary journals being published at the time.

The scene, both in setting and movement, is a ritual, and its central action, a persistent attempt by the king to urge Johnson to continue writing, enacts what had long been the central motive of courtly letters. His Majesty opens the subject by courteously inquiring if Johnson "was then writing anything," to which Johnson responds that "he was not, for he had pretty well told the world what he knew."[4] Not to be put off, the king urges him "to continue his labours," and at this point Johnson says rather sharply that "he thought he had already done his part as a writer." King George still carries it off very gracefully—"I should have thought so too . . . if you had not written so well"—and then he drops the subject for a moment, only to return to it at the end of the conversation when he "expressed a desire to have the literary biography of this country ably executed, and proposed to Dr. Johnson to undertake it."[5]

The setting, the action, and the parts played out in this library scene were shaped by a multitude of forces, not the least of which were such personal factors as the new young king's conservatism and Johnson's exhaustion in the midst of his second major attack of mental depression.

But whatever the personal circumstances, the library scene was primarily a literary ritual in which a monarch determined to restore old ways in many areas tries to play out once more the traditional royal authority over letters. That authority is silently expressed by the setting of the noble library and its magnificent collection of books, the sacred objects that assert through the king's ownership of the best books, his implied control of all books. Royal authority over letters is *actively* expressed by the king's command to one of his subjects to write, voicing symbolically the long-exercised and unquestioned right of kings to determine who could write and what could and could not be written. These same powers had been exercised *de facto* for five centuries by strong European monarchs who had literally called Renaissance art into being by commissioning the architects who built their palaces, great houses, and churches, and the painters and sculptors who decorated them. Theirs too were the writers who had filled their libraries with books celebrating the prince, his kingdom, court, and native language, legitimating the aristocratic ethos and the hierarchical social structures that centered the entire political and artistic enterprise. In the palace, church, university, and great house, all those bastions of the established courtly order, art had existed to testify to and in turn be justified by the power, wealth, and grandeur of the king, the state religion, and the court aristocracy.

The power that princes had over art had been practically exercised through a number of very forceful social arrangements that were all present, just at or below the surface of the scene, in the king's library. Most obviously, there was the legal power of the crown to exercise censorship, establishing as fact the king's ownership of all writing by determining which books could and could not be printed. This absolute authority over the existence of books had been extended by the traditional prerogative of the king to license presses and to sell exclusive rights to certain particularly profitable sacred books—bibles, primers, law books—to a printer or bookseller. In England, official censorship ended legally in 1694, except for stage plays, but the power remained very much alive through the eighteenth century as the government continued to exercise its authority in this regard through various indirect methods such as invoking the libel laws. Defoe had stood in the pillory for displeasing his queen by writing ironically on religious questions, and the crucial case of John Wilkes was in the courts about the time Johnson and the king talked. Print and censorship, which was a restraint of trade, were at odds, and as a Gutenberg author Johnson had attacked censorship early in life, though later in his life of Milton he hedged on the issue.

The king's authority in the library was further backed up by patronage, an elaborate system of payments, operating on several levels and in complex ways, that the European courts and churches had used for centuries to manage their relationships with their subjects, not in the arts alone but in all areas of life, political, economic, and personal. Power was exercised, in an age before civil services and meritocracies, and subjects tied to their rulers by gifts of many kinds—gifts of money sometimes, but more often titles, appointments to office, land, grants, wardships, and special privileges. The fortunate writers were those who managed, in an age before a living could be made by writing books for sale, to exchange their writing for some reward as substantial as Spenser's land grant and official position in Ireland, Donne's appointment as Dean of St. Paul's, Ben Jonson's as writer of the annual masque for the court, or Dryden's poet laureateship. The *quid pro quo* needed not always be so concrete, and for courtiers such as Sidney, Lovelace, and Suckling, poetry served primarily to establish their reputations as courtiers accomplished in this area as in others, and thus worthy of royal notice and favor. With a few obvious exceptions, notably Puritans like Bunyan and Milton, and to some extent the playwrights who worked in the public theater between 1580 and 1640, writing, from about 1300 to the early 1700s and in some cases beyond, was closely tied to the court by the patronage system. Macaulay's brilliant description of patronage in the late seventeenth and early eighteenth centuries gives an excellent picture of its extent and complexity just before the professional writer, like Johnson, who could make a living by selling his writing appeared. Never, Macaulay says, was there a time at which the rewards of literary merit were so splendid—at which men who could write well found such easy admittance into the most distinguished society and to the highest honours of the state. The chiefs of both the great parties into which the kingdom was divided patronized literature with emulous munificence. Congreve, when he had scarcely attained his majority, was rewarded for his first comedy with high places that made him independent for life. Edmund Neale Smith, though his *Phaedra and Hippolitus* failed, would have been consoled with 300 pounds a year but for his own folly. Rowe was not only poet laureate, but land-surveyor of the customs in the port of London, clerk of the council to the Prince of Wales, and secretary of the Presentations to the Lord Chancellor. John Hughes was secretary to the Commissions of the Peace. Ambrose Phillips was judge of the Prerogative Court in Ireland. Locke was Commissioner of Appeals and of the Board of Trade. Newton was master of the Mint. Stepney and Prior were employed in embassies of high dignity and importance. Gay, who commenced life as apprentice to a silk mercer, became a secretary of legation at five-and-twenty. It was to a poem on the death of Charles II, and to the City and Country Mouse, that Charles Montague owed his introduction into public life, his earldom, his garter, and his auditorship of the Exchequer. Swift, but for the unconquerable prejudice of the queen, would have been a bishop. Oxford, with his white staff in his hand, passed through the crowd of his suitors to welcome Parnell, when that ingenious writer deserted the Whigs. Steele was a commissioner of stamps and a member of Parliament. Arthur Mainwaring was a commissioner of the customs and auditor of the imprest. Tickell was secretary to the Lords Justices of Ireland. Addison was secretary of state.[6] Johnson himself was not entirely free of the patronage system. He had, it is true, declared the independence of writing from patronage in ringing terms in his famous letter to Lord Chesterfield in 1755. But he had been in possession of a pension from the crown of 300 pounds a year since 1763. King George was, in fact, making a last effort to resuscitate patronage in order to further his publicly stated intention "to be a king," that is to restore power to the monarch lost in 1688 and since, and besides Johnson he had pensioned Gibbon, Hume, Robertson, and Home and made John Hill, author of the *Vegetable System,* royal gardener at Kensington at 2,000 pounds per annum.

But perhaps the most powerful actuality behind the king's command to Johnson to write was the long tradition acknowledging poetic service to church and state. Dante established the archetypal role of the heroic poet whose genius, aided by the pagan classics, particularly Vergil, and Christian love and beauty, Beatrice, allowed him to walk living through the realms of the highest truth where other men could go only by dying. The great line of heroic poets who followed him—Petrarch, Ariosto, Ronsard, Spenser, and Milton, to mention only the most luminous—thought no less of their poetic powers, and all conceived of their poetry as an art of service. If Dante's vision lifted him above earthly limits, what he saw and taught as a poet were the established iconography and ethics of his church: hell, purgatory, and heaven, all achieved and suffered in doctrinally orthodox ways. Petrarch presented himself in his coronation with laurel on the Capitoline Hill on Easter Sunday, 1341, as a Christ figure redeeming with his poetry a fallen world, and a classical poet restoring the greatness of Roman literature, but he designed the ritual so that the civic authorities of the city of Rome crowned him, and afterwards he crossed the Tiber and laid his laurels on the altar of St. Peter's, the central shrine of the church he served and was supported by all his life. Ariosto's *Orlando Furioso* exalted, not without chafe, the greatness of his patrons, the Este dukes and cardinals of Ferarra, while Ronsard was the court poet of the monarchs of France and celebrated them in his *Franciade*. Spenser's epic, *The Faerie Queene,* celebrated the great Queen of England by praising her as the embodiment of all English history and all Reformation moral virtue; and Milton, politically and philosophically the most radical of all these heroic poets, after long service to the commonwealth and an official position in its government, saw his poetic task in *Paradise Lost* as the social work of explaining God's ways to man and revealing beneath the confusion and distortion of his historical moment the enduring order of human life in mainly familiar terms of the biblical story and its traditional elaborations.

These were the high moments of courtly letters, the points at which its largest claims were made and its largest services rendered to the state. Ordinarily it functioned in less heroic but no less serviceable ways. Castiglione provided in his *Courtier* (1528) a model for generations of gentlemen poets for whom writing was only one social accomplishment, comparable and ancillary to other courtly skills such as dancing, horsemanship, dress, manners, and speaking well. Poetry was used by Castiglione's aristocratic amateur to implement courtly interests, praising a lady or tactfully advising a prince, and in its style it always enacted linguistically the same grace, skill, learning, wit, and good manners which were the ethical ideals of courtly life in all spheres.

"There were very few writers," J. W. Saunders states, "who could not have been said to be, in a very real sense, courtiers first and writers second . . . half the writers of the age [1520–1659] earned their living wholly at Court, . . . most of the others were dependent for a major part of their income, in various ways, upon courtly patronage, and . . . nearly all the great important writers were either courtiers in their own right or satellites utterly dependent upon the courtly system."[7] Maintaining the appearance of being such a courtier writer for whom poetry was only one of many courtly accomplishments was difficult but still necessary for writers of limited means and high ability, like Donne, for example, and it was even more of a problem, while remaining equally necessary, for the new professional writers who began first to appear in England in the late sixteenth century, men like Nashe, Spenser, Marlowe, Shakespeare, and Jonson, who really earned their livings by writing but tried in various ways, such as Shakespeare's buying a coat of arms, to cultivate an appearance of gentility. Pope and Gray were still at the same game a century or more later, and even some of Johnson's Grub-Street contemporaries like Savage and Goldsmith still tried, with grotesque consequences, to pretend in the most straitened circumstances that they were still Castiglione's gentlemen poets who wrote only for amusement and circulation among friends.

This long continuing role of the poet as gentleman courtier enacted in one way the close link between writing and the dominant social order that was somewhat less evident but equally at work in courtly poetics. The neoclassical aesthetic values, which progressively replaced the old native or Gothic traditions of folk art during the Renaissance, were artistic transformations of the hierarchical principles central to the politics and social order of the *ancien régime*. Criticism was not the major literary genre in the Renaissance that it became during the romantic period. Literature was legitimated by the political and religious order and therefore did not need to be justified in other terms. But in a wide variety of critical pieces—e.g., Dante's letter to Can Grande, Boccaccio's *Genealogy of the Gentile Gods,* Cinthio on tragedy, Sidney's *Apology,* Dryden's *Essay of Dramatic Poesy,* Boileau and Pope on the rules—the classical texts were idealized, obedience to the authority of these ancients established, the use of the vernacular justified by mandating imitation of the form and style of the classics, a hierarchy of genres with epic and tragedy at the top constructed, and the teaching of the official morality made the primary purpose of poetry. These and other forms of literary piety, order, restraint, rules, tradition, and subordination, tied poetry as firmly to the court in the aesthetic realm as patronage linked it economically and censorship legally to the strong centralized monarchies and their expanding bureaucracies.

The mismatch between the king's and Samuel Johnson's assumptions about letters must have been startlingly apparent in the library in Johnson's failure as a person—huge, grotesque, badly scarred, ridiculously small wig, shabby clothes, compulsive tics and starts, a professional writer who made his living by selling his skills—to fill the traditional poetic roles of courtly amateur, like Sidney, or the Dantean apologist for orthodoxy. The irony was not so obvious but it was even more profound in the king's relation to the printed books in his library. Standing in their rich leather bindings with gold titles, stamped with the royal arms, rank on glowing red rank—like the king's soldiers—along the shelves, the fine collection and its noble setting were sacred objects in the cult of courtly art symbolizing ownership of all books by the king. But the relationship between absolute monarchs and printed books had never been easy, as the long, troubled history of censorship and continual efforts of the crown to control printers and limit the number of presses testify. The antagonism between print and absolute monarchs first appeared in aesthetic terms at the beginning of the age of print. E. B. Fryde tells us that "Authors in search of Medici patronage presented splendidly illuminated copies of their works. But printed books were not welcome. Like his contemporary, Duke Federigo of Urbino, who did not possess a single printed book in his library, Lorenzo had no use whatsoever for this new technique."[8] This aristocratic contempt for print lingered on long, it is interesting to note, in poetry. Sir Philip Sidney, who printed none of his own writings, speaks scornfully in his *Apology* of "base men with servile wits . . . who think it inough if they can be rewarded of the Printer," and he laughs at the writer whose "name shall flourish in the Printers Shoppe."[9] Professional poets like Spenser, Shakespeare, Chapman, Daniel, Drayton, and, most scandalously, Ben Jonson, however, tended to publish their poetry in their lifetimes. Among those who published, a certain religious emphasis is also noticeable—Crashaw, Vaughan, Milton—and perhaps a trace of middle-class scrambling for favor in the court—Carew, Cowley, Samuel Butler, Waller, and perhaps even Dryden. On the other hand, some religious poets like Herbert did not publish, and Traherne was not printed until this century. Some middle-class writers who were trying to get ahead politically, like Marvell and Donne, were also content to circulate their poems in manuscript. Donne, in fact, was greatly distressed at the thought of having to print some of his work in order to raise money a few years before his death. The complete list of English poets who did not print but were content to circulate their poetry in manuscript is instructively long and contains such further names as Wyatt, Surrey, Sidney, Ralegh, the Shakespeare of the sonnets and all the plays, Herbert, Suckling, and Lovelace. There clearly was a fashionable and long-continuing, though by no means universally observed, antipathy to print that reveals some of the basic values of courtly letters. Manuscript circulation carried the courtly values of limit, privacy, handcraft, and rarity, while large numbers of identical printed copies of a work for sale in the marketplace carried democratic and commercial values. The aristocratic attitude of the courtly poet towards what J. W. Saunders has called "The Stigma of Print" remained a literary ideal until well into the eighteenth century, and Samuel Johnson could still observe that "Swift put his name to but two things, (after he had a name to put,) 'The Plan for the Improvement of the English Language,' and the last 'Drapier's Letter.' "[10] The example of Swift is instructive, for he needed to and did print his works, like many another gentleman writer, but by keeping his name off the title page, as in the elaborate game with *Gulliver,* he maintained at least the outward appearance of the gentleman amateur that Sidney exemplified. Not until the mideighteenth century could a professional writer openly laugh at the amateur poet circulating his writings in manuscript, as Johnson did when he remarked that "the highest praise" some bad poems "deserved was, that they were very well for a gentleman to hand about among his friends."[11]

So long as the court or the great house remained the ideal social setting of poetry, print with its democratic associations of mechanic trade, money, and a vulgar public audience of readers, not listeners, could never be the medium of letters. Conservative courtly attitudes toward print now seem to us only quaintly snobbish, but there was in them a real recognition that print was a democratic medium, making many books available to many readers, and therefore at odds in important ways with the central value of the literary system and ultimately the political values of the court world. Avoidance of print was the gentlemanly way of dealing with the problem, but the King's Library represents the long-continued and more forceful efforts of the old regime to control print technology by censorsing printed books, licensing presses, taxing paper, and generally absorbing books into a literary system centering in the royal palace and the monarch. But the printed book was finally no more under George III's control than were the actual books in his own royal library. When George IV "came to the throne," Arundell Esdaile tells us, "he employed Nash to remodel Buckingham Palace, and probably found the books in the way."[12] The new king first tried to sell the library, and according to one story, offered it, appropriately enough, to the last of the great autocrats, the Czar of Russia. The sale was said to have been blocked by public indignation, and the king, making the best of his losses by saying that he was "by this means advancing the literature of my country," gave the books to the growing collection of the national library of the British Museum, where they can still be seen gathered together in a long gallery specially built for them to the right of the Great Russell Street entrance. The change of context and thereby of meaning are the same as those of many other royal and ducal libraries and art collections, such as the Uffizi, the Louvre, the Prado, which became national collections, open to the public, where art became, as in romantic ideology, the property of the people, a manifestation of the national genius, and, in time, of the aesthetic achievements of mankind.

Both the forces that would destroy it and the social complex that made up courtly letters—the poetics of hierarchy, the role of gentleman amateur as poet, patronage, crown censorship, the efforts to control the printed book, the setting of the royal palace, all centering in the king—were still in place in the King's Library when George III and Johnson met, symbolically represented in the architecture and the collection, enacted ritually in a king's command to one of his subjects on when and what to write. But in the social history of Western literature, this scene in the library between Johnson and King George divides the old regime of courtly letters in the service of the established hierarchical order from, eventually, the new romantic literature of the modern industrial liberal state, centered not on a king but on the creative imagination of the individual. The old order did not, of course, precisely end at this moment, no more than the new literary order entirely began here, but Boswell's dramatic scene is very like a painting encountered in a chronologically arranged art gallery which makes it suddenly clear that a crucial point has somehow been passed. The formal subject may remain the same, the Annunciation, the Crucifixion, a royal portrait; but perspective, the elaboration of realistic detail, the increased importance of the landscape, an emphasis on painterly technique, perhaps the inclusion of an image of the artist, all accumulate to show that art has shifted its focus from service to church and state to a concern with itself, the artists who make it and the fullness of the world.

Royalists both, Johnson and Boswell did not consciously know that a transfer of literary power from the king to the author was being symbolically enacted in the library. The scene "gratified [Johnson's] monarchical enthusiasm," Boswell believed, and to the king's final request for "the literary biography of this country . . . Johnson signified his readiness to comply with his Majesty's wishes. During the whole of this interview, Johnson talked to his Majesty with profound respect but still in his firm manly manner, with a sonorous voice, and never in that subdued tone which is commonly used at the levee and in the drawing-room. After the King withdrew, Johnson shewed himself highly pleased with his Majesty's conversation and gracious behaviour."[13] But authorial independence is openly stated, politely but firmly, in the opening of the scene when Johnson says that "he thought he had already done his part as a writer." It is more concealed but still nonetheless there at the end of the scene if we remember that Johnson complied with his Majesty's wishes to write "the literary biography of this country" only some ten years later, and then at the solicitation of a group of booksellers and printers who needed short prefaces to the collected works of a group of poets in whom they were trying, futilely, to preserve copyright. Once started on the project Johnson, out of his personal interest in literary biography and criticism, and out of a need to fill his declining days with some worthy and congenial work, extended it far beyond what had originally been requested, and finally made *The Lives of the Poets* a free-standing book in which the writer, not kings or booksellers, creates other writers by collecting their lives and linking them to their writings. *The Lives* thus became themselves the symbolic statement of modern literature, declaring that the poetic self is the sole source of the author and his writing.

Appendix: The Caldwell Minute

There is another description of the meeting of Johnson and King George that gives a very different interpretation of the scene than Boswell does. The "Caldwell Minute," which was probably dictated by Johnson to a copyist shortly after the event, describes some parts of the scene such as the entrance of the monarch to the library in a much more casual way: "The King came in and after having walked by Mr. Johns talked for some time to other persons in the Library, turned to Dr. Johnson and asked him if he were not lately come from Oxford."[14] The conversation that follows, including the urgings and refusals to write, is substantially the same in the Minute and in Boswell, who, in fact, used a copy of the Minute to construct his account, but changed the beginning to make the king come specifically to see Johnson, centered the scene on Johnson and added at the end the King's request that Johnson undertake "the literary biography of this country" to anticipate the writing of *The Lives of the Poets.* And instead of Boswell's magnificent conclusion in which the king withdraws, leaving the great cham in serene possession of the library and of English letters, the Minute tells us that "the Princes Dowager came in and put an end to the conversation."[15] The passages with a line drawn through them indicate early editing of the Minute, perhaps at Johnson's direction as he was dictating, in an effort, says Taylor, to save his "dignity by removing the possible implications that the King *deliberately* walked by him or that the Princess Dowager *deliberately* put an end to the conversation."[16] Boswell saves even more of Johnson's dignity. He doesn't really change very much, dropping a deflating detail here and adding a proleptic reference to *The Lives of the Poets* there, pointing up the scene by showing it always from the Johnsonian perspective and making it more dramatic by providing a powerful beginning and ending. The changes were slight, but in the end what was according to the Minute a fairly ordinary morning in the royal household becomes one of the great symbolic scenes of literary history in which control of writing passes from kings to writers. From the point of view of positivist history this kind of tampering with the facts both discredits Boswell and makes doubtful any use of his version, at least in the detailed way I have been reading the scene, as a typological event in modern literature. Positivism would simply close the situation off by declaring Boswell's scene to be a fictional distortion of prior facts more likely to be known from the less suspect Minute. From the point of view of a social history of literature, however, with its interest in the complex ways in which literary reality is socially constructed in the world, it is the contrast between the two versions, three really, and the indubitable fact that Boswell's doctored version has become and maintained itself as truth that are of central interest. Who after all, even among scholars, has so much as heard of the Caldwell Minute? The facts are not in question; insofar as anyone can really tell, the Minute probably renders the bare events of the meeting more accurately than Boswell, given his usual tendency to portray Johnson as epic hero of print. But when viewed from the angle of cultural history, certain further and more interesting questions appear, such as, for example, Why the fictional version has prevailed as truth and become typological—the author or artist defying established authority? Why a compulsive writer and hero-worshiper like Boswell should have been able to make Johnson more real and meaningful in a printed biography than he was in his own life and writing? Whether Boswell's dramatization of the meeting with the king did not catch a kind of truth about an actual transfer of literary and other kinds of power from kings to writers that the bare facts of the Minute blur?

Notes

1. Samuel Johnson, *The Letters of Samuel Johnson*, ed. R. W. Chapman (Oxford: Clarendon Press, 1952), 1:218.
2. Arundell Esdaile, *The British Museum Library* (London: George Allen & Unwin, 1946), 189.
3. James Boswell, *Life of Johnson*, ed. G. B. Hill, rev. L. F. Powell (Oxford: Clarendon, 1934), 2:33–34.

4. Ibid., 2;35.
5. Ibid., 2:40.
6. Thomas Babington Macaulay, "Crocker's Edition of Boswell's *Life of Johnson,*" in *Critical and Miscellaneous Essays* (New York: D. Appleton, 1896), 2:36.
7. J. W. Saunders, *The Profession of English Letters* (London: Routledge and Kegan Paul, 1964), 34–35.
8. E. B. Fryde, "Lorenzo de Medici," in *The Courts of Europe,* ed. A. G. Dickens (London: Thames and Hudson, 1977), 96.
9. Sidney's *Apology* is cited from *Elizabethan Critical Essays,* ed. Gregory Smith (Oxford: Clarendon, 1904), 194, 196.
10. Boswell, *Life of Johnson,* 2:319.
11. Ibid., 3:15.
12. Esdaile, *The British Museum Library,* 19.
13. Boswell, *Life of Johnson,* 2:33.
14. F. Taylor, "Johnsoniana from the Bagshawe Muniments," *Bulletin of the John Rylands University Library of Manchester* 35 (1952): 235.
15. Ibid., 238.
16. Ibid., 239.

Contributors

LORRAYNE Y. BAIRD-LANGE, Professor of English at Youngstown State University, has published on literature and iconography and is coeditor of *A Bibliography of Chaucer, 1974–1985*. She currently serves as Director of the Bibliographic Division of the New Chaucer Society.

EMERSON BROWN, JR., who teaches English at Vanderbilt University, is a specialist in Chaucer, Dante, and Arthurian literature. The author of numerous articles and reviews, he is currently completing a study of Epicureanism in ancient and medieval thought and literature.

ROBERT C. EVANS, Associate Professor of English at Auburn University at Montgomery, has published articles on various Renaissance writers and is the author of *Ben Jonson and the Poetics of Patronage*.

GEORGE GARRETT is the Hoyns Professor of English at the University of Virginia and the author of, among many other works, *Death of the Fox* and *The Succession*.

RICHARD R. GRIFFITH, Professor of English at C. W. Post College of Long Island University, has published widely on Middle English literature.

JAY L. HALIO, Professor of English at the University of Delaware, has published widely on Shakespeare. He is the author of *Understanding Shakespeare's Plays in Performance,* the editor of the Cambridge *King Lear,* and the Chair of the Board of Editors of the University of Delaware Press.

ROBERT W. HALLI, JR., an associate professor of English at the University of Alabama, is a specialist in Renaissance literature and has published articles on Herrick, Herbert, and Milton. He is also the editor of *Ballads, Folksongs, and Spirituals of Alabama.*

DAVID W. HISCOE has taught at North Carolina State University, the University of North Carolina at Greensboro, Duke University, Rice University, and Loyola University in Chicago. He has published articles on Chaucer, Augustine, Gower, Whitman, and Mark Twain and is now employed as a writer of marketing materials in the telecommunications industry.

R. E. KASKE is Avalon Foundation Professor in the Humanities at Cornell University, founder of Cornell's distinguished program of Medieval Studies, a Fellow in the Medieval Academy of America, and chief editor of *Traditio.* He is the author of *Medieval Christian Literary Imagery: A Guide to Interpretation* (Toronto, 1988) and of over sixty articles on medieval literature, especially *Beowulf,* Dante, *Piers Plowman,* and Chaucer.

DOROTHEA KEHLER, Associate Professor of English at San Diego State University, is the author of over a dozen notes and articles on Shakespeare and other Renaissance writers. The third edition of her reference guide, *Problems in Literary Research,* appeared in 1987. Currently, she is coediting an anthology of feminist criticism on Renaissance drama.

KATHLEEN A. KELLY is an associate professor of English at Babson College, Wellesley, Massachusetts, where she coordinates the writing program. In addition to several articles on the teaching of writing, she has written on Berryman and Donne.

ALVIN B. KERNAN teaches English at Princeton University. Among his many books are *The Cankered Muse: Satire of the English Renaissance* and *Printing, Technology, Letters and Samuel Johnson.*

HARRIET KRAMER LINKIN is an Assistant Professor of Nineteenth Century Literature at New Mexico State University who specializes in British Romanticism. Currently engaged on a book-length study of "Hieratic Language in Herbert, Blake, and Hopkins," she has published articles on Herbert, Blake, and Yeats.

PAMELA ROYSTON MACFIE is an assistant professor of English at the University of the South. Among her publications are essays on Marlowe, Donne, and Dante.

H. W. MATALENE, an associate professor of English at the University of South Carolina, specializes in eighteenth-century literature. His special interest is in new historicist perspectives, and he concentrates particularly on how literature portrays "face to face" authority.

WARD PARKS, an assistant professor of English at Louisiana State University, has published articles on Old and Middle English literature and has recently completed an extensive study on flyting in heroic narrative.

DEBORA SHUGER is an associate professor of English at the University of Arkansas. She is the author of *Sacred Rhetoric: The Christian Grand Style in the English Renaissance*.

CHARLOTTE SPIVACK is a professor of English at the University of Massachusetts, specializing in Tudor-Stuart drama and contemporary fantasy fiction. A frequent contributor to scholarly journals and a member of the editorial board of *English Literary Renaissance,* she has published five books: *Early English Drama* (co-author, 1966), *George Chapman* (1967), *The Comedy of Evil on Shakespeare's Stage* (1978), *Ursula K. Le Guin* (1984), and *Merlin's Daughters* (1987). Currently she is working on a study of female roles in Jacobean drama.

NATHANIEL STROUT, an associate professor of English at Hamilton College, has published on Ben Jonson and is at work on a full-length study of Ford's portrayal of women.

MICHAEL WENTWORTH is an associate professor of English at the University of North Carolina at Wilmington. His book *Thomas Heywood: A Reference Guide* was published by G. K. Hall in 1986, and he is currently working on an annotated bibliography of modern studies on Sir Thomas More. He has also published articles on Machiavelli and William Inge as well as numerous articles on the teaching of writing and literature.

Index